We Wear the Mask

We Wear the Mask

Paul Laurence Dunbar and the Politics of Representative Reality

Edited by Willie J. Harrell Jr.

The Kent State

University Press

KENT, OHIO

© 2010 by The Kent State University Press, Kent, Ohio 44242
ALL RIGHTS RESERVED
Library of Congress Catalog Card Number 2010000360
ISBN 978-1-60635-379-0
Manufactured in the United States of America

Library of Congress Cataloging-in-Publication Data
We wear the mask : Paul Laurence Dunbar and the politics of representative reality /
edited by Willie J. Harrell Jr.
p. cm.
Includes bibliographical references and index.
ISBN 978-1-60635-046-1 (hardcover : alk. paper) ∞
1. Dunbar, Paul Laurence, 1872–1906—Criticism and interpretation.
2. Dunbar, Paul Laurence, 1872–1906—Language.
3. African Americans in literature. I. Harrell, Willie J., Jr.
PS1557.W4 2010
811'.4—dc22
2010000360
British Library Cataloging-in-Publication data are available.

Contents

Introduction: Dunbar and the Ethics of Black Identity
Willie J. Harrell Jr. ix

Part I. Poetry

1. The Poetry of Paul Laurence Dunbar and the Influence of African Aesthetics: Dunbar's Poems and the Tradition of Masking
Lena Ampadu 3

2. National Memory and the Arts in Paul Laurence Dunbar's War Poetry
Nassim W. Balestrini 17

3. "Sing a Song Heroic": Paul Laurence Dunbar's Mythic and Poetic Tribute to Black Soldiers
Sharon D. Raynor 32

4. Minstrelsy and the Dialect Poetry of Paul Laurence Dunbar
Elston L. Carr Jr. 49

5. Dunbar, Dialect, and Narrative Theory: Subverted Statements in *Lyrics of Lowly Life*
Megan M. Peabody 59

Part II. Race, Rhetoric, and Social Structure

6. Rhetorical Accountability: Paul Laurence Dunbar's Search for "Representative" Men
Coretta M. Pittman 73

7 "Jump Back, Honey, Jump Back": Reading Paul Laurence Dunbar
   in the Context of the *Century Magazine*
   Mark Noonan   82

8 The Glamour of Paul Laurence Dunbar: Racial Uplift, Masculinity,
   and Bohemia in the Nadir
   Matt Sandler   98

9 Kemble's Figures and Dunbar's Folks: Picturing the Work of
   Graphic Illustration in Dunbar's Short Fiction
   Adam Sonstegard   116

10 "We Know de Time Is Ouahs": The Power of Christmas in the
   Literature of Paul Laurence Dunbar
   Amy Cummins   138

11 Creating a Representative Community: Identity in Paul Laurence
   Dunbar's *In Old Plantation Days*
   Willie J. Harrell Jr.   154

Part III. Novels, Identity, and Representation

12 Memory and Repression in Paul Laurence Dunbar's *The Sport
   of the Gods*
   Jeannine King   173

13 A Little Something More Than Something Else: Dunbar's
   Colorist Ambivalence in *The Sport of the Gods*
   Dolores V. Sisco   191

14 Mobile Blacks and Ubiquitous Blues: Urbanizing the African
   American Discourses in Paul Laurence Dunbar's *The Sport of
   the Gods*
   Michael P. Moreno   210

15 "With Myriad Subtleties": Paul Laurence Dunbar's Constructions
of Social Identity in *The Sport of the Gods*
Jayne E. Waterman   230

16 "Nemmine. You Got to Git Somebody Else to Ring Yo' Ol' Bell
Now": Nigger Ed and the Rhetoric of Local Color Realism and
Racial Protest in Dunbar's *The Fanatics*
Willie J. Harrell Jr.   242

CONTRIBUTORS   255
INDEX   259

Introduction
Dunbar and the Ethics of Black Identity
WILLIE J. HARRELL JR.

> I want to know whether or not you believe in preserving by Afro-American ... writers those quaint old tales and songs of our fathers which have made the fame of Joel Chandler Harris, Thomas Nelson Page, Ruth McEnery Stuart and others! Or whether you like so many others think we should ignore the past and all its capital literary materials.
> —PAUL LAURENCE DUNBAR,
> LETTER TO ALICE RUTH MOORE, APRIL 17, 1895

> [Dunbar's] brilliant and unique achievement was to have studied the American negro objectively, and to have represented him as he found him to be, with humor, with sympathy, and yet with what the reader must instinctively feel to be entire truthfulness.
> —W. D. HOWELLS, INTRODUCTION TO *LYRICS OF LOWLY LIFE* (1896)

OF THE INNUMERABLE ACCOMPLISHMENTS that secured Paul Laurence Dunbar's footing as America's "poet laureate of the Negro Race," perhaps none is more significant than the fact that he fashioned two distinct voices in his works—the traditional English of the conventional poet and the renowned, redolent dialect of African Americans at the turn of the century. Between the publication of his first collection of poetry, *Oak and Ivy,* in 1892 and his death from tuberculosis and the publication of his last volume of poetry, *Joggin' Erlong,* in 1906, Dunbar would write three librettos, eleven volumes of poetry, four novels, songs, and more than a few short stories and essays, rightfully leaving behind a legacy that would inspire many writers to come. By and large, Dunbar's legendary corpus has been highly praised as an extraordinary representation of black life in early twentieth-century America, which is the subject of this collection. *We Wear the Mask: Paul Laurence Dunbar and the Politics of Representative Reality* builds upon the already significant body of research published over the past two decades on Dunbar's extraordinary creativity. What distinguishes this volume from previous collections discussing Dunbar's artistic evolution is its focus. Supplementing the work of early examinations of Dunbar's life and works,[1] *We Wear the Mask* picks up where Jay Martin's *A Singer in the Dawn: Reinterpretations of Paul Laurence Dunbar* left off in 1975. An assessment of some of the earliest scholarship of Dunbar's artistic ability demonstrates how crucial it is to compile these rereadings and critical approaches to his works.

Drawing on an array of approaches to analyzing Dunbar's poetic creations; most representative novel, *The Sport of the Gods;* and other works, the essays in this volume exemplify the kinds of issues being addressed in the twenty-first century, among them Dunbar's war verse, the influence of African aesthetics in his poetry, Dunbar's use of dialect and minstrelsy to represent his race, and his depiction of African American masculinity. The contributors concentrate on the politics of black representation and identity to advance Dunbar studies on two fronts: contributors situate Dunbar's works within the age of contemporary literary studies while locating his artistry in relation to various contextualizations of the politics of black reality that proliferated at the turn of the century, and they engage earnestly in the process of evaluating Dunbar's works, closely examining the self-motivated and dynamic effect of his use of dialect, language, rhetorical strategies, and narrative theory to promote racial uplift. Although the topics of the contributions vary, if read together, they offer valuable insights into why Dunbar has become one of America's most celebrated, widely taught African American authors. Indeed, the essays as a whole reveal the ability of Dunbar's works to spark enlightening discussions of the vexing and conflicting cultural conditions of turn-of-the-century America.

The evolution of Dunbar's representation of black reality meant that the poor reception of *The Uncalled* (1898), Dunbar's first novel, had an adverse effect on his racial consciousness. The story of a young white man who refuses to enter the ministry, *The Uncalled* lacked the local color of the African American community. After the publication of *The Uncalled*, Dunbar published his first collection of short stories, *Folks from Dixie,* which included stories about southern blacks, and some about African Americans who were trying to traverse the terrain of the Northeast. *Folks from Dixie* was immensely more popular than *The Uncalled*. It's not hard to see why Dunbar shifted his attention from nonracial themes in *The Uncalled* to matters of race interests in *Folks from Dixie* and later works.[2] To effectively represent the black voice in his works, Dunbar illustrated his awareness of the black struggle to triumph over the legacy of slavery and prejudice while affirming the civil liberties, responsibilities, and advantages of freedom. Since American society had previously disadvantaged blacks by denying them respect and the presupposition of integrity, Dunbar characterized black reality by extracting his voice from the previous white representations to combat the negative stereotyping to which his people had been subjugated. Desiring not only self-determination for himself but also his race's liberation from the constraints of nineteenth-century American prejudice, Dunbar's most recognizable poem, "We Wear the Mask," was evidence of this racial manifestation.

Written during Reconstruction, "We Wear the Mask" epitomized the angst African Americans found themselves experiencing while attempting to construct an identity amid the preexisting racial hierarchy not long after the Civil War. Dunbar's usage of the metaphorical mask suggested that African Americans were preeminently commodities, and citizens only marginally as far as their rights as human beings were concerned. Employing a pre–Du Boisian "double consciousness" approach, Dunbar sought to assist white America in acknowledging the trials and tribulations blacks faced on a daily basis. Institutionalized racism of Reconstruction dictated that black writers had to silence or else *mask* their voices to be accepted by white audiences.[3] Dunbar believed, then, that African Americans had to wear a mask to hide their "torn and bleeding hearts." "We Wear the Mask" insinuates that the world never really sees blacks for their contributions to society. Instead, the dominate culture only sees "the mask" that "hides our cheeks and shades our eyes." The mask, then, conceals the pain, the anguish, the suffering of those who don it. By composing the poem, Dunbar "took a chance that could have cost him his life" had his white nineteenth-century reading audience fully comprehended the poem's multilayered meanings.[4] But what was the motivation behind the mask? Did Dunbar mean to convey the message that blacks were ultimately seeking acceptance in white America? Was he suggesting that blacks needed to find a voice and be heard amid the racial injustices that plagued them? Or was his message that wearing the mask was a part of the American experience, and that when African Americans wear it, it bespeaks their longing for a representative identity?

The search for a representative black identity and reality in Dunbar's works is a far-reaching subject, which is evident throughout this volume. While the contributors to *We Wear the Mask* have developed a greater understanding of African American literary and cultural studies, they have also developed a genuine appreciation for Dunbar's artistry. Although Dunbar believed in the morality of oppressed blacks, readings of his work have seemingly neglected this aspect of his oeuvre. This volume not only encourages a greater understanding of the complex readings surrounding the evolution of Dunbar's artistry but also emphasizes that he was actively engaged in the representation of the black community, which he saw as an ever-evolving phenomenon (one that did not, however, begin with him). This volume is also premised on the fact that there has not been enough attention given to the ways in which Dunbar's representation of a black identity was positioned and conditioned in his works.

If, as Kwame Anthony Appiah argues in *The Ethics of Identity*, the contemporary use of the term "identity" "refer[s] to such features of people as their race, ethnicity, nationality, gender, religion, or sexuality" gained notoriety "in the social psychology of the 1950s,"[5] how does identity for turn-of-the-century African Americans fit into the ethical scope of American democracy? If a black identity was to be recognized, and furthermore *represented*, what kind of demands could African Americans genuinely make as citizens of a society that did not view them as equal? Dunbar understood that there were no straightforward answers to these issues and that championing equality for his people would be a difficult task: the preexisting labels applied to African Americans ("ideals about people who fit the label") "come to have social and psychological effects."[6] Dunbar felt the call to eliminate not only the labels applied to blacks but also the effects that came along with them. On December 13, 1890, Dunbar wrote that "a great mistake that has been made by the editors of the race is that they only discuss one question, the race problem." Although he believed that "the race question" was indeed still important to the advancement of the race, Dunbar felt that a quarter of a century of discussion had "worn it thread-bare." Indeed, a new focus needed to be addressed. "Your cry is 'we must agitate, we must agitate.' So you must but bear in mind that the agitation of *deeds* is tenfold more effectual than the agitation of *words*," Dunbar wrote. Therefore, he called to the architects of the race's public image to "stop saying, and go to doing. Find other things," he suggested, "than this one question to talk about. . . . Cease feeding your weary readers on an unbroken diet of the race problem."[7] His struggle with representing his race seems to anticipate W. E. B. Du Bois's declaration that racism was not the foreseeable consequence of primordial bigotry but was engrained or perpetuated by ignorance. Dunbar too felt his "dogged strength alone" kept his soul "from being torn asunder": his marked attempt to represent his people pulled him toward literature and, at the same time, toward discomfiture amid the "politics and prejudices of the white community."[8]

Dunbar's continuing exploration of black identity sheds light on the courses of action that African Americans encountered while they attempted to construct a public identity. His works addressed the complicated questions of advancement during Reconstruction, the hazards of the exodus of blacks from southern rural areas to northern cities, and the contradictions of realistically representing the black experience amid surviving stereotypes that held a strong influence over society at large. However, his popularity as a dialect poet led him to feel that "I am tired, so tired of dialect. I send out graceful little poems, suited for any of the magazines, but they are returned to me by editors who say, 'We would be very glad to have a dialect poem, Mr. Dunbar, but we do not care for the language compositions.'"9

We Wear the Mask challenges facile interpretations of the role Dunbar played in representing the black community around the turn of the century. The contributors explore an array of topics on Dunbar's artistry and raise a variety of crucial questions relevant to ongoing discussions on Dunbar. While the essays in this volume are fully reflective of the vibrant diversity by which Dunbar critical studies are characterized, they are nonetheless striated by some common concerns: How did Dunbar create personal and group identity? What roles do dialect, urbanization, and movement play in the formation of a representative black identity? How does the interpretation of war affect mainstream national identity, ethnic identity, and race relations? *We Wear the Mask* seeks to respond to these questions by shedding light on the processes through which Dunbar sought to construct a black identity and to examine how this identity in turn supplied his reading public with answers to the questions surrounding his community. Not only is this volume a long-overdue reexamination of Dunbar's influential works, but above all else, *We Wear the Mask* challenges the superficial interpretations of the role Dunbar's prose played during the complex period of turn-of-the-century America, reassessing his works and introducing new paradigms for understanding the unfolding evolution of his artistry.

Part I: Poetry

Because Dunbar's reputation is primarily based on a sizable body of poetry presented in the dialect of southern blacks, some critics have accused him of portraying negative stereotypes to satisfy a white reading public. The essays in this section denounce this notion and, instead, suggest that Dunbar used dialect not only to represent his race in a positive light but also to show that beneath the surface lay a disguised protest against their treatment as second-class citizens. Suggesting that Dunbar's poems owe a debt to African traditions and aesthetics, Lena Ampadu, in "The Poetry of Paul Laurence Dunbar and the Influence of African Aesthetics: Dunbar's Poems and the Tradition of Masking," argues that by preserving the legacy of the African griot, Dunbar created poems in the genre of the African praise poem written in celebration of an honorable community member or leader.

Nassim W. Balestrini and Sharon D. Raynor explore Dunbar's war poetry in their contributions. In "National Memory and the Arts in Paul Laurence Dunbar's War Poetry," Balestrini suggests that approximately twenty of Dunbar's four hundred poems deal with the topic of war. The majority of these works, Balestrini argues, adhere to long-established poetic styles; even the poems written in dialect are presented in traditional metrical and stanzaic forms. In "'Sing a Song Heroic': Paul Laurence Dunbar's Mythic and Poetic Tribute to Black Soldiers," Raynor investigates several of Dunbar's war poems and concludes that Dunbar uses myth, memory, and folklore to both memorialize and pay tribute to the identity of black soldiers. She examines various aspects of Dunbar's tribute poetry and concludes that Dunbar's poetry historicizes, mythologizes, and memorializes the stories and sacrifices of black soldiers.

In "Minstrelsy and the Dialect Poetry of Paul Laurence Dunbar," Elston L. Carr Jr. suggests that there is little question that Dunbar's dialect poetry can be read as a mask in motion that presents oppositional and subversive themes within the signifying system as described by Henry Louis Gates Jr. and, to a lesser degree, within the blues matrix as described by Houston A. Baker. Carr proposes an additional way of reading Dunbar's work that amplifies the motif of masking by considering the cultural context and implications of dialect writing in the late nineteenth century. Megan M. Peabody, in "Dunbar, Dialect, and Narrative Theory: Subverted Statements in *Lyrics of Lowly Life*," provides insight into Dunbar's use of a multileveled, dialect-driven narrative that proves that not all utterance can be trusted and that readers must look to the narrative gaps for answers and truths. Peabody encourages a rereading of Dunbar within this context as a means of reckoning with historical and critical marginalization and examining his importance as a purveyor of black experience. In doing justice to these dual modes, Peabody utilizes Gérard Genette's narrative theories in a close study of selections from *Lyrics of Lowly Life*.

Part II: Race, Rhetoric, and Social Structure

The authors of the essays in this section open new avenues for reading Dunbar's works by bringing together several significant readings on issues ranging from his polemics from minstrel performances to his works published in popular magazines to representations of Christmas as a means of racial uplift. To begin, in "Rhetorical Accountability: Paul Laurence Dunbar's Search for 'Representative' Men," Coretta M. Pittman explores Dunbar's essay "Representative American Negroes" to discuss why character and respectability were twin components that drove the rhetorical message in Dunbar's search for what was representative of blacks during his time. Pittman suggests that the recognition and examination of racial schism that would define America in the twentieth century is important in explaining the value of W. E. B. Du Bois's *The Souls of Black Folk* (1903) relative to Dunbar's essay on representative African Americans.

Mark Noonan, in "'Jump Back, Honey, Jump Back': Reading Dunbar in the Context of the *Century Magazine*," examines the apparent influence of Clarence Edmund Stedman and James Whitcomb Riley on Dunbar to show that much of what is viewed as his "natural" pastoral inclinations and inherent lyricism was in fact gleaned from his readings in a genteel publication interested in promoting "the folk" and "the ideal," in part, as antidotes to urbanism and industrialization. Meanwhile, Matt Sandler, in "The Glamour of Paul Laurence Dunbar: Racial Uplift, Masculinity, and Bohemia in the Nadir," seeks to map Dunbar's work in what has been called the age of Washington and Du Bois by examining his relationship with one of the most prominent white editors of the late nineteenth and early twentieth centuries, George Horace Lorimer at the *Saturday Evening Post*. The possibility that Dunbar might have been a representative of a newly forming black bohemia during this time, Sandler argues, is thinkable only if we consider the existence of a fully fleshed-out community with teachings and culture to preserve, not merely based on the fact that he was an aesthete.

Tracing the politics of restoring Edward Windsor Kemble's almost forgotten illustrations to critical conversations, and of attempting to reconstruct their appearance before audiences, Adam Sonstegard's essay, "Kemble's Figures and Dunbar's Folks: Picturing the Work of Graphic Illustration in Dunbar's Short Fiction," offers a unique examination in which he suggests that reading these tales as they were written *and* illustrated resurrects Dunbar's struggle for authority over his own texts, reveals his work with as well as against stereotypes of slaves and the Old South, and animates his dialect-speaking characters.

In "'We Know de Time Is Ouahs': The Power of Christmas in the Literature of Paul Laurence Dunbar," Amy Cummins focuses on an area that has not yet been addressed by scholarship: the meaning of Christmas in Dunbar's writings. Dunbar utilized the subject and setting of this holiday in numerous poems. Cummings concludes that Dunbar used the topos of Christmas to express truths about life under slavery, to document the impact of racism and economic injustice on African Americans, and to urge reconciliation and charitable giving. Finally, "Creating a Representative Community: Identity in Paul Laurence Dunbar's *In Old Plantation Days*" adds a much-needed discussion to Dunbar studies as I examine race, representation, and identity in Dunbar's second volume of short fiction. Dunbar attempted to create a viable black community through tales that highlight the strength of women and introduce gender politics, tales that illustrate the strength of religion as a community-building vehicle, tales that illustrate the rebellious slave, and tales that illustrate the importance of conjuring to the slave community.

Part III: Novels, Identity, and Representation

The Sport of the Gods is Dunbar's final and most representative novel. In one of the first novels to callously depict the reality of ghetto life in the North, Dunbar clearly asserts that it is impossible for African Americans to escape the shadows of slavery. Jeannine King, Dolores V. Sisco, Michael P. Moreno, Jayne E. Waterman, and my discussion on *The Fanatics* offers modern readings of *Sport* by illustrating that Dunbar sought to reveal the forces that subjugated blacks in both the North and the South. In "Memory and Repression in Paul Laurence Dunbar's *The Sport of the Gods*," King examines memory and migration in *Sport*. Though many consider *Sport* to be typical of the plantation tradition, King argues that it both represents and challenges this genre. King concludes that a close examination of *Sport* reveals a dark portrayal of post-emancipation declension, violence, and traumatic memory as Dunbar, "beneath the cloak of the plantation novel," confronts the injustice of slavery and the possibility of freedom.

Sisco, in "A Little Something More Than Something Else: Dunbar's Colorist Ambivalence in *The Sport of the Gods*," seeks to reveal the ways in which Dunbar indirectly modeled black masculinity based on white supremacy. *Sport* was a personal endeavor for Dunbar, who struggled with issues of race. Sisco concludes that *Sport* was Dunbar's first attempt at eliminating "intraracial color and class bias."

Moreno, in placing the emphasis on migration in "Mobile Blacks and Ubiquitous Blues: Urbanizing the African American Discourses in Paul Laurence Dunbar's *The Sport of the Gods*," argues that part of what constructs black identity in the migration narrative can be comprehended through examination of the disparate spaces generated by postbellum dichotomies: North and South, city and country, black and white, spirituality and the blues. As such, locales constructed throughout Dunbar's *The Sport of the Gods* serve to establish discourses from which notions of postbellum bodies and identities are manufactured and reconfigured.

Waterman challenges previous readings of *The Sport of the Gods* by focusing on the sociologist Erving Goffman's identification of the self, its "dramaturgical" stage management, and the shame that forms the basis of social interaction. In "'With Myriad Subtleties': Paul Laurence Dunbar's Constructions of Social Identity in *The Sport of the Gods*," Waterman suggests that performance, in its illusionary deception, and the ensuing embarrassment and consequence of wearing the wrong performative mask, characterizes key episodes in the narrative of *The Sport of the Gods* and the "myriad subtleties" of Dunbar's constructions of self-projection and identity.

The book ends with my discussion of Dunbar's third novel, *The Fanatics*. In "'Nemmine. You Got to Git Somebody Else to Ring Yo' Ol' Bell Now': Nigger Ed and the Rhetoric of Local Color Realism and Racial Protest in Dunbar's *The Fanatics*," I argue that Dunbar's portrayal of Nigger Ed was deliberate. Although Ed's character is presented through the eyes of the white community, Dunbar portrays Ed as a productive figure who aids in bridging the racial gap in the community. I conclude that through his use of local color realism, Dunbar's celebration of Ed's acceptance in the face of racial discrimination ultimately gains him the admiration of the white community at the end of the novel.

In 1892, early in his writing career, Dunbar insisted to James Newton Matthews, "I hope there is something worthy in my writings and not merely the novelty of a black face associated with the power to rhyme that has attracted attention."[9] What might we learn if we transpose this line of thinking to Dunbar's representation of black identity and reality? Readers will note that the sequence of essays in this collection attempts to follow the development of Dunbar's oeuvre of black representation, from his innovative dialect poems to his forays into fiction. The contributors to *We Wear the Mask* all agree that Dunbar's representations of a black identity deserve renewed investigation and analysis. They challenge lingering assessments of Dunbar's works and connect literary and rhetorical strategies that give authority to his diverse literary techniques. In all, *We Wear the Mask* offers considerable new ways of rethinking the artistry of America's preeminent pre–Harlem Renaissance poet and bears witness to the powerful effects of Dunbar's language, dialect, representation, and vision.

Notes

1. Addison Gayle, *Oak and Ivy: A Biography of Paul Laurence Dunbar* (Garden City, NY: Doubleday, 1971); Pearle Hendrikson Schultz, *Paul Laurence Dunbar: Black Poet Laureate* (Champaign, IL: Garrard, 1974); Jay Martin and Gossie H. Hudson, eds., *The Paul Laurence Dunbar Reader: A Selection of the Best of Paul Laurence Dunbar's Poetry and Prose, Including Writings Never before Available in Book Form* (New York: Dodd, Mead, 1975); Peter Revell, *Paul Laurence Dunbar* (Boston: Twayne, 1979); Herbert Woodward Martin, *Paul Laurence Dunbar: A Singer of Songs* (Columbus: State Library of Ohio, 1979); Joanne M. Braxton, ed., *The Collected Poetry of Paul Laurence Dunbar* (Charlottesville: University of Virginia Press, 1993), Catherine Reef, *Paul Laurence Dunbar: Portrait of a Poet* (Berkeley Heights, NJ: Enslow, 2000); Eleanor

Alexander, *Lyrics of Sunshine and Shadow: The Tragic Courtship and Marriage of Paul Laurence Dunbar and Alice Ruth Moore* (New York: New York University Press, 2001); Herbert Woodward Martin and Ronald Primeau, eds., *His Own Voice: The Dramatic and Other Uncollected Works of Paul Laurence Dunbar* (Athens: Ohio University Press, 2002).

2. Dickson D. Bruce Jr., *Black American Writing from the Nadir: The Evolution of a Literary Tradition, 1877–1915* (Baton Rouge: Louisiana State University Press, 1988), 88.

3. Rafia Zafar, *We Wear the Mask: African Americans Write American Literature, 1760–1870* (New York: Columbia University Press, 1997), 4.

4. Daniel P. Black, "Literary Subterfuge: Early African American Writing and the Trope of the Mask," *CLA Journal* 48 (2005): 388.

5. Kwame Anthony Appiah, *The Ethics of Identity* (Princeton, NJ: Princeton University Press, 2005), 4.

6. Ibid., 66.

7. *In His Own Voice*, 171–72.

8. Jay Martin, "Paul Laurence Dunbar: Biography through Letters," foreword to *A Singer in the Dawn: Reinterpretations of Paul Laurence Dunbar* (New York: Dodd, Mead, 1975), 17.

9. *Dunbar Reader*, 412.

Part I

Poetry

1
The Poetry of Paul Laurence Dunbar and the Influence of African Aesthetics

Dunbar's Poems and the Tradition of Masking

Lena Ampadu

His fame having rested mostly on his dialect poems, which have origins in the minstrel tradition, many critical studies examine Paul Laurence Dunbar's work and its relationship to the slave past in America and to the tradition of minstrelsy popularized in nineteenth-century America. By 1899, Dunbar was widely acknowledged as a master of poetic technique who commanded respect in the literary world at home and abroad. He began losing his prestigious status in 1922 during the Harlem Renaissance with the publication of Johnson's *Book of American Negro Poetry,* which made way for the poetry of the New Negro. Later, after the civil rights movement, consistent with the tenor of the times, which called for more direct social protest and often comic depictions of blacks, Dunbar continued losing popularity and was often heavily criticized because of the absence of racial affirmative pride in his poetry. He was generally cited as a kind of tragic black figure desiring to be accepted by predominantly white audiences.[1] A close and careful examination of the breadth of Dunbar's poems, both the standard and vernacular varieties, reveals an often neglected link to the oral traditions of the African past and shows his poetry to convey the tenets of racial consciousness and pride that would later characterize the Harlem Renaissance. To rectify this lack of attention to the debt that Dunbar's poems owe to African traditions and aesthetics, this chapter will examine his poetry by identifying the African retentions in his poetry and examining the transformation and revision many of these retentions underwent after arriving in the New World to become African American vernacular cultural forms.

In 1921, James Weldon Johnson, in his preface to *The Book of American Negro Poetry,* lauds Dunbar as a poet whose skill and artistry had their beginnings outside dialect poems. However, Dunbar lamented the restrictive role that larger society had given him as an author of dialect poems: he launched a public protest against this in the often-quoted lines of one of his poems: "But ah, the world, it turned to praise / A jingle in a broken tongue."[2] His explanation for why he seemed to placate white audiences by assuming the minstrel role and writing poems advancing black stereotypes and glorifying life on the plantation can be found in his poem "We Wear the Mask." In the tradition of African verbal discourse filled with dualities, he explains that one wears "the mask that grins and lies" to prevent the world from being "over-wise, / In counting all our tears and sighs."[3] Having originated in Dunbar's poem, this use of the term "masking" serves in literary and language conventions today "as both a rhetoric of deception and a kind of cultural 'shibboleth.'"[4] Revisionist criticism of Dunbar's dialect poems considers them to be "masks in motion" that act as facades for the messages communicated in the poems as well as the cryptic messages central to the African American experience.[5]

Although Dunbar probably did not have the African mask in mind when he wrote this poem, if one views his poem purely within an African context, one can interpret it as both a literal and figurative reference to a mask. The mask, a decorative carving usually made of wood or stone, can be worn during African ceremonies for different functions and can have the same kinds of dualities as language. In Africa, which one thinks of as traditionally having a purely oral culture, a mask can be considered a form of writing; such a view thus elevates African societies to ones of "mixed orality," in which writing coexists with orality.[6] We might view Dunbar's poems in a similar way: they are produced within a literate mainstream culture, but they reflect the oral culture of the people about whom they are written. His poems are also infused with the various strategies of orality, some being written strictly in dialect, while others are written strictly in Standard English. Still others are a fusion or a mixture of the two varieties of English.

The word "masks" can refer to the types of face coverings that people wear at celebrations throughout the African diaspora, for example, during Mardi Gras in New Orleans or Carnival in Brazil or Trinidad. When I introduce this poem in my literature classes and ask students to define the word "mask," the consensus usually is that the mask is a facade, and they usually admit that the poem could refer to a mask of revelry much like that of the clown in Smokey Robinson's "Tears of a Clown." The lyrics of Robinson's song facilitate their comprehension of the message of "grinning and lyin'" in comparison to the character of the clown in the song, who wears a mask that shows a happy outward appearance but masks the clown's true feelings of sadness and unhappiness.

Further drawing from an aesthetic originating in the African homeland, Dunbar, preserving the legacy of the African griot, created poems in the genre of the African praise poem (poems written in celebration of an honorable community member, leader, or event). An important dimension of African oral poetry, the praise poem is best understood and appreciated when preached, sung, or recited. African poems are direct and immediate but celebrate heroes and historical events and are concerned with the poetry's immediate effects.[7] Several of Dunbar's poems paid tributes in this fashion, including "Black Samson of Brandywine," "Douglass," "Booker T," "The Colored Soldiers," and "When Malindy Sings."

As African praise poems, his "Black Samson of Brandywine" and "The Colored Soldiers" examine the plight of black soldiers individually and collectively. In the 1930s, literary critic, poet, and professor Sterling Brown labeled these "race-conscious poems," and Dunbar labeled himself a "race representative." He declared of his role, "My ambition is to make closer studies of my people."[8] In the poems, Dunbar heaps praises upon the soldiers, "the noble sons of Ham,"[9] who, like his father, gallantly fought in the Civil War wearing the uniform of the Union army. These brave soldiers often fought just as courageously as the white soldiers but faced more imminent danger of being executed by rebel soldiers, who would kill them rather than take them as prisoners of war.[10] Since the heroic deeds of the black soldiers were never publicly acknowledged, Dunbar bestows this honor upon them in his "The Colored Soldiers." In the same vein, he praises Black Samson, who fought mightily against the British in the Revolutionary War in southeastern Pennsylvania. Using words that convey pride in Samson's and his own heritage, Dunbar labels him

> An ebony giant,
> Black as the pinions of night.
> Swinging his scythe like a mower
> Over a field of grain.[11]

In his description of Samson, Dunbar anticipates the positive comparisons of blackness to the night that later writers like Langston Hughes used to extol the beauty of blackness:

> I am a Negro:
> Black as the night is black
> Black like the depths of my Africa.[12]

Though Dunbar uses the term "colored" in his poem valorizing the soldiers who fought in the Civil War, a term that originated among the mixed-race group, he reverses the earlier negative connotations of the word "black" that writers like the eighteenth-century poet Phillis Wheatley and the nineteenth-century political writer Maria Stewart had used in their writings. In the line "Remember Christians, Negroes black as Cain," from Wheatley's "On Being Brought from Africa,"[13] blackness is associated with the evil Cain, the first man to commit a murder in the Bible. Later, Stewart would write, "Though black your skin as shades of night, / Your hearts are pure, your souls are white."[14] Although she, like Dunbar and Langston Hughes, compares blackness to the night, she contrasts blackness with the purity and whiteness of the soul. Stewart, therefore, links darkness with sin and evil, as does Wheatley.

During his exceptional career as a poet, Dunbar came into contact with several nationally known leaders in the African American community, including Frederick Douglass, Alexander Crummell, W. E. B. Du Bois, Mary Church Terrell, James Weldon Johnson, Charles Chesnutt, and Booker T. Washington, all of whom advanced the educational goals and/or political aspirations of African Americans. Since all these leaders were engaged in social and political struggles for African Americans, Dunbar's friendship and association with them helped counteract the belief that he was merely a minstrel who avoided social protest. In fact, Du Bois, who often appeared at programs with Dunbar, labeled him a "protest writer."[15] Mary Church Terrell, a women's rights activist and spokesperson against lynching, was a neighbor and friend who maintained a lifelong correspondence with him. She dubbed him "poet laureate of the Negro Race," a title that survives today.[16]

Dunbar wrote poems extolling the virtues of several of these activist leaders. In 1893, Frederick Douglass praised Dunbar when he read his poetry at the World's Columbian Exposition in Chicago. In turn, Dunbar praised Douglass in the poem "Frederick Douglass," originally called "Old Warrior," which he dedicated to him upon his death in 1895. In "Frederick Douglass," Dunbar calls Douglass "a spirit brave" who "has passed beyond the mists."[17] Calling him a son of Africa, using the Ethiopian biblical reference to Africa, Dunbar in the same poem says of him, "And Ethiopia, with bosom torn / Laments the passing of her noblest born."[18] In "Douglass," he compares Douglass to the captain of a ship in the midst of a storm, a metaphor for the days of racial strife and segregation. Dunbar asserts that we need Douglass's "voice high-sounding o'er the storm," his "strong arm to guide the shivering bark / to give us comfort through the lonely dark."[19]

Episcopal priest Alexander Crummell, his advisor and mentor, who espoused firm, unshakeable beliefs that Africans and African Americans should ban together because of their shared heritage, made Dunbar a member of the American Negro Academy, which Crummell had cofounded. Upon the death of Crummell, Dunbar lauded him in "Alexander Crummell Dead" as a "learned one and a leader," describing his fame as intertwined with the light of the dawn of day.[20]

Booker T. Washington, considered the spokesperson for African Americans, invited Dunbar to a convention at Tuskegee Institute for black farmers in 1890. Though Dunbar sometimes assisted Washington in fund-raising for this black institution, he did not embrace Washington's philosophy of industrial education. Feeling moved to honor Washington's accomplishments, however, Dunbar wrote a poem honoring him, calling him one who had risen from his humble beginnings in a lowly West Virginia cabin to become "a peer of princes in the world's acclaim / A master spirit for the nation's need."[21]

In addition to praising Washington, Dunbar wrote the school song for Tuskegee, glorifying the institution founded by Washington. In similar praise language, Dunbar paints a picture of the school as an enduring mother whose children shall not abandon her: "Oh long striving mother of diligent sons / And of daughters, whose strength is their pride / We love thee forever, and ever shall walk / Thro' the oncoming years at thy side." He concludes with similar praise: "Oh, Mother Tuskegee, thou shinest to-day / As a gem in the fairest of lands; Thou gavest the Heav'n-blessed power to see / The worth of our minds and our hands."[22] In emphasizing these two themes in the song, Dunbar sustains the African tradition of holding mothers and education in high esteem.

Continuing this reverence for mothers, his poem "When Malindy Sings," written in praise of Dunbar's mother, who had the gift of song, extends a tribute to those black musicians who delivered music in an emotionally expressive style learned aurally. In this regard, the poem examines the musical traditions and aesthetics linked to the African motherland by sharply contrasting the Western classical tradition of learning and producing music by strict note reading with the African-inspired form relying on improvisation and the ear. Music plays a pivotal role in West African culture, as expressed by Olaudah Equiano: "We are almost a nation of dancers, musicians, and poets. Thus every great event, such as a triumphant return from battle, or other cause of public rejoicing, is celebrated in public dances."[23] True to Equiano's declaration about the Ibos' reverence for music, Dunbar's poem examines the primacy of music, a potent remnant of African culture found in African American culture. Thus music is an integral part of many social events and entertainments, occupying a place of prominence in African American culture in slave quarters.

The narrator of Dunbar's "When Malindy Sings" offers valuable commentary about the production of music in the plantation life of slaves. Many parallels exist between the singing style of gospel and soul singers, like Aretha Franklin and Mahalia Jackson, or a jazz singer like Billie Holiday, and the style of Malindy, who "jes' spreads huh mouf and hollahs."[24] Closely allied with the oral tradition, musicians like Mahalia Jackson and Billie Holiday had no formal musical training and were unable to read music, yet they are widely regarded as having almost perfect musical styling and phrasing. They symbolize a lineage of African singers and musicians who have the gift of the ear. The poem's narrator observes that Malindy's robust voice, which delivers music that "strikes yo' hea't and clings," is far superior to that of Miss Lucy, the white woman whose musical training has her rely on "lines an'dots."[25]

Dunbar summarizes one of the key elements of black music: its ability to touch the heart or move the people—the emotional effect that the singer has on his or her audience, one that fills people with spirit. Having originated in the music of the church, this quality was carried over into the secular singing style called soul singing, best exemplified by Aretha Franklin, known as the Queen of Soul, whose earliest musical training was in her father's church in Detroit. A deacon reared in a traditional church in South Carolina during the 1930s aptly expresses the emotional effect this singing style has on the audience: "If you want people to be moved, let the spirit hit you then let it go to them. Because my Bible tells me that the spirit runs from heart to heart. Strike your heart first, then mine. It'll go from me to you and from you to somebody else—that's just how it goes."[26] The poem's narrator identifies this spiritual effect by pronouncing, "An you fin' yo' teahs a-drappin' / When Malindy sings."[27]

The narrator criticizes Miss Lucy for not having the "tu'ns an' twistin's / Fu' to make [the sound] sweet an' light."[28] One can imagine that those "tu'ns an' twistin's" are equivalent to the embellishments that the gospel singer uses to elongate words and lines in the song in the same way that the blues singer extends or prolongs the blue note.[29] The qualities that cause the narrator to declare this music superior to the music that Miss Lucy produces parallel those of importance in African music: robustness of voice, sometimes with a raspy timbre; stylistic expressiveness; and improvisation.[30] One might get a better sense of the comparison that the narrator is making by listening to a recording of "America the Beautiful" by Judy Garland and comparing it to that of Ray Charles. Although his voice is hoarse and raspy, and he embellishes notes, using improvisation, Charles's version, a soulful performance rooted in gospel, is more rhythmic and syncopated than Garland's version.

One can compare the performance of the college marching band from a traditionally white institution that plays classical and pop tunes with that of the marching band from historically black colleges and universities, which march soulfully onto the field with intricately rhythmic moves, playing the most contemporary rhythm-and-blues and hip-hop tunes. The contrasts between Ray Charles and Judy Garland and the white college band and the black college band are very much like the contrast between the white Miss Lucy's singing and the black Malindy's. Similarly, in another of Dunbar's poems, "The Colored Band," Dunbar contrasts these differences between the two musical traditions. He distinguishes ragtime and other music peculiar to the "colored" band from that of the white band:

> You kin hyeah a fine perfo'mance w'en de white ban's serenade,
>   An' dey play dey high-toned music mighty sweet
> But hit's Sousa played in ragtime, an' hit's Rastus on Parade
>   W'en de colo'ed ban' comes ma'chin' down de street.[31]

The narrator pays the highest compliment to Malindy by describing how the greatest natural singers, birds, hush their singing, along with the most accomplished percussionists on the plantation, the fiddlers and the banjoists, to listen to the talented Malindy sing:[32]

> Fiddlin' man jes' stop his fiddlin',
>   Lay his fiddle on de she'f;
> Folks a-playin' on de banjo
> Draps dey fingahs on de strings—
>   Bless yo'soul—fu'gits to move 'em,
> When Malindy sings.[33]

Other elements of African aesthetics include Dunbar's use of the sermon and the rhythmic preaching style of the black preacher, as in his poem "An Antebellum Sermon" and in a short story, "The Fruitful Sleeping of the Rev. Elisha Edwards." Dunbar describes the interactive style of the black church in his story about a pastor caught snoring in church during a fellow preacher's sermon. When he has awakened and the time comes for him to speak, instead of getting the usual response from his congregation, the Reverend Edwards gets "Not a cry, not a moan, not Amen."[34] Although during the era in which Dunbar wrote he was linked to the minstrel tradition because of his emphasis on pathos and humor, we can look beyond these limitations in this poem: the poem provides an in-depth look at the complexities of communication in black culture. We have the black preacher comically portrayed, a ridiculing of the black preacher showing him as a buffoon, but the poem can also be interpreted in the context of the old folk saying within the African American community, "Got one mind for white folks to see, 'nother for what I know is me." Although some of the strongest examples of humor are found in the story of the black preacher, this story is designed to make the white audience laugh at the black preacher, while the black one laughs at and with him.

In the black language tradition, the preacher in "An Ante-bellum Sermon" highlights Moses as the subject of his sermon and appeals to the double audience. Black preachers, like the spirituals, use double-voiced language strategies: on one level the story is, in a biblical sense, about the prophet Moses delivering the Hebrews from Pharaoh's bondage, appealing to a white audience. On another level, it underscores freedom and its relevance to the black audience. By beginning the sermon with the communal "We," addressed to a gathering of "brothas," Dunbar places the action of the poem in a site of resistance, one emphasizing this cry for freedom. Using "hush harbor rhetoric,"[35] Dunbar situates the poem in a secret hiding place where people gather to seek freedom:

> We is gathahed hyeah, my brothas,
>   In dis' howlin' wildaness,
> Fu' to speak some words of comfo't
>   To each othah in distress.[36]

Indeed, one of Dunbar's accomplishments is the number and variety of people inspired to memorize and recite his poems in post–World War I America. Dunbar gave many public recitals of his own poetry and served as a model for many in the black community who followed in his footsteps. Like the griots in the African homeland, these New World storytellers, sometimes called elocutionists, continued this oral tradition, interweaving art into the fabric of society in black communities. When these griots delivered these poems, they were usually in black communities and performed for black audiences, thus altering the racial composition of Dunbar's intended audience.

These New World griots dramatized and performed his poems, bringing alive the vernacular and the cadences of the black preacher, often setting in motion the call and response associated with the kind of oral delivery to an African audience. In Africa, however, the griots often compose before a live audience, with the audience co-creating the text. From church pulpits and basements to classrooms and cafeteria/auditoriums in urban and rural communities in the South, the Northeast, and the Midwest and in states ranging from Mississippi to Maryland and Michigan, there were always those men and women who distinguished themselves by reciting a repertoire of Dunbar's poems, mostly the dialect poems. Popular ones are "In the Morning," "Little Brown Baby," and "When Malindy Sings." At the height of the popularity of Dunbar's poems, these griots were central to social gatherings, and Florence Borders, who grew up in uptown New Orleans during the 1930s, recollects that whenever there was a gathering of her father's generation at neighborhood parties, church programs, picnics, or family reunions, Dunbar's poems were recited as the primary entertainment.[37]

Sometimes the recitations were planned, but at other times they were spontaneous. According to Borders, at the cooking demonstrations held at the AME church in the neighborhood, whenever there was a break, instead of buying refreshments or participating in a raffle, audience members would spontaneously recite Dunbar's poems. Part of Dunbar's genius was his use of a language with which many blacks, especially the everyday working folks, were familiar. Borders's observation supports this view of Dunbar's relevance to the community. She recalls, "The older generation related to the dialect poems more than to Standard English ones because they reflected their experiences more authentically."[38] In the neighborhood in which she grew up, not many of the people in her father's generation had a high school or college education. Her father would recite his favorites, among them "The Party" and "In the Morning." Similarly, Lois Taylor recalls that her mother, in the 1940s and 1950s in rural Ridgeland, South Carolina, would recite poems at social gatherings, mostly "The Party" and "In the Morning," as part of the evening entertainment at the learning and quiz programs at the local elementary school.[39] They would recite poems, and afterward, they would go outside and roast wieners. When John Gissendanner was growing up in Saginaw, Michigan, at the age of eleven or twelve, he began reciting Dunbar's poems, mostly at church fund-raising events.[40] Gloria Scott fondly recalls how her mother would pack churches in east Baltimore and sometimes in her native South Carolina, as well, with people who came to hear her recite his poems at special programs.[41]

These griots made lasting impressions, according to Johnnie Mae Harris of New Orleans, who recalls how her aunt Josie Nell Moore's performances of Dunbar's poetry in Jackson, Mississippi, could transport the listeners vicariously to the locales in the poems. Harris fondly remembers, "She could bring the setting alive; she could make you feel as if you were there on that plantation."[42] As a child during the late 1950s and early 1960s, I recall hearing recitations of Dunbar's "In the Morning," which would sometimes involve a griot literally taking on the persona of Lias's mother, wearing long dresses and kerchiefs typifying the dress of a woman on the plantation, and a boy dressed as Lias. Expressive body movements would complement their dress and speech. Often the poets would wear costumes or some other striking dress to help bring the performance to life. The performers would use what linguists call tonal semantics, rhythmical language with emphasis on the sound of certain words and phrases.[43] Central to the oral tradition, the Dunbar griots would sometimes substitute words or add new ones to augment the text. For example, a variation I have heard in public performances adds the word "lazy" before "scamp," a word not present in Dunbar's original version: "Ef you don' git up, you *lazy* scamp, / Dey'll be trouble in dis camp." Each performer had a unique style and flair that would make the performance his or her own, true to the black performance tradition. As in the gospel tradition, no two performances were alike because of improvisation.

Live performances sometimes would incorporate song and movement, as in the African tradition, into the poems. Thus, when reciting "Negro Love Song," performers would dance in synchronization to the rhythm of the words. Or when reciting "When Malindy Sings," one would sing the lyrics of the hymns and spirituals incorporated into the poem. In Margaret Walker's recorded rendition of the poem, she sings the words of the hymns "Come to Jesus" and "Rock of Ages" and the spiritual "Swing Low, Sweet Chariot" expressively when reciting the poem.[44] Clearly, Dunbar's poems anchored community activities aiding socialization, as well as preserving and passing on a love of and respect for traditional oral culture to subsequent generations.

In a vastly different world with few television sets, if any, one could easily find examples of the role Dunbar's poems played in memorization, family socialization and bonding, and handing down traditionally oral culture. Borders says her father, while holding her little sister on his knee, rocking her back and forth, would recite "Little Brown Baby" to calm her when she was fretful. This account supports Braxton's assertion that "Dunbar refutes the myth that slave fathers did not love their children."[45] Gloria Scott recalls how when she was a child, she and her relatives would busy themselves by reciting Dunbar's poetry while sitting in the kitchen when meals were being prepared.[46] This tradition of reciting Dunbar's poems, as Henry Louis Gates Jr. recalls, aided him in waking up his own children, who were born in 1980 and 1982. He would recite "In the Morning" to them, as his father had done for him.[47] Thus the use of a number of Dunbar's poems emphasizes the primacy of the family in African American culture and demonstrates that, like African art, Dunbar's poetry is not merely appreciated for its aesthetic value but often has functional value.[48]

Often Dunbar's poems were recited at social functions and community gatherings, but for many older adults, they may have been standard fare in the school curriculum and were integral components of literacy programs in schools and homes during the era of racial segregation. Some famous African Americans recall how their familiarity with Dunbar's poems influenced their love of literature and learning. Maya Angelou acknowledges Dunbar as one of her favorite writers. In fact, her grandmother insisted that she study black poets, whom her grandmother placed above writers like Shakespeare, Kipling, and Poe.[49] Perhaps Maya Angelou recited Dunbar's poems in church and school, and her recitations of his poems may have influenced her poetry readings, which helped her find her voice as a professional poet. In her autobiography *You May Plow Here*, Sara Brooks, who was born in 1911, observes that Dunbar is one of the poets whom women of her generation most often name among those they studied in elementary school.[50] Vernon Jordan Jr., who served as an advisor to Bill Clinton, acknowledges "In the Morning," which he learned to recite as a child and he can easily recite today, to be his favorite poem.[51] Gates says of his observation of Jordan's recitation that "his face lit up when he began to recite."[52] This poem is cited as one memorized by thousands of schoolchildren. Dunbar's poems seem to have fostered a love of learning and respect for the oral tradition.

Several oral accounts tell of teachers and students who had an affinity for poems by black writers, with Dunbar poems cited as popular ones that helped maintain oral culture in the "separate but equal" classrooms of the South. In true African fashion, such teachers became a vital and inseparable part of the community in which they taught and transmitted their appreciation for literature to the members of these communities. During the 1930s, there was a literature teacher at John Wesley Hoffman Junior High in New Orleans who would give her students opportunities to earn extra credit on Fridays by reciting Dunbar's poems. They would recite these poems during Black History Week as well.[53] When Ruth Thornton, a middle school teacher in Washington, D.C., attended the all-black Jennie Dean combined elementary and high school in Manassas, Virginia, in the 1960s, students were required to learn poems by black poets, including those of Dunbar.[54] Taking their spoken-word talents into the communities in which they served, Thornton's teachers would, at times, assume the role of Dunbar griots in the local communities. Thornton also recollects her experiences listening to her teachers perform Dunbar's dialect poems at Sunday morning services and special programs in Prince William County, Virginia.[55] Willie Mae Kilgore, who enthralled community audiences in Baltimore with her rousing performances, had been a teacher in her home state of South Carolina.[56]

Dunbar was also celebrated in institutions of higher education. Borders recalls that when she worked as a librarian at Bethune-Cookman College (now

Bethune-Cookman University) in Daytona Beach, Florida, the president's wife would routinely recite Dunbar's poetry in the 1930s and 1940s at community meetings attended by whites until faculty became disgruntled and criticized her for reciting those embarrassing dialect poems.[57] According to Borders, people were self-conscious about Dunbar's poetry and felt "we could do better."[58] This attitude change began to pave the way for attacks on Dunbar's work as representing the accommodationist school of thought, which became prevalent during the 1960s. This new attitude reflected the tension between high and low culture, a tension that had been central to a black value system as far back as the Harlem Renaissance. Advocates of high culture prize the art and culture of white society and view art and culture through a lens of European standards. Advocates of low culture value black aesthetics, accept their blackness, and are not ashamed of indigenous art forms that originated among the black working class.

Dunbar was an exceptional poet whose work as a poet of the people influenced other distinguished poets who honored this oral tradition, including James Weldon Johnson, Langston Hughes, Gwendolyn Brooks, Nikki Giovanni, Michael Harper, and Sonia Sanchez. Though in his poetry Dunbar was not militant or outspoken in addressing racial themes, he capitalized on the oral traditions of his African ancestors to produce a unique and rhythmically beautiful body of poetry praising black heroes, leaders, and activists; black music; and black cultural traditions rooted in Africa. As a race poet, he wrote of community love and unity, and his poetry served to foster a sense of community via the many griots or storytellers who dramatized his poems at events integral to the life of post–World War I communities across America.

As chief poet of the people, he read his poems publicly with intense feeling and expression and initiated a tradition among black folks, who would, like him, memorize his poems and would dramatize and recite them, but at all-black community gatherings instead of for white audiences. Clearly, many in the African American community first learned to love Dunbar's poems by hearing them recited before ever seeing them in print. Indeed, today's surviving vernacular tradition in African American poetry remains one of Dunbar's most enduring contributions to poetry.

Notes

1. Felton O. Best, "Crossing the Color Line: A Biography of Paul Laurence Dunbar, 1872–1906" (PhD diss., Ohio State University, 1992), 12.

2. *The Collected Poetry of Paul Laurence Dunbar*, ed. Joanne M. Braxton (Charlottesville: University of Virginia Press, 1993), 191, lines 13–15.

3. Ibid., 71, lines 6–7.

4. William W. Cook, "Found Not Founded," in *African American Rhetoric(s): Interdisciplinary Perspectives*, ed. Elaine B. Richardson and Ronald L. Jackson II (Carbondale: Southern Illinois University Press, 2004), 259.

5. *Collected Poetry*, xxii.

6. Paul Zumthor, *Oral Poetry: An Introduction* (Minneapolis: University of Minnesota Press, 1990), 25.

7. Landeg White and Jack Mapanje, eds., *Oral Poetry from Africa: An Anthology* (New York: Longman, 1983), 5–6.

8. Best, "Crossing the Color Line," 211, 212.

9. *Collected Poetry*, 50, line 6.

10. Ibid., xix.

11. Ibid., 206, lines 19–22

12. "The Negro," in *The Collected Poems of Langston Hughes*, ed. Arnold Rampersad and D. Roessel (New York: Vintage Classics, 1995), 338, lines 1–3.

13. "On Being Brought from Africa to America," in *Poems of Phillis Wheatley: A Native African and a Slave* (Bedford, Mass.: Applewood Books, 1995), 12, line 7.

14. Maria Stewart, "Lecture Delivered at the Franklin Hall," in *With Pen and Voice: A Critical Anthology of Nineteenth-Century African-American Women*, ed. Shirley Wilson Logan (Carbondale: Southern Illinois University Press, 1995), 7.

15. Best, "Crossing the Color Line," 204.

16. Ibid.

17. Ibid., 114, line 3.

18. *Collected Poetry*, 208, line 11.

19. Ibid., 114, line 3.

20. Ibid., 113, line 20.

21. Ibid., 209, lines 8–9.

22. "The Lyrics of the Tuskegee Song," in *The Booker T. Washington Papers*, vol. 6, 1901–2, ed. Barbara R. Kraft, Raymond W. Smock, and Louis R. Harlan (Urbana: University of Illinois Press, 1977), 403, 404, lines 5–6, 17–20.

23. Olaudah Equiano, *The Interesting Narrative and Other Writings*, ed. Vincent Carretta (1789; New York: Penguin, 2003), 34.

24. *Collected Poetry*, 82, line 41.

25. Ibid., 82, lines 18, 21–22.

26. Bernice Johnson Reagon, *If You Don't Go, Don't Hinder Me: The African American Sacred Song Tradition* (Lincoln: University of Nebraska Press, 2001), 47.

27. *Collected Poetry*, 82, lines 48–49.

28. Ibid., 82, lines 11–12.

29. The blue notes (flatted third and seventh scale degrees) have been linked to African musical production. For an extended discussion, see Portia Maultsby, "Africanisms in African American Music," in *Africanisms in American Culture*, ed. Joseph E. Holloway (Bloomington: Indiana University Press, 2005), 328.

30. Ibid., 334.

31. *Collected Poetry*, 178–79, lines 11–14.

32. The banjo has been established as an instrument of indisputable African origin, as documented by Dena Epstein in "The Folk Banjo: A Documentary History," *Ethnomusicology* 19 (1975): 347–71. For a thorough discussion of the banjo's origin and place in American culture, see John Edward Philips, "The African Heritage of White America," in *Africanisms in American Culture*, 2nd ed., ed. Joseph Holloway, 225–239 (Bloomington: University of Indiana Press, 2005). Although brought to America and used by slaves in seventeenth-century America, today the instrument is played mostly by Appalachian whites. Dunbar celebrates the banjo in several other poems, including "A Banjo Song" (*Collected Poetry*, 20).

33. *Collected Poetry*, 82, lines 33–40.

34. Paul Laurence Dunbar, "The Fruitful Sleeping of the Rev. Elisha Edwards," in *African American Humor: The Best Black Comedy from Slavery to Today*, ed. Mel Watkins (Chicago: Lawrence Hill Books, 2003), 83.

35. For an in-depth discussion of "hush harbor rhetoric," see Vorris L. Nunley, "From the Harbor to the Academic Hood: Hush Harbors and an African American Rhetorical Tradition," in *African American Rhetoric(s)*, 221–41.

36. *Collected Poems*, 13, lines 1–4.

37. Personal interview, March 20, 2007.

38. Personal interview, February 10, 2006.

39. Personal interview, March 15, 2007.

40. Personal interview, February 25, 2006.

41. Personal interview, February 25, 2006.

42. Personal interview, February 10, 2006.

43. Tonal semantics is sometimes defined as "conveying meaning through an emphasis on sound by altering the rhythm of one's speech and inflecting the voice." For an expanded discussion, see Geneva Smitherman, *Talkin' and Testifyin': The Language of Black America* (Detroit: Wayne State University Press, 1986).

44. Margaret Walker, "When Malindy Sings," *Every Tone a Testimony* (Smithsonian Folkways Recordings, 2001).

45. *Collected Poetry*, xxviii.

46. Personal interview, February 25, 2006.

47. Henry Louis Gates Jr., foreword to *In His Own Voice: Paul Laurence Dunbar*, ed. Herbert Woodward Martin and Ronald Primeau (Athens: Ohio University Press 2002), xi.

48. Robert Brain, *Art and Society in Africa* (New York: Longman, 1980), i–iii.

49. Maya Angelou, *I Know Why the Caged Bird Sings* (New York: Bantam Books, 1969), 3–14.

50. *You May Plow Here: The Narrative of Sara Brooks*, ed. Thordis Simonsen (New York: Norton, 1986), 128.

51. Gates, foreword, xi.

52. Ibid., xii.

53. Personal interview, March 20, 2007.

54. Personal interview, March 21, 2007.

55. Personal interview, March 21, 2007.

56. Personal interview, March 25, 2006.

57. Personal interview, March 20, 2007.

58. Personal interview, March 20, 2007.

2
National Memory and the Arts in Paul Laurence Dunbar's War Poetry

NASSIM W. BALESTRINI

APPROXIMATELY TWENTY OF Paul Laurence Dunbar's four hundred poems deal with the topic of war. The majority of these works adhere to long-established poetic styles; both the poems in dialect and in Standard English are clothed in traditional metrical and stanzaic forms. As is the case with other prevalent themes in his poetry, Dunbar sometimes clearly identifies his lyrical "I" or the described characters as African American, whereas in other instances he excludes all references to race and skin color in order to emphasize a general human perspective or at least an all-American outlook. Dunbar's war poems reflect both his love for the African American heritage and his insistence on shared cultural values, such as long-standing types of English-language poetry. The creation of a national tradition of, on the one hand, remembering all people who suffered through war and, on the other hand, appreciating the contributions and sacrifices of specific race- or gender-defined groups bespeaks the poet's awareness of the influence of cultural and national memory on future generations. How, then, do late nineteenth- and early twentieth-century Americans commemorate the Revolutionary War, the Civil War, the Spanish-American War, and the role of black soldiers in each of these conflicts? How does the interpretation of a war affect mainstream national identity, ethnic identity, and race relations? How can artists participate in creating traditions of remembrance that foster interracial harmony on the basis of equality and mutual respect?

Two goals recur throughout Dunbar's war poems. First, the extinction of race prejudice and of the perceived blemish of slavery will foster the integration of African Americans into American society; this will occur once all Americans acknowledge the suffering and appreciate the achievements of the black population. Second, a dignified and appropriate manner of keeping the memory of the African American soldiers' contributions to American glory alive will evolve in the arts and in historiography. Numerous instances of bitterness or irony in the poems indicate the stony path to be overcome before reaching these goals.

Several critics describe "Black Samson of Brandywine," Dunbar's poem about an American hero of the Revolutionary War, as an example of the assertion of the manliness and the prowess of black soldiers.[1] To Jean Wagner, however, "the poem breathes an authentic racial pride, though for some tastes it lays rather too much stress on the loyalty of the black hero. . . . He could fight for the freedom of his country, while his black brothers were still enslaved."[2] This six-stanza poem deserves a closer look, as it goes beyond merely praising a hero; rather it addresses Dunbar's concern with historiography and cultural memory created through the arts.

A quotation from C. M. Skinner's *Myths and Legends of Our Own Land* (1896) precedes the first stanza, as if to authenticate the subsequent statements on Black Samson's unearthly physical powers.[3] The imagery of colorlessness and of faulty vision found in the opening lines implies that historiography only provides partial truth: "Gray are the pages of record, / Dim are the volumes of eld; / Else had old Delaware told us / More that her history held."[4] The speaker thus states in the second stanza that personified Delaware would then have proudly elaborated on Black Samson's feats. Ranking the war hero with "your chiefs and your nobles, / Saxon and Celt and Gaul"[5] makes his achievement part and parcel of an ancient military tradition associated with European rulers and explorers, who, by implication, are the ancestors of the American revolutionaries and their French associates.

Whereas the description of scythe-swinging Black Samson as "a mower" and "the reaper" evokes conventional images of grim death, the speaker plays with the irony of a "human harvest,"[6] which focuses on killing rather than on providing physical nourishment. As Black Samson caused the deaths of numerous British soldiers, his heroism ultimately contributed to American victory and independence. But the persona does not reveal that the Americans lost the 1777 battle at Brandywine Creek and, thus, control over Philadelphia. In other words, Dunbar expects his audience to applaud a hero for his courage and devotion to a cause without judging the immediate outcome of a specific battle.

The fifth stanza confirms this appreciation of personal qualities without considering the circumstances: "Was he a freeman or bondman? / Was he a man or a thing? / What does it matter? His brav'ry / Renders him royal—a king."[7] These lines have been criticized as an inappropriate dismissal of the question as to whether Black Samson, an American slave, should have fought for the independence of a country that held him as "a chattel."[8] The persona argues that the soldier's loyalty and courage are timeless and thus ennobling qualities. The monarchical imagery obviously serves as a metaphor that elevates the slave to the highest possible social position. As he fought for the establishment of a republic based on equality, his royal status refers to his place within the pantheon of national heroes. It also shows that inherent qualities of character override man-made categories of class based on skin color.

Black Samson's name invites interpretation. If he survived to see the American republic, does this republic then represent his Delilah? Is this Delilah responsible for eventually blinding and torturing Samson, for depriving him of his hitherto useful God-given strength? The final stanza encourages the reader to imagine that Black Samson's story has more dimensions than a mere account of a battle. The lyrical "I" claims that, in contrast to the extant "Gray" and "Dim" historiography, his tale is so "Noble and bright"[9] that it can inspire all artists. These artists' works will then achieve the speaker's goal of securing the memory of Black Samson for the entire world.

The fact that Dunbar was interested in the role of African Americans during the Revolutionary War or in the significance of the Revolutionary War for African Americans is also indicated in the lyrics of a song entitled "On Emancipation Day," which he wrote in 1898.[10] At the end of this exuberant song about a parade celebrating the freeing of the slaves, we learn that some of the celebrants are "Generals stiff as hick'ry sticks / In de dress of sev'nty six."[11] The ahistorical projection of an American revolutionary general's uniform onto an African American celebrating the emancipation of 1863 implies analogies between the legitimacy and necessity of both the independence from Britain and the abolition of slavery. It also represents one way of dating African American history back to the beginnings of U.S. history and of reminding white audiences of the long-standing presence of slaves and, eventually, free blacks in American society. Ultimately the ahistoricity of a black general in the Revolutionary Army provokes the implied viewer of the parade to rethink ideology-based patterns of inclusion and exclusion in American historiography.[12]

Dunbar's poems on the American Civil War can be grouped as follows: poems on African American soldiers in general, poems on individual experiences, interpretations of the Civil War as a whole, and poems without reference to the race of the soldiers. In the discussion of the fourth group, I also include poems that deal with remembering soldiers of unspecified American wars.

James A. Emanuel regards "The Colored Soldiers" as Dunbar's "strongest war poem," and he discusses the battles mentioned in the work.[13] William M. Ramsey concurs when he states that the poem exudes "strong racial assertiveness,"[14] whereas Jean Wagner concludes that although the persona addresses whites directly, "here [Dunbar] too persists in his timidity, expressing no open indignation at injustice and limiting himself to dropping hints."[15] The structure, the diction, and the speaker's reading of American history contradict Wagner's assertion. Within the aesthetic parameters of Dunbar's poetic style, "The Colored Soldiers" belongs to the group of poems that clearly delineate the necessity of commemorating the contributions of black soldiers in historiography and in the arts.

The closing three lines of the first and the last of the ten stanzas describe African American soldiers as "those noble sons of Ham—/ The gallant colored soldiers / Who fought for Uncle Sam!"[16] The persona reinterprets the belief that Africans descended from Noah's rejected son, a genealogy that was used as a justification for permanent enslavement based on divinely ordained inferiority, with the use of the adjective "noble." From a pro-slavery perspective, "noble sons of Ham" would be oxymoronic. The speaker confirms this reinterpretation by referring to "*gallant* colored soldiers," that is, by applying a term formerly reserved—at least in the southern plantation tradition—to white gentlemen. The worthiness of these African American soldiers is further validated through the rhyme "Ham" / "Sam," which seems to imply progressive development or at least congruence between the African Americans' background and their engagement in the Union army, which eventually contributed to the abolition of slavery. This rhyme strikes me as rather bold for a time when post-Reconstruction racists competed with each other in their efforts to deny African Americans allegiance to "white" American values and to keep them permanently oppressed and subservient.

The poem clearly points out the initial haughty rejection of African American contributions to the struggle against the Confederacy (second stanza), the demand for black soldiers once all-white efforts were on the brink of collapse (third stanza), and the superlative contributions of valiant African American soldiers (fourth and fifth stanzas). In the fifth and sixth stanzas, the speaker refers to the locations of several famous battles. The indirection with which the lyrical "I" expresses his disdain for the massacre and murder of captured black soldiers by Confederate soldiers against all rules of warfare (sixth stanza) may be ascribed to Dunbar's expectation that these events are still sufficiently vivid in the nation's memory; on the other hand, he may have been worried about offending his audience to the extent that the central point of the poem would be lost.[17]

The main sociopolitical criticism in this poem is twofold. First, Dunbar rejects national amnesia regarding the crucial role of African American soldiers in winning the Civil War (seventh through tenth stanzas). Second, he addresses the regressive developments since the end of the war: "They were comrades then and brothers, / Are they more or less to-day?" And, as in the characterization of Black Samson, he asserts that "the traits that made them worthy,—/ Ah! those virtues are not dead." For this reason, the persona is certain that "their deeds shall find a record / In the registry of Fame; / For their blood has cleansed completely / Every blot of slavery's shame."[18] In these lines reside the crucial notions this poem promotes. As the African American soldiers proved their valor and other generally desired virtues, historiography will eventually remember and immortalize them. Furthermore, the positive evaluation of their sacrificial blood goes beyond the immediate context of the Civil War, as it removed any stigma associated with enslavement. The washing away of this mark then serves as their entry into mainstream society as citizens and siblings to all. The progression from the persona's humble *captatio benevolentiae* in the opening stanza ("If the muse were mine to tempt it / And my feeble voice were strong")[19] to the forceful assertion in the final stanza regarding the appreciation of the soldiers' deeds contradicts the impression of timidity and rather confirms the clarity of Dunbar's programmatic interest in historiography and commemoration in the arts.

"The Unsung Heroes" represents such an attempt at artistic homage,[20] but the speaker again proclaims his inability and desires "some seer" to "tell of their virtues as minstrels did of old, / Till the pride of face and the hate of race grow obsolete and cold."[21] The title of this poem again raises awareness of the silence of historiographers and artists concerning African American soldiers. The use of the term "minstrels" probably struck readers at the time (who were aware of the difference between the medieval minstrel singer of ballads and the racist intentions of minstrel show depictions of stereotyped "darkies") as bold. The desire for heroic ballads of folk minstrels, for ballads that would be part of the shared cultural heritage, implies the integration of black heroes into national lore. While this poem again refers to various battles and to the eager contribution to Union victories, it also—like "The Colored Soldiers"—stresses a metaphysical dimension of history. In "The Unsung Heroes," God appears as an observer of black heroism, which makes him pronounce: "I have made them men."[22] These twice-created soldiers "fought their way from night to day and struggled up to God."[23] The metaphysical quality of their achievement makes the fact that they are "unsung" on a larger scale even more jarring. This religious dimension implicitly provides a basis for the concrete social goal: the removal of man-made and race-based feelings of supremacy and hatred.[24]

"When Dey 'Listed Colored Soldiers" and "Whistling Sam" deal with the Civil War experiences of specific fictional characters. In the first poem, the persona is an African American slave woman whose partner, Elias, joins the Union army. She describes two instances of changing emotions: while she initially pleads with Elias not to go away, she subsequently supports him when he marches off in his blue uniform; while she at first cannot mourn for the Confederate dead within the family of her white owners, she does empathize with them when Elias is at war, and especially when she learns of his death on the battlefield. Her main comfort resides in the conviction that "Gawd had called him"[25] to serve in the Union army. In "Whistling Sam," the title character is a private whose gift of whistling comes in handy on all occasions. He can cheer up his peers; he can also move them to tears by whistling a church hymn during a burial on a battlefield. Whistling Sam survives the war and joins his love, Dinah, at the end.

In her response to "When Dey 'Listed Colored Soldiers," Nancy B. McGhee points out that the "dramatic contrasts of Blacks with whites" and "the pain and suffering of the war-ravaged plantation people, the Blacks as well as the whites,"[26] do not deny the speaker's ability to mourn loved ones on both sides. Jean Wagner criticizes Dunbar's seemingly unclear allegiance: "Here Dunbar is dancing on a tightrope, and he sheds a revealing light on the art of compromise he had to practice to avoid angering either of his two publics, the black or the white. The reader can but lament his embarrassment."[27] To Wagner, any form of empathy with slaveholders is to be rejected, even if this means that a black widow cannot share the pain experienced by a white widow. On the contrary, I would argue that Dunbar's depiction of the persona's learning process appeals to black and white readers alike. Pride in sacrifices on the battlefield as well as shared mourning of the casualties can be learned. Dunbar's depiction of shared feelings of loss among women of both races resembles the strategy used in abolitionist essays by Angelina Grimké Weld and Sarah Grimké, and in Harriet Beecher Stowe's sentimental novel *Uncle Tom's Cabin*; this strategy recurs in postbellum literary texts into the twentieth century, as seen in Angelina Grimké Weld's 1916 play *Rachel*.

Like "When Dey 'Listed Colored Soldiers," "Whistling Sam" is written in dialect. As is well known, critics have been debating the implications of Dunbar's work in black dialect (and others). To cite two extreme perspectives: Wagner describes Dunbar's use of what the former calls the plantation tradition as proof of the adverse psychological effects of "the mark of oppression."[28] John Keeling regards the switch between Standard English and dialect as part of Dunbar's "dialogic" poetics based on the idea of "deliberate 'masking.'"[29] "Whistling Sam" illustrates Keeling's notion of dialogic poetry in that the speaker—through whom we learn about Sam—uses diction and implies ways of thinking that derive partially from his experience as a slave and partially from his enjoyment of freedom. In the first category, the reader will notice that Sam is not given a last name but rather is defined through the slave owner's full name ("ol' Ike Bates's Sam").[30] The speaker also refers to African Americans as "da'kies" (for instance, in line 3). In contrast, the lyrical "I" expresses pride in Sam's participation in the emancipation process by calling the Union forces "Gawd's great ahmy," and the proudly enlisted Sam "a king."[31] During the war, Sam rests assured that Jesus is "de Mastah" with a capital *M;* after the war, all blacks know that "souls an' bodies was freed"[32] and that Christ himself may have accomplished this feat. As a result, Whistling Sam—whom the speaker humorously and repeatedly describes as being rather ugly when puckering up his face to whistle—emerges not only as an all-American Sam but also as a counterimage to the stereotype of the minstrel slave, the happy-go-lucky Jim Crow.[33] The speaker's emphasis on Sam's religiousness and on his close ties to his parents and his bride combats antebellum stereotypes concerning the absence of familial and social coherence within the African American community. The healing function of Sam's whistling equips his music with a spiritual strength that transcends entertainment or even the mere enjoyment of music as such.

If one looks at "Whistling Sam" and "When Dey 'Listed Colored Soldiers" as companion pieces and as complements to the poetic tributes to African American soldiers as a group, the complexity of Dunbar's approach becomes clear. These poems promote a kind of historical memory of individual and shared experiences that acknowledges predicaments and solutions and illustrates the human potential for violence and—more importantly—for transracial human brother- and sisterhood.

"The Veteran" recounts a parade of veterans and follows the speaker's reverie about a crippled veteran's possible thoughts. Several other poems address traditional ways of honoring dead soldiers by, for instance, visiting their graves on Memorial Day. One might argue that Dunbar wrote these poems without references to the soldiers' racial backgrounds because he wanted them to appeal to all Americans. At the same time, it appears plausible that Dunbar is suggesting the necessity of shared moments of memory regardless of race, and thus inclusive of all Americans. These poems have been mostly ignored by critics, possibly because they deemed poems without a specific race-related topic negligible.

"The Veteran," "Dirge for a Soldier," "Remembered," "Our Martyred Soldiers," "Memorial Day," and "Ode for Memorial Day" share tendencies that are fundamental to Dunbar's notion of public remembrance of history. The speakers often express the notion that honoring the dead should take the form of praying for their resurrection and that an optimistic outlook on the future based on a joyous appreciation of the heroes' glory should be in the foreground. By believing that the Civil War had a transcendent purpose, all celebrants can look forward to and work toward a better future.

Dunbar's insistence on future-oriented ways of remembering the past certainly does not mean that he wants to ignore past suffering. As "The Veteran" shows, the speaker is torn between perceiving the veterans' parade as "a dirge" and imagining joyful bands applauded by exuberant viewers: "Shout, hurrah and laugh and jest, / This is memory at its best."[34] The speaker then notices a veteran standing on the side, lifting his cane, "Longing to be with the rest."[35] In the attempt to imagine the old man's thoughts, the speaker engraves the veteran's image in his own memory and thus ensures remembrance of a dying generation. The *figura etymologica* "He stood and stands"[36] emphasizes the merging of past and present in the speaker's recollection. Thus the war experience is imaginatively kept alive in a young individual, possibly an observer like Dunbar who was also born after the Civil War. Again, as in "When Dey 'Listed Colored Soldiers," empathy creates an intersubjective bond regardless of age or race.

The issue of which events in a nation's history should be commemorated and immortalized in the arts is treated in different ways. In the 1888 poem "Our Martyred Soldiers," sixteen-year-old Dunbar confirms the peaceful (albeit cold) refuge that soldiers have found in their graves, but in the final stanza the speaker cries out for better reasons for national moments of remembrance: "And when this memory lost shall be, / We turn, oh Father, God, to thee! / Oh find in heaven some nobler thing / Than martyrs of which men can sing."[37] In his later poems, Dunbar modifies his outlook and stresses the necessity of always remembering these martyred soldiers, but he continues to create visions of positive endeavor resulting from such acts of remembrance.

Accordingly, the poet repeatedly contrasts the unproductiveness of tears with the productiveness of doing something constructive. Even in "Dirge for a Soldier," in which the narrator describes a soldier's burial, the mourning mother is cheered by her patriotic convictions, and the stoic soldiers avoid shedding tears because "Now [is] no time for grief's pursuing, / Other work is for the doing, / Here to-day."[38] Both "Memorial Day" and "Ode for Memorial Day" stress the metaphysical dimension of suffering. In the former poem, which consists of two stanzas of seven and eight lines respectively, lines 7 and 8 begin identically but differ in their continuations. The eighth line thus transforms the statement of the previous line into a spiritual claim and serves as the turning point of the poem—that is, the point at which we turn from focusing on graves, flowers, and tears to acknowledging the soldiers' heavenly home: "Flesh is but dust when parted from the breath. / Flesh is but dust, but worth of soul is gold!"[39] The assonance linking "soul" and "gold" stresses this transformation. "Ode for Memorial Day" similarly illustrates the contrast between "fraternal estrangement" and "a conflict fraternal," on the one hand, and the virtues that the Union army defended ("truth," "Right," "charity, peace, and devotion," "Love"), on the other hand. Simply referring to the soldiers as "our fathers" and "our heroes" subsumes all soldiers under the umbrella of the previous generation.[40]

Dunbar uses blossoming flowers as symbols for the positive outcome of letting the nation's soil drink the soldiers' blood. These flowers again represent a heavenly dimension that is to influence the future. In "Remembered," the speaker applies the flower image to ongoing memory ("Fresh as these blossoms shall their [the killed soldiers'] memories keep, / With fragrance sweet, eternal and divine").[41] In "Ode for Memorial Day," metaphorical flowers represent newly developed virtues that replace hatred and enmity: "Flowers of charity, peace and devotion / Bloom in the hearts that are empty of strife."[42]

How, then, does Dunbar view the Civil War and its legacy? Wagner argues that Dunbar's sonnet on Robert Gould Shaw expresses "bitterness and disillusionment."[43] Emanuel concurs, whereas Ramsey sees this poem as an example of works that convey "strong racial assertiveness."[44] In his discussion of "Speakin' at de Cou'thouse," Emanuel finds that Dunbar satirically shows the unreliability of white politicians and, thus, the uncertain situation of African Americans after the Civil War.[45] In "Lincoln" and in "A Spiritual," Dunbar also interprets the war. In this group of poems, feelings of despair and hope mingle with hints at the possibility of remembering the war in constructive ways.

The most encouraging interpretation of the Civil War, at least at first sight, is "A Spiritual." The speaker reads the "'cession"[46] as a foreboding of the Second Coming of Christ. He thus exhorts the sinner to stop crying and to hope for release from his burdens (second stanza), and the mourning widow as well as orphans to stop mourning and to recognize Christ as both mother and father (third and fourth stanzas). The poem thus focuses on the spiritual dimension of the war and the wonderful opportunity it provides to see the Lord. The speaker, however, merely announces Christ's imminent return as recompense for the current horrors. It remains unsaid whether this longed-for event comes to pass. As in the genre of the spiritual, the poem is a song of hope for a better future and for release from suffering.

The eighteen-line poem "Lincoln" describes the president as an epic author endowed with mythical powers: "The mighty Homer of the lyre of war. / 'Twas he who bade the raging tempest cease, / Wrenched from his harp the harmony of peace. / Muted the strings, that made the discord,—Wrong, / And gave his spirit up in thund'rous song."[47] By implication, Lincoln wrote and composed the outcome of the war; his death resembled a roar of thunder that gave the earth some heavenly knowledge. This rather bombastic imagery depicts Homer's epics as analogous to Lincoln's writing in the book of history. However, if Lincoln "Muted the strings, that made the discord," his action appears ambiguous. A mute on a string can merely muffle sounds by depriving them of their overtones, and this muffling would make the—in this case—unpleasant sounds less loud; in the context of the poem, these muted sounds would be less audible than the unmuted harmonious ones. If one interprets muting as complete silencing (in the sense of a person who cannot speak), only the pleasant harmonies would remain. The added word "Wrong" could imply a value judgment: Lincoln silenced wrong assumptions, that is, assumptions that led to discord and war. Or does the speaker intend to dismiss his own verse and to conclude that Lincoln's murder proves the president's failure at muting the discord? Although the four closing lines metaphorically lift Lincoln up to heaven, the second interpretation of the problematic line could be a commentary on the unresolved legacy of the Civil War. Muting discordant sounds does not equal rooting out their sources. In this case, part of the work still needs to be done as the discords still rumble under the surface of supposed harmony.

"Speakin' at de Cou'thouse" and "Robert Gould Shaw" possibly support the interpretation of "Lincoln" as merging praise for the man with awareness of the tragically unaccomplished task. In the first poem, the black speaker goes to hear a white politician's speech in the courthouse. The speaker is disturbed by the pageantry of the political rally, but the orator's accounts of Civil War battles and his claim that "de colah question" has been "solved" put him at ease—until one of the white listeners announces next week's speech by a political opponent.[48] In other words, the postbellum period has not produced consensus, or—in the words of the "Lincoln" poem—harmony and agreement on race relations. In "Robert Gould Shaw," Dunbar uses sound and fire imagery reminiscent of "Lincoln."[49] The speaker asks why "the thunder voice of Fate" drew the young scholar from his study onto the battlefield and why he decided "To lead th' unlettered and despised droves / To manhood's home and thunder at the gate." Shaw's decision results in death and in the loudly voiced request for admittance to heaven, a request that echoes the strength of Fate's summons. The sestet then contradicts these two lines, as the speaker claims that, whereas learning is a quiet and comparatively cool flame, "this hot terror of a hopeless fight" has been, according to what "the Present teaches, / but in vain!"[50] These closing words have been interpreted as an expression of complete surrender to despair and disappointment. However, the context of all of Dunbar's poems on war encourages a different reading. While the final lines of the octet outline the speaker's perspective on Gould and his black soldiers' achievement, albeit as the culmination of wonder at the contrast between Gould's social background and his willingness to fight for the downtrodden, the sestet depicts a currently visible predicament as well as a currently prevalent view of history. Segregation, lynchings, and unconstitutional laws and behaviors bespeak the lack of practical consequences of Gould's sacrifice, but they cannot invalidate the spiritual dimension described in the sestet. At the same time, the appositional remark—"the Present teaches"—may also be read as a reflection of the fact that the American public ignores what the fate of the Fifty-fourth Massachusetts Infantry should have taught them. "Robert Gould Shaw" was published in the 1903 volume *Lyrics of Love and Laughter,* six years after the dedication of Saint-Gaudens's sculpture in honor of Shaw and his regiment. The poem implies that this site of national memory in Boston is not consistent with the current predicament of African Americans. Whereas official public and national memory appears to honor black soldiers and their commander, the descendants of these very soldiers do not live in equality and harmony. Again, celebrating heroes only makes sense if these heroes' values are practiced.

Dunbar shows in his poetry that individuals sacrificed their lives in the defense of laudable eternal principles. Despite the sacrifices of the famous and the unknown, human frailty has prevented the realization of the high ideals fought for. Possible remedies for a selective and faulty national historiography and art are remembering the ideals, the struggle, and its outcome and assessing the present by the original high standards developed in the American revolutionary era and based on both Enlightenment and Christian thought.

Dunbar's war poetry includes "The Conquerors: The Black Troops in Cuba," a lyrical reflection on the Spanish-American War similar to his depictions of African American soldiers in the Civil War and of Black Samson of Brandywine. In "The Conquerors," found in *Lyrics of the Hearthside* (1899), the persona describes the sight-inhibiting battle conditions, which, however, do not impede general awareness of the soldiers' military achievements. Their fame is comparable, for instance, to that of "Lincoln," metaphorically made audible: "Bravely you spoke through the battle cloud heavy and dun. / Tossed though the speech toward the mist-hidden sun, / The world heard."[51] Conventional contrasts between night and day, darkness and light, hell and heaven again—as in some of the Civil War poems—indicate a type of progress linked to the growing awareness of the soldiers' courage (see second stanza). But the persona then returns to sound and voices, particularly to the voice of "Truth." This voice will, once "fear" has been overcome, be heard "Loud and clear" above "noises of trade and the turbulent hum" and above the sound of "the militant drum."[52] Thus, just as clear vision must follow distorted vision, the sound of truth will drown out the hubbub of other noises.

The fourth and final stanza explains these metaphorical perceptions as expressions of the nation's ability to appreciate the African American troops for more than just their military feats: "Then on the cheek of the honester nation that grows, / All for their love of you, not for your woes, / There shall lie / Tears that shall be to your souls as the dew to the rose; / Afterward thanks, that the present yet knows / Not to ply!"[53]

This stanza features elements found in the majority of Dunbar's war poems. First, the speaker's reference to "the honester nation" suggests the necessity to develop a higher degree of truthfulness. Second, appreciating black troops not because of their horrific experiences but because of genuine love lends such appreciation a spiritual dimension rather than merely reflecting awe at their courage and gore. Third, the symbolic rose indicates the potential beauty that may grow out of something as destructive and ugly as war. Fourth, the speaker knows that such gratitude is not yet granted and that—he hopes—it will evolve over time. As in "Robert Gould Shaw," Dunbar indicts contemporary society for insufficient, unjust, dishonest, and superficial modes of memory. The description of heavenly appreciation for the black troops establishes a standard of gratitude that, as in other poems, takes into account the importance of the arts in the nation's culture of memorializing heroes: "Heaven would have crowned you, with crowns not of gold but of bay."[54] Celestial justice thus envisions a reward not in material or monetary terms but rather in the symbol of the poet's and the victor's laurels. This symbol declares the African American soldiers worthy of being artistically represented (as demanded in the final stanza of Dunbar's "Ode to Ethiopia"),[55] and it appreciates their deeds in a manner reminiscent of model republics.

"The Conquerors" complements Dunbar's newspaper article entitled "Recession Never," which was published in the Chicago *Record* in December 1898. As Jay Martin points out, this and similar dispatches unmistakably illustrate Dunbar's "positive view of the black community"[56] and his awareness of discrepancies between praise for black military heroes fighting abroad and dogged demands for African Americans' disenfranchisement in the country for whose ideals they are dying. Dunbar sarcastically writes, "The new attitude may be interpreted as saying: 'Negroes, you may fight for us, but you may not vote for us. You may prove a strong bulwark when the bullets are flying, but you must stand from the line when the ballots are in the air. You may be heroes in war, but you must be cravens in peace. . . . America strides through the ashes of burning homes, over the bodies of murdered men, women and children holding aloft the banner of progress.'"[57] It seems as if Dunbar reserved this degree of direct political indictment for his essays, whereas in his poems he considered subtle poetic means of expressing such thoughts more appropriate. Upon close scrutiny, his stance is clear in both genres.

Dunbar's war poems bespeak his love of both his race and American ideals. The poet who, during his short life, was hailed as the African American poet laureate and who was applauded in the United States and abroad was keenly aware of the role the arts play in both distorting historical memory and honestly portraying a nation's conflicts and achievements. The recurring theme of demanding just assessments of African American soldiers' sacrifices and making such assessments part of a national culture of remembrance demonstrates Dunbar's intention to go beyond encouragement of African Americans. His poems are a clarion call to artists, legislators, and citizens to grapple with national history in a candid and constructive fashion in order to close the gap between American ideals and American reality for all.

Notes

1. See James A. Emanuel, "Racial Fire in the Poetry of Paul Laurence Dunbar," in *A Singer in the Dawn: Reinterpretations of Paul Laurence Dunbar*, ed. Jay Martin (New York: Dodd, Mead, 1975), 84, and Gossie Harold Hudson, "Paul Laurence Dunbar: Dialect et la Negritude," *Phylon* 34, no. 3 (1973): 242.

2. Jean Wagner, *Black Poets of the United States: From Paul Laurence Dunbar to Langston Hughes*, trans. Kenneth Douglas (Urbana: University of Illinois Press, 1973), 98.

3. This method of (pseudo-)authentication recalls white philanthropists' introductory remarks to the poetry volumes of, for instance, Phillis Wheatley. Such acts of vouching for someone who is deprived of social equality are questioned in the course of Dunbar's poem.

4. *The Collected Poetry of Paul Laurence Dunbar*, ed. Joanne M. Braxton (Charlottesville: University of Virginia Press, 1993), 205, lines 1–4.

5. Ibid., 206, lines 9–10.

6. Ibid., 206, lines 21, 29, and 25.

7. Ibid., 206, lines 33–36.

8. Ibid., 206, line 37.

9. Ibid., 205, 206, lines 1, 2, and 39.

10. *In His Own Voice: The Dramatic and Other Uncollected Works of Paul Laurence Dunbar*, ed. Herbert Woodward Martin and Ronald Primeau (Athens: Ohio University Press, 2002), 158.

11. Ibid., 158, lines 19–20.

12. This is not to say that Dunbar took the discrepancy between the ideals of the Declaration of Independence and the legal and social situation of African Americans lightly. In a letter to the *New York Times* published on July 3, 1903, Dunbar follows the approach of Frederick Douglass's famous 1852 Fourth of July speech. Just as Douglass scolded his audience for celebrating natural rights while consistently denying them to parts of the population, Dunbar contrasts Fourth of July celebrations with the ongoing brutality toward African Americans. See Jay Martin, "Paul Laurence Dunbar: Biography through Letters," foreword to *A Singer in the Dawn*, 30.

13. Emanuel, "Racial Fire," 86, 85.

14. William M. Ramsey, "Dunbar's Dixie," *Southern Literary Journal* 32, no. 1 (1999): 38.

15. Wagner, *Black Poets*, 99.

16. *Collected Poetry*, 52, lines 78–80; cf. 50, lines 6–8.

17. Commenting on the sixth stanza (especially lines 42–43), Emanuel argues: "One cannot be certain . . . why Dunbar asks for mercy on the *souls* of the black victims, but requests mercy on the *deeds* of the Confederate killers. Mercy is bestowed upon humans, not upon things and actions. The poet seems either cautious about damning the whites directly, or subtly unwilling to invoke mercy for them" ("Racial Fire," 87).

18. *Collected Poetry*, 51–52, lines 57–58, 63–64, 73–76.

19. Ibid., 50, lines 1–2.

20. Ramsey groups "The Unsung Heroes" with the poems that convey "strong racial assertiveness" ("Dunbar's Dixie," 38).

21. *Collected Poetry*, 197, lines 25 and 27–28.

22. Ibid., 196, line 8.

23. Ibid., 198, line 32.

24. Emanuel also interprets this passage as an expression of "Dunbar's optimistic purpose in praising the might of black soldiers" (84).

25. *Collected Poetry*, 184, line 39.

26. Nancy B. McGhee, "Portraits in Black: Illustrated Poems of Paul Laurence Dunbar," in *Stony the Road: Chapters in the History of Hampton Institute*, ed. Keith L. Schall (Charlottesville: University of Virginia Press, 1977), 94.

27. Wagner, *Black Poets*, 86.

28. Ibid., 95.

29. John Keeling, "Paul Dunbar and the Mask of Dialect," *Southern Literary Journal* 25, no. 2 (1993): 38.

30. *Collected Poetry*, 156, line 4.

31. Ibid., 157, lines 14, 19.

32. Ibid., 157, lines 26, 31.

33. Parallel to endowing Sam with positive characteristics, Dunbar calls Sam's loved one Dinah, a name stereotypically used for female characters in minstrel shows. Similar to the eponymous title character in his poem "Dinah Kneading Dough" (*Collected Poems*, 188–89), she is a complex woman.

34. Ibid., 256, line 8.

35. Ibid., 257, lines 13–14.

36. Ibid., 256, lines 4, 13–14, 24, and 33.

37. Ibid., 294, lines 29–32.

38. Ibid., 199–200, lines 25–32, 40, and 43–45.

39. Ibid., 311, lines 7–8.
40. Ibid., 23, lines 7, 25, 24, 29, 31, 14, and 35.
41. *In His Own Voice*, 277, lines 15–16.
42. *Collected Poetry*, 23, lines 29–30. "After the Struggle" (*In His Own Voice*, 282) is identical with the third and final stanza of "Ode for Memorial Day."
43. Wagner, *Black Poets*, 99.
44. Emanuel, "Racial Fire," 81; Ramsey, "Dunbar's Dixie," 38.
45. Emanuel, "Racial Fire," 82.
46. *Collected Poetry*, 194, line 1.
47. Ibid., 184, lines 10–14.
48. Ibid., 205, lines 37, 38, and 47–48.
49. In "Lincoln," the speaker describes Lincoln's "strains of fire" (ibid., 184, line 16), thus linking melody and fire.
50. Ibid., 221, lines 1, 7–8, 11, 13–14.
51. Ibid., 112, lines 4–6.
52. Ibid., 112–13, lines 17, 15, 18, 16, 17.
53. Ibid., 112–13, lines 19–24.
54. Ibid., 112, line 10.
55. Wagner bemoans that Dunbar does not fulfill the vision of "Ode to Ethiopia" (ibid., 16, lines 43–48), because his soldier-heroes "are *American* heroes, not racial heroes" (*Black Poets*, 100). Saunders Redding argues that "in such pieces as 'Black Samson of Brandywine' and 'The Conquerors' he [Dunbar] tried to establish his people's rightful claim to their humanity and their share in the American heritage." Saunders Redding, "Portrait against Background," in *A Singer in the Dawn*, 43.
56. See Martin, "Paul Laurence Dunbar," 24.
57. Dunbar, qtd. in ibid., 25, 26.

3
"Sing a Song Heroic"
Paul Laurence Dunbar's Mythic and Poetic Tribute to Black Soldiers

SHARON D. RAYNOR

> If the muse were mine to tempt it
> And my feeble voice were strong,
> If my tongue were trained to measure,
> I would sing a stirring song.
> I would sing a song heroic
> Of those noble sons of Ham,
> Of the gallant colored soldiers
> Who fought for Uncle Sam!
> —PAUL LAURENCE DUNBAR, "THE COLORED SOLDIERS," 1895

IN 1989, HOLLYWOOD'S RECOGNITION of the Fifty-fourth Massachusetts Regiment in the blockbuster film *Glory* sparked a resurgence of interest in the Civil War and black participation in several historic battles. This film tells the stories not just of the commander, Colonel Shaw, but also of the "six hundred freedmen" who, "motivated by a call to arms by abolitionist Frederick Douglass, . . . offered their services."[1] Unfortunately, up to this point, the recognition of black participation in the Civil War had been minimal at best, and Civil War–era blacks were often portrayed "as a downtrodden and displaced people, dependent for their freedom and liberty on the genteel 'white boys in blue.'"[2] The story is the same for tribute poetry honoring black participation in the Civil War, which had been continually overlooked and overshadowed, relegated to the bowels of history, along with those black servicemen who fought and died for a country that, until this pivotal moment, never considered honoring their sacrifice or granting them full citizenship. With an all-star cast giving America its first glimpse of blacks in one of America's early wars, it was easy to forget about those who first honored those men, such as the poet Paul Laurence Dunbar, in his poems "The Colored Soldiers," "When Dey 'Listed Colored Soldiers," "Ode for Memorial Day," "The Warrior's Prayer," and "The Veteran."

In his poetry, it is obvious that Dunbar possesses the gift of storytelling. His tribute poetry functions in a manner similar to myth as "an expression of social power," and it helps "justify and explain the dominant order" as well as "transcend habits of prejudice and domination."[3] In two other poems, "Robert Gould Shaw" and "Black Samson of Brandywine," Dunbar succeeds in mythologizing these men as larger-than-life humans. Jerry Lembcke defines myths "as a way to help people come to terms with difficult periods of their past. They provide explanations for why things happened. Often, the explanations offered by myths help reconcile disparities between a group's self-image and the historical record of the group's behavior."[4] Dunbar's poetry, like myth, acts as "a network of stories and images by which systems of oppression and violence are made to seem inevitable."[5] Dunbar began documenting these stories through poetry as a reaction to the compassion he felt for those who served in these important battles, like his father, Joshua Dunbar.

This chapter examines how Dunbar's poetry functions in a mythical capacity as it both memorializes and mythologizes the black soldiers and the sacrifices they made to serve their country and their struggles to obtain full rights of citizenship. Whether written in Standard English or Black English vernacular, the multiple meanings embedded in Dunbar's poetry mark the significance of their fight. Dunbar captures the essence of why and how these soldiers fought and died for their rights, despite tremendous efforts to prevent them from joining American armies. In this tribute, Dunbar also succeeds in mythologizing the black soldier as both warrior and hero. His poetry debunks the myths (1) that "black men, especially ex-slaves, were too cowardly and servile to be good soldiers" and (2) that "the American Negroes are the only people in the history of the world . . . that ever became free without any effort of their own."[6] Dunbar's poetry historicizes, mythologizes, and memorializes the stories and sacrifices of black soldiers. Through historical allusions, diction, narrative myth, and imagery, Dunbar references the curse of Ham, the battles at Wagner and Olustee, and the massacre at Fort Pillow; he tells the story of "W'en dey 'listed colo'ed sojers an' my 'Lias went to wah"; and he also mythologizes Black Samson of Brandywine and Robert Gould Shaw, whose legendary acts give them an important place in the history of the war. His poetry, which is both a literal and mythical memorial to black soldiers, tells the story of their history, their struggles, and the sacrifices that they made despite having to face and endure the same inequalities that existed in civilian life.[7] Dunbar answered the call to erect a memorial that would prove everlasting not only in black history but also in American history.

Because cultural studies, as it relates to historical criticism, teaches scholars to approach a work in terms of the social, cultural, and historical contexts in which it was produced, the historical critic should attempt to re-create the meaning and values of the work for its own time. Dunbar's poetry plays an important role in helping us understand contemporary black American culture and the importance of black participation in America's wars. According to Donald Hall, cultural studies "is a field that fixes its critical eye firmly on the past. [It] makes a strong case for the important role played by literary texts in the creation and replication of systems of power" and gives scholars "an ability to understand a text's reflection of multiple, co-existing systems of meaning, thereby emphasizing textual and historical complexity to a greater degree."[8] Dunbar's poetry illustrates the hierarchies of the social structure during this time and how America had to adjust to the participation of slaves and freed blacks in this war. Despite America's collective amnesia about black participation in the war, it would be difficult to erase it from cultural memory. The image of the strength and sacrifices of blacks who fought in the war has become a major component of black American culture: discussing Dunbar's poetry from a thematic perspective offers literary insight into Dunbar's personal connection to the Civil War and what black participation meant not only to his father but also to so many other men as well. Their participation set a precedent on the battlefield that defined a warrior not by the color of his skin but more by his actions and loyalty.

Dunbar pays homage to both real and mythical soldiers who fought for freedoms they had yet to experience themselves, who never got the opportunity to tell their own stories because of the devastating silence of America's distorted history, and who paved the way for other black servicemen, like the Smoked Yankees, the Buffalo Soldiers, Harlem's Own 369th Infantry, the 761st Tank Battalion, the Tuskegee Airmen, the Montford Point Marines, the Triple Nickels, and the Bloods. His poetry tells the stories of heroes who defined patriotism according to their own rules as well as their desire to prove their bravery and loyalty. He memorializes the black soldier as a real hero who "is not the one who simply states and defends the accepted rules of society, but the one who reaffirms those rules only after questioning and redefining them in his own terms."[9] Perhaps it was Joshua Dunbar's decision to return to America from Canada to fight in the Fifty-fourth Massachusetts Infantry that both influenced and motivated this poetry that redefined patriotism and bravery. Or perhaps it was Dunbar's curiosity about why his father, after escaping slavery by way of the Underground Railroad and establishing a new life in Canada, would return to fight for the very country that first enslaved and then disenfranchised him that motivated him to write about the significance of their sacrifices. Since the quota for the Fifty-fourth Regiment had already been met, Joshua Dunbar and other recruits were enlisted in the Fifty-fifth Massachusetts Infantry (the second black regiment organized by the Union army). According to Bernard Nalty, "In the ranks . . . was Joshua Dunbar. Apparently the soldier was not discouraged by the broken promises concerning pay and the swift punishment for protest, since the son would celebrate in his poetry the interracial camaraderie of the battlefield."[10] Dunbar puts a voice to their experiences, thereby memorializing their presence on America's battlefields.

Dunbar was writing during a revolutionary period of time in American history. A revolution has both the power and potential to produce myth, and the heroes of that revolution may then perhaps embody the (masculine) ideologies of that movement—habits of domination therefore exist. If this power and potential do exist and a myth is produced, does the hero/soldier/warrior embody the same dominant ideologies of that revolutionary movement? Dunbar's poetry speaks to this question, because it, like myth, evolves from silence. At last, he makes audible those voices that have yet to be heard. He memorializes their fight and bravery while debunking the myths of their cowardice in battle. Dunbar indeed surpasses his patriotic duty of merely honoring those who served. He brought national attention to what at first appeared to be a regional and geographical issue but soon escalated into yet another race war (both moral and ethical) over who should be allowed to wear the patriotic "blue suits," to carry weapons, and to ultimately defend the country. According to Noah Trudeau, "they would reflect honor to our race, and . . . become the representative of men of color in the North."[11] James Henry Gooding, a corporal in the Fifty-fourth, stated, "Our people must know that if they are ever to attain any position in the eyes of the civilized world, they must forego comfort, love, fear, and above all, superstition, and fight for it. . . . Consider that on this continent, at least, their race and name will be totally obliterated unless they put forth some effort now to save themselves."[12] Dunbar's decision to memorialize the soldiers so soon after their great sacrifices helped answer many questions about the men's desire to join the fight. They were already fighting against such insurmountable odds that joining the war effort seemed appropriate and a means of elevating their status from slave to citizen.

Because the army interpreted the 1792 Militia Act as "banning black enlistment" and President Lincoln "saw no reason to change this,"[13] blacks still were not allowed to fight for the Union army even after the attack on Fort Sumter. Both the Confiscation Act and the Militia Act, which Congress passed on July 17, 1862, allowed the president to employ as many people of African descent as needed to suppress the rebellion and authorized the employment of free Negroes and freedmen as soldiers.[14] Such organizations as the Prince Hall African Masonic Lodge (the nation's first black Masons) formed their own regiments and offered their services, while other black leaders offered to "assemble and finance three black regiments."[15] Because their willingness to serve became essential to victory, it was important to document their participation and casualties. According to Kai Wright, "Few historical moments encapsulate America's relationship with its black military heroes as well as that of the first nationally recognized engagement between black Union regiments and Confederate troops. In all, 209, 145 served in the Civil War, an estimated 174,000 of them former slaves. The 166 USCT regiments that served throughout the war fought in 449 engagements. Somewhere between 38,000 and 68,000 lost their lives."[16] Dunbar captures in his verses those critical moments in time when the strength for the fight was there on the battlefield and eloquently portrays these tremendous efforts in his poetry. This analysis will provide but a brief journey through some of the most moving verses of Dunbar's poetry as he paints a picture of the majestic deeds of black servicemen that have so often been forgotten.

Dunbar employs a vernacular dialect to tell the story of "W'en dey 'listed colo'ed sojers an' my 'Lias went to wah." In this particular poem, Dunbar's use of the Black English vernacular pays homage to a specific historical period. He skillfully masters the written use of the dialect to tell the story or, better yet, to remember the time when the country began enlisting "colored" soldiers. In this poem, it is important that this dialect was used because Dunbar both needed and wanted to capture the voice and memory of the narrator. Not only does the poem capture that particular historical moment in time—when master and slave were able to fight for the same cause—but it also captures the dialect of both the culture and community.

This poem can also be read as a love poem that details both the trauma and loss told by the voices of those women left behind. Their remembrance of loss is captured by lines such as "Oh, I hugged him, an' I kissed him, an' I baiged him not to go";[17] "So he kissed me, an' he lef' me, w'en I'd promised to be true";[18] "W'y my hea't nigh broke wid grievin' twell I seed him on de street";[19] and "Den I felt lak I could go an' th'ow my body at his feet."[20] The poem eloquently describes a brief meeting between the lovers when he struggles to tell her that he has enlisted to go to war. Even her begging and pleading have no power in the face of his deepest desire to fight in the war. Dunbar writes, "But he tol' me dat his conscience, hit was callin' to him so / An' he couldn't baih to lingah w'en he had a chanst to fight / For de freedom dey had gin him an' de glory of de right."[21] She promises to be true until his return and gives him "pap's ol Bible f'om de bottom of de draw."[22] Ultimately she shares his pride in his only opportunity to enlist and join the fight. The colored soldier's pride in his enlistment is symbolized by his allegiance to "his coat o' sojer blue."[23] The narrator's experience of her love leaving for war and then the trauma of her master's demise and her love's death in battle is portrayed through her sorrow song. Dunbar writes:

> Mastah Jack come home all sickly; he was broke for life, dey said;
> An' dey lef' my po' young mastah some'r's on de roadside,—dead.
> W'en de women cried an' mou'ned 'em, I could feel it thoo an' thoo,
> For I had a loved un fightin' in de way o' dangah, too.
> Den dey tol' me dey had laid him some'r's way down souf to res',
> Wid de flag dat he had fit for shinin' daih acrost his breas'.
> Well, I cried, but den I reckon dat's whut Gawd had called him for,
> W'en dey 'listed col'ed sojers an' my 'Lias went to wah.[24]

The power of this poem lies in the fact that the sadness that the enlistment of black soldiers brought to their loved ones, because they were so eager and proud to fight a battle that was not considered their own, is described in the narrator's authentic and distinctive voice. Dunbar succeeds in writing about these heroic deeds in poems that read as both myth and legend.

In "The Colored Soldiers," Dunbar pays homage to the colored soldiers who fought and died at the battles of Fort Wagner, Olustee, and Fort Pillow. He recalls the desperation and the need to be victorious and the simultaneous attempt to avoid having to arm the slaves, "those noble sons of Ham,"[25] to help fight the war. Dunbar remarks, "Then you called the colored soldiers / And they answered to your call."[26] Their willingness to fight came despite all the ridicule and doubt born of the belief that the war was not one that black men should be fighting:

> In the early days you scorned them,
> And with many a flip and float
> Said, "Those battles are the white man's,
> And the whites will fight them out."

> Up the hills you fought and faltered,
> In the vales you strove and bled,
> While your ears still heard the thunder
> Of the foes' advancing tread.[27]

This poem moves the reader beyond believing that just the human power with which they were endowed could help them be victorious in battle. Dunbar focuses on the righteousness in the hearts of the servicemen so scorned by others. They proved triumphant despite the mythical curse of Ham.

Referring to the colored soldiers as the sons of Ham harkens back to the biblical myth (contemporarily called the curse of Canaan) that God placed a curse on Ham, the son of Noah, for seeing his father naked while the latter was drunk. Historically, this curse was referenced in justification of racism and the enslavement of those of African descent, who were thought to be the descendants of Ham. According to the myth, the descendants of Ham were cursed with black skin. The poem reminds the reader of the unjust treatment of the black soldiers before they were asked to join the fight. Despite being viewed with doubt and scrutiny, they were present at some of the most important battles of the war: "They were foremost in the fight / Of the battles of the free."[28] Throughout the poem, Dunbar describes their heroic participation and feats during battle. He portrays the "colored soldiers" as "hounds unleashed and eager for the life blood of the prey"[29] who were present where the "fight was hottest, where the bullets fastest fell."[30] He describes these soldiers, "unblanched and fearless at the very mouth of hell,"[31] as the "stronger in their labors and braver in the fight."[32] He asks the question, "They were comrades then and brothers / Are they more or less to-day?"[33] What of those men who fought alongside whites for a common goal? Dunbar continues: "They were citizens and soldiers / When rebellion raised its head / And the traits that made them worthy? Ah! Those virtues are not dead."[34] The narrator seems to speak to those Americans who doubted the abilities of the black soldiers—who questioned their eagerness and ability to fight:

> They have shared your nightly vigils,
> They have shared your daily toil;
> And their blood with yours commingling
> Has enriched the Southern soil.
> They have met as fierce a foeman,
> And have been as brave and true.[35]

The poem takes on a tone of resolution and tenacity when Dunbar writes:

> And their deeds shall find a record
> In the registry of Fame;
> For their blood has cleansed completely
> Every blot of Slavery's shame.
> So all honor and glory
> To those noble sons of Ham—
> The gallant colored soldiers
> Who fought for Uncle Sam![36]

History also teaches us that the black man in America has always been at odds with his existence in a country that devalued him. According to W. E. B. Du Bois,

> The Negro is a sort of seventh son, born with a veil, and gifted with second-sight in this American world,—a world which yields him no true self-consciousness, but only lets him see himself through the revelation of the other world. It is a peculiar sensation, this double consciousness, this sense of always looking at oneself through the eyes of others, of measuring one's soul by the tape of a world that looks on in amused contempt and pity. One ever feels his two-ness,—an American, a Negro; two souls, two thoughts, two unreconciled strivings; two warring ideals in one dark body, whose dogged strength alone keeps it from being torn asunder.[37]

A significant parallel can be drawn with Dunbar's poetry as he moves the reader beyond the realms of praise and into the perimeters of strength and courage that have yet to be witnessed. Black soldiers had to be willing to fight multiple battles simultaneously in order to prove their loyalty and dedication to the very country whose intentions were to keep them disenfranchised and oppressed. Their honor, however, endured beyond their victories on the battlefields; it was evident in their sheer determination to fight.

In "The Veteran," Dunbar creates a stark portrayal of the aged soldier who is once again ready to answer the call to duty. He remarks in the poem, "This is memory at its best,"[38] as he watches a parade of veterans "as when first they marched away / Smile on lips and curl on brow / Only white-faced gray beards now."³⁹ The emotion Dunbar captures in the poem with such poignant lines as "Did you notice at your quip / That old comrade's quivering lip?"⁴⁰ reveals the honor of their service. Dunbar portrays the aged soldier as

> Stumbling with the rumbling drum;
> But a sight more sad to me
> E'en than these ranks could be
> Was that one with cane upraised
> Who stood by and gazed and gazed
> Trembling, solemn, lips compressed
> Longing to be with the rest.⁴¹

As he remarks that perhaps a bystander expressed a desire to be among these men, this becomes a sadder thought than the men's positions in society. Despite their position in society, these great soldiers were still willing and ready to answer that call again. Was their desire to fight that profound? What could have been at the root of this desire to join the ranks of the others? Dunbar poses these questions in the following lines:

> Did he dream of old alarms,
> As he stood, "presented arms"?
> Did he think of field and camp
> And the unremitting tramp
> Mile on mile—the lonely guard
> When he kept his midnight ward?
> Did he dream of wounds and scars
> In that bitter war of wars?⁴²

Historically, black soldiers were honored to serve for civil liberties that most white Americans thought that they did not deserve. "What of that?" he asks.⁴³ "As if to question these men who are actually waiting for the call once again: 'To arms, my sons' / And his ears hear far-off guns / Roll of cannon and the tread / Of the legions of the Dead!" ⁴⁴ Honoring those who served called for national recognition by those who enjoyed the freedoms of their sacrifices; Dunbar challenged his readers to fully contemplate the meaning of such recognition. For many black servicemen, the question must be asked: Can true recognition come without the actual acknowledgment of service?

Dunbar's "Ode for Memorial Day" speaks in tribute to what has occurred: "DONE are the toils and the wearisome marches / Done is the summons of bugle and drum."⁴⁵ He recalls that at the end of the day, a significant question remains: "What did it cost for our fathers to gain / Bought at the price of the heart's dearest treasure / Born out of travail and sorrow and pain."⁴⁶ His ode to this day of remembrance is dedicated to those who fought to protect "a land where Rebellion is dumb"⁴⁷ in the dark days of "derangement, conflict and fraternal estrangement."⁴⁸ Their joy and contentment came simply with the right to fight and what this would ultimately mean in regards to achieving their civil liberties: "Ah, but this joy which our minds cannot measure."⁴⁹ Dunbar's poem also captures the vivid realities of battle while sharing the sentiment that these soldiers were

> Born out of travail and sorrow and pain;
> Born in the battle where fleet Death was flying,
> Slaying with saber-stroke bloody and fell;
> Born where the heroes and martyrs were dying,
> Torn by the fury of bullets and shell.
> Ah, but the day is past; silent and rattle,
> And the confusion that followed the fight.
> Peace to the heroes who died in the battle,
> Martyrs to truth and the crowning of Right!⁵⁰

The black soldier was stereotyped as "'child-like,' 'careless,' 'shiftless,' 'irresponsible,' 'secretive,' 'superstitious,' and 'more likely to be guilty of moral turpitude.' The Negro soldier was 'a comic,' 'emotionally unstable,' 'musically inclined with good rhythm,' and 'if fed, loyal and compliant.'" He was viewed as "'lacking in physical courage and psychological characteristics,' which made him 'inherently inferior.'"⁵¹ It was important that Dunbar offered a different story as well as some recognition of those legendary figures who rose above all battles of war and scrutiny and perhaps lived only in the imaginations of those who created them.

Black Samson of the Battle of Brandywine in Delaware, a mythical hero whose name never actually appears in any historical record, is the main character in Dunbar's poem "Black Samson of Brandywine." The legend of Black Samson was created as a myth and evolved into legend. According to Kai Wright,

> Black Samson plays a bit role in a regional tale of patriot betrayal and vengeance. A white man named Isaac Maryland was betrayed by a British spy whom he and his daughter had taken into their confidence, leading to Maryland's death by burning while hiding from British troops. Maryland had caught Samson,

and his daughter had given him food when he was down on his luck. So the "giant Negro" took the murder personally. As legend has it, during the Battle of Brandywine the following day, Samson, "armed with a scythe," heroically "sweeps his way through the red ranks like a sable figure of Time." Later, "in the height of the conflict," Samson reenters the American ranks with the treacherous spy as his prisoner. Following the battle, the patriots tied the spy's arms and legs to a pair of hickory trees they had bound on top. After lashing him, they cut loose the trees and allowed his body to be torn apart.[52]

The following lyrical stanza from the poem portrays this heroic image:

> There in the heat of the battle
>   There in the stir of the fight
> Loomed he, an ebony giant,
>   Black as the pinions of night
> Swinging his scythe like a mower
>   Over a field of grain
> Needless the care of the gleaners
>   Where he had passed amain.[53]

The collective effort of all the black soldiers who served and fought contributed to this grand image of Black Samson of Brandywine. The need to believe and trust in the possibility of the existence of a soldier of his stature among their ranks fueled the creation of Dunbar's poem. This particular poem emphasizes the actual rationale of myths—to "become an expression of social power" and to "justify and explain the dominant order," to "transcend habits of prejudice and domination,"[54] as well as "to help people come to terms with difficult periods of their past."[55] His grand efforts to be brave and unafraid create the premise of possibility present in this poem. He redefines the heroic ideal of the great warrior. Black Samson was not the only soldier Dunbar mythologized in his poetry. He decided to pay homage to a twenty-five-year-old "Boston Brahmin abolitionist"[56] who, under doubt and scrutiny, took command of the Fifty-fourth Massachusetts Regiment and led them into great historical battles.

Dunbar's poem "Robert Gould Shaw," written in the form of a sonnet, appeared in the October 1900 edition of the *Atlantic Monthly*. Dunbar was one of four black American poets who wrote about Shaw. According to Allen Flint in "Black Response to Colonel Shaw," "this is—a startling poem. No poems written before 1900 even hint at the possibility that Colonel Shaw's sacrifice was in vain. But this poem thrusts him into a hopeless fight."[57] Dunbar opens the sonnet with a question: "WHY was it that the thunder voice of Fate / Should call thee, studious, from the classic groves / Where charge thee seek the turmoil of the state?"[58] He seems to be questioning Shaw's intentions and motivations in the next line of the sonnet: "What bade thee hear the voice and rise elate / Leave home and kindred and they spicy loaves / To lead th' unlettered and despised droves / To manhood's home and thunder at the gate."[59] Flint suggests that since Shaw had already dropped out of Harvard in March 1859, joined the New York Seventh Regiment in 1861, and commanded the Fifty-fourth in 1863, these portions of the sonnet are an exaggeration.[60] Despite how the war ended, Shaw clearly chose this path. Even though he assumed command of the "the unlettered and despised droves"[61] and led them into "this hot terror of a hopeless fight,"[62] Dunbar suggests in the final lines of the poem that he did not deserve to die in vain: "This bold endurance of the final pain / Since thou and those who with thee died for right / Have died, the Present teaches, but in vain."[63] This poem's initial exaggeration mythologizes Colonel Shaw as a hero even in death for the sacrifices he made to fight in a war that should have epitomized the true meaning of freedom. He, however, sacrificed more than his life when he decided to lead the "colored soldiers" of the Fifty-fourth. The criticism from others, especially other men of his rank, contributed to the need to glorify his service. Trudeau writes:

> Robert Gould Shaw initially rejected Andrew's offer (to command the 54th Massachusetts Regiment). "If I had taken it," he explained to his sister, "it would only have been from a sense of duty; for it would have been anything but an agreeable task." But after a few days' reflection, he changed his mind. The more he thought about it, the more convinced he became that the "undertaking will not meet with so much opposition as was at first supposed." Shaw had also warmed to the higher purpose of the whole enterprise—"to prove that a negro can be made a good soldier."[64]

Nalty writes, "Killed, wounded, or captured during the evening's fighting were half the officers and men of Shaw's regiment. The Confederates, out of hatred for any white man who would lead black troops into battle, threw Shaw's body into a pit, then heaped the dead troops on top of his corpse—a mass grave shared by the dead of a gallant regiment."[65] His legend will always remind us that he was willing to share his bravery with those honorable men he commanded, even in death. Dunbar does not fail to recognize the spiritual perseverance of those who fought the battles.

In "The Warrior's Prayer," the phrase "strength for the fight" is repeated at the close of the second through fourth stanzas. The warrior is praying for the strength to endure the fight: "I do not ask that thou shalt front the fray / And drive the warring foeman from my sight / I only ask, O Lord, by night, by day / Strength for the fight." [66] This poem "written shortly before his death in 1906 identified the fight against racism as the critical battle when victory would bring not medals and parades but full citizenship."[67] Dunbar insinuates in the poem that he prays for the strength to fight multiple battles. He never specifically names the battles at Fort Pillow, Wagner, or Olustee, as he does in "The Colored Soldiers," so his plea for courage could also be meant to be for the battles on the home front for civil liberties: freedom and citizenship. Black soldiers since the American Revolution had to fight on two fronts even after they assumed that their service would grant them freedoms that they had yet to experience. He closes the poem with four very powerful and poignant lines: "And when, at eventide, the fray is done / My soul to Death's bedchamber do thou light / And give me, be the field lost or won / Rest from the fight."[68] The poem suggests that the soldiers were willing to fight until the bitter end, and regardless of whether the battle was lost or won, they would proudly accept their fates, even if their service took them to death's door. The surviving black soldiers of these battles were merely seeking to become a part of democracy and enjoy full civil liberties as recognized and acknowledged citizens. According to Kai Wright, "By the war's end, fully twelve percent of the Union's forces were black. For many of these men, enlistment was not just an opportunity to fight for their own freedom; it was also a chance to immediately improve the lives of their families. They joined in search of housing, education, and income."[69] Their prayers would be answered when their civil liberties were granted to them. Their sacrifices were met by grave disappointment after the war ended, so their fight continued.

The participation of those men who served and refused to be forgotten or erased from America's collective memory in their own recognition was similar to Dunbar's portrayals. Trudeau writes:

> May 31, 1897, brought the unveiling in Boston of a bronze-relief memorial created by Augustus Saint-Gaudens, depicting Colonel Robert Shaw and twenty-three soldiers of the 54th Massachusetts. A contingent from the 54th did attend the unveiling ceremony, however, and the moment when they marched past the monument was said to be unforgettable, "They seemed to be returning from the war, the troops of bronze marching in the opposite direction, the direction in which they had left for the front, and the young men there represented now showing those veterans the vigor and hope of youth. It was a consecration."[70]

Dunbar's tribute poetry succeeds in fully honoring and recognizing those men who fought with the same great intent and courage as his father. In a letter that Colonel Shaw wrote to his mother before the Battle of Antietam Creek, he stated, "We fight for men and women whose poetry is not yet written."[71] Ironically, shortly afterward, Abraham Lincoln announced the Emancipation Proclamation, which began the freedom process for enslaved blacks. Despite the fact that many soldiers were captured, imprisoned, tortured, and killed by the Confederacy, their efforts were remembered as brave and courageous. After the Battle at Fort Wagner, a Christian worker who witnessed the arrival remembered: "The wounded of the Fifty-fourth Massachusetts came off the boat first, and, as those sad evidences of bravery and patriotism of the colored man passed through the lines of spectators, every heart was melted with tenderness and pity. We will vouch for it . . . that no word of scorn or contempt for negro soldiers will ever be heard from any who beheld that spectacle."[72] Frederick Douglass stated, "In that terrible battle, under the wing of the night, more cavils in respect of the quality of Negro manhood were set at rest than could have been during a century of ordinary life and observation."[73] Their efforts in such historic battles persuaded the many who doubted their service and even their ability to withstand the endurance of battle. The doctor who treated the mangled servicemen recalled, "The only thing that sustained us was the patient endurance of those stricken heroes lying before us, with their ghastly wounds, cheerful, courageous, many a poor fellow signing that his right arm was shattered beyond hope of striking another blow for freedom."[74] Their bravery became legendary in the stories that shaped America's myths and remembrance of the Fifty-fourth. "Yet," according to Hoberman, "the fact that slaves and their descendants did make good soldiers in war after war did little to change the black man's status and American society. The federal government's treatment of [black] troops during WWI and II was a disgrace, yet it was rationalized by ideas about the deficiencies of black men that whites have found more convincing than black sacrifices on the battlefield. These stereotypes have left a disabling legacy that remains poorly understood."[75] Dunbar, in his poetic tribute, offers a greater recognition of sacrifices that were silenced by cultural memory.

Is Dunbar's poetry "a network of stories and images by which systems of oppression and violence are made to seem inevitable"?[76] Do his poems function "as a way to help people come to terms with difficult periods of their past [or do] they provide explanations for why things happened or help reconcile disparities between a group's self-image and the historical record of the group's behavior"?[77] Does he properly capture the tumultuous battles of those soldiers as they happened and honor them with a memorial of interconnected stories of their courageous lives? Dunbar did what so few poets during his time even attempted to do: he had the compassion and the courage to shed light on such a significant moment in American history. His poetry succeeds in reminding America of what is so easily forgotten with the passing of time and so many other American wars that have been fought, whether won or lost. Dunbar's poetry celebrated then and continues to celebrate now black participation in the Civil War. Because black servicemen are still deemed the "seventh son" and are still experiencing some difficulties within the armed forces, Dunbar's poetry holds great significance to attempts to fully understand their sacrifices. Black servicemen have continued to defy all stereotypes and myths about their cowardice. Dunbar's remedy for America's collective amnesia about black participation in America's early wars is his tribute poetry, which memorializes and mythologizes exactly what should not have been long forgotten.

Notes

1. Torriano S. Berry and Venise T. Berry, *The 50 Most Influential Black Films: A Celebration of African American Talent, Determination, and Creativity* (New York: Citadel Press, 2001), 207.
2. Ibid., 208.
3. Joy Connolly, "Global Mythologies" (seminar, NYU Faculty Resource Network, June 5, 2005).
4. Jerry Lembcke, *The Spitting Image: Myth, Memory, and the Legacy of Vietnam* (New York: New York University Press, 1998), 184.
5. Connolly, "Global Mythologies."
6. Jay David and Elaine Crane, *The Black Soldier from the American Revolution to Vietnam* (New York: William Morrow, 1979), 12.
7. Ibid.
8. Donald Hall, *Cultural and Literary Theory: From Basic Principles to Advanced Applications* (New York: Houghton Mifflin, 2001), 299–301.
9. Mary Blundell and Kirk Ormand, "Western Values or the Peoples Homer: *Unforgiven* as a Reading of the *Iliad*," *Poetics Today* 18, no. 4 (1997): 533–69.
10. Bernard Nalty, *Strength for the Fight: A History of Black Americans in the Military* (New York: Free Press, 1989), 10.
11. Noah Andre Trudeau, *Like Men of War: Black Troops in the Civil War, 1862–1865* (Edison, N.J.: Castle Books, 2002), 72.
12. Qtd. in ibid.
13. Kai Wright, *Soldiers of Freedom: An Illustrated History of African Americans in the Armed Forces* (New York: Black Dog & Levental, 2002), 59.
14. David and Crane, *The Black Soldier*, 53
15. Ibid., 59.
16. Wright, *Soldiers of Freedom*, 56, 71.

17. *The Complete Poems of Paul Laurence Dunbar* (New York: Dodd, Mead, 1922), 182, line 9.
18. Ibid., 182, line 13.
19. Ibid., 182, line 19.
20. Ibid., 182, line 21.
21. Ibid., 182, lines 10–12.
22. Ibid., 182, line 15.
23. Ibid., 182, line 22.
24. Ibid., 182, lines 33–40.
25. Ibid., 50, line 6.
26. Ibid., 50, lines 23–24.
27. Ibid., 50, lines 9–16.
28. Ibid., 50, lines 39–40.
29. Ibid., 50, lines 25–26.
30. Ibid., 50, lines 29–30.
31. Ibid., 50, lines 31–32.
32. Ibid., 50, lines 35–36.
33. Ibid., 50, lines 57–58.
34. Ibid., 50, lines 59–62.
35. Ibid., 50, lines 64–69.
36. Ibid., 50, lines 70–78.
37. W. E. B. Du Bois, *The Souls of Black Folk* (Boston: Bedford, 1997), 38.
38. *Complete Poems*, 256, line 14.
39. Ibid., 256, lines 4–6.
40. Ibid., 256, lines 15–16.
41. Ibid., 256, lines 18–24.
42. Ibid., 256, lines 25–32.
43. Ibid., 256, line 33.
44. Ibid., 256, lines 36–40.
45. Ibid., 22, lines 1–2.
46. Ibid., 22, lines 14–16.
47. Ibid., 22, line 4.
48. Ibid., 22, lines 5–6.
49. Ibid., 22, line 13.
50. Ibid., 22, lines 17–24.
51. John Hoberman, *Darwin's Athletes: How Sport Has Damaged Black America and Preserved the Myth of Race* (New York: Houghton Mifflin, 1997), 67.
52. Wright, *Soldiers of Freedom*, 15.
53. *Complete Poems*, 22, lines 17–24.
54. Connolly, "Global Mythologies."
55. Lembcke, *The Spitting Image*, 184.
56. Berry and Berry, *Most Influential Black Films*, 297.
57. Allen Flint, "Black Response to Colonel Shaw," *Phylon* 45, no. 3 (1984): 210–19.
58. Ibid., 212.
59. *Complete Poems*, 222, lines 1–4.
60. Ibid., 221, lines 5–8.
61. Ibid., 221, line 7.
62. Ibid., 221, line 11.
63. Ibid., 221, lines 11–14.
64. Trudeau, *Like Men of War*, 72.

65. Nalty, *Strength for the Fight*, 38.
66. *Complete Poems*, 123, lines 9–12.
67. Nalty, *Strength for the Fight*, 1.
68. *Complete Poems*, 123, lines 21–24.
69. Wright, *Soldiers of Freedom*, 73.
70. Qtd. in Trudeau, *Like Men of War*, 467.
71. Qtd. in Berry and Berry, *Most Influential Black Films*, 207.
72. Qtd. in Trudeau, *Like Men of War*, 86.
73. Qtd. in ibid., 87.
74. Qtd. in ibid.
75. Hoberman, *Darwin's Athletes*, 62.
76. Connolly, "Global Mythologies."
77. Lembcke, *The Spitting Image*, 18.

4
Minstrelsy and the Dialect Poetry of Paul Laurence Dunbar

Elston L. Carr Jr.

He sang of life, serenely sweet,
With, now and then, a deeper note.
From some high peak, nigh yet remote,
He voiced the world's absorbing beat.

He sang of love when earth was young,
And Love, itself, was in his lays.
But, ah, the world, it turned to praise
A jingle in a broken tongue.
—Paul Laurence Dunbar, "The Poet"

In the preface to *The Book of American Negro Poetry*, James Weldon Johnson articulates his now famous position that dialect poetry, which grew out of the plantation and minstrel traditions, was not a viable means of African American literary expression.[1] For him, dialect poetry had, at best, a marginal place in the evolving African American literary aesthetic that would lead to the Harlem Renaissance. Johnson goes on to qualify, if not complicate, his position by stating that he is not as opposed to dialect itself as he is opposed to its use within the context of American popular culture: "Negro dialect is at present a medium that is not capable of giving expression to the varied conditions of Negro life in America, and much less is capable of giving the fullest interpretation of Negro character and psychology. This is not an indictment against the dialect as dialect, but against the mold of convention in which Negro dialect in the United States has been set."[2]

Though Johnson does not explicitly mention Paul Laurence Dunbar here, it is likely that Dunbar's dialect poetry is part of his consideration in this case.

Johnson's direct assessment of dialect poetry in *The Book of American Negro Poetry* makes Dunbar's importance to American and African American letters clear. While suggesting that Dunbar's dialect poetry is passé, Johnson simultaneously lionizes him as "the first American Negro poet of literary distinction."[3] Johnson's ambivalence about the significance of dialect poetry continued well after his initial assessment of Dunbar. In *To Wake the Nations: Race in the Making of American Literature,* Eric Sundquist points out that Johnson reversed himself several times on the merits of dialect poetry: "But Johnson himself would largely repudiate [his statement on dialect] ten years later in his preface to Sterling Brown's *Southern Road,* which employed dialect in a masterful way."[4]

Since Dunbar's death, the critical concern about his dialect poetry has only been encouraged by the poet's ongoing popularity and by recent attempts to reassess his work. Much of the work began with Joanne Braxton's *The Collected Poetry of Paul Laurence Dunbar.* "We reclaim, in Paul Laurence Dunbar, a significant American author whose career transcends race and locality even while he makes use of racialized and regional cultural material to create . . . a unique black poetic diction."[5] Although Dunbar scholars such as Jay Martin argue that it is a myth that Dunbar was ever marginalized or discarded,[6] Braxton's project of reclamation addresses a deep ambivalence among African American literati regarding Dunbar's dialect poetry. Houston A. Baker Jr. and Henry Louis Gates Jr., for example, have done excellent jobs of vindicating Dunbar—Gates perhaps more than Baker.

Gates's critical paradigm described in *The Signifying Monkey: A Theory of African-American Literary Criticism* suggests that Dunbar's work engages the characteristic rhetorical improvisation of black speech.[7] He also suggests that such rhetorical improvisation has the ability to speak simultaneously and distinctively to both white and black audiences. Gates calls this aspect of American literature and popular culture "linguistic masking"—"the verbal sign of the mask of blackness that demarcates the boundary between the white linguistic realm and the black, two domains that exist side by side in a homonymic relation signified by the very concept of Signification."[8] I suggest that signification, though primarily concerned with language, can also be related to Freud's ideas on the unconscious—"that an idea may exist simultaneously in two places in the mental apparatus."[9]

In "Paul Dunbar and the Mask of Dialect," John Keeling summarizes Baker's blues ideology in the blues matrix by elaborating on Jacques Derrida's ideas.[10] For Baker, blues literature can be a transforming source of cultural agency and change. Ultimately, Keeling suggests that even though there are transforming elements in some of Dunbar's dialect poetry, the nostalgia of the plantation tradition moved toward the essentialism and fixity in racial meaning that Baker rejects.[11]

There is little question that Paul Laurence Dunbar's dialect poetry can be read as a mask in motion that articulates oppositional and subversive themes within the signifying system as described by Gates and, to a lesser degree, within the blues matrix as described by Baker. I suggest an additional way of reading Dunbar's work that amplifies the motif of masking by considering the cultural context and implications of dialect writing in the late nineteenth century. That is, much of Dunbar's dialect poetry evolved from and re-creates the performative space of minstrelsy. The dialect in his poetry, which bears little resemblance to African American speech in the nineteenth century, is really the result of conscious and unconscious projected, hegemonic anxieties of a nation moving toward and eventually recovering from the Civil War—a nation imagining and fantasizing blackness as means to self-definition.[12]

Elaborating on the concept of behavioral vortices in *Cities of the Dead: Circum-Atlantic Performance* by Joseph Roach, I view Dunbar's work as having been read and published in a cultural and performative vortex that was both oral and literary. According to Roach, "The vortex is a kind of spatially induced carnival, a center of self-invention through the restoration of behavior. In such maelstroms, the magnetic forces of commerce and pleasure suck the willing and the unwilling alike. Although such a zone or district seems to offer a place for transgression, for things that couldn't happen otherwise or elsewhere, in fact what it provides is far more official: a place in which everyday practices and attitudes may be legitimated, 'brought out into the open,' reinforced, celebrated, or intensified."[13] For Roach, these behavioral vortices include British newspapers that covered theater. In the American context, I suggest that the vortex could include the liminal cultural space of the minstrel show and the publications in which Dunbar's work was published and read: Dunbar published his poetry, including his dialect poetry, in the *New York Times*, the *Atlantic*, *Harper's Weekly*, the *Century*, *Good Housekeeping*, the *Outlook*, and the *Saturday Evening Post*. These publications were instrumental in nation building in that, as Benedict Anderson explains in *Imagined Communities: Reflections on the Origin and Spread of Nationalism*, "the convergence of capitalism and print technology on the fatal diversity of human language created a new form of imagined community, which in its basic morphology set the stage for the modern nation."[14]

Dunbar's dialect poetry occupies and performs American ambivalence and contradiction concerning national and racial identity—as well as notions of freedom and of enslavement, of integration and of segregation, of attraction and of repulsion, of pleasure and of anxiety. It is a space concerned with marking black bodies, occupying black bodies, and ventriloquizing black bodies with hyperbolic jingles in broken tongues. In *Black American Writing from the Nadir: The Evolution of a Literary Tradition, 1875–1915,* Dickson D. Bruce Jr. suggests that Dunbar was somewhat aware of the broader cultural context in which he produced his work: "One may most profitably look at Dunbar as a poet who, whatever his motives for doing dialect work, recognized that such work was intimately tied to the direction that ideas about racial identity were taking in a segregated society. His dialect work reveals the kinds of tensions, at an emotional level, that such a society could produce."[15]

Dunbar's dialect poetry entertained large black and white audiences: "It is true, certainly, that his dialect verse was more popular than his poetry in standard English. But this was true for his black as much as for his white readers."[16] Consequently, his dialect poetry articulates a liminal space of racial and cultural contradiction and ambivalence. Masking introduces the useful binary of double consciousness, but cultural context and performance allow us to consider the agency of poet and of audience. This approach may be helpful in that Dunbar's dialect poetry, at its most unredeemable, could be signifying in the same way as a black minstrel applying whiteface and then blackface. The very edges of whiteness under blackface may well implicate an audience that is comfortable with comic subversion and transgression as entertainment only when a mask of blackness, the mask of dialect, is in place. That is, the suspension of reality and the performance would be over if the mask were removed. Ann Douglas makes a similar argument in *Terrible Honesty: Mongrel Manhattan in the 1920s:*

> For both black Manhattan moderns and the white, theater was the only means of turning danger into profit and art; drama allows its participants to find whatever meaning, whatever measure of safety, that danger allows. For the Negro, however, danger was constant, omnivorous fluid, and unstable; it necessitated the use of that plurality of masks Africa had donated and minstrelsy had elaborated and Americanized. The chosen mode of black Manhattan was one of contrasting, shifting rhythms as a fractured but infinite series of impersonations never culminating in the dénouement of unmasking.[17]

Victor Turner in "Are There Universals of Performance in Myth, Ritual, and Drama?" refers to performances that exist in such a cultural limen or margin, to which Douglas refers as "being in the 'subjunctive mood' of culture, the mood of maybe, might-be, hypothesis, fantasy, conjecture, desire."[18] In "Space and Context," Yi-Fu Tuan claims that within the realm of comedy, laughter is the form of active participation that breaches the distance between performance space, spectator, and performer. As Dunbar and James Weldon Johnson realized the limits of dialect poetry as a form, Yi-Fu Tuan also speculates on the limits of such comedy: "Nothing truly threatening or awesome occurs in social comedy. The audience does not feel the need to maintain a protective or deferential distance."[19]

Sigmund Freud's ideas in "The Unconscious" regarding simultaneity, repression, displacement, and timelessness suggest another way to read Dunbar's dialect poems that is not ostensibly oppositional. That is, if the actual minstrel performance exists in the space of the preconscious, a space that is often marked by regression, this could be one way to explain the sentimentality and nostalgia in the plantation tradition. In this discursive space, it then becomes possible to talk of masters, of deserted plantations, of beautiful banjo and fiddle music, and of joyous celebrations without addressing the oppressive nature of slavery. It is precisely at this preconscious site that cultural behavior such as a minstrel show or the reading of a dialect poem "appears 'comic' and excites laughter."[20] The unconscious and comedic processes, according to Freud, "pay just a little regard to reality." Moreover, the unconscious often "consists of wishful impulses."[21]

I will consider the aforementioned ideas about performance, the unconscious, and the cultural and historical context in a close reading of "Accountability," "The Deserted Plantation," and "A Virginia Reel," Dunbar dialect poems that fall within the plantation tradition. These close readings will also draw on John Keeling's work in "Paul Dunbar and the Mask of Dialect." In that essay, Keeling demonstrates how Dunbar often constructs poetic form that is similar to a dramatic monologue in which a dramatic situation can subvert the speaker's narrative: "If we pay close attention to the distance between the poem's speaker and listener (who is not the reader or audience), if we look at the narrative details which seem to contradict the speaker's portrait, then we shall find a bleaker vision rupturing the surface of the poem."[22]

While Keeling's reading is appropriate when we consider dialect poems that are oppositional and subversive, we are still left to wonder about poems that are more firmly situated in the plantation tradition and in minstrelsy. In such poems, it is useful to consider the dramatic monologue or element within the context of a minstrel show, in order to understand how and why blackness is being performed. With minstrelsy as a context, it is not, as Lott suggests in *Love and Theft*, always possible to distinguish between subversion and exploitation, pleasure and anxiety, in minstrel performance in general and in Dunbar's dialect poetry in particular.

"A Virginia Reel," published in the *Century* in 1901, is one example of a dialect poem by Dunbar that may fall within the performative tradition of minstrelsy. Though the poem is a dramatic monologue with a speaker, or interlocutor in the minstrel tradition, directing dancers through the pattern of a reel, a Scottish folk dance, there is very little that is obviously oppositional in this poem, which has an AABB rhyme scheme. With highly apostrophized dialect and its portrayal of happily dancing blacks, this work also exemplifies the recurring themes of the plantation tradition. There is a hint of subversion, of signifying, in the second and third stanzas:

> No th'ow dem window open wide,
> An' fo'ma line f'om side to side;
> Bow to de lef', bow to the right,
> An' lif' yo' feet lak dy was light.
>
> Now all togedah bow an'vance,
> No draggin' feet in dis heyah dance;
> Lay all yo' sorrows on de she'f
> An' sta't to enjoy yo'se'f.[23]

That the speaker insists that the dancers lift their feet as if they were light and indicates that they are tired ("No draggin' feet") but should put their worries and sorrows aside ("Lay all yo' sorrows on de she'f") and enjoy the dance suggests that these are not carefree and unburdened people. Aside from this hint that these bodies are far more than the stereotypical dancing black people of the plantation tradition and minstrel show, nothing occurs in the poem to undermine the speaker's dramatic monologue, nothing to rupture the placid surface of the verse.

There are several ways to read this poem. The early reference to "De banjo done commence de schune" alludes to minstrelsy, in which the banjo was the stock instrument for many shows. In stanza 4, the speaker presents the stereotype of the lazy black man, so lazy that he is almost dead: "A body'd t'ink dat you had foun' / A'int'rus in a burying-groun'." It is also interesting that the comic stanza comes immediately after stanzas 2 and 3, with their intimations of a more serious side of life. In stanza 4, Dunbar personifies the banjo: "An' listen to dat banjo sing." Also in stanza 4, "Wipe all de shine f'om off yo' face" can be read as an allusion to blackface—incidentally the only physical marker, besides dialect, that identifies the dancers as black.[24]

The reference to a Scottish folk dance in the title should make the reader suspect that Dunbar is creating the fantasy world of minstrelsy. According to Lott, such dances usually occurred in the third act of a minstrel show: "The third part was a narrative skit, usually set in the South, containing dancing, music, and burlesque."[25] Though not impossible, it is historically unlikely that antebellum or postbellum blacks would have danced reels. John W. Blassingame, in *The Slave Community: Plantation Life in the Antebellum South*, suggests as much: "Apparently the European reels, minuets, and schottisches were too sedate and formalized for the slave."[26] That there are no historical references in this poem to indicate whether this event occurs before or after the Civil War may also indicate the atemporality of fantasy, of the unconscious desire to, perhaps, lock black bodies into perpetual performance and servitude: "The processes of the [unconscious] system are timeless; i.e. they are not ordered temporally, are not altered by the passage of time; they have no reference to time at all."[27] I suggest that the penultimate stanza, "Nex' couple forrard, do de same; / Ef you gits mixed, I ain't to blame,"[28] may allude to the idea of miscegenation and the concomitant "vagaries of racial desire" that Lott says are "fundamental to minstrel-show mimicry."[29] Especially in the context of turn-of-the-century lynching and in the context of minstrelsy, it is difficult to read the word "mixed" as racially and sexually neutral. As Lott points out, "It was cross-racial desire that coupled a nearly insupportable fascination and a self-protective derision with respect to black people and their cultural practices that made blackface minstrelsy less a sign of absolute white power and control than a panic, anxiety, terror, and pleasure. As it turned out, the minstrel show worked for over a hundred years to facilitate safely an exchange of energies between two otherwise rigidly bounded and policed cultures, a shape-shifting middle term in racial conflict."[30]

In "Accountability," the Dunbar speaker/interlocutor creates an antebellum atmosphere in line with the plantation tradition and minstrel performance. Here, the interlocutor creates, elevates, and sustains tension and expectation in a sermonic tone that is satiric and appears to parody the serious intent of the black preacher in "An Ante-bellum Sermon." Though "Accountability" is not a burlesque performance, it alludes to the inextricable connection between high and low culture, with references to God's creations: "Him dat made de streets an' driveways wasn't shamed to make de alleys." As in a comedic monologue, the speaker leads the reader, the audience, to some answer to God's grand plan: "When you come to think about it, / How it's all planned out it's splendid." Here, we have the speaker as creator, and the creative artist as God: "Nuthin's done er evah happens, 'dout hit's somefin' dat's intended." In this case, I suggest that the speaker is almost boastfully declaring his mastery of the performance of a poem with a punch line, a punch line that revolves around the standard minstrel gag of the black chicken thief, who all along has been justifying his actions by couching them in the Christian discourse of moral bankruptcy during slavery: "Viney, go put on de kittle, I got one o' mastah's chickens."[31] Such performances, whether poetic or dramatic, were not unfamiliar to Dunbar. In 1898, he and Will Marion Cook co-wrote an all-black musical, *Clorindy,* that was a close relation to all-black minstrelsy. Although the lyrics of the songs often had nothing to do with their titles, as in "All Coons Look Alike to Me" and "Who Dat Say Chicken in Dis Crowd?" the latter song, like "Accountability," as Sundquist points out, "voices the racial hierarchy of society through the comic stereotype of the darkey chicken thief."[32]

In "The Deserted Plantation," Dunbar presents a maudlin speaker who equates plantation life to heaven on earth: "'Twell de othah Mastah thinks it's time to end it, / An' calls me to my qua'ters in the sky." The speaker presents stock images of mourning birds, a solemn plantation house, singing banjos, prancing children, a "da'ky fiddlah," and happy days gone by. While the poem's nostalgia would have appealed to fans of the plantation tradition, it could be argued that the speaker may not be nostalgic for slavery itself—he does not present the reader with any brutal imagery of the institution—but mourns the loss of a community that developed a means of survival, that preserved an inner sense of self and cohesiveness despite violent racism: "But it hol's in me a lover till de las', / Fu' I fin' hyeah in the memory dat follers / All dat loved me an' dat I loved / in de pas.'"[33] It is important to note that the speaker, however sentimental, gives no indication that he mourns the loss of the master or his family, but rather that he mourns the loss of his own community. Here memory animates the past and brings back the dead, at least in this ludic performance space, the site that can accommodate experimental theater, surrealism, comedy, and clowning and that develops rules of structure, subversion, and grotesque spectacle.[34]

At the end of "A Virginia Reel," the interlocutor calls for the dancers to show their feelings, and the tone of "Deserted Plantation" demonstrates an almost supernatural level of pathos. Lott suggests that regardless of a minstrel show's theme, there is always the implication that blacks are "special" people imbued with deep feelings, akin to race gifts, and exemplary spirituality, a view similar to the romantic racialism portrayed in Harriet Beecher Stowe's *Uncle Tom's Cabin*: "Like women, blacks were considered creatures of feeling at a time when feeling was paramount in the culture; what fund of emotion the 'go-ahead-ative,' aggressive Anglo-Saxon lacked, blacks would surely supply."[35]

While there is ample evidence to support the contention that much of Dunbar's dialect poetry falls in the minstrel and plantation traditions, one must still ask why Dunbar chose to write using manufactured dialect that perpetuated the performance of black speech as caricature. Perhaps there can be no single answer to this question, because Dunbar was the first African American literary figure who gained considerable access to American popular culture with a diverse reading audience, and he was subject to the attendant contradictions and exploitation of that culture. His choices may be less a capitulation to racist expectations than an indication of the literary market's expectations. In the context of local color, Braxton, Martin, and other critics point out that Dunbar was an experimenter who wrote in Western, Irish, and German dialects. However, there is no evidence to indicate whether Dunbar read Frances Harper's dialect poetry. The fact remains that unlike Harper, Dunbar did not alter the dialect of the plantation poets in his poetry. Unlike Harper, who embraced a didactic pedagogical agenda, Dunbar, the experimenter and entertainer, was far more interested in the dramatic possibilities of exaggerated black speech than he was in any modicum of verisimilitude.

If at times subtlety can tease out dramatic irony—and it does in some of Dunbar's best poetry, such as "We Wear the Mask"—his dialect seems to operate under the assumption that hyperbole can also betray subtle irony in a society fraught with racial tension, anxiety, and ambivalence. The hyperbolic jingles in broken tongues may have been a dramatic, albeit commodified, tool that was not necessarily indicative of racial essentialism. If blackness is a cultural performance like whiteness, then anyone can hypothetically don any array of masks to some degree. This choice gained Dunbar national attention but also denied him the artistic status that would have given all his poetry equal critical consideration. The irony for Dunbar is not that he wore the mask of dialect all too well, but that he could not discard it even if he had the inclination. Reiterating the words of Audre Lorde, Braxton points out in the introduction to Dunbar's collected poetry that the limitations of this dialect say less about Dunbar's abilities and motives than about the near impossibility of dismantling "the master's house using the master's tools."[36] If anything, minstrelsy was always about entertaining a conflicted American population engaged in occupying and transforming the master's house.

Notes

1. James Weldon Johnson, *The Book of American Negro Poetry, with an Essay on the Negro's Creative Genius* (New York: Harcourt, Brace & World, 1959).

2. Ibid., 42.

3. Ibid., 50.

4. Eric J. Sundquist, *To Wake the Nations: Race in the Making of American Literature* (Cambridge, Mass.: Belknap Press at Harvard University Press, 1993), 304.

5. Joanne M. Braxton, introduction to *The Collected Poetry of Paul Laurence Dunbar*, ed. Joanne M. Braxton, ix–xxxvi (Charlottesville: University of Virginia Press, 1993).

6. *The Paul Laurence Dunbar Reader: A Selection of the Best of Paul Laurence Dunbar's Poetry and Prose, Including Writings Never before Available in Book Form*, ed. Gossie H. Hudson and Jay Martin (New York: Dodd, Mead, 1975), 261.

7. Henry Louis Gates Jr., *The Signifying Monkey: A Theory of African-American Literary Criticism* (New York: Oxford University Press, 1988).

8. Ibid., 75–76.
9. *The Freud Reader*, ed. Peter Gay (New York: Norton, 1995), 579.
10. John Keeling, "Paul Dunbar and the Mask of Dialect," *Southern Literary Journal* 25 (1993): 24–38.
11. Ibid., 26–28.
12. Eric Lott, *Love and Theft: Blackface Minstrelsy and the American Working Class* (New York: Oxford University Press, 1993), 29.
13. Joseph Roach, *Cities of the Dead: Circum-Atlantic Performance* (New York: Columbia University Press, 1996), 28.
14. Benedict Anderson, *Imagined Communities: Reflections on the Origin and Spread of Nationalism* (London: Verso, 1991), 46.
15. Dickson D. Bruce Jr., *Black American Writing from the Nadir: The Evolution of a Literary Tradition, 1875–1915* (Baton Rouge: Louisiana State University Press, 1989), 60.
16. *Dunbar Reader*, 261.
17. Ann Douglas, *Terrible Honesty: Mongrel Manhattan in the 1920s* (New York: Farrar, Straus and Giroux, 1995), 105.
18. Victor Turner, "Are There Universals of Performance in Myth, Ritual, and Drama?" in *By Means of Performance: Intercultural Studies of Theatre and Ritual*, ed. Richard Schechner and Willa Appel, 8–18 (New York: Cambridge University Press, 1990); Douglas, *Terrible Honesty*, 11.
19. Yi-Fu Tuan, "Space and Context," in *By Means of Performance*, 236.
20. *The Freud Reader*, 582.
21. Ibid.
22. Keeling, "Dunbar and the Mask," 31.
23. *Collected Poetry*, 326, lines 8–12.
24. Ibid., 327, lines 16, 19.
25. Lott, *Love and Theft*, 5–6.
26. John W. Blassingame, *The Slave Community: Plantation Life in the Antebellum South* (New York: Oxford University Press, 1972), 44.
27. *The Freud Reader*, 582.
28. *Collected Poetry*, 327, lines 25–26.
29. Lott, *Love and Theft*, 6.
30. Ibid.
31. *Collected Poetry*, 5, lines 4, 13, 14, 16.
32. Sundquist, *To Wake the Nations*, 283, 284.
33. *Collected Poetry*, 68, lines 35–36, 30–32.
34. Victor Turner, "Are There Universals?" 14.
35. Lott, *Love and Theft*, 32.
36. Braxton, introduction, xxx.

5
Dunbar, Dialect, and Narrative Theory
Subverted Statements in Lyrics of Lowly Life

Megan M. Peabody

Paul Laurence Dunbar's black dialect poetry brought him immense popularity with the publication of *Lyrics of Lowly Life* in 1896. Though fewer than a quarter of the 105 poems in the collection are written at least partially in black dialect, it is these poems for which Dunbar is remembered and, at the same time, derided. William Dean Howells lauded Dunbar in his introduction to the volume, noting that "his brilliant and unique achievement was to have studied the American negro objectively, and to have represented him as he found him to be, with humor, with sympathy, and yet with what the reader must instinctively feel to be entire truthfulness." Howells goes on to say, however, that Dunbar "reveals in these [poems] a finely ironical perception of the negro's limitations."[1] Though Dunbar would later lament Howells's focus on his dialect poems, Howells in many ways gets at the heart of them: Dunbar's poetic creations are experiments in what can be said and what must remain unsaid, what can be revealed and what must remain concealed.

Much of this dichotomy is based on Dunbar's interest in oral traditions and his subsequent literary renderings of oral speech. Myron Simon notes, "One of the reasons for Dunbar's great importance in the history of black poetry is that in his books the two channels through which black poetry emerged in America—the literary and the oral traditions—begin to come together: they inhabit the same mind, are bound between the same covers."[2] Composing in writing what was once verbal utterance allowed Dunbar to explore the voice of his people to a larger degree than any black poet before him. In doing so, Dunbar unfortunately fell into the modes utilized by purveyors of the plantation tradition, postbellum writers who used stock tropes to deride black figures and imply that slavery was not as dehumanizing as abolitionists had argued. As Holger Kersten notes, "Critics of his dialect poems saw him as a successor to Irwin Russell, Joel Chandler Harris, Thomas Nelson Page, and other white writers who had assumed an African voice. Although these authors made use of African-American folk material, the purpose of their writing is usually identified with an ideology that attempted to valorize and idealize life in the antebellum South."[3]

Many critics, whether writing contemporarily or a century later, disparaged Dunbar's reliance on the stereotypical plantation representations and spelling alterations he utilized in *Lyrics of Lowly Life*. William M. Ramsey, writing at the close of the twentieth century, believes that Dunbar "does not fully seize the issues of southern critique" because of his seeming glorification of black southern life.[4] Valerie J. Wheat reminds us that "Dunbar expresses only quiet, subtle statements against the wrongs of slavery in his dialect poems,"[5] which is why leading African American voices like James Weldon Johnson and Sterling Brown questioned his artistic integrity and rhetorical goals even decades after his death. True, some of his dialect poems ostensibly celebrate life on the plantation and in their dialect spellings seem to emphasize African Americans' historical inability to access traditional education. What this reductionist view disregards, though, is Dunbar's careful craft. As he wrote prolifically in many genres, his attention to narrative structure offers a means to appreciate his veiled pro-black sentiment.

A handful of dialect poems in *Lyrics of Lowly Life* serve as Dunbar's experiments with multilayered narratives. Poems like "Discovered," "A Coquette Conquered," and "The Delinquent" feature speakers interacting with an unrepresented listener as well as the poems' readers. In "The Delinquent," for instance, Dunbar's speaker is late getting home to Mirandy and tries to blame Suke for his tardiness. What the reader sees, though, just as Suke likely does, is that the speaker's actions reveal that his meandering, as uttered and physically enacted, is what makes him late. These are three densely layered poems focused on secrets, gossip, and escaping blame, but others use a multilayered narrative for more politicized means. There are, in "The Party" and "An Antebellum Sermon," not only narrators/speakers but also narratees/characters and diegetic audiences with different expectations and knowledge bases than the reader. These levels of discourse create spaces where solid facts and cultural truths become mere vagaries, allowing Dunbar to assert a new perspective on the plight of postbellum black America. These two representative poems, though written in plantation tradition dialect, defy sentimental conventions by utilizing narrative schemes that question a black speaker's ability to speak whole truths, and by creating dialogic systems that reflect a burgeoning black community rebelling against white power.

Dunbar's poems are most apparently unique in the manner in which his speakers convey messages within a carefully constructed world. In both "The

Party" and "An Ante-bellum Sermon," the speakers deliver their ideas and experiences not only to a reader but also to an audience that exists within the poem. To borrow terminology from Gérard Genette, Dunbar's speakers are narrators; the characters within the world created by the poem, or within the diegesis, are intradiegetic narratees and intradiegetic listeners; and finally, when Dunbar's narrators relay others' speech, they are engaging in mimesis. Though generally reserved for prose analysis, Genette's narrative theories apply to these two poems since they are not standard lyric poems and the many levels of discourse necessitate a thorough study. On the surface level, there is an automatic relationship between the narrator and the reader, frequently treated as the poet speaking to his reading audience. Beneath this there are narrator-narratee and narrator-listener relationships, situations when narratees and listeners interrupt the narrator's speech, instances when the narrator replicates past speech from an intradiegetic character, and a few moments when the narrator engages in self-censorship and understatement. Darwin T. Turner dispels the myth of Dunbar as a "natural versifier" and asserts that critics who see Dunbar's craft as no more than "easy, spontaneous writing which is all that might be expected from a young black elevator operator whose formal education ended with graduation from high school" disregard the time and care that went into Dunbar's writing.[6] Granted, he wrote many poems, stories, essays, and speeches over the course of his short lifetime, but Dunbar's easy tone and musical style are more than happy accidents. Utilization of narrative theory to explore the levels of meaning does justice to this often maligned poet so in tune with meter, pattern, rhyme, and rhythm.

In exploring Dunbar's poem "The Party," all the above narrative levels are used early on in order to covertly reveal the ability of raced poetry to speak whole historical truths. In the first six lines, Dunbar's narrator interacts with both an intradiegetic narratee and an intradiegetic listener:

> Dey had a gread big pahty down to Tom's de othah night;
> Was I dah? You bet! I nevah in my life see sich a sight;
> All de folks f'om fou' plantations was invited, an' dey come,
> Dey come troopin' thick ez chillun when dey hyeahs a fife an' drum.
> Evahbody dressed deir fines'—Heish yo' mouf an' git away,
> Ain't seen no sich fancy dressin' sense las' quah'tly meetin' day.[7]

While a surface read would show this to be merely a black slave recounting a party "de othah night," Dunbar's narrative manipulations deserve further scrutiny. Since the second line begins with, "Was I dah? You bet!" what is missing is the direct discourse of an intradiegetic narratee, or the person to whom this narrator is recounting his tale. Filling in the blanks, one can assume that this narratee asked the narrator if he was present, with line 2 indicating he was. In the fifth line, the narrator interrupts his own narrative when he says, "Heish yo' mouf an' git away," indicating that his narrative has been halted by an intradiegetic listener, a character within the poem who has obviously interrupted the speaker and forced him to momentarily shift his focus from the recounting of the party. The narrator regroups, though, in line 6, reiterating the statement made at the beginning of line 5, but with an added focus on the "fancy dressin'."

Analysis of this construction offers a lens through which to view Dunbar's ideas regarding the power of language. If this were lyric poetry, and the narrator were merely acting as a speaker, there would be no deeper narratological levels to explore. The first six lines of "The Party" already hint at the difficulty a black voice has in presenting a statement in a dialogic system where interruptions, questions, and calls for reiteration abound. While the intradiegetic figures are likely black and therefore not fracturing the narrative out of malice, Dunbar relies on these figures to address the way in which statements shift when a voice is not permitted autonomy. For instance, the narrator describes the revelers' dress in detail up through line 12, when he tells his narratee, "I cain't tell you nothin' 'bout it, y' ought to seen it fu' yo'se'f." If this were a poem with only one narrative level, a poem with a standard speaker-reader relationship, then it would end here. But as Dunbar allows questions and interjections from intradiegetic narratees, line 13 begins with "Who was dah? Now who you askin'? How you 'spect I gwine to know?"—obviously responses to an unwritten question. While the narrator explicitly states that he "cain't tell you nothin' 'bout it," he does. He holds the power as storyteller, but his objectivity is questionable since he was provoked.

The purpose of the narrator's tale has shifted from what he intended to relay to what his intradiegetic audience expects: further detail. In an effort to oblige his narratee, the narrator states, "You mus' think I stood an' counted evahbody at de do."[8] Meeting the expectations of the narratee, the narrator dives into cataloging all the partygoers. These narrative shifts focus on two aspects: narratee questions and narrator desires. While this narrator has no outward aversion to sharing the details of the party, he would have had no purpose for continuing his narrative without intradiegetic provocation. As he is constantly prodded for more information, his descriptions become even more fantastic. The narrator describes the lavishness of the party: "Gals all dressed in silks an' satins, not a wrinkle ner a crease, / . . . Men all dressed up in Prince Alberts, swaller-tails 'u'd tek yo' bref!"[9] He claims that all these lower-class black men and women are dressed in finery that would be historically beyond their financial means. Then both the reader and the narratee learn about characters like the feeble ole man Johnson, a man who is "hittin' clost onto a hunder,"[10] who manages to swing a woman around the dance floor. This is no average woman, of course; she's Aunt Marier, a woman who the narrator claims "weighs th'ee hunder mo' er less."[11] John Keeling points out that "judging from this summary alone, it seems easy to view the poem as satirizing these revelers."[12] Based upon the social class system in place that prevented blacks from being able to afford "silks an' satins," in addition to certain physical constraints that ole man Johnson must suffer, it is obvious that the narrator grossly exaggerates the goings-on. Keeling thinks that Dunbar creates a narratee in the poem in order to communicate the negative feelings that surround the stereotypical plantation sentimentality, but Dunbar's motives are apparent just in the narrator's actions and conveyances. When confronted with a situation where he is forced to act, the narrator can do nothing but bend to the will of his listeners, be they narratees or readers, and feed them exaggerations.

Also telling are the mimetic features of "The Party." When the narratee prods for even more information, the narrator takes on the speech of other partygoers to magnify the scene and establish a degree of authority. When the narrator tells of Ike's unrequited love for Lindy, he says,

> Ike he foun' a cheer an' asked huh: "Won't you set down?" wif a smile,
> An' she answe'd up a-bowin', "Oh, I reckon 't ain't wuth while."
> Dat was jes' fu' style, I reckon, 'cause she sot down jes' de same,
> An' she stayed dah 'twell he fetched huh fu' to jine some so't o' game;
> Den I hyeahd huh sayin' propah, ez she riz to go away,
> "Oh, you raly mus' excuse me, fu' I hardly keers to play."[13]

This direct quotation is coming from a narrator who claimed only a few lines earlier that he could not possibly be expected to recount each and every detail of the party. His claims could be mere understatements motivated by his desire to incite more intradiegetic participation, but the mimetic quality of the quoted discourse must certainly be fabricated; even if the narrator were privy to Ike and Lindy's conversations, he is not a reliable chronicler since he cannot be expected to directly replicate speech acts uttered "de othah night."

Additionally, there is dialogic conflict at a metadiegetic level in the exchange between Ike and Lindy. Ike offers Lindy a chair even though it is obvious that she does not want to sit with him. As she rises to leave once his back is turned, she makes an excuse for her departure that does not account for her later actions. Just as Lindy tells Ike half-truths, so does the narrator to his narratee and the reader. Dunbar's assertion of the subjectivity of memory and its methods of dissemination is multileveled.

In an effort to engage not only with narratees but with readers, twice in "The Party" the narrator sings songs. The first song comes from Lindy's mouth, yet another voyeuristic rendering of a partygoer's speech. A number of revelers, though, sing the second song. The narrator fuses this song with his conversation with his narratee in order to ground the narratee—and, on another level, the reader—in traditional music:

> You know when dey gits to singin' an' dey comes to dat ere paht:
> "In some lady's new brick house,
> In some lady's gyahden.
> Ef you don't let me out, I will jump out,
> So fa' you well, my dahlin.'"[14]

The introductory statement, in which the narrator assumes his narratee will remember the context in which this song is often sung, emphasizes the solidity of the black community. Since the reader is allowed to peek into this world, just as the narrator peeks in on the partygoers and recounts their discourse, the use of dialectal song helps unite the reader with the diegetic figures. The narrator's song is more than the mimicry he utilized when recounting Ike and Lindy's dialogue. Here, he offers the reader a means to engage directly with the party.

Dunbar's reader, then, is invited into a diegesis propagated by a dialect-speaking narrator whose inconsistent, embellished, and fantasy-oriented narrative raises questions about the ability of such a raced presentation to speak the truth about the life and conditions of blackness in the South. Keeling writes: "The listener's [i.e., narratee's] responses and interruptions, as well as the somewhat dubious details of the narrative itself, undermine the narrator's intentions and hint of a different reality. The poem almost invites the reader to act, with even more vigor than the listener, to question and subvert the speaker's narrative. And though the reality beneath the party can only be glimpsed at . . . we should not be fooled by our narrator's 'mask.'"[15] Through the representation of a dialect-uttering narrator speaking half-truths, the reader must question the conventions of sentimental traditions as a whole, possibly flawed, genre. In "The Party," Dunbar creates an outwardly sentimental world in order to juxtapose with it his own purposes of proving this world false. He sets up this sketch as a reminder of traditional apologist works that stereotype and minimize blacks so that the reader will then question the validity and truth of those works as well. It is through this chain that Dunbar makes his veiled statements about the black condition throughout their history in America and why "The Party" functions both in terms of structure and content as a denunciation of the plantation tradition. Dunbar's use of a multileveled, dialect-driven narrative proves that not all utterance can be trusted and that readers must look to the narrative gaps for answers and truths.

Kersten asserts that in American literature, "Unconventional language served as a device to extend an author's creative possibilities. It permitted him or her to engage in role-playing: speaking from the perspective of an ethnic character offered the advantage of presenting American life from the outside, thus creating an opportunity for revealing things otherwise invisible to members of the dominant culture."[16] Dunbar's use of dialect, though personally and professionally conflicted, allows him to render this portrait of black life that defies the expectations of his reading audience. His ultimate failure, though, is in his complexity. Just as he tries to confound his intradiegetic characters with a fractured narrative leading to communication bypasses, so does he his readers. In these scenarios in "The Party" that convolute the intradiegetic characters' expectations, perhaps these bypasses confuse readers who simply desire to skim the work for its lyrical style and seemingly simplistic situation, leaving the grand political statements undetected.

"An Ante-bellum Sermon" achieves more success than "The Party" because the many narrative levels work toward a common goal, preventing a complete extradiegetic communication bypass. As Dickson D. Bruce Jr. writes, "'An Ante-Bellum Sermon' is a thinly disguised articulation of the slaves' hope for freedom, expressed in the story of Moses and the pharaoh.... The focus of the poem, and what gave it its punch, was the slaves' need to keep anything other than the religion imposed upon them by the plantation owners under wraps."[17] The narrator, a southern black preacher, begins the poem by calling out to his intradiegetic narratees:

> We is gathahed hyeah, my brothahs,
> In dis howlin' wildaness,
> Fu' to speak some words of comfo't
> To each othah in distress.
> An' we chooses fu' ouah subjic'
> Dis—we'll 'splain it by an' by;
> "An' de Lawd said, 'Moses, Moses,'
> An' de man said, 'Hyeah am I.'"[18]

In the first six lines, the narrator establishes the character of his intradiegetic narratees: they are a black congregation. By using the all-encompassing "We" throughout the poem, Dunbar's narrator identifies with his narratees but also attempts to forge ties between himself and the reader. Cultivating a multi-leveled relationship is in keeping with the oral tradition of the sermon, since the goals of a clergyman center around piquing his audience's interest and engaging their participation. This narrator defies standard linear discourse since he speaks on many levels.

In lines 7 and 8, the narrator uses mimesis to reach out even more to the narratee and the reader. Within this quoted passage, there are even embedded quotations, revealing not only a metadiegetic narrative, but also a meta-metadiegetic narrative. Simply put, the narrator infuses his narrative with even deeper levels of discourse in order to garner attention and reverence (Bruce notes the importance of this sermon's topic to the plight of the southern black slave). What Dunbar scripts in these first lines of "An Ante-bellum Sermon" is a scenario in which a black narrator uses many levels of narrative in black dialect to connect narratees and readers to the slavery situation. Had he written this poem in Standard English, the effect would be lost; it is the combination of dialect and diegetic movement that bolsters the narrator's statements.

The narrator in "An Ante-bellum Sermon" goes even further into his intradiegetic landscape when he relays the Bible story of Moses and the Pharaoh. He states,

> Now ole Pher'oh, down in Egypt,
> Was de wuss man evah bo'n,
> An' he had de Hebrew chillum
> Down dah wukin' in his co'n;
> 'Twell de Lawd got tiahed o' his foolin',
> An' sez he: "I'll let him know—
> Look hyeah, Moses, go tell Pher'oh
> Fu' to let dem chillun go."[19]

In this passage, not only does the narrator mimic God's speech in biblical passages and relay it in spoken black dialect, but the Bible story enters the diegesis since the narrator paraphrases the Hebrew children's experiences. When this Bible story becomes part of the diegesis, it becomes part of the black congregation's world and occupies an even more crucial space because it fuses with antebellum life. Whereas the use of black dialect in "The Party" reveals the subjectivity of black language in a white world, here it bolsters black sentiment by rendering white words black. Bruce asserts that "in 'An Ante-bellum Sermon,' Dunbar caught more than just the superficial aspects of the religious language of the slaves for, in this and other religious poems, he also showed himself to be aware of the beliefs that lay behind the language."[20] This use of a religious setting to convey black tensions about slavery and freedom helps assuage the communication bypasses between the poet and the reader that rendered "The Party" a less effective denunciation of racial stereotypes.

"An Ante-bellum Sermon" also conveys Dunbar's understanding of the necessity of restraint when a black voice speaks against white doctrine. He achieves this by forcing his narrator to censor himself. As the narrator continues relaying the Bible tale, he builds intensity, telling his narratees that "enemies may 'sail you / In de back an' in de front; / But de Lawd is all aroun' you, / Fu' to ba' de battle's brunt."[21] The "you" in the first line is heavily emphasized since the narrator encourages his narratees to see how the Bible can help them to unite and fight against the "chains an' shackles" binding them, both literally and figuratively. But just as the narrator's sermon is brimming with fire, he halts his narrative and asserts:

> But fu' feah some one mistakes me,
> I will pause right hyeah to say,
> Dat I'm still a-preachin' ancient,
> I ain't talkin' 'bout to-day.[22]

This narrator's acute awareness of the extent to which he can use speech to invigorate and mobilize his black congregation forces him to halt his call to arms for fear of negative repercussions from white society. Keeling notes that "In a humorous move we might expect from Dunbar, the preacher interrupts his own narrative to deny this revolutionary theme's relevance to his listeners. . . . By doing so, of course, he reinforces their relation to his audience's [i.e., narratees'] circumstances."[23] In case both the narratees and the reader misunderstand this passive reinforcement, the narrator next states, "But I tell you, fellah christuns, / Things'll happen mighty strange." He redirects both audiences, his narratees and his reader, and relies on religious ideas about the will of God to bolster a subverted assertion that changes in the battle of black versus white will come. The reasons for subverting his statements have to do with contemporary politics; the narrator reminds his narratees, "Now don't run an' tell yo' mastahs / Dat I's preachin' discontent."[24]

This is not the only instance in "An Ante-bellum Sermon" when the narrator must self-censor. After touching on themes of freedom and truth in the Moses and Pharaoh tale, the narrator pulls back and reminds the narratees and the reader that he is "talkin' 'bout ouah freedom / In a Bibleistic way."[25] He must pepper his narrative with these asides in order to protect himself. The self-censoring act has come full circle by the end of the poem, when the narrator says,

> But when Moses wif his powah
> Comes an' sets us chillum free,
> We will praise de gracious Mastah
> Dat has gin us liberty;
> An' we'll shout ouah halleluyahs,
> On dat mighty reck'nin' day,
> When we'se reco'nised ez citiz'—
> Huh uh! Chillun, let us pray![26]

The narrator's gallant sermon holds God, not white slaveholders, as "Mastah." It is this "Mastah"—not white slaveholders—who imparts "liberty." His rousing speech emboldens both narratee and listener and further reveals the connections between the Bible and the antebellum South. But again, the narrator knows just how far he can take these connections when, in the closing lines, he says, "An' we'll shout ouah halleluyahs, / On dat mighty reck'nin' day, / When we'se reco'nised ez citiz'—." He forces himself to halt referring to the members of this black congregation as citizens because doing so would be too militant. The narrator's self-imposed limitations prove him to be a deft user of language, as he understands what he can get away with saying and what he must leave his audience to infer.

Just as in "The Party," Dunbar uses narrative gaps in "An Ante-bellum Sermon" to address the limitations of black speech. While his narrator can imply connections between biblical freedom and the antebellum South, he cannot overstep racial boundaries and call for revolution. Had Dunbar relayed this sermon in Standard English or in a single-leveled narrative, hidden statements about the ways black voices are constrained and restrained could not exist. The metadiegetic construction allows the narrator's statements to speak volumes about his place in society. He is aware of the constraints imposed by society in terms of what he can plainly divulge, so he uses the accepted tongue to subversively battle against these conventions; his call for action does not fall aside since both the narratees and the reader understand his subverted narrative. Dunbar's multileveled discourse shows how use of dialect can actually shift the sentimental tradition because it can encode veiled messages while protecting the narrator.

Dunbar himself claimed that his goal was "to be able to interpret my own people through song and story, and to prove to the many that after all we are more human than African."[27] Dunbar achieves this aim by relying on black voices, which removes an oppressor's direct powers of speech. These narrators, though flawed, are humanized for that exact reason. When they embellish and self-censor, they are acting within their social constraints and therefore seeking protection within diegetic spaces. When viewed as a series of carefully constructed narrative levels, "The Party" and "An Ante-bellum Sermon" promote Dunbar's belief that his people are "more human than African," since they maneuver through their dialect in order to change the way readers perceive black culture.

Dunbar's dialect creations were no mistake; he had a subversive purpose in using a stereotypically sentimental voice to perpetuate new ideas about a black narrator's powers of speech and representation. His critics claim that he maintains too much southern quaintness in his dialect pieces, but this is a surface judgment. His narrators both actively and passively cast off the plantation tradition conventions by acknowledging their immersion in southern black culture, presenting the limitations of the dialect discourse, and urging readers and narratees to move beyond surface judgments. These narrators feel; they muse; they embellish; they defy. And they encourage their intradiegetic narratees, and by proxy the reader, to do the same. Their presence alone as complex black characters, as well as their multileveled narratives, proves that there is indeed hope for change, both within the boundaries of the narrator-narratee relationship and beyond.

Notes

1. William Dean Howells, introduction to *The Complete Poems of Paul Laurence Dunbar* (New York: Dodd, Mead, 1921), viii–ix.
2. Myron Simon, "Dunbar and Dialect Poetry," in *A Singer in the Dawn: Reinterpretations of Paul Laurence Dunbar*, ed. Jay Martin (New York: Dodd, Mead, 1975), 115.
3. Holger Kersten, "The Creative Potential of Dialect Writing in Later-Nineteenth-Century America," *Nineteenth-Century Literature* 55, no. 1 (2000): 99.
4. William M. Ramsey, "Dunbar's Dixie," *Southern Literary Journal* 32, no. 1 (1999): 31.
5. Valerie J. Wheat, "Nineteenth Century Black Dialect Poetry and Racial Pride: Candelario Obeso's *Cantos populares de mi tierra* and Paul Laurence Dunbar's *Lyrics of Lowly Life*," *Afro-Hispanic Review* 15, no. 2 (1996): 31.
6. Darwin T. Turner, "Paul Laurence Dunbar: The Poet and the Myths," in *A Singer in the Dawn*, 60.
7. *Complete Poems*, 83, lines 1–6.
8. Ibid., 83, line 14.
9. Ibid., 83, lines 7, 11.
10. Ibid., 84, line 36.
11. Ibid., 84, line 39.
12. John Keeling, "Paul Dunbar and the Mask of Dialect," *Southern Literary Journal* 25, no. 2 (1993): 31–32.
13. *Complete Poems*, 84, lines 21–26.
14. Ibid., 84, lines 44–48.
15. Keeling, "Dunbar and the Mask," 33–34.

16. Kersten, "The Creative Potential," 97–98.
17. Dickson D. Bruce Jr., "On Dunbar's 'Jingles in a Broken Tongue': Dunbar's Dialect Poetry and the Afro-American Folk Tradition," in *A Singer in the Dawn*, 99.
18. *Complete Poems*, 13, lines 1–8.
19. Ibid., 13, lines 9–16.
20. Bruce, "On Dunbar's 'Jingles,'" 101–2.
21. *Complete Poems*, 14, lines 25–28.
22. Ibid., 14, lines 29, 37–40.
23. Keeling, "Dunbar and the Mask," 36.
24. *Complete Poems*, 14, lines 41–42, 47–48.
25. Ibid., 14, lines 71–72.
26. Ibid., 15, lines 81–88.
27. Qtd. in Ramsey, "Dunbar's Dixie," 30.

Part II

Race, Rhetoric, and Social Structure

6
Rhetorical Accountability
Paul Laurence Dunbar's Search for "Representative" Men
Coretta M. Pittman

In 1903, Paul Laurence Dunbar's "Representative American Negroes" was published in a book titled *The Negro Problem,* a compilation of essays written by such men as Booker T. Washington, W. E. B. Du Bois, Charles W. Chesnutt, and T. Thomas Fortune. Lesser-known figures such as Wilford H. Smith and H. T. Kealing also contributed essays. As the title and essays in the compilation indicated, finding a solution to the so-called Negro problem was a serious and complex endeavor in the early 1900s. By the time this compilation was published, opportunities for individual and collective success for African Americans were limited primarily by white hatred and bigotry, which meant that more often than not, African Americans were unable to obtain the same kind of economic and political successes as their white peers. Without a doubt, the men with whom Dunbar shared a textual platform in *The Negro Problem* were "successful" men. Although their individual successes could be applauded, the reality was that their successes were not necessarily economic or political, but rather social in that they were identifiable leaders who led the charge for social uplift for African Americans. If success was defined by public recognition and intellectual acumen, then all the contributors to the book qualified as successful. However, if success was defined in economic and political terms as well as in terms of possessing the ability to move outside one's racial-geographical space without risking physical harm, then these men were not entirely successful. In other words, success was narrowly defined for African Americans, and in the essays in *The Negro Problem,* the writers vociferously pointed out the limits imposed on their and other African Americans' lives by white supremacy.

Even amid the turmoil discussed in the essays in *The Negro Problem,* the possibilities for African American reinvention were almost always front and center. In one sense, the compilation was a critique of the failures of democracy. In another way, the compilation was a celebration of African American achievement. This was evident in Dunbar's essay, in which he described the best representations of African Americans. According to Dunbar, there were successful African American men and women, some of whom he admitted were not widely known but were important to highlight. Dunbar defined a "representative" man as one who "achieved something for the betterment of his race rather than for the aggrandizement of himself."[1] As Dunbar suggested, there were African Americans who were successful but not representative. Those "non-representative" African Americans gained success, but neither their success nor their character helped to uplift the collective African American people. As African Americans attempted to emerge from the stain of enslavement, representation both symbolic and literal had to publically present the best and the brightest. In the early 1900s, there was little public space where African Americans could afford to embark on public campaigns that did not highlight the superior intellect, proper behavior, and strict moral code of African Americans who held leadership positions. Dunbar knew that the public representations of those representative African American men and women were often the standard by which other African Americans were judged. Therefore, in his essay, he praised African Americans who represented the race well.

Defining and praising the best representative African American men and women in prose form was complicated. On the one hand, Dunbar was forced to evaluate African Americans' intellect, behavior, and attitudes by standards most associated with white men and women who had already deemed African Americans to be second-class citizens. Stated differently, since the traditional model by which all African Americans were measured in the early twentieth century was based on a white ideal, those who rose to or above the model were deemed exceptional. Thus "exceptional" was defined according to rules African Americans did not create. On the other hand, those African American men and women who did not conform to the model might be good and respectable in their own right, but since the traditional model often did not recognize their characteristics, they were not considered good and respectable and, most importantly, representative. The challenges that writers like Dunbar encountered as they attempted to effectively evaluate representative African American men and women's characters were not directly addressed by Dunbar, but the fact that he did not address these issues does not indicate that this was not a problem. It was in fact part of a larger problem he and other African American writers and intellectuals encountered in the 1900s as they set out to reinvent African American life and possibilities.

In this chapter on Dunbar's "Representative American Negroes," I highlight a few men and one woman whom Dunbar considered representative American

Negroes. I discuss why character and respectability were twin components that drove the rhetorical message in his essay. I also discuss another pivotal text that was also published in 1903: Du Bois's *The Souls of Black Folk*. Because Du Bois's *The Souls of Black Folk* described the racial schism that came to define America in the twentieth century, it is important to explain the impact of his text relative to Dunbar's essay on representative African Americans.

Like other visible African American leaders in the late 1890s and early 1900s, Dunbar was subjected to many of the constraints imposed by society due to his racial heritage. One of the constraints he had to deal with as a public figure was the necessity of being mindful of his responsibility to his race. That is to say, Dunbar knew that he had to be a respectable man. He "had" to be a credit to his race. His public persona could not conflict with his intellectual or artistic pursuits. In other words, as a representative man, Dunbar held himself and other African American men and women accountable for their public actions.

Interestingly enough, while he was investigating these issues, Dunbar himself was becoming the representative poet for "his people."[2] Excelling in the creation of representations of harmonious and elegiac black voices, Dunbar zealously yearned to represent his people in a way that would be beneficial to them and not purely for white entertainment.[3] Much of his "Representative American Negroes" was a tribute to African American leaders who were providing respectable public leadership in their communities. The first African American man whom Dunbar described as a good representative leader was Bernard Taylor, a young man in Baltimore. Dunbar castigated "the 'Judges,' 'Colonels,' 'Doctors,' and 'Honorables' whose stock cuts burden the pages of our Negro journals week after week" but applauded Taylor for his "quiet and unobtrusive" demeanor.[4] According to Dunbar, Taylor's positive contribution to the African American community and society at large was predicated not on his individual accomplishments but rather on his commitment to his community.

For Dunbar and many other African Americans living during the late nineteenth century and the beginning of the twentieth century, public leadership was an important but no less interesting topic than debates about the kinds of cultural representations—both good and bad—of black people's experiences in America. Struggling to gain both literal and figurative independence in communities throughout the United States after the Civil War, African Americans sought to become a sovereign people. Yet many who wanted the ability to control their physical bodies and their economic lives soon realized that freedom was a heavy burden. Some of the newly freed went back to their former plantations, others eked out a living where they could, some had entrepreneurial acumen, and a few became elected officials. It was clear to Dunbar that the elected officials who represented African Americans in Congress shortly after the Civil War were not always representative men. Dunbar made this clear repeatedly in his essay when he criticized what he viewed as ineffective leadership in Congress. For example, Dunbar argued that it was necessary to make distinctions between "attainment," "achievement," and "values." Writing about African Americans who were public servants after the Civil War, Dunbar sardonically argued, "The illiterate and inefficient black man, whom circumstance put into Congress, was a 'representative' but was not representative. So the peculiar conditions of the days immediately after the war have made it necessary to draw fine distinctions."[5] Mere attainment of a specific job or status did not guarantee that one would be representative. Without the right type of values, achievement only meant that one had attained, not that one had the moral fortitude to lead.

Throughout his essay, Dunbar asserted that moral leadership was the driving force that propelled African American leadership in the right direction, not money or social status. To illustrate his point, Dunbar described a moral quandary encountered by Robert Smalls, a slave during the Civil War. According to Dunbar, Smalls was forced to decide whether to pilot the *Planter* over to the Union side or leave it with the Confederate army. Smalls chose to steer the ship to the Union forces. In Dunbar's estimation, Smalls's act of bravery made him a representative man. Even though Dunbar recognized Smalls's commitment to his individual freedom and, by extension, the freedom of all African Americans, he acknowledged the complexity of his act. In the complex world of slavery, slaves were taught to obey their masters, even when their masters forced them to engage in morally reprehensible behavior. That meant that slaves might have to whip other slaves for transgressions the slave master or overseer found offensive, slaves might have to tell the master if another slave was attempting to flee the plantation, or a male slave might even engage in sexual acts with slave women with whom he had no social connection and to whom he felt no physical attraction. If slaves resisted the commands of their masters or overseers, they were considered disobedient. If slaves failed to act on their own moral codes and instincts, they were failing themselves. When Smalls was faced with a moral dilemma—to remain loyal to his master or to seek freedom for himself—he made a decision that would help him attain his freedom. In the eyes of his master and those who did not want to abolish slavery, Smalls acted most disrespectfully and immorally. But Dunbar interpreted

Smalls's behavior differently. He wrote, "Robert Smalls had done something, something that made him loved and hated, praised and maligned, revered and despised, but something that made him representative of the best that there is in sturdy Negro manhood."[6] Smalls's appeal to Dunbar was his act of good faith. Dunbar recognized that, too often, slaves and freed men were given titles and respect for deeds that benefited the oppressors instead of the oppressed. Put another way, sometimes African American leaders who were accepted and lauded by members of the white community were accepted merely because they "got in the way of progress" or, if in positions of power, because they did little to help fight for equality. In Dunbar's estimation, Smalls did not disrupt African Americans' pursuit of equality and respect.

After Dunbar explained why Smalls was a representative African American leader, he described qualities that made Booker T. Washington an important and representative figure. By the time that Dunbar's essay was published, Washington was already a prominent African American leader. In an essay titled "Industrial Education for the Negro" included in *The Negro Problem*, Washington theorized that African Americans' path to success would be best helped by investment in industrial education. He wrote, "For two hundred fifty years, I believe the way for redemption of the Negro was being prepared through industrial development." Washington believed that slavery had given African American men and women specific labor skills they could capitalize on in the South. He maintained that "to a large degree, ... this business contact with the Southern white man, and the industrial training on the plantations, left the Negro at the close of the war in possession of nearly all the common and skilled labor in the South."[7]

Furthermore, Washington asserted: "The industries that gave the South its power, prominence and wealth prior to the Civil War were mainly the raising of cotton, sugar cane, rice and tobacco. Before the way could be prepared for the proper growing and marketing of these crops forests had to be cleared, houses to be built, public roads and railroads constructed. In all these works the Negro did most of the heavy work."[8] Although Washington was vilified by Du Bois for theorizing that African Americans should seek economic progress by way of an industrial education, Dunbar understood the value of Washington's theory. In spite of Du Bois's and other prominent African Americans' criticism of Washington, Dunbar did not fail to view Washington as another representative African American man. In his essay, Dunbar wrote eloquently about Washington's "one idea": "They say of this man that he is a man of one idea, but that one is a great one and he has merely concentrated all his powers upon it; in other words, he has organized himself and gone forth to gather in whatever about him was essential."[9] Dunbar realized that there were many different ways that African American leadership could represent the collective race well, and he even acknowledged the differences among the men and women in his essay. Robert Smalls was socially different from Washington, and Washington's educational philosophy was antithetical to Du Bois's; however, Dunbar never asserted that one leadership quality or philosophy was better than another. He merely described the differences and allowed his readers to decide with which of the models they mostly identified.

After Dunbar explained why Washington qualified as a representative African American leader, he described the positive leadership characteristics of Du Bois. None of the men discussed in Dunbar's essay is probably more widely known than Du Bois, whose book *The Souls of Black Folk* and whose essay "The Talented Tenth" described the sociopolitical and intellectual crossroads many African Americans faced at the dawn of the twentieth century. Du Bois articulates many insights in *The Souls of Black Folk*. However, there are two I want to point out here, as they relate to his representative status. Du Bois was a man of keen insight. In *The Souls of Black Folk* he argued prophetically that "THE PROBLEM OF THE TWENTIETH CENTURY is the problem of the color-line."[10] Of course there were many problems and challenges Americans faced during the twentieth century; however, none was probably more explosive than racial conflicts during the second half of the century. W. E. B. Du Bois's prophecy was realized in a civil rights movement that attempted to eradicate the problems associated with the color line.

Du Bois's intellectual acumen did not just allow him to foresee the color-line problem. He was also able to keenly articulate the psychological damages of enslavement. For example, in a famous passage from *The Souls of Black Folk*, Du Bois passionately wrote: "The Negro is a sort of seventh son, born with a veil, and gifted with second-sight in this American world,—a world which yields him no true self-consciousness, but only lets him see himself through the revelation of the other world. It is a peculiar sensation, this double-consciousness, this sense of always looking at one's self through the eyes of others, of measuring one's soul by the tape of a world that looks on in amused contempt and pity."[11] This passage is often quoted by scholars who write about the black experience in America. Du Bois argued fervently and correctly that African Americans were examining and evaluating themselves through the eyes of the "other." For millions of African Americans, such a constraint both protected and limited their psychological selves. Although Du Bois wrote that passage more than a hundred years ago, it remains as relevant today as it was in 1903. Because Du Bois was such an important figure, it would have been absurd for Dunbar to ignore Du Bois's contribution to African American life.

Du Bois was an intellectual giant, and his understanding of African Americans' position in American life gave credence to his scholarly achievements.

In addition to helping African Americans understand their double consciousness, Du Bois also attempted to help African Americans gain intellectual and political equality at the turn of the century. His well-known "Talented Tenth" theory articulated a way to guarantee the educational and political rise of the African American people. His philosophy also served as a foil to Washington's industrial education theory. Du Bois's Talented Tenth theory argued that 10 percent of the educated elite should help lead the masses. He surmised: "The Negro race, like all races, is going to be saved by its exceptional men. The problem of education, then, among Negroes must first of all deal with the Talented Tenth; it is the problem of developing the Best of this race that they may guide the Mass away from the contamination and death of the Worst, in their own and other races."[12] Throughout his career as a public intellectual, Du Bois was an exceptional theorist. Although Dunbar was unable to see the full trajectory of Du Bois's accomplishments, certainly he knew that Du Bois would always be an influential and representative leader.

After Dunbar completed his description of Du Bois's accomplishments, he described lesser-known but no less important representative figures such as the Honorable Richard Theodore Greener, Judge Mifflin Wistar Gibbs, George H. White, Granville T. Woods, and Daniel H. Williams. Near the end of his essay, Dunbar discussed representative African American women. Unfortunately, he does not spend a great deal of time describing the positive attributes of representative African American female leadership. In fact, what he wrote is a brief two paragraphs that attribute the women's significance to their ability to inspire men rather than to the women's own intellectual abilities. He remarked, "I have spoken of 'men and women,' and indeed the women must not be forgotten, for to them the men look for much of the inspiration and impulse that drives them forward to success."[13] The best-known African American woman mentioned in his essay is Mary Church Terrell, although Dunbar wrote very little about her. She was a prominent African American woman who fought passionately for women's rights in the late nineteenth and early twentieth centuries. In 1896, Terrell was the first president of the National Association of Colored Women. She was a lecturer, activist, and writer. Dunbar called Terrell "the one fully in the public eye, with learning and eloquence, telling the hopes and fears of her kind."[14]

Dunbar finished the essay by praising qualities that make great representative men. He remarked: "All these of whom I have spoken are men who have striven and achieved and the reasons underlying their success are the same that account for the advancement of men of any other race: preparation, perseverance, bravery, patience, honesty and the powers to seize the opportunity."[15] Dunbar mused, "It is a little dark still, but there are warnings of the day and somewhere out of the darkness a bird is singing to the dawn."[16] Although the last line of Dunbar's essay lamented the fact that opportunities to represent the race well were limited by racism, it is apparent that he was optimistic about African Americans' future possibilities.

The title of my chapter suggests that Dunbar aspired to hold African American men and women accountable for their public actions. Since he lacked the political or economic power to hold men and women accountable, he used his essay as a way to point to behavior appropriate for African American leadership. Put another way, words and descriptions of respectable and representative African Americans was his way of holding his brothers and sisters accountable. Dunbar's desire to do so was prompted by an abiding faith in the future of his people but also by his recognition that African American people needed representative African American men and women in their communities and in public life. Leadership for African Americans in the early twentieth century was of paramount importance. What better way to show the masses how to change their lives than to use words to describe the dynamic lives of African American people? Perhaps his essay about representative men and women could inspire as well as give an historical account of a group of people whose successes were often ignored by society at large.

Dunbar was careful to point out in his essay that positive representation came in different forms. Dunbar esteemed not those African Americans who had acquired money or those who had questionable reputations. He valued African Americans who worked hard for the group and who also had a good character. He knew better than most that an individual's moral character and public persona were often used as an indicator of respectability. Dunbar took seriously the challenge to represent his race well. He expected others to do the same.

Notes

1. Paul Dunbar, "Representative American Negroes," in *The Negro Problem*, ed. Norm R. Allen Jr., Molefi Kete Asante, and Toyin Falola (New York: Humanity Books, 2003), 189.

2. Jay Martin, "Paul Laurence Dunbar: Biography through Letters," foreword to *A Singer in the Dawn: Reinterpretations of Paul Laurence Dunbar* (New York: Dodd, Mead, 1975), 17.

3. Lida Keck Wiggins and William Dean Howells, *The Life and Works of Paul Laurence Dunbar* (Naperville, Ill.: Nichols, 1907), 109.

4. Dunbar, "Representative American Negroes," 189.
5. Ibid., 192.
6. Ibid., 193.
7. Booker T. Washington, "Industrial Education for the Negro," in *The Negro Problem*, 10.
8. Ibid., 11–12.
9. Dunbar, "Representative American Negroes," 194.
10. W. E. B. Du Bois, *The Souls of Black Folk* (New York: Dover, 1994), 9.
11. Ibid., 2.
12. W. E. B. Du Bois, "The Talented Tenth," in *The Negro Problem*, 33.
13. Dunbar, "Representative American Negroes," 206.
14. Shirley Wilson Logan, *"We Are Coming": The Persuasive Discourse of Nineteenth-Century Black Women* (Carbondale: Southern Illinois University Press, 1999), 84–85.
15. Dunbar, "Representative American Negroes," 209.
16. Ibid.

7
"Jump Back, Honey, Jump Back"
Reading Paul Laurence Dunbar in the Context of the Century Magazine

MARK NOONAN

> I found [Dunbar] seated in a chair on the lower landing hastily glancing at the July *Century,* and jotting down notes in a handy pencil tablet. . . . He stated he had been writing rhymes since he was 13. His favorite authors are Whittier and James Whitcomb Riley.
> —JAMES NEWTON MATTHEWS, *INDIANAPOLIS JOURNAL* (1892)

ACADEMIC CRITICISM HAS RECENTLY recovered Paul Laurence Dunbar from William Dean Howells's influential claim in 1896 that the author of *Lyrics of Lowly Life* was at his best working in "negro dialect" and "describing the range between appetite and emotion . . . which is the range of [his] race."[1] Today, Dunbar is rightly viewed as a complex and subtle author adept at working in a variety of literary genres and forms. Despite such reassessments, the authenticity of his black voice and the extent to which he subverted plantation myth conventions remain at the fore of criticism of his work. In his landmark book *The Signifying Monkey,* Henry Louis Gates Jr., for example, focuses on the poet's use of dialect to address his alleged acquiescence to racist stereotypes. For "Dunbar to draw upon dialect as a medium through which to posit this mode of realism," Gates writes, "suggests both a certain boldness as well as a certain opportunism, two qualities that helped to inform Dunbar's mixed result, which we know so well, he lamented to his death."[2] Gates's claim that his art is *both* bold and baldly opportunist captures the dilemma that scholars face in looking at Dunbar well and partially addresses it. Yet to advance our understanding of the mixed impulses in Dunbar's poetry, we still need a clearer understanding of his apprenticeship as a poet, as well as a careful consideration of the material context and reception of his poems when they first appeared for public consumption, often in major magazines and newspapers.

Still underacknowledged, in particular, is the significant role the *Century Illustrated Monthly Magazine* played in developing Dunbar's talent and interests during his formative years and introducing his poetry to the American public when his poems began to regularly appear in it from 1895 to 1901. The *Century* was Dunbar's literary handbook and Holy Grail. During the 1880s and 1890s, the young poet devoured each monthly issue, paying particular attention to the regional works of James Whitcomb Riley and the literary criticism of Edmund Clarence Stedman. In light of this fact, this chapter examines the clear influence of Riley and Stedman on Dunbar to show that much of what is viewed as his "natural" pastoral inclinations and inherent lyricism was, to a great extent, gleaned from readings in a genteel publication interested in promoting "the folk" and "the ideal" during a time of rapid urbanization and industrialization. Equally significant was the reception of Dunbar's poetry in the context of the periodical he appeared in. In its initial years (1870–80), when it was called *Scribner's Monthly*, the *Century* sought to promote reconciliation between the North and South by publishing a seemingly endless stream of plantation myth fiction celebrating an antebellum social order with well-demarcated gender, class, and—most notably—racial distinctions by the likes of James Lane Allen, Thomas Nelson Page, Irwin Russell, and Joel Chandler Harris. When Dunbar began publishing his dialect poems in the *Century* in the 1890s, his work often appeared alongside a new cadre of Southern sympathizers including Richard Malcolm Johnston, F. Hopkinson Smith, Ruth McEnery Stuart, and Grace King. Individually, Dunbar's poems can often be read as rustic variations on Riley from the viewpoint of a black laborer or farmer exuding humor, pathos, homespun intelligence, and resolute spirit. But in the context of the *Century*'s plantation myth propaganda machine, his poems appear to contribute to reactionary social views and stereotypes the author clearly wished to distance himself from.

Well known in Dunbar criticism is Howells's famous introduction to *Lyrics of Lowly Life* (based on a review published in *Harper's Monthly* in 1895), but consideration is rarely given to the fact that many of these collected poems first appeared in periodicals and newspapers. Accordingly, it is important to recognize that Howells's commentary is a response to a series of poems that, when read in book form, produce a unique reading experience. Read collectively, these poems, as Howells so clearly recognized, respond to the late nineteenth-century rage for local color writing by documenting "what passes in the hearts and minds of a lowly people whose poetry had hitherto been inarticulately expressed." Rather than reading the mostly dialect poems as demeaning, Howells understood the collection as a "brilliant and unique achievement" attesting to the manner in which the author "studied the negro objectively, and . . . represented him as he found him to be, with humor, with sympathy, and yet with what the reader must instinctively feel to be entire truthfulness."[3] When we disregard the context in which the poems were originally published, and the actual history of their composition, it is easy to see how Howells came to his influential conclusions. But if we return to the source of many of Dunbar's ideas and influences, the *Century*, which also published much of his work, a different story emerges. His poetry was not simply the result of a careful study of black life. It was meant to be read not realistically, as Howells, the dean of American realism, believed, but *ideally*, as Edmund Clarence Stedman proposed in his *Century* essays. Howells's review also did not consider that no matter how "truthful" Dunbar's poems may have felt, they were generally entrenched in the wildly distorting, racialized context of the periodical press.

Born to freed Kentucky slaves who had come north to settle in Dayton, Ohio, Dunbar's understanding of black life on the plantation quite clearly came to him secondhand. It was from his father, who had served in the second all-black regiment of the Union army, that he heard stories of the war as well as life under slavery. His mother, too, relayed her experiences of the past and instilled in her son a love for literature and an understanding of the value of a good education. Growing up, he had a great deal of contact with black southerners who had come north after the war and briefly attended a black district grade school. His formative schooling, however, took place at Central High School in Dayton, where blacks were a distinct minority. Despite his minority status, he graduated with notable distinctions, including editor in chief of the *High School Times*, president of the Philomathean Society (a literary club), class poet, and founder of the *Dayton Tattler*, the town's first newspaper aimed at a black audience. Largely sheltered from the effects of racism in high school, he quickly encountered the color line upon graduation. Though Dunbar had hoped to eventually earn enough money to study law at Harvard, good job prospects eluded him and he resigned himself to taking a position as an elevator hop in an office building at four dollars a week. It was at this job that he found the time to read his favorite poets and critics—usually as their work appeared in the *Century*—and his true apprenticeship as a writer began.

In July 1892, Dunbar became an overnight sensation after reading a welcome address in verse at the Western Association of Writers' annual conference. Arranged by one of his former teachers, his recitation was so impressive that James Newton Matthews, editor of the *Indianapolis Journal*, sought him out the following day. The article Matthews wrote about his new discovery, whom he found eagerly devouring the July issue of the *Century*, was read by none other than James Whitcomb Riley, the most popular poet of the day. In November, Riley wrote directly to Dunbar in words that would prove prophetic: "See how your name is traveling, my chirping friend. And it's a good, sound name, too, that seems to imply the brave, fine spirit of a singer who should command wide and serious attention."[4]

That Riley was the first major writer to pay Dunbar any mind is extraordinarily apt, for the young poet had already been trying to learn as much as he could from Indiana's poet laureate since he published his first poem at the age of sixteen. A key figure in the regionalist literary movement during the last quarter of the nineteenth century, Riley, over the course of his career, published more than fifty poems in the *Century*, where Dunbar certainly encountered them. Harkening back to preindustrial America and looking to the common folk as a source of purity and inspiration, Riley's poems—flush with populist sentiment, sentimental love scenes, and colloquial speech—were perhaps the most popular and financially remunerative an American has ever produced. As Jean Wagner writes, Riley's success "awakened in young Dunbar the ambition to emulate the Indiana poet laureate. Coldly and industriously he began to dismantle Riley's devices, with an eye to appropriating them."[5]

Riley's *Century* poems, collected in *Poems Here at Home* (1893), served in part as an antidote to growing commercialism, industrialism, and urbanism following the Civil War. As America became increasingly modern, literature that harkened back to simpler times in the disappearing countryside came into favor. As cultural historian T. J. Jackson Lears writes, the vitality and simplicity of pastoral living portrayed in regionalist writing provided "educated bourgeoise" readers an "alternative to modern unreality"[6] and the alienation it wrought. Regionalist writing such as Riley's also served to promote an authentically American literature and, in turn, democratic ideals. Following the Civil War, America's cultural custodians sought to induce social harmony and national pride by encouraging the work of domestic writers and artists. Leading the charge was the *Century*, begun as *Scribner's Monthly* under the editorship of Josiah G. Holland and his associate Richard Watson Gilder. Beginning in the 1870s, the magazine actively sought writers from every part of the country, including southerners such as George Washington Cable, Joel Chandler Harris, Thomas Nelson Page; westerners such as Bret Harte, John Muir, and Mary Halleck Foote; and Hjalmar Hjorth Boyesen, Edward Eggleston, and Hamlin Garland from the Midwest.

Riley's title poem, "The Poems Here at Home," first published in the *Century* in 1892, testifies to what the editors of the magazine desired in promoting regional literature in their pages:

The Poems here at Home!—Who'll write 'em down,
Jes' as they air—in Country and in Town?—...

> What We want, as I sense it, in the line
> O' poetry is somepin' Yours and Mine—
> Somepin' with live-stock in it, and out-doors,
> And old crick-bottoms, snags, and sycamores:
> Putt weeds in—pizenvines, and underbrush....
>
> Putt in old Nature's sermonts—them's the best,—
> And 'casion'ly hand up a hornets' nest....
>
> We want some poetry 'at's to Our taste,
> Made out o' truck 'at 's jes' a-goin' to waste
> 'Cause smart folks thinks it's altogether too
> Outrageous common—'cept fer me and you!—[7]

What Riley calls for in these lines is local color writing on natural, everyday themes presented in the regional dialect of the common man. His contributions, along with those of so many other local color writers flooding the major periodicals at the time, opened America's eyes to its own dynamic diversity and provided reassurance that literature could still resonate with their own modern lives.

Riley's own poetry published in the *Century* embodies his vision of utilizing local voices and themes to showcase America's regional vitality while combating a disconcerting modern world. The pleasures of country life over city life, for example, are captured in "Back from Town" (Feb. 1891), in which a speaker who has been away for many years is glad to return to "These old comforts waiting here—/ These old friends; back to the hands / 'At a feller understands."[8] In "Our Hired Girl" (Dec. 1890) and "The Raggedy Man" (Dec. 1890), Riley glorifies day laborers for the simple cheer they bring to their work and those they work for. The revitalizing effects of being in nature are celebrated in "In Swimming-Time" (Sept. 1883) with lines such as "Ah! The glorious carnival! / Purple lips and chattering teeth—/ Eyes that burn—but, in beneath, / Every care beyond recall."[9] The themes of domestic bliss and childhood innocence too are rendered in a variety of works, including "The All-Kind Mother" (Feb. 1889), "A Boy's Mother" (Dec. 1890), "Some Poems by Boys" (Dec. 1890), and "Home Again" (Aug. 1894). Almost always in Hoosier dialect, Riley's *Century* poems also speak to the joys of courtship, as in "When She Comes Home" (June 1887): "When she comes home again! A thousand ways / I fashion, to myself, the tenderness / Of my glad welcome."[10]

For Riley, the poet's role was to use the language of everyday speech to capture sentiments familiar to everyone. As he writes in "The Poet of the Future" (Jan. 1889), the ideal poet "will come as man to man, / With the honest arm of labor, and the honest face of tan, / The honest heart of lowliness, the honest soul of love / For human-kind and nature-kind about him and above."[11] Despite our contemporary view of Riley as a backward-looking sentimentalist, his poetry in fact consciously strove for an authentically American voice that celebrated the nation's regional diversity in democratic terms.

Allied to Riley and his efforts to clear a new path for poetry was Edmund Clarence Stedman, another enormous yet underacknowledged influence on Dunbar. A Wall Street broker by day, Stedman began establishing his reputation as one of America's most astute literary critics in the pages of *Century* with revisionist essays on the hallowed names of literature, including Lowell (May 1882), Emerson (April 1883), Longfellow (Oct. 1883), Holmes (Feb. 1885), and Whittier (May 1885). In general, Stedman spoke appreciatively of these writers as unique American voices, but he also criticized these writers' tendency to be excessively didactic and moralistic. More sympathetic were his essays on Poe (May 1880) and Whitman (Nov. 1880), writers who had long suffered at the hands of inferior critics (including the *Century*'s first editor, Josiah G. Holland). Insightfully, for the time, Stedman heralded Poe's emphasis on beauty of expression as well as Whitman's "prophetic gift of song."[12] Unlike their overly didactic counterparts, Stedman argued, Poe and Whitman rightly viewed beauty, feeling, and imagination as the highest aims of art. Despite their achievements, however, Stedman in "The Twilight of the Poets" (Sept. 1885) conceded that American poetry, by and large, had yet to flourish. As he sees the field, "There is, if not a decadence, at least a poetic interregnum." His advice to future poets is to learn from novelists who "depict Life as it is, though rarely as yet in its intenser phases."[13] Looking at reality and capturing it in all its intensity, Stedman predicted, would inaugurate a "new dawn" of poetic greatness.

While it is not clear whether the essays that would later comprise his famous *Poets of America* were read by Dunbar in the pages of *Century*, his next series of critical essays (collected in *The Nature and Elements of Poetry* in 1892) certainly was. Interestingly, the impetus for these writings was Howells's review of *Poets of America* in the March 1886 issue of *Harper's Monthly*. In it, Howells took issue with Stedman's call for a bardic "genius" in poetry and argued that social consciousness was the writer's provenance. As such, the novel, not poetry, was the most useful genre in the modern age of realism. Stedman's response to Howells in the *Century* was impressive and thorough. In "Oracles Old and New" (March 1892), "What Is Poetry?" (April 1892), "Creation and Self-Expression" (May 1892), "Melancholia" (June 1892), "Faculty Divine" (Oct. 1892), and "Imagination" (Sept. 1892), he countered that the spiritual elements of poetry were what distinguished it as the highest art form. In "Truth" (Aug. 1892), he goes so far as to speak of the divine powers of the poet: "As far as the poet, the artist, is creative, he becomes a sharer of the divine responsibility." Stedman proposes in essence that the poet should strive for idealist aims. Unlike the realist novelist, he sees the poet's function as portraying the elements of the world not "as they are, but as they are or may be at their best. This lifts them out of the common, or, rather, it is thus we get at the power and mystery of common things."[14] In other words, for Stedman, the poet's role is an imaginative one in which he or she dramatizes life's ideals rather than merely capturing prosaic reality.

According to Matthews, in Dunbar's hands when he was discovered as an elevator hop was the July issue of the *Century*, which contained Stedman's essay "Beauty." In it, Stedman continues his defense of poetry on spiritual grounds that the realist prose writers have overlooked. He begins with the argument that "No work of art is worth considering unless it is more or less effective through beauty, feeling, and imagination; and in the consideration of art, truth and ethics are a part of beauty's fidelity to supreme ideals."[15] Stedman pursues his case on behalf of romantic idealism by asking why these three elements have been overlooked in recent literary criticism of the novel. "Why," he asks, "in order to advance the banner . . . of realism . . . should we assume the task of denying beauty altogether?" Stedman next turns to a discussion of the short lyrical poem as the finest poetical form for extolling beauty. In lyrical poetry, he writes, one finds "the music of speech" and the appropriate rhythm and verbal expression for the most poignant themes. For Stedman, "the tuneful plaint of sorrow, the tears 'wild with all regret,' the touch that consecrates, the preciousness of that which lives but in memory and echo and dreams, move the purest spirit of poesy to sweep the perfect minstrel lute."[16]

Certainly, Riley and Stedman's effect on Dunbar was strong. It is clear that, following the advice of Stedman, Dunbar, in his rhythms, sentiments, and style, sought lyricism and beauty, not necessarily realist accuracy. That he learned this also from Riley is illustrated by his paean to his mentor, "James Whitcomb Riley":

> No matter what you call it,
> whether genius, or art,
> He sings the simple songs that come
> The closest to your heart.
> Fur trim an' skillful phrases,
> I do not ker a jot;
> 'Tain't the words alone, but feelin's,
> That tech the tender spot.

....
He paints our joys an' sorrers
In a way so stric'ly true,
That a body can't help knowin'
that he has felt them too.
....
There's none of them kin tech the heart
Like our own Whitcomb Riley.[17]

Of course, it was not just sentiment but themes and plots that Dunbar directly borrowed from his mentor. Despite Howells's claim that Dunbar's source of inspiration for much of his dialect work was the "objective study of black life," it is apparent that his *Century* poems are very much in the tradition of Riley, though almost all of them have blacks as central characters and are written in African American vernacular.[18] Like Riley, Dunbar has his share of exquisite love poems. In "Lover's Lane" (Oct. 1898), for example, a young lover hopes that a romantic trail exists for him and his lady in heaven. Unable to ever imagine life without his mate, the protagonist wonders "whetah in de skies / Dey's a lovah's lane. / Ef dey ain't, I tell you true, / 'Ligion do look mighty blue, / 'Cause I do' know whut I'll do / 'Dout a lovah's lane."[19] In "Parted" (Dec. 1896) the pain of separation from a lover is evoked as we overhear a black narrator explain how "Old Mas' done sol' me down de stream." Despite the unreality of the claim (given historical realities surrounding the plight of slaves), the poem promises an idyllic ending: "Jes' wait, jes' b'lieve in whut I say, / My lady, my lady; / D' ain't nothin' dat kin keep me 'way, / My lady, my lady."[20] Dunbar's paeans to domestic bliss such as "At Candle-Lightin' Time" (May 1897) also recall his mentor. In this particular poem we overhear the protagonist speak of "de happy hours dat foller . . . when I come in f'om de co'n-fiel aftah wukin' ha'd all da."[21] Similarly, in "Foolin' Wif de Seasons" (Oct. 1897), Dunbar privileges life on the farm over the cares and tribulations associated with the city. Reminiscent of the sentiments expressed in Riley's "Home Again," Dunbar's protagonist, a black rustic, asks: "Why don't foks quit movin' forrard? Ain't it better jest to stan', / An' be satisfied wif livin' in de season dat's at han'?"[22]

What is clear about Dunbar's dialect poetry, which the *Century* regularly welcomed, is that artistically it is of the highest order within the parameters of the school of romantic idealism. Following Riley and Stedman's lead, Dunbar strove to create poems of deep feeling drawn directly from the vicissitudes of life. As he writes in "The Poet,"

He sang of life, serenely sweet,
    With, now and then, a deeper note.

> From some high peak, nigh yet remote,
> He voiced the world's absorbing beat.
>
> He sang of love when earth was young,
>   And Love, itself, was in his lays.[23]

While it is clear that Dunbar succeeded in his aims, it is equally true that the critics, including contemporary ones, have been unable to allow that his work often met expectations different from his own. When Howells, for example, praised Dunbar for how his dialect so truthfully captured black life, he missed the more universal note that the poet strove for. As Dunbar, wiser than his critics, concludes,

> But ah, the world, it turned to praise
>   A jingle in a broken tongue.[24]

Though the ending of "The Poet" is generally read as Dunbar's lament that his more formal English poems had not been accepted, a close reading of the full poem actually tells us something different. Dunbar understood most of his oeuvre to have achieved lyrical greatness. However, critics have rarely been able to see his work beyond the dialect he so often employed.

Even today critics tend to undervalue his elegant lyricism and artistry, focusing instead on the extent to which his work has perpetuated stereotypes. In so doing, they fail to see that he quite clearly sought to distance himself from the work of the plantation myth tradition. In a letter to Frederick Douglass's widow, Helen, for example, he explicitly rejected the view that his work was indistinguishable from that of writers such as Thomas Nelson Page: "I am sorry to find among intelligent people those who are unable to differentiate dialect as a philological branch from the burlesque of Negro minstrelsy."[25] What is often missed is that Dunbar, in his dialect poems, wished to depict an accurate yet sympathetic and somewhat idealized representation of black life, just as Riley had achieved for the Hoosier. Indeed, what primarily distinguishes Dunbar from Riley is the very fact that his characters are black. Unfortunately, despite Dunbar's clear intentions, a poem that strives, like Riley's do, to valorize the country over the city or to venerate rest at the end of a long day, when narrated by an African American in the late nineteenth century, takes on an obvious racial dimension. This dimension is only enhanced in the context of a magazine deeply committed, by the 1890s, to plantation myth propaganda.

Generally speaking, the aim of regional writers published by first *Scribner's Monthly* and then the *Century* beginning in the 1870s was to promote native American literature to ease the pains of modernization and showcase a heterogeneous yet united society. Its southern writers, however, often had an added political agenda, which the *Century* tacitly supported. One can see the role the editors played in the last quarter of the nineteenth century in assisting southern writers to perpetuate the myth of the "Lost Cause," which sought to recover a once harmonious society marked by a docile workforce, loyal and obedient "true" women, and racial segregation.

From its earliest issues, *Scribner's* pro-southern sympathies were apparent in the dialect verses of Thomas Dunn English, a southerner committed to depicting Reconstruction as a failure of misguided idealism. In "Caesar Rowan" (July 1871), English's first work to appear in *Scribner's,* an elderly black slave hears of the Emancipation Proclamation but refuses to leave his master's plantation because of all his fond memories and his love for "Mas' Jeemes." As Caesar explains,

> Yes, I heen about de proclamation—
> Ole Mas' Linkum's—dessay, boss, it's right;
> But fo' seventy yeah on dis plantation,
> Young Mas' Jeemes an I have fit de fight—
> Whah I've bin I mean to stay.[26]

In the second stanza, the reader learns that Caesar and his master grew up together as "pardners ev'ry day." Caesar accompanies Mas' Jeemes, for example, when he goes off to college and is at his side when he marries Nancy, a lady with "spirit . . . full o' grace an' pride." The saddest moment of Caesar's life occurs when his master's young son, Randolph, rescues him from the river and drowns in the process. Master Randolph's death causes both Mas' Jeemes and his wife great sorrow, the latter dying on the day of the funeral. From that day forth, Caesar has seen his role as the comforter and caretaker of his former owner, "who sits all day wropt up in fancy."[27]

Written entirely in Negro dialect and containing the lugubrious pathos that would become a trademark of the genre, "Caesar Rowan" is an early but classic example of the postbellum school of plantation myth fiction. As we see, the poem exhibits many of the school's classic motifs, including the portrayal of loving master-slave relationships, the beautiful and proudly loyal southern belle (a mythical image perfected in Margaret Mitchell's *Gone with the Wind*), the handsome and noble plantation owner, and his devoted black foot servant, who is unwilling (or rather unable) to live independently. In issue after issue, southern writers in the vein of English portrayed blacks as foolish, superstitious, lusty, lazy, and/or excitable—in short, running the entire gamut

Figure 7.1: From Irwin Russell's "Nebuchadnezzar" (July 1876).

of "darkie" stereotypes. An actual list of the submissions accepted for publication in the *Century* alone would number well over five hundred (an average of several per issue); this includes some classic examples of the genre, such as Russell's "Christmas-Night in the Quarters" (Jan. 1878), Harris's "A Rainy Day with Uncle Remus" (June, July, Aug. 1881) and "Free Joe and the Rest of the World" (Nov. 1884), Page's "Marse Chan: A Story of Ole Virginia" (April 1884) and "Meh Lady" (June 1886), Allen's "Two Kentucky Gentlemen of the Old School" (April 1888), F. Hopkinson Smith's *Colonel Carter of Cartersville* (Nov. 1890–April 1891), and Grace King's "Balcony Stories" (Jan. 1893–Dec. 1893), as well as works by Richard Malcolm Johnston, Mary Johnston, J. A. Macon, Julia Pickering, Ruth McEnery Stuart, and countless others.

Given the context of so much black caricature, Dunbar's pastoral poems that appeared in the *Century* are, by and large, barely distinguishable from the plantation myth fiction that literally surrounded his work and, one can only presume, must have been read as such. For example, when read side by side with the *Century*'s demeaning cartoons, such as those accompanying the work of Irwin Russell (figure 7.1), "Foolin' Wif de Seasons" can no longer be read merely as a poem elevating country life over city life but must be read as concerning distinct types of races.

In the poem the black narrator mocks those who "nevah t'inks o' nuffin only but to plot an' plan." For himself: "Hit's enough fu' me to listen when de birds is singin' roun', / 'Dout a-guessin' whut 'll happen when de snow is on de groun'. / In de springtime an' de summah I lay sorer on de she'f / 'Cause I know ol' Mistah Winter gwin to bustle fu' hisse'f." In the context of the *Century*, the work seems to juxtapose a somewhat lazy and less-than-rational black with the white populace, who obsessively "plot an' plan."[28] Similarly, one could not read the artful "Noddin by the Fire," which deftly captures the comfort of the hearth and was first published in the *Century* in 1901, without the stereotype of the sleepy black hand in mind.

> Some folks t'inks hit's right an' p'opah,
>   Soon ez bedtime come eroun',
> Fu' to scramble to de kiver,
>   Lak dey'd hyeahed de trumpet soun'.
> But dese people dey all misses
>   Whut I mos'ly does desiah;
> Dat's de settin' roun' an' dozin',
>   An' a-noddin' by de fiah.[29]

Of course, like Riley, Dunbar's aim is to make his characters appealing, not foolish. Dunbar's race and the racial makeup of his protagonists, however, make his poetry "folk" poems with a highly charged, culturally constructed racial dimension.

While the sheer lyricism and rhythm of much of Dunbar's work in dialect should dispel notions of black inferiority, it is impossible to read his *Century* poems in racially progressive terms. Though a strong case can be made that the poet does often present his black characters humanely and positively, and that notes of protest against racism are occasionally sounded, Dunbar, to his disadvantage, *seems* to promote racial stereotypes associated with the plantation myth tradition all too regularly. In "At Candle-Lightin' Time," for example, the black protagonist looks forward to finishing his work, not simply because it is against his true nature, but so he can play his banjo. In "On the Road" (April 1897), the black poet longs to get home to his lover but is most concerned that it is getting dark (of which he is desperately afraid). His frequent association of blacks and possums in a comic vein is equally disconcerting in a highly racialized context. The central point of "Possum" (March 1898), for example, is expressed by a black speaker who pities "White folks [who] t'ink dey know 'bout eatin'" when in fact "dey ain't a t'ng dey knows of / Dat I reckon cain't be beat / When we set down at de table / To a unskun possum's meat!"[30] In a magazine that also printed such work as E. W. Kemble's obviously demeaning cartoon "The Possum Hunt" (figure 7.2), the irony of Dunbar's humor is clearly dissipated.

The notion that blacks not only talk and eat differently but court differently is also illustrated in Dunbar's *Century* poems. In "A Coquette Conquered" (July 1896) a black man named Sam tries to make overtures to his "gal," who

Figure 7.2: E. W. Kemble, "The 'Possum Hunt" (June 1890).

rejects him until she finds out he has brought her a possum. Another poem suggesting that, in love, blacks are concerned with baser concerns than their white counterparts, who supposedly practice "pure" mating rituals, is "A Frolic" (Oct. 1899). In it, a slave looks forward to the fact that his master is going to be away for a few days and duly warns Miss Lucy that she will "be cotched an' kissed / 'Fo' de night is done."[31] Though this poem, out of context, could (and should) be read as a case study in black subversion of white authority, it instead recalls the plantation myth stereotype of the sexually aggressive black male, such as Daddy Jack lustily chasing Tildy in Joel Chandler Harris's "Night with Uncle Remus." Even the exquisitely rendered "Negro Love Song" (April 1895) takes on negative racial implications when read in the context of the plantation myth fiction swarming the *Century* at this time. In this poem, a black man escorts his lover home and anticipates the pleasures he will soon encounter, echoing the refrain "Jump back, honey, jump back":

Put my ahm aroun' huh wais',
   Jump back, honey, jump back.
Raised huh lips an' tuck a tas'e,
   Jump back, honey, jump back.[32]

Despite the rhythmic elegance and exquisite sensuality of this poem, the known racial makeup of the author and its serial context even here transform art into sociology.

In general, the *Century* preferred Dunbar's poems in Negro dialect, which seemed to conform to and reinforce the plantation myth tradition. However, on two occasions it did publish two of his more outspoken poems written in Standard English that call for recognition of the continuing struggle for black rights in the post-Reconstruction era. In "Harriet Beecher Stowe" (Nov. 1898), Dunbar pays tribute to "this fearless woman's voice" who "at one stroke ... gave / A race to freedom."[33] And in the truly haunting "The Haunted Oak" (Dec. 1900), he protests the growing number of lynchings the South is responsible for from the perspective of a tree. As it recalls, "I feel the rope against my bark, / And the weight of him in my grain, / I feel in the throe of his final woe / The touch of my own last pain."[34] Both poems are powerful and should place the *Century* in an honorable and progressive light. But this is only if one removes from the picture the magazine's long history of promoting the racist ideology behind the segregation and continued violence against blacks in the South. By publishing work such as James Lane Allen's "Mrs. Stowe's 'Uncle Tom' at Home in Kentucky" (Oct. 1887), which essentially takes Stowe to task for allegedly misconstruing the abuse of blacks in the South, a place where Uncle Tom could only have been content, the *Century* had already forfeited its credibility.

The cage that racist America during the Gilded Age had built for itself, as well as for its first black poet to reach a national audience, is only now becoming apparent. As Gavin Jones writes, even so prescient a reader as Howells could not undo the shackles of race thinking when introducing Dunbar's second book of poems. Dunbar himself was caged, "caught in a theory of literature and an institutional matrix tragically inadequate to his poetic resources."[35] In order to reach a wide audience, he had to continue producing dialect poems and utilizing black subjects, even though he preferred writing in a more classical style on an open range of broadly literary topics. Yet no matter what pitch of greatness these poems achieved (and many of them *are* aesthetic masterpieces), they would inevitably be considered the work of a "black" artist, especially when read in the context of wildly distorting racialized venues. Eventually, Dunbar would establish his true voice with the brilliant naturalist novel *The Sport of the Gods,* but in doing so, he found that both his mainstream audience and the support of genteel publishers were, by and large, gone. By the turn of the century, the refrain "Jump back, honey, jump back" would refer not to black joy and release, but to the reactionary racial policies of a "new" America, to which the *Century* had clearly contributed over a thirty-year period. It may have helped produce a young aspiring writer and helped to make him famous, but it also ultimately contributed to the unjust demise of his reputation.

NOTES

1. William Dean Howells, introduction to *Lyrics of Lowly Life,* by Paul Dunbar (New York: Dodd, Mead, 1896), ix.

2. Henry Louis Gates Jr., *The Signifying Monkey: A Theory of Afro-American Literary Criticism* (New York: Oxford University Press, 1988), 115.

3. Howells, introduction, ix, x.

4. Qtd. in Virginia Cunningham, *Paul Laurence Dunbar and His Song* (New York: Dodd, Mead, 1971), 74.

5. Jean Wagner, *Black Poets of the United States: From Dunbar to Langston Hughes,* trans. Kenneth Douglas (Urbana: University of Illinois Press, 1973), 76.

6. T. J. Jackson Lears, *No Place of Grace: Antimodernism and the Transformation of American Culture, 1880–1920* (Chicago: University of Chicago Press, 1981), 5.

7. James Whitcomb Riley, *Poems Here at Home* (New York: Century, 1893), 7, lines 1–2, 17–21, 25–26, 38–40.

8. Ibid., 640, lines 21–22.

9. Ibid., 798, lines 46–49.

10. Ibid., 175, lines 1–3.

11. Ibid., 450, lines 33–36.

12. Robert J. Scholnick, *Edmund Clarence Stedman* (Boston: Twayne, 1977), 50.

13. Ibid., 794, 796.

14. Ibid., 622, 616.

15. Ibid., 366.

16. Ibid., 366, 374.

17. *The Collected Poems of Paul Laurence Dunbar,* ed. Joanne M. Braxton (Charlottesville: University of Virginia Press, 1993), 287, lines 1–21.

18. It should be kept in mind that Dunbar, like all *Century* writers, was writing for a particular venue with a particular audience in mind, and thus his use of dialect makes sense for the time. Interestingly, one of his dialect poems appears next to "The Dialect Store" (April 1897), a metacritical essay satirizing the fact that in order to be published in the magazines, American writers were essentially required to add a "dose" of dialect to their work. In it, Charles Battell Loomis discusses an actual store where various dialects (from Swedish to Scotch to Yankee to German to French-Canadian) can be found. The largest department is the Negro department, a favorite of "Tawmas Nelson Page . . . de fustes' one ter see how much folks was dyin' ter git a leetle di'lect." Entirely sold out is the "Western dialect" department, for James Whitcomb Riley had "just engaged the whole output of the plant" (959).

19. *Collected Poems,* 132, lines 39–44.

20. Ibid., 145, line 6, 27–30.

21. Ibid., 155, lines 1–2.

22. Ibid., 139, lines 33–34.
23. Ibid., 191, lines 1–7.
24. Ibid., 191, lines 8–10.
25. Qtd. in Dickson D. Bruce Jr., *Black American Writing from the Nadir: The Evolution of a Literary Tradition, 1877–1915* (Baton Rouge: Louisiana State University Press, 1989), 60.
26. *The Select Poems of Dr. Thomas Dunn English,* ed. Alice English (Newark, N.J.: Published by Private Subscription, 1894), 418, lines 1–6.
27. Ibid., 421, line 93.
28. *Collected Poems,* 140, lines 36–45.
29. Ibid., 201, lines 1–10.
30. Ibid., 141–42, lines 28–32.
31. Ibid., 200, lines 10–12.
32. Ibid., 49, lines 25–28.
33. Ibid., 119, lines 3–4.
34. Ibid., 220, lines 52–55.
35. Gavin Jones, *Strange Talk: The Politics of Dialect Literature in Gilded Age America* (Berkeley, Calif.: University of California Press, 1999), 206.

8
The Glamour of Paul Laurence Dunbar
Racial Uplift, Masculinity, and Bohemia in the Nadir

MATT SANDLER

IN 1903, PAUL LAURENCE DUNBAR was asked to contribute an essay on "Representative American Negroes" to an anthology entitled *The Negro Problem*, which featured commentary from T. Thomas Fortune, Charles W. Chesnutt, Booker T. Washington, and W. E. B. Du Bois. He took the assignment seriously, researching and inquiring into the lives of the men whose lives he sketched. By way of introduction, Dunbar provides a laconic definition of his framing term: "Some men are born great, some achieve greatness, and others lived during the reconstruction period. To have achieved something for the betterment of his race rather than for the aggrandizement of himself seems to be a man's best title to be called representative."[1] The first sentence, a renovation of a line from Shakespeare's *Twelfth Night* (2.5), captures Dunbar's pessimism about success in the period called the "nadir" of African American history.[2] The third clause of the sentence is deadpan and ambiguous, suggesting that the standard circuitry among circumstance, greatness, and achievement cannot be assumed by those who "lived during the reconstruction period." Dunbar's allusion to the English author most often identified with Anglo-Saxon greatness is in the service of a stricture that African American achievement should also be identified only when it is a credit to the race. This ironic reconfiguring of cultural forms might have been called "symbolic action" by the great modern literary theorist Kenneth Burke, whose work is frequently cited by Albert Murray and Ralph Ellison for its usefulness for thinking about African American life. In his 1941 collection, *The Philosophy of Literary Form*, Burke writes about the way proverbs form a mutable social algebra that works as "equipment for living."[3] Dunbar's own work has occasioned urgent debate about the stylization of folk culture and whether his aesthetic forms an appropriate set of tools for negotiating modern life. In the face of nearly impossible contradiction, he brokers a compromise among the requirements of bohemianism, racial uplift, and the vernacular mode.

Dunbar was disappointed with his tremendous popularity. That his poetry in Standard English met with disinterest was a source of severe confusion, and he occasionally felt trapped by his audience's demand for dialect writing. This situation presents a jagged paradox: his own success as an African American poet is predicated on literary work that was taken to be an insult to his race. In his introduction to *Lyrics of Lowly Life,* William Dean Howells sets the terms of this entanglement: "He reveals in [the dialect poems] a finely ironical perception of the negro's limitations, with a tenderness for them which I think so very rare as to be almost quite new."[4] The progressive newness of Dunbar's vision is based on his penetration of the "negro's limitations." The latent contradiction would only be visible to later readers of Dunbar's work. Langston Hughes has Howells's support in mind when he writes in his seminal essay, "The Negro Artist and the Racial Mountain," that Dunbar was read with "the same kind of encouragement one would give a side-show freak."[5] Dunbar came to feel that by the end of the nineteenth century, the newly scientific ideology of race had become more pernicious.[6] This examination of Dunbar's ideas of uplift, bohemia, and folk culture will demonstrate that he was often much more interested in the potential than the limitations of black people. In his elegy to Frederick Douglass, Dunbar's antiquated usage neatly but suggestively characterizes the situation of African American achievement during the height of American racism: "We ride amidst a tempest of dispraise."[7]

Dunbar's critics associated his success with Booker T. Washington's agrarian-mechanical doctrine of racial uplift, and his dialect writing came to be seen as a capitulation to stereotype. His status as "the rejected symbol," in Darwin Turner's useful phrasing, is the result of his supposedly accomodationist cant.[8] Victor Lawson, author of the first book of literary criticism of Dunbar, writes, "The very popular jingles of courage and success, like the poems of race spokesmanship, emphasized an optimism based on a short-sighted part-vision of the needs, hopes, and aims of the Negro."[9] This diagnosis is based on some assumptions about literature and African American life in general, and Dunbar in particular, that need updating.

In the American literary tradition, it has been customary to see themes of uplift or improvement as the sign of bad writing. This view has its origins in Poe's concept of the "heresy of *The Didactic,"* and in the opposition of the American Renaissance writers to what they saw as the excessively prescriptive ethics of the "d——d mob of scribbling women."[10] By the 1940s, when Lawson wrote his book and the American Renaissance had formed the looming consensus vision of nineteenth-century poetry, this view had found a home in New Criticism, which restricted the work of reading to examination of the text itself, and which saw the search for morals as fallacious or, again, "heretical." The occlusion of improvement from the high brow was meant to bulwark a new religion of literature or simply art for art's sake.

August Meier's *Negro Thought in America, 1885–1915* describes a development that must be seen as adjacent for the purposes of understanding Dunbar's project.[11] In this period, during which intellectual history is traditionally divided between the academic social criticism of W. E. B. Du Bois and the more practical program of Booker T. Washington, African American leaders across the spectrum turned to the idea of economic as well as intellectual and moral self-help to supplement the loss of their political efficacy.[12] In an essay criticizing the black press, Dunbar's complaint is part of this tendency: "The space that might contain some story or poem that would inspire the young reader to do or be something is given over to twaddle about the merits of the candidate for sheriff. The column that might be filled with helpful household hints to the girls whose mothers have so lately returned from toiling in the cotton fields, is devoted to exploiting the merits of the man who wants to be county prosecutor."[13] It is fair to argue that this repels, inasmuch as Dunbar appears to value "helpful household hints" over the development of real African American political culture or civil society. However, the inexpediency of this sacrifice should not prevent us from trying to understand what Dunbar "would inspire the young reader to do." With southern states seeking to limit suffrage through property and literacy requirements, this tactic was urgently political even as it appeared to refuse politics.

Nevertheless, because of his involvement with this aspect of the difficult terrain of black public life at the turn of the century and his engagement with the problem of the didactic in poetry, Dunbar's work came to bear the stigma of self-help twice over. He has never been treated as a parvenu, *arrivant*, or pretender by the African American cultural establishment that uneasily bears his legacy, although he certainly was by the white hotel clerks whom he met on his reading tours. The way that his work is diminished by the prejudice against self-help is evident in Sterling Brown's searing critique of Benjamin Brawley's biography of Dunbar in "The Literary Scene" column of *Opportunity*. In noting that Brawley has failed to situate Dunbar frankly in relation to other black leaders or to the problem of labor, he writes with visible disappointment that "the biography before us is uncomfortably close to Horatio Alger."[14] In the 1930s, such an association, however conditional, would have been deadly among the left-wing literary circles that might have been sympathetic to a black poet.

Since the publication of Meier's work in 1970, however, a number of scholarly projects have begun to provide ways of evaluating the rich array of responses to the nadir.[15] Dunbar saw himself as responding to a deeply felt need in African American culture. In the short story "One Man's Fortunes," about a young black college graduate who tries and fails to become a lawyer in his hometown, he writes, "All the addresses and all the books written on how to get on, are written for white men. We blacks must solve the question for ourselves."[16] Perhaps the most common theme of contemporary black self-help writing is this frustration with the absence of more writing of its kind, especially in the face of the flood of publications by white authors.[17] To get a sense of what Dunbar thought his readers needed, I'll turn to the work of his friend and editor George Horace Lorimer, a white self-help philosopher with his own ideas about folk culture and bohemianism.

Lorimer was the dynamic editor of the *Saturday Evening Post* from 1899 to 1937. The *Post* had been in circulation for around seventy years when it was purchased in 1898 by Cyrus Curtis, the owner of the *Ladies' Home Journal*, one of the most successful monthly magazines in America. Lorimer was brought on to differentiate the magazine from its towering sister publication. His strategy was to align the *Post*, which falsely claimed to have been started by Benjamin Franklin, with the kind of exaggerated masculinity that was fashionable at the turn of the century, following the lead of Teddy Roosevelt, dime novels, Bill Riordan's *Plunkitt of Tammany Hall*, and the evangelist Billy Sunday. These works presented themselves in the rough veneer of common sense and common living but were unerring in their focus on progress. Lorimer writes, "To get any sense of a proverb, I usually find that I have to turn it wrong side out."[18] The nostalgic patriotism for which the magazine is known, most closely associated with the covers of Norman Rockwell, who started at the *Post* in 1916, was not precisely the tone of these earlier issues. Lorimer courted the imaginations of young men with dreams of success in business, but he did not shy away from its ugly side. Frank Norris's novels *The Pit* and *The Octopus* appeared in the *Post* under his stewardship. Somehow, Paul Laurence Dunbar fit into this strategy: he was published in the *Post* no fewer than seventeen times between 1900 and his death in 1906. The height of the poet's career coincided with the meteoric rise of the magazine's fortunes.

Dunbar dedicated his collection of short stories, *In Old Plantation Days* (1903), to Lorimer, thanking him for suggesting its subject matter. The relationship appears not to have just been one of simple professional courtesy. In a letter to his agent, Paul Reynolds, Dunbar explains why he continued to offer his work to Harrison S. Morris of *Lippincott's* and Lorimer once his popularity would have allowed him to find more lucrative venues: "Both are my personal friends and I should feel myself rather niggardly if I should withhold from them first sight of the things that are in their line merely because now that my things are selling better I could get better prices elsewhere. . . . I feel a sense of honor and obligation towards these men which is a little beyond price."[19] The word "niggardly" is not etymologically related to the ethnic slur that is its homonym—it has a Scandinavian and German origin meaning "narrow," unlike the Latin root *niger*, which gives us the ethnic slur. However, *The Oxford English Dictionary* does say that "coincidence in form and pronunciation in some regional varieties with 'nigger' have enlarged the definition of 'niggard' to include not only the sense of 'miserly' but also 'barbaric.'" The "sense of honor and obligation . . . is a little beyond price" but follows a mysterious aristocratic protocol. At once cautiously and flagrantly skirting internalized racism, Dunbar informs his editor that the character of his publishing practices reflects on his race. As in his poetry, plays, and fiction, he does so with a deft use of double language that belies settled prescriptions for the behavior of African Americans.

One place to look for a sense of the rules of conduct that Dunbar thought he might break by seeking better prices for his work is Lorimer's own series of advice columns in the *Post*, published contemporaneously with Dunbar's work. Lorimer took on the persona of a Chicago packing magnate writing letters to his effete son at Harvard University. Lorimer distills a vision of the modern captain of industry barreling into the machine age with native American brawn. But he also depicts a character who has learned to bring careful skepticism and humility to the rapidly differentiating and future-oriented business world. His willingness to adapt ostensibly folksy wisdom to the exigencies of a new situation is neatly exemplified in improvised proverbs that double as jokes: "Business is a good deal like nigger's wool—it doesn't look very deep, but there are a heap of kinks and curves in it."[20] So at the same time that Dunbar is taking less money for his work because he perceives that he has been initiated into a mutually beneficial order of businessmen, Lorimer uses antiquated caricatures of black bodies to fill out his image of the business world.

The column's epistolary form has a long and venerable tradition in conduct writing from at least the eighteenth century; both Benjamin Franklin's autobiography and the wildly popular work of Lord Chesterfield were published as letters to their sons. In the eighteenth century, these works provided the middle class with a window onto the inheritance of power—personal, social, political, and economic. Think of it in counterpoint with Dunbar's "Representative

American Negroes," which is a series of discrete biographical sketches quite unlike the intimate passing on of practical knowledge and useful structures of feeling that characterize the letters between father and son.

Lorimer's use of this form at the dawn of the twentieth century brings into question the insistent significance of genealogy, family, and race for a supposedly monadic modern individual trying to help himself. Pierrepont "Piggy" Graham comes in for all kinds of verbal abuse from his father, John "Old Gorgon" Graham. Old Gorgon begrudges the ease and privilege his son is afforded by his success. The prejudice against inherited wealth and the liberal arts education that often accompanied it was common among the newly moneyed robber barons. They didn't need new-fangled professional training or esoteric classical learning to get on in the world, just native grit. Of Pierrepont's desire to go on to graduate school, Old Gorgon says, "There's a chance for everything you have learned from Latin to poetry, in the packing business, though we don't use much poetry here except in our street-car ads., and about the only time our products are given Latin names is when the Board of Health condemns them. So I think you'll find it safe to go a little short on the frills of education; if you want them bad enough you'll find a way to pick them up later, after business hours."[21] After all, Richard Hofstader calls the *Post* an "unimpeachable source of anti-intellectualism" in his classic history.[22] But in bullying his son into the family business, Old Gorgon is compelled to indicate where his arcane skills might find be useful. To leave room for compromise, Graham imagines meatpacking as a potentially humanistic activity—"There's a chance for everything you have learned." It is an odd concession, given the character's comical blustering throughout. But it appears to be a necessary one, motivating Pierrepont to come back home to Chicago. In later columns, father and son are still communicating by mail because Old Gorgon, in physical need of some of the Old World culture he sought to limit to his son, is traveling to European spas to rest his overworked body. Despite the one-sidedness of the conversation—only Old Gorgon's letters are presented—there is real conflict to be reckoned with between education and industry, history and race, privilege and disadvantage, leisure and work.

Lorimer and his paragon both know, however, that the natural order of competition will remain preserved beneath the shifting terrain of culture. In the letters, courtesy is always a way of placating opponents, or seeming to be considering opposition:

> Tact is the knack of keeping quiet at the right time; of being so agreeable yourself that no one can be disagreeable to you; of making inferiority feel like quality. A tactful man can pull a stinger from a bee without getting stung.[23]

> Superiority makes every man feel its equal. It is courtesy without condescension; affability without familiarity; self-sufficiency without selfishness; simplicity without snide. It weighs sixteen ounces to the pound without the package, and it doesn't need a four-colored label to make it go.[24]

These insights are not unique to Lorimer; there are shades of Franklin here, and a whole history of self-help writing that preaches dissimulation as the way to win in a hierarchical society.[25] In this case, Pierrepont needs his father's help in coping with the resentment of his co-workers at the meatpacking plant, who have worked longer to get the job that he finds waiting for him after college. "Of course, everybody's going to say you're an accident. Prove it. Show that you're a regular head-on collision with anything that gets in your way. They're going to say you've got a pull. Prove it—by taking up all the slack they give you."[26] The manipulated language of these punned proverbs indicates the framing of force in the presentation of the self. Their individuality is in the way they sound both immanent, trans-historic vernacular honesty and interrupted, futuristic modernist irony.

The place that Dunbar's work might have in a world like this is difficult to imagine; unlike his contemporary Mark Twain, he never put his name to products and he was an unabashed classicist. In the 1910s and 1920s, Lorimer went on to become a rabid anti-immigrationist and turned the *Post* into an organ of aggressive racism and nativism. Responding to the regular appearance of the work of Octavus Roy Cohen, W. E. B. Du Bois wrote him a frustrated letter: "We are continually receiving by word of mouth and by letter, protests against the treatment of the colored people in the *Saturday Evening Post*." Lorimer responded, first defensive and then insulting: "There is not the slightest intention or wish on our part to be unfair in our treatment of the colored people. When Paul Lawrence Dunbar was alive he was a regular contributor to our columns and we would welcome to our pages another colored writer with his abilities."[27] In this private exchange between two very public men, Dunbar's misspelled name flashes up as an insult, his greatness again used to detract from that of "the colored people." His worries about seeming "niggardly" are finally allayed, but at the sacrifice that his talent is supposed to be unrecognizable among black poets of the 1920s.

Whatever betrayal may have been the conclusion of this story, it is important to note that Dunbar was able to find space in Lorimer's vision of the American literary imagination. While Lorimer was certainly looking for representations of African America that fit plantation nostalgia, he published "Negro Society in Washington," Dunbar's famous essay describing the lives of upper-class professional black families. His sense of the variety of American life, especially during Dunbar's career, cannot be underestimated as plainly xenophobic. At the very least, Dunbar and Lorimer share a recognition of the irony of self-help: to get ahead, you must have a vision of your origins that is as obscure and terrifying as it is lovely. For the poet, this meant rendering African American life in an extremely aesthetic lyric form.

Despite his frustrations with the appraisal, Dunbar was unwilling to let go of what Howells saw as his "distinctly modern consciousness."[28] In explaining his decision not to send a promised magazine to his future wife because of its erotic content, he writes declamatorily: "I am a Bohemian. . . . There is much purity of thought, motive and action in Bohemia as elsewhere—perhaps more. In this world it isn't so much among what people one lives or where one lives,—it is more *how* one lives."[29] In this self-description Dunbar allies himself with the still unformulated modernist emphasis on form and art as a way of life, in opposition to the romantic search for an expression of the spirit of a people or place. In a more speculative mood, he asks an interviewer: "Do you think it is possible now to invent a new form?"[30] Dunbar has a problematic and unconscious kinship with modern aestheticism—a decadent and blasé bohemianism.

As a poet working two decades before what David Levering Lewis has called "civil rights by copyright,"[31] Dunbar could not have been sanguine about the prospect that literature could resolve the tension between the realities of black life and the requirements of racial uplift. In a typical complaint about his audience's desire for dialect, he alludes to his ambition in conversation with the young James Weldon Johnson: "I have never gotten to do the things I really wanted to do."[32] He was often given to extremes of despair, which found their place within his poetry's wide range of sentiment, as in the short poem "Resignation":

> Long had I grieved at what I deemed abuse;
> But now I am as grain within the mill.
> If so be thou must crush me for thy use,
> Grind on, O potent God, and do thy will![33]

The contrast here with what Lawson views as optimism is almost too stark to mention. It is worth noting the rhetorical turn: Dunbar's speaker offers himself—"now I am as grain"—but then asks again for mercy—"If so be thou must crush me"—in consideration of his pitiful spectacle. Dickson D. Bruce Jr. writes definitively, "Here was the real paradox of Dunbar's writing. Known as the poet of joy and simplicity and as one of the first poets to make a conscious effort to explore the black folk heritage, he was also the first black writer to create a literature of pessimism and despair.... In this creation he made an important break with the middle-class black literary tradition that had preceded him."[34] This assessment is useful in that it casts Dunbar's work in terms of innovation. However, it is not the syncopation of "joy and simplicity" with "pessimism and despair" that makes Dunbar's dramatic rupture with "the middle-class black literary tradition."[35] Take, for example, "The Poet and His Song":

> Sometimes the sun, unkindly hot,
> My garden makes a desert spot;
> Sometimes a blight upon a tree
> Takes all my fruit away from me;
> And then with throes of bitter pain
>   Rebellious passions rise and swell;
> But—life is more than fruit or grain,
>   And so I sing, and all is well.[36]

Here it is not simply the existence of the "folk" scene of the garden or the "rebellious passions" that comprise the interest, but rather the intrusion of the song itself, the capitalizing of culture within the emotional arc. The innovation is in the use of literature as a palliative—rather than as a tool for social advancement—a turn whose politics are necessarily obscure even as they are desperately political.

Two characters from Dunbar's fiction sketch out his understanding of bohemianism usefully for our concerns about racial uplift and the vernacular. Sadness Williams of *The Sport of the Gods* and Taylor of *The Uncalled* each play the role of an immoral monitorial friend to the troubled young male protagonist. The setting of *The Uncalled* (1898)—Dexter, Ohio, a small but burgeoning town loosely based on Dunbar's hometown of Dayton—presages the work of Sinclair Lewis, Sherwood Anderson, and Willa Cather, who often include a yearning aesthetically minded youth in their diagnoses of the modernizing Midwest. Fred Brent is adopted by a staunchly Methodist woman, Miss Hester Prime, after the death of his alcoholic mother. An older woman set in her ways, Miss Prime is not prepared to be flexible with a young boy, scolding or whipping him for giggling in church, fighting, or playing baseball, and she eventually forces him into the seminary. In the course of his heated meditations on vocation, morality, and hypocrisy in small-town Ohio, Fred turns to Taylor for advice as he tries to decide whether he is satisfied by the liberating poverty his choice to become a poet provides. Acting as the exemplar of hopeless *poète maudit* commitment, Taylor responds with a cryptically naturalistic metaphor: "I chose the [calling] that gave me the most time to nurse the serpent that had stung me."[37] This occult foreboding fails to deter Fred, who is drawn to the lurid streets of Cincinnati in search of sin to test his own poisonous capacities. He eventually settles down to a more liberal Congregationalist home life and a clerkship at a meatpacking business, but Dunbar never subjects Taylor's influence to the moral judgment he reserves for the more conformist Midwesterners. His venom is categorizable as a kind of necessary antidote to the prohibitions of Fred's vaguely Calvinist upbringing.

A more fleshed-out but less directly artistic vision of the bohemian life is discernable in the character Sadness Williams of Dunbar's classic final novel *The Sport of the Gods* (1903). Sadness is a roustabout who hangs out at the Banner Club, "an institution for the lower education of negro youth" in the Tenderloin district of Manhattan, where the Hamilton family's final destruction takes place. He introduces himself with campy flamboyance: "Better known as Sadness.... A distant relative of mine once had a great grief. I have never recovered from it." The biological improbability of this idea of affect, detachment, and personality is his trademark and has echoes of Oscar Wilde and Mark Twain: "It's a pity you weren't born older. It's a pity that most men aren't. They wouldn't have to take so much time and lose so many good things learning."[38] Sadness's peculiar combination of flippancy and mournfulness becomes dangerous when he counsels Joe Hamilton in his artfully beggary lifestyle. For Joe, Sadness's style is profound. "The only effect that the talk of Sadness had upon him was to make him feel wonderfully 'in it.' It gave him a false bravery.... It was plain to him now that to want a good reputation was the sign of unpardonable immaturity, and that dishonor was the only real thing worthwhile."[39] His sophisticated enticement seals Joe's identification with a "great hulking, fashionably uniformed fraternity of indolence": "A peculiar class,—one that grows larger and larger each year in New York and has imitators in every large city in this country. It is a set that lives, like the leech, upon the blood of others,—that draws its life from the veins of foolish men and immoral women, that prides itself upon its well-dressed idleness and has no shame in its voluntary pauperism."[40] There is certainly no indication here of the sweet and light love of his verse, nor is there any hint of the fact that this "peculiar" vampiristic class has its origins in the sphere of art. In this bleak picture of the world, the artistic coteries of the Banner Club fail to produce any beauty besides the "coon shows" and the yellow journalism that gets the aged Berry Hamilton released from jail. Likewise, the moralizing in the novel about the theater and its influence does not square with Dunbar's own extensive and groundbreaking work with William Marion Cook and James Weldon Johnson in that genre.

Here in Sadness's lecture to Joe, just as in *The Uncalled*, the denizens of café society are characterized as diseased:

> It's dangerous when you're not used to it; but once you go through the parching process, you become inoculated against further contagion. Now, there's Barney over there, as decent a fellow as I know; but he has been indicted twice for pocket-picking. A half-dozen fellows whom you meet here every night have killed their man. Others have done worse things for which you respect them less. Poor Wallace, who is just coming in, and who looks like a jaunty ragpicker, came here about six months ago with about two thousand dollars, the proceeds from the sale of a house his father had left him. He'll sleep in one of the club chairs to-night, and not from choice. He spent his two thousand learning. But, after all, it was a good investment. It was like buying an annuity. He begins to know already how to live on others as they have lived on him. The plucked bird's beak is sharpened for other's feathers. From now on Wallace will live, eat, drink, and sleep at the expense of others, and will forget to mourn his lost money. He will go on this way until, broken and useless, the poor-house or the potter's field gets him. Oh, it's a fine, rich life, my lad. I know you'll like it. I said you would the first time I saw you. It has plenty of stir in it, and a man never gets lonesome. Only the rich are lonesome. It's only the independent who depend upon others.[41]

In this dynamic passage, the ironic way that Dunbar's bohemian characters describe themselves is given several figurative incarnations. Sadness draws a parallel between the Wild West of Twain and the dime novelists: "a half-dozen fellows whom you meet here every night have killed their man." The poverty of vagabondage is turned around as an "investment" in street knowledge—the Protestant work ethic of the starving artist. The prophetic is the rhetorical mode played out in a series of sharply dialectical epigrams, which have at once the ring of common sense and the scratching tone of an unforgiving modernism. It remains to be seen what experience gives these detached and exhilarating lines their bitter force.

Many of Dunbar's would-be bohemian characters—Sadness, Walter, and Taylor—are presented as detached from their homes and families. Sadness's father has been lynched, for instance, and so he has "aspired to the depths without ever being fully able to reach them."[42] Then the Hamilton family is evicted from their rooms because Minty Brown, a vengeful and gossipy young woman, brings the story of their shame to New York. His mother disowns Joe in disappointment and rage, sending him on the binge that culminates in his murder of Hattie Sterling, his dissolute actress-girlfriend. "It's been a long time sence you been my son."[43] Before concluding, I'll turn to a poem about black family life to tease out a conception of what is lost to the perverse characters to whom he gives such woeful life.

In "Little Brown Baby," from the collection *Poems of Cabin and Field* (1899), a man affectionately addresses his child, whose face and hands are covered with molasses. The poem was well liked enough to be made the title of one of Dunbar's unique art nouveau illuminated photo books. Joanne Braxton, in her introduction to the current scholarly edition of Dunbar's *Collected Poetry*, takes the poem as an example of his hidden cultural politics: "Dunbar refutes the popular myth that slave fathers did not love their children. . . . Here in his own subtle way, Dunbar argues that the black family did survive enslavement and that black fathers bonded with their children and attempted to shield them from painful encounters with racist oppression."[44] This reading misses some key accents in the poem that are integral to understanding Dunbar's sense of self-help within the context of an aesthetically rendered vernacular culture. If the poem is to be taken as an argument for the survival of the black family and as a record of that survival, then these themes should be understood in the terms that would have framed them at the time of the poem's composition. The survival of the black family and its protection from racist oppression would have been discussed in terms of racial uplift, a furiously contested set of ideas that are now politically unpalatable.

Racial uplift in "Little Brown Baby" is encoded in a tender scene unconsciously layered with social import. The father calls his wife to tidy the little boy while musing on his messiness. He arrives at a teasing conceit: that the boy will be eaten up by bees because he's covered in sweet molasses. Taking this further into playful teasing, he pretends not to recognize the baby:

My, you's a scamp!
Whah did dat dimple come f'om in yo' chin?
Pappy do' know you—I b'lieves you's a tramp;
Mammy, dis hyeah's some ol' straggler got in![45]

The father then goes on to summon the "buggah-man" to carry off the vagrant he has conjured into their midst. The appearance of the "buggah-man" in Dunbar's work is not unique to this poem; "The Buggah Man" and "At Candle-Lightin' Time" feature adult figures telling ghost stories to frighten their children. Even more horrifying, the speaker asks him to eat the baby:

Buggah-man, buggah-man, come in de do',
   Hyeah's a bad boy you kin have fu' to eat.
Mammy an' pappy do' want him no mo'.[46]

In these lines, which address neither the baby nor his mother, the indentation is subtly altered to indicate the change in voice for an imagined addressee. The boy is so bad that a ghostly and presumably grotesque sentry must be called to make him disappear. But once he has thoroughly terrified the object of his teasing, the man begins to assure the baby,

> Dah, now, I t'ought dat you'd hug me up close.
>   Go back, ol' buggah, you shan't have dis boy.
> He ain't no tramp, ner no straggler, of co'se;
>   He's pappy's pa'dner an' playmate an' joy.
> Come to you' pallet now—go to yo' res';
>   Wisht you could allus know ease an' cleah skies;
> Wisht you could stay jes' a chile on my breas'—
>   Little brown baby wif spa'klin eyes![47]

The boy is reinvited into the family. That the man "wisht" his boy could "allus know ease an' cleah skies" is paradoxical given that he has just staged this scary scene. Here a threat masquerades as play. Braxton assumes that the buggah man is an apparitional white man. If so, why would a protective father want to frighten his infant son with an amalgamated incantatory figure of the world system that makes their lives contingent, violent, and impoverished?

It is left to the reader to speculate on the significance of this intimate and overdetermined little scene. In a narrow sense, the racial content of the poem is difficult to ascertain: it is not clear whether the boy's brown color is due to the molasses or his race. To what end is the boy exposed to the distinction between paternity and paternalism? Does the poem preoccupy itself with cleanliness and therefore white respectability? These questions are answered finally only at the peril of grisly pragmatism.[48] That the poem may have been composed in response to the flirtations of Dunbar's then-fiancée, Alice Ruth Moore (later Alice Dunbar-Nelson), complicates things immensely: "Do you know that I have had occasion to laugh at myself a number of times since your letter came. I cannot help feeling I am again an uncle and in fancy I see myself trotting little Alice Ruth upon my knee and singing lullabies to her. The best and tenderest bit of verse that I have done since I came here is a little lullaby called 'Little Brown Baby with Sparkling Eyes.'"[49] Dunbar-Nelson's letter is unfortunately lost. This sketchy conversational exchange about the poem does hint that it refers to their own affections through several layers of masquerade and transposed relation—parent and child to lovers, father and son to man and woman.

To restore a sense of aestheticism to Dunbar's work requires that one address the ludic element of his work, however morbid it may sometimes seem. The problem here is that the idea of play in Dunbar cuts too closely to the image of happy slave. But this cannot disqualify the existence of play on the level of form. Dunbar's work, and his relevance to literary history is in his acute sense of the various possibilities available in the social exchange between black poet and reader. His agility with the permutations of the lyric scene is formidable.[50] The social critique and ethical rhetoric ("meter-making argument" in Emerson's phrase, racial uplift in the African American public sphere of Dunbar's moment) are disguised in half-tone ironies and dense nostalgic mist. In "Little Brown Baby," Dunbar superimposes a set of relations (artist-lovers, black and white society) onto a detached sequence of loving family life. Paul Valéry, in an essay on a well-known poem of his own, "Le Cimetière marin," offers a statement of his goals that may well have described Dunbar's as well: "In the lyric universe each moment must consummate an indefinable alliance between the perceptible and the significant.... There is not one time for the 'content' and another for the 'form'; and composition in this genre is not only opposed to disorder or disproportion but also to decomposition. If the meaning and the sound can easily be dissociated, the poem decomposes."[51] Valéry demands of himself a union of form and content so absolute that it takes into its sweep the parallel dichotomy of "the perceptible and the significant." The question of analysis—the parsing of technique and meaning—is to be left to some moment after the poem. Dunbar shares some of this commitment to the holism of poetic experience, to the breaking forth of the lyric. It is in this way that he is able to maintain the compromise between the very disparate concerns of his literary work—uplift, improvement, and self-help; the vernacular language and folk culture of African Americans; and finally the requirements of the cult of art, or bohemia, as he calls it.

The word "glamour" appears four times in *The Sport of the Gods* in reference to the sordid attractions of New York City life. There is a strange wrinkle in its etymology, which will provide a fitting conclusion to these remarks. The use of the word "glamour" to signify beauty and high living was an American development roughly contemporaneous with Dunbar's writing. The word is of Scottish origin, originally signifying magic, enchantment, or the occult. It is a derivative of the English word "grammar," meaning the system of linguistic inflection and syntax. This connection between grammar and witchcraft goes back to the Middle Ages, when "grammar" (*gramer* in Old English and *gramarye* in Old French, though both occur in English) signified both general knowledge—in a sense like philology—and specifically the knowledge of Latin in particular. Both Walter Scott and Robert Burns used the term "glamour" in this sense, carrying with it a longtime understanding of language as imported evil magic. The word "spelling" has a similar double meaning.

For Dunbar, poetry experiments in deep histories of language and cultural knowledge. In a letter to Helen Douglass about his elegy for her husband, Dunbar defends his writing: "As to your remarks about my dialect, I have nothing to say save that I am sorry to find among intelligent people those who are not able to differentiate dialect as a philological branch from the burlesque of negro minstrelsy."[52] He came to know that he could not protect his "philological" inquiry from the necromancy of racism and so became a dark artist himself. In "The Paradox," he is at his most vatic: "I am the mother of sorrows, / I am the ender of grief; / I am the bud and the blossom, / I am the late-falling leaf. / I am thy priest and thy poet, / I am thy serf and thy king."[53] These lines, confident and melancholic, declare an essence at once aligned with and overarching the categories of contemporary identity. The powers reserved therein by poetry were left outside the reach of the institutional languages of racial uplift and vernacular culture. Dunbar's sad grace left a choreography for American poetry that is not yet fully danced out.

Notes

Thanks to Courtney Boissonnault and Marcellus Blount, without whom this essay could not have been written.

1. Paul Laurence Dunbar, "Representative American Negroes," in *The Paul Laurence Dunbar Reader: A Selection of the Best of Paul Laurence Dunbar's Poetry and Prose, Including Writings Never Before Available in Book Form*, ed. Jay Martin and Gossie H. Hudson (New York: Dodd, Mead, 1975), 51.

2. Dunbar's periodization is perhaps different from our own; following contemporary convention, he assumes that Reconstruction is still going on at the turn of the century. For "the nadir," see Rayford Logan's *The Negro in American Life and Thought: The Nadir, 1877–1901* (New York: Dial Press, 1954).

3. Kenneth Burke, "The Philosophy of Literary Form" and "Literature as Equipment for Living," in *The Philosophy of Literary Form* (Berkeley: University of California Press, 1973). In associating Dunbar with American modernism, I have also taken cues from larger framings of the term "modernism" found in Matei Calinescu's *Five Faces of Modernity: Modernism, Avant-Garde, Decadence, Kitsch, Postmodernism* (Durham, N.C.: Duke University Press, 1987) and Marshall Berman's *All That Is Solid Melts into Air* (New York: Simon & Schuster, 1982). As well, I have also benefited from the perspective of Cary Nelson's *Repression and Recovery: Modern American Poetry and the Politics of Cultural Memory, 1910–1945* (Madison: University of Wisconsin Press, 1992).

4. William Dean Howells, introduction to *The Complete Poems of Paul Laurence Dunbar* (New York: Dodd, Mead, 1921), xvii–xviii.

5. Langston Hughes, "The Negro Artist and the Racial Mountain," *Nation*, June 23, 1926, 693. Having been christened "poet 'low-rate' of [the] Harlem," by the *Chicago Whip* (Feb. 26, 1927), a backhanded compliment to Dunbar and his immediate predecessor, Albery Allson Whitman, the "Poet Laureate of the Negro Race," Hughes was in a good position to comment on this situation. On Whitman, see Joan R. Sherman, ed., *African-American Poetry of the Nineteenth Century: An*

Anthology (Champaign: University of Illinois Press, 1992), 236; for Hughes, see Arnold Rampersad's "Langston Hughes's *Fine Clothes to the Jew*," *Callaloo* 26 (Winter 1986): 151.

6. See especially George Frederickson's *The Black Image in the White Mind: The Debate on Afro-American Character and Destiny, 1817–1914* (New York: Harper & Row) and C. Vann Woodward's *The Strange Career of Jim Crow* (New York: Oxford University Press, 1955).

7. *The Collected Poetry of Paul Laurence Dunbar*, ed. Joanne M. Braxton (Charlottesville: University of Virginia Press, 1993), 208.

8. Darwin T. Turner, "Paul Laurence Dunbar: The Rejected Symbol," in *The Journal of Negro History* 52, no. 1 (1967): 1–13; E. Franklin Frazier, in *Black Bourgeoisie: The Rise of a New Middle Class* (New York: Free Press, 1957), tells how "the small Negro elite, comprised mostly of mulattoes, had reacted ... against" Dunbar's dialect poetry (124). However, this passing comment contradicts the numerous contemporary accounts and the poet's own famous exposé in the *Saturday Evening Post*, "Negro Society in Washington." Also see Willard B. Gatewood's voluminous *Aristocrats of Color: The Black Elite, 1880–1920* (Fayetteville: University of Arkansas Press, 2000). My sense of the way that these scenes of reading inform one another successively and dialectically is based on the work of two critics: Jonathan Arac, especially his *Critical Genealogies: Historical Situations for Postmodern Literary Studies* (New York: Columbia University Press, 1989), and Jerome McGann, especially an essay on one of Dunbar's influences, "Keats and the Historical Method in Literary Criticism," *MLN* 94, no. 5 (1979): 988–1032.

9. Victor Lawson, *Dunbar Critically Examined* (Washington, D.C.: Associated Publishers, 1941), 48.

10. Edgar Allan Poe, "The Poetic Principle," in *Essays and Reviews* (New York: Library of America, 1984), 75; Nathaniel Hawthorne to William D. Ticknor, Jan. 19, 1855, in *The Centenary Edition of the Works of Nathaniel Hawthorne*, ed. William Charvat, Roy Harvey Pearce, and Claude M. Simpson (Columbus: Ohio State University Press, 1962), 17:304.

11. August Meier, *Negro Thought in America, 1880–1915: Racial Ideologies in the Age of Booker T. Washington* (Ann Arbor: University of Michigan Press, 1970).

12. There was some disagreement as to the place of the arts in this program. Alexander Crummell, for instance, in *Africa and America* (New York: Negro Universities, 1969), voiced his concern about what he saw as "an addiction to aesthetical culture as a special vocation of the race" (22), qtd. in Kevin Gaines's *Uplifting the Race: Black Leadership, Politics, and Culture in the Twentieth Century* (Chapel Hill: University of North Carolina Press, 1996). In *Negro Thought in America*, Meier notes that Dunbar's celebrity should be viewed alongside the contemporary institutionalization of African American culture through elite literary societies and magazines (266–69).

13. "Of Negro Journals," in *In His Own Voice: The Dramatic and Other Uncollected Works of Paul Laurence Dunbar*, ed. Herbert Woodward Martin and Ronald Primeau (Athens: Ohio University Press, 2002), 174–75.

14. Sterling Brown, "The Literary Scene," *Opportunity*, Sept. 1937, 216.

15. Kenneth Warren has reminded readers of Howells and James that the work of Anna Julia Cooper and Charles Chesnutt was integral to those writers' sense of American life in his *Black and White Strangers: Race and American Literary Realism* (Chicago: University of Chicago Press, 1993). The anthologies edited by Joan R. Sherman as well as her *Invisible Poets: Afro-Americans of the Nineteenth Century* (Urbana: University of Illinois Press, 1974); Dickson D. Bruce Jr.'s *Black American Writing from the Nadir: The Evolution of a Literary Tradition, 1877–1915* (Baton Rouge: Louisiana State University Press, 1989); Jean Wagner's *Black Poets of the United States: From Paul Laurence Dunbar to Langston Hughes*, trans. Kenneth Douglas (Urbana: University of Illinois Press, 1973); and Chidi Ikonné's *From DuBois to Van Vechten: The Early New Negro Literature, 1903–1926* (Westport, Conn.: Greenwood Press, 1981) are all useful for filling in the literary historical context for Dunbar's work.

16. *Dunbar Reader*, 140.

17. A great deal of the growing scholarly literature on black self-help and the doctrine of racial uplift takes literature as at least a partial focus. Gaines's *Uplifting the Race* is the only work to give substantial treatment to Dunbar, treating the way his views of urbanization both overlap with and diverge from uplift ideology. See also Meier, *Negro Thought*; Saidiya Hartman, "Fashioning Obligation," in *Scenes of Subjection: Terror, Slavery, and Self-Making in Nineteenth Century America* (New York: Oxford University Press, 1997); William L. Andrews, "The Representation of Slavery and the Rise of Afro-American Literary Realism," in *Slavery and the Literary Imagination*, ed. Deborah McDowell and Arnold Rampersad (Baltimore: Johns Hopkins University Press, 1989), 62–80; Ralph Luker, *The Social Gospel in Black and White: American Racial Reform 1885–1912* (Chapel Hill: University of North Carolina Press, 1991); Carla Peterson, *Doers of the Word: African-American Women Speakers and Writers in the North (1830–1880)* (New York: Oxford University Press, 1995); and Jacqueline Moore, *Booker T. Washington, W. E. B. Du Bois, and the Struggle for Racial Uplift* (Wilmington, Del.: SR Books, 2003).

18. George Lorimer, *Letters from a Self-Made Merchant to His Son* (Boston: Small, Maynard, 1902), 116.

19. Paul Laurence Dunbar to Paul Reynolds, Oct. 25, 1901, courtesy of the Schomburg Center for Research in Black Culture, New York Public Library. Most of what has survived of Dunbar's business correspondence languishes at the Ohio Historical Society in a difficult-to-translate species of shorthand that was indigenous to Ohio. Two more letters to Lorimer, as well as a number of others to public figures like W. E. B. Du Bois, are in that collection, but I've been unable as yet to decode them. The story of Dunbar's relationship to Lorimer is mentioned in passing by Peter Revell in what is perhaps the most comprehensive book-length study of Dunbar: *Paul Laurence Dunbar* (Boston: Twayne, 1979), 107–9.

20. Lorimer, *Letters*, 151.

21. Ibid., 29–30.

22. Richard Hofstadter, *Anti-intellectualism in American Life* (New York: Vintage, 1962), 218.

23. Lorimer, *Letters*, 163.

24. Ibid., 89–90.

25. See especially chapters 1 and 2 of Karen Halttunen's *Confidence Men and Painted Women: A Study of Middle-Class Culture in America, 1830–1870* (New Haven, Conn.: Yale University Press, 1982).

26. George Lorimer, *Old Gorgan Graham: More Letters from a Self-Made Merchant to His Son* (New York: J. H. Sears, 1927), 34.

27. George Lorimer to W. E. B. Du Bois, Dec. 22, 1922, *The Correspondence of W. E. B. Du Bois: Selections, 1877–1934* (Amherst: University of Massachusetts Press, 1997), 259.

28. Howells, introduction, xvi.

29. *Dunbar Reader*, 434.

30. *In His Own Voice*, 206.

31. David Levering Lewis, *When Harlem Was in Vogue* (New York: Penguin, 1997), xxviii.

32. Qtd. in James Weldon Johnson, *Along This Way: The Autobiography of James Weldon Johnson* (New York: Da Capo, 2000), 161.

33. *Collected Poetry*, 106, lines 1–4.

34. Bruce, *Black American Writing*, 98. This view of Dunbar is consonant with William L. Andrews's repeated insistence that Dunbar's work is much more cynical than both the hopeful self-help ideology of Frances E. W. Harper's *Iola Leroy* and the calls for progressive social reforms that conclude Charles W. Chesnutt's *The Marrow of Tradition*. See his introduction to Dunbar's *The Sport of the Gods* (New York: Signet Classic, 1999), xi, and *The Literary Career of Charles W. Chesnutt* (Baton Rouge: Louisiana State University Press, 1980), 87.

35. The black middle-class literary tradition is difficult to identify from the context here: are happy poems middle class? In a work with significantly different priorities from Bruce's, Wilson J. Moses refers to Dunbar's "Ode to Ethiopia" in his *The Golden Age of Black Nationalism, 1850–1925* (Hamden, Conn.: Archon Books, 1978), partly in support of his halting axiom: "Black nationalism is a genteel tradition in English letters."

36. *Collected Poetry,* 5, lines 25–32.

37. Dunbar, *The Uncalled* (New York: Dodd, Mead, 1898), 140.

38. Dunbar, *Sport,* 66, 64, 83.

39. Ibid., 85–86.

40. Ibid. The scholarly writing on black bohemia and its cognates before the New Negro movement is, happily, growing. William J. Maxwell's essay on Dunbar's bohemianism was not published in time for me to consult for this piece but is forthcoming in the *African American Review*. Monica Miller's project on the black dandy is also due out soon, but see her "W. E. B. Du Bois and the Dandy as Diasporic Race Man" in *Callaloo* 26, no. 3 (2003): 738–65. Also important is Houston Baker's reading of *The Sport of the Gods*, which does not take notice of Sadness Williams or his bohemianism but does emphasize the importance of form as it is figured in the novel. Baker's argument is that the theft blamed on Berry Hamilton by the artist Frank Oakley is replicated in the destruction of his family by the phantasmagoric life of the city epitomized in the coon shows' "sea of sense"—each an artistic corruption. For Baker, this unity opens up the possibility that Dunbar's indication of the vast will that controls the fate of his characters signals an awareness of authorial power as much as it does resignation before social circumstances. "The characters of Dunbar's work are, finally, victims of their own individual modes of processing reality. Their failings are paradoxical results of their peculiarly human ability (and inclination) to form theories of knowledge," which are corrected by the white "blues detective" and yellow journalist Skaggs. An emphasis on Sadness shifts the focus away from the progressive social reform at which his whistle-blowing presumably aims, toward a character who is a sort of counter-imaginary, or "buggah-man," of black self-help. See Baker, *Blues, Ideology, and Afro-American Literature: A Vernacular Theory* (Chicago: University of Chicago Press, 1987), 124–25.

41. Dunbar, *Sport,* 84–85.

42. Ibid., 84.

43. Ibid., 80.

44. *Collected Poetry,* xxvii.

45. Ibid., 134, lines 13–16.

46. Ibid., 134, lines 21–23.

47. Ibid., 134, lines 25–32.

48. Booker T. Washington's implausibly superficial "gospel of the tooth-brush" in *Up from Slavery* (New York: Norton, 1996) resonates with the father's joking disapproval of the child's over-indulgence (80).

49. *Dunbar Reader,* 442.

50. This has been most forcefully demonstrated by Marcellus Blount in his "The Preacherly Text: African American Poetry and Vernacular Performance," *PMLA* 107, no. 3 (1992): 582–93.

51. Paul Valéry, "Concerning 'Le Cimetière marin,'" in *The Art of Poetry* (Princeton, N.J.: Princeton University Press, 1958), 150.

52. "Paul Dunbar," in *Poetry Criticism: Excerpts from Criticism of the Works of the Most Significant and Widely Studied Poets of World Literature,* vol. 5 (Detroit: Gale Research, 1992), 143.

53. *Collected Poetry,* 89, lines 1–4, 6.

9
Kemble's Figures and Dunbar's Folks
Picturing the Work of Graphic Illustration in Dunbar's Short Fiction

ADAM SONSTEGARD

SUMMER 1896 MARKED A TURNING POINT in Paul Laurence Dunbar's career in two ways. In the June issue of *Harper's*, William Dean Howells brought national attention to Dunbar's verse, and in the July issue of the *Century*, Richard Watson Gilder printed a visual illustration to accompany Dunbar's poem "A Coquette Conquered" (figure 9.1).[1] Howells's career-making review had a greater impact than Peter Newell's cartoon, but both initiated the decade of Dunbar's greatest success in American letters: from that summer until his death in 1906, Dunbar's work would be frequently published, widely discussed, and graphically illustrated.

The poem, Dunbar's first work to appear with illustrations, is narrated by a flirtatious young woman and written in a heavily rendered dialect; the subject of the dramatic monologue is a familiar minstrel motif: an African American's insatiable appetite for a possum dinner. The poet who had written "We Wear the Mask" is managing multiple masks indeed. In the illustration, the only one to accompany a poem in this issue of *Century*, Newell depicts the possum in a gentleman's coat, creeping toward the man's provocatively opened legs. The coquette, who wears an attractive formal gown and is carefully and respectfully depicted by the artist, sits beside the man and reaches eagerly for the possum—or salaciously toward the man's lap. Emphasizing the characters' sexuality and imagining a setting for Dunbar's dramatic monologue, the illustrator clearly offers his own visual interpretation of the poet's work. The artist and editor exhibit more control than the poet over the work's appearance. Thus readers have not encountered Dunbar working in isolation to manipulate masks so much as received his work in a dialogue between publisher and poet, verbal work of art and graphic (mis)interpretation—all played out in an elaborate masquerade.

This chapter attempts to revisit part of Dunbar and his illustrators' masquerade. Recuperating a group of illustrations that accompanied the writer's work,

A Coquette Conquered.

Yes, my ha't 's ez ha'd ez stone—
Go 'way, Sam, an' lemme 'lone.
No; I ain't gwine change my min'—
Ain't gwine ma'y you—nuffin' de kin'.

Phiny loves you true an' deah?
Go ma'y Phiny; whut I keer?
Oh, you need n't mou'n an' cry—
I don't keer how soon you die.

Got a present! Whut you got?
Somef'n fu' de pan er pot!
Huh! yo' sass do sholy beat—
Think I don't git 'nough to eat?

Whut 's dat un'neaf yo' coat?
Looks des lak a little shoat.
'T ain't no possum! Bless de Lamb!
Yes, it is, you rascal, Sam!

Gin it to me; whut you say?
Ain't you sma't now! Oh, go 'way!
Possum do look mighty nice,
But you ax too big a price.

Tell me, is you talkin' true,
Dat 's de gal's whut ma'ies you?
Come back, Sam; now whah 's you gwine?
Co'se you knows dat possum 's mine!

Paul Laurence Dunbar.

DRAWN BY PETER NEWELL.

Figure 9.1: Dunbar's first illustrated work, "A Coquette Conquered," from the July 1896 issue of the *Century*.

it reads part of Dunbar's career as a series of negotiations founded on unequal power relations between an African American working in verbal art and Euro-American publishers dealing in visual art. Dodd, Mead and Company of New York published Dunbar's novels without illustrations, but the company issued his poetry books with photographs by the Hampton Institute Camera Club.[2] It published all four of Dunbar's short-fiction collections with illustrations by white artists. For three of these collections, it employed Edward Windsor Kemble, who had illustrated Mark Twain's *The Adventures of Huckleberry Finn* (1885) and regularly contributed caricatures to the *Century*.[3] Dunbar once indicated he approved of the *Century*'s comic treatment of African Americans, and he returned to Dodd, Mead for each of his subsequent short-fiction collections— and thereby returned to their choice of Kemble as illustrator of his work.[4]

Kemble's work has attracted the attention of Twain scholars, who have assessed his illustrations for *Huckleberry Finn*.[5] Writing most forcefully of these scholars, Earl F. Briden determines that "in retaining Kemble, Twain was in effect authorizing a pictorial narrative which runs counter to major implications of his verbal text. For Kemble's drawings rewrite the Huck-Jim relationship by reducing Jim, whom Huck gradually recognizes as an individualized human being, to a simple comic type, a stock figure in an emerging pictorial tradition."[6] Even within the inherent limitations of Kemble's visual medium, Kemble's work diminishes Twain's black protagonist and constitutes a "countertext," in Briden's words, to the prose novel's more progressive spirit. Briden concludes that "in approving Kemble's countertext for *Huckleberry Finn*," which Briden calls "a pictorial text that holds the black hero fast in the grip of comic typification," Twain "might be said to have sold Jim down the river himself."[7] But if so, why would Dodd, Mead choose to retain Kemble as Dunbar's illustrator more than a decade later, and why in turn would Dunbar choose Dodd, Mead for his three subsequent story collections, if this also meant including Kemble's countertexts?[8] If Twain's publishers "sold Jim down the river," what did Dodd, Mead do in using the same illustrator to sell the works of Dunbar?

Most readers have deferred such questions. Most publishers have taken steps to omit Kemble's imagery from Dunbar's reissued fictions, and most editors have given the same visual appearance to Dunbar's work that they give to the work of such strident black arts movement writers as Amiri Baraka and Audre Lorde.[9] But presenting Dunbar's work in this way discounts its original context, obscures the vexed visual politics of Dunbar's day, and leaves the impression that Dunbar independently incorporated white stereotypes into his work—when, in fact, Dodd, Mead superimposed them when it published Kemble's figures with Dunbar's fictions. A leading early Dunbar advocate once remarked that Dunbar "produced stereotypes—devoted slaves and comic darkies—that later generations could not distinguish from the disparaging stereotypes created by Joel Chandler Harris, Thomas Nelson Page, Thomas Dixon, and other romancers of the plantation myth."[10] Indeed, Dunbar's "stereotypes" were so indistinguishable from the work of these white writers that these works all featured the same artist: Kemble illustrated Harris, Page, and Dunbar alike. But for his part, Dunbar did not produce these stereotypes so much as work from the assumption that they already existed, within plantation fiction's conventions, and within Kemble's "comic" representations. Editing Kemble out of Dunbar's critical histories means deleting a crucial visual dimension of his work. It risks misleadingly attributing Anglo-Americans' racial stereotypes to an African American writer who in fact knew his fictional folks would appear in print with Kemble's figures and thereby wrote his later stories bearing Dodd, Mead's marketing and Kemble's art in mind.

Reviewing Dunbar's publishing career means recuperating images that originally appeared within readers' visual fields as they read Dunbar's work. These images comprised a set of theatrical backdrops against which Dunbar learned to stage his fictional racial masquerade. Dunbar devised his southern folks to perform crucial cultural work in opposition to Kemble's "work" of art. The writer initially penned stories he knew would invite the artist's kind of caricatures; he went on to balance tales that seemed ripe for Kemble's art with more militant stories that evaded Kemble's typical subject matter. Finally, with his nimble verbal artistry, Dunbar showed he could handle the minstrel mask more dexterously than Kemble, with his comparatively crude visual artistry, could. Re-creating these original verbal and visual dimensions of Dunbar's published performances shows that he not only donned masks in his fiction but sought to manipulate the additional masks that Dodd, Mead and Kemble imposed.

"Kemble is ready to illustrate my book," Dunbar wrote to Alice Ruth Moore, soon to be his wife, the day after Valentine's Day 1898. "I enclose the names of the stories and want you to try and choose a name for the book—see Mr. Dodd's letter. Let me hear from you at once. Don't forget about the journal story."[11] Dunbar's urging sounds impatient, as Kemble's readiness interrupted the young couple's complicated courtship.[12] Moore was not to keep Kemble waiting but assemble Dunbar's newspaper clippings, remember to send a story that had appeared in the *Sunday Journal,* and choose a name for the collection. Two of Dunbar's previous letters to Moore, which say that two other artists were willing to illustrate his work for newspapers, suggest that illustrations were not incidental but instrumental in providing Dunbar and Moore with occasions and financial incentives for publication.[13] Kemble's availability precipitates the collection of Dunbar's stories from scattered periodicals and prompts Moore to gather her fiancé's fiction.

Though Moore chose "'The Ordeal at Mt. Hope' and Other Stories" for a title, Dodd, Mead published the collection as *Folks from Dixie* and included eight illustrations from Kemble. The peripheral characters and marginal subjects that appear in these illustrations suggest that Kemble chose his own subjects to illustrate. He seems to have approached the writer's work by singling out the moments in Dunbar's fictions that most emphatically reinforce white stereotypes of black behavior and, conversely, by ignoring the moments in Dunbar's fictions that most directly reflect the characters' efforts to chart their courses through dizzying social change. Kemble renders a mammy smoking a pipe in a scene reminiscent of *Uncle Tom's Cabin,* but a missionary from the same story, who rescues this woman's son from gambling and drinking, is not depicted by Kemble. Kemble draws a man who has devoured most of the possums a church congregation had wanted to save for Christmas dinner (incriminating possum grease still smudges the man's mouth); this is all Kemble pictures from the entire congregation's Christmas season (figure 9.2). He shows a rustic angler grinning at his bait and hook (figure 9.3) but never depicts the more magnanimous title character of the story "Nelse Hatton's Vengeance." Nelse achieves financial independence after emancipation, gives shelter to a wandering white hobo, and soon discovers the hobo is in fact his impoverished former master. Both men have experienced extremes of economic fortune; both defy stereotypes of rich masters and dirt-poor former slaves. But Kemble draws a fisherman who still looks at home on the Old Suwannee in antebellum days. In short, his drawings give no hint of the social change these stories depict.

Dunbar draws his fictional characters from widely dispersed demographic groups, but Kemble exclusively visualizes impoverished rural blacks. In "A Family Feud," Aunt Doshy, speaking in heavy dialect, recounts her white family's ongoing squabbles. In "The Intervention of Peter," the narrator describes a slave who comically forestalls a duel between feuding masters. Such tales highlight slaves who dare to influence, interfere in, and then independently chronicle a white family's affairs. In "The Ordeal at Mount Hope," the Reverend Howard Dokesbury heads south across the Mason-Dixon Line and finds southern blacks so culturally different that he wonders if he can call them his own people. "At Shaft 11" treats striking white miners, as well as their black replacement laborers; it concludes with a white foreman, Jason Andrews, and his black assistant, Big Sam, leading a racially integrated mining team. The Mason-Dixon Line, stratifications of social class, and common vocational bonds complicate these stories' familiar racial divides. Unlike the "folks" in W. E. B. Du Bois's *The Souls of Black Folk* (1903), Dunbar's "folks from Dixie" are both black and white.

All of Kemble's illustrations for the story collection depict blacks; none depict whites. They give evidence of neither racial interaction nor socioeconomic mobility but reflect the march of social progress in these stories as a series of discrete snapshots showing Kemble's reactionary politics instead. Critiquing the politics of this era's periodical illustrations, Henry B. Wonham has determined that "as a technique of realist literary performance, both within and in relation to the literary text, caricature served to insulate readers from the politically unnerving social 'reality' that the magazine made a point of opening to view."[14] Prose realism exposed social realities, visual caricature functioned to distract white readers, and both tendencies extend from the margins of periodicals to Dunbar's collections of short fiction. Dunbar's characters live through epochal social change, fumbling with its personal implications, but

"I SEE POSSUM GREASE ON YOU' MOUF."

Figure 9.2: One of the images Kemble drew for Dunbar's first volume, *Folks from Dixie*.

"WHA'D YOU CATCH?"

Figure 9.3: One of the images Kemble drew for Dunbar's first volume, *Folks from Dixie*.

Kemble transports them to nostalgic settings that erase social advances. He instead reassures Euro-American readers that pastoral plantations endure into 1898's more turbulent political climate.

Dunbar even anticipates exaggerated and sensationalist caricatured reactions in his tales. When the Reverend Dokesbury glimpses "a group of idle Negroes exchanging rude badinage with their white counterparts across the street," Dunbar's narrator steps in to clarify: "After a while this bantering interchange would grow more keen and personal, a free-for-all friendly fight would follow, and the newspaper correspondent in that section would write it up as a 'race war.'"[15] This particular tale departs from white readers' sensational expectations. In "Nelse Hatton's Vengeance," Dunbar carefully differentiates between these readers' assumptions and the less fanciful interior setting he wishes to describe. "If this were a story chronicling the doings of some fanciful Negro, or some really rude plantation hand," Dunbar writes hypothetically, "it might be said that the 'front room was filled with a conglomeration of cheap but pretentious furniture, and the walls covered with gaudy prints'—this seems to be the usual phrase. But in it the chronicler too often forgets how many Negroes were house servants, and from close contact with their master's families imbibed aristocratic notions and quiet but elegant tastes."[16] Dunbar mobilizes an interracial understanding of socioeconomic affiliation in order to disrupt a common misinterpretation of racial identity. He differentiates the comments of a misguided "chronicler" from the more informed observations of narrator "who knows better than to make such overgeneralizations"; he also "documents the actual differences from stereotypical norms that Nelse represents."[17] Dunbar, who submitted his work to the richly illustrated *Saturday Evening Post,* and who knew that artists like Kemble influenced the appearance of his work, writes such passages to wrest control of the appearance of his own published prose. If the artist assigned by the publisher to interpret these tales could select imagery that ran counter to the author's politics, the author could brace himself and his readers against racist distortions.

The second volume to combine Dunbar's stories and Kemble's images, *The Strength of Gideon and Other Stories* (1900), reflects this strained relationship between visual and written media. Kemble renders another mammy figure "marching in like a grenadier" (figure 9.4); a preacher pausing amid brimstone exhortations; and a cute quartet of children peeking warily at readers. But readers of this volume go for hundreds of pages without seeing an illustration from Kemble, and reading these intervening pages means apprehending a reason for Kemble's omissions. If the artist looked for comforting motifs and familiar plantation imagery, seeking assurances of an enduring antebellum social order, he instead found stories told in an increasingly strident tone, evading Kemble's trademark subject matter. Dunbar balances tales that would occupy Kemble with stories that offered little conventional subject matter he could depict.

The opening illustration imbricates Gideon, hero of the title story, in an American flag; the brim of his hat roughly parallels the Union army's stripes (figure 9.5). Viewers who perceive the illustration to be patriotic receive a different impression than the story's readers: Gideon remains loyal to his Confederate master in the tale but is combined with the Union flag in the picture. Gideon suffers from a surfeit of loyalty to his master and remains on the plantation when all the other slaves, including his wife, escape at emancipation. Gideon witnesses the departure of the army wearing blue, tearfully obeys his plantation mistress's call, and experiences a pyrrhic victory in the concluding line, "Gideon had triumphed mightily."[18] Sounding such hollow tones of supposed triumph, the tale can only offer cold comfort for his consistency. Kemble refuses to leave him alone in his excessive fidelity but combines him with nationalist iconography. In Dunbar's tale, Gideon seems a lonely figure meant to be a warning to others; in Kemble's image, he seems strangely transformed into a cause for national celebration.

"MAMMY PEGGY CAME MARCHING IN LIKE A GRENADIER."

Figure 9.4: Kemble's image of a mammy character from *The Strength of Gideon and Other Stories*.

Kemble reinterprets Gideon's history but passes over tales that register social protest. If Kemble sought familiar plantation motifs, he found several tales in this collection that departed from conciliatory themes and offered little to inspire his signature caricatures. In "One Man's Fortunes," Bertram Halliday, an educated black man, cannot secure the jobs for which his white peers are easily hired. Eventually he is employed by a white jurist as the jurist campaigns for a place on the bench, but Bertram is dismissed (and replaced by a white worker) as soon as the judge persuades enough of the black voting block to elect him. In "Cornelius Johnson, Office Seeker," a would-be political operative visits his congressman, hoping for an appointment to a government bureau. Eventually he discovers the politician has lied to him and has allowed the term to pass without arranging Cornelius's appointment. In "The Tragedy at Three-Forks," Jane Hunster, an impoverished white woman, sets fire to her rival's house but then feels pity for the two blacks whom the town blames for Jane's crime. When the townspeople lynch the accused arsonists, two of Jane's white suitors grotesquely fight one another for pieces of the gallows rope. One suitor murders the other, the townspeople call for the murderer to be lynched,

"'IT'S FREEDOM, GIDEON.'"

Figure 9.5: Kemble's image of Gideon, one of the protagonists of *The Strength of Gideon*.

and an "imperious voice" from the mob calls out, "Who knows what may have put him up to it? Give a white man a chance for his life."[19] Careful readers note that no one granted such a chance to the falsely accused blacks. Dunbar does not paper over discrimination or excuse racism but leaves characters shouting (as in the final line of "Cornelius Johnson, Office-Seeker"), "Damn your deceit, your fair cruelties; damn you, you hard, white liar."[20] The visual artist would have expected droll minstrel "darkies" well suited to belittling graphic representation, but instead Dunbar supplies strident African American militants who demand political representation. Kemble does render a sketchy image for "Jim's Probation," in which the face hovers vaguely above a blank background, the man's outline fails to extend to the edge of the image, and a rifle emerges from the surrounding fog to lead the viewer's gaze diagonally across Jim's face (figure 9.6). The hero depicted in this image renounces his sinful ways for the

JIM.

Figure 9.6: Kemble's image of Jim, one of the protagonists of *The Strength of Gideon*.

sanctity of the church (and for relief from arthritis, which his pastor claims is a manifestation of God's displeasure). When an insatiable hunger for possum leads him to quit his church probation, the story prompts readers to laugh off, not lament, his relapse. One hundred pages separate this image of Jim from the previous drawing in the collection; another hundred pages pass before the appearance of the following one. Kemble passes up the opportunity to depict several black heroes in the intervening pages but sketches Jim faintly, making his slight sneer the only visual correlative to Bertram Halliday's agony, Cornelius Johnson's defeat, and two falsely accused blacks' execution.

Such loud silences from Kemble—pages he leaves blank, stories he does not illustrate—show the publishing industry colluding with the businesses and bureaus these stories depict. "Even at the height of his literary career," according to Dunbar and Moore's biographer, Eleanor Alexander, Dunbar "would face a form of job discrimination. Critics would love his dialect work and happy tales of life on the old plantation, but novels deviating from the formula would be denigrated."[21] Stories "deviating from the formula," even those appearing in the collections with stories that fit the pattern, would also be dismissed. White political bosses and business leaders in Dunbar's stories do not notice or appreciate behaviors from blacks that defy expectations. Nor do the illustrators of Dunbar's tales graphically depict stories that run counter to those expectations. Kemble's inattention begins to register ironically: Dunbar's efforts on behalf of fictional black heroes, who are ignored, get ignored in turn.

The crafty, subtle "Council of State" deserves not to be ignored for these very reasons. It merits attention for the unusual character Kemble chooses not to illustrate, for the conventional illustration he supplies instead—and for the story's function as a meta-text for the uneasy combination of Dunbar's and Kemble's art. Political operative Miss Kirkman conspires with white politicians, impugning her identity both racially and politically. "One might have looked at her for a long time and never suspected the truth, that she was allied to the colored race," says the story's narrator, who then explores her allegiance and appearance:

> Neither features, hair, nor complexion showed it, but then "colored" is such an elastic word, and Miss Kirkman in reality was colored "for revenue only." She found it more profitable to ally herself to the less important race because she could assume a position among them as a representative woman, which she could never have hoped to gain among the whites. So she was colored, and, without having any sympathy with the people whom she represented, spoke for them and uttered what was supposed by the powers that be to be thoughts that were in their breasts.[22]

Her ambiguous physiognomy and subtle duplicity might have inspired a fascinating illustration, but Kemble passes up the opportunity.[23] He renders instead a bishop who speaks benignly but articulately as he offers bland platitudes that neither alienate nor fully satisfy anyone. Kemble's unimaginative image aptly matches the character's dull, derivative address (figure 9.7). He chooses the less threatening, unambiguous figure over what could have been an innovation.

The story also distinguishes between a "majority opinion," a benign and conciliatory consensus that does not disturb powerful white leaders, and a "minority report," a truer record of a party's anger, which is phrased so defiantly that it risks alienating white politicians. A black leaders' assembly passes its official majority report, in which it flatters the white leadership and represents blacks as unified in their good-natured passivity. As several characters voice

THE BISHOP'S ADDRESS.

Figure 9.7: Kemble's rendering of a bishop engaged in public speaking, from "Council of State"

thunderous exceptions to the bland majority report, Miss Kirkman takes down their names, has them blacklisted, and sees that they are dismissed from their jobs. These speeches culminate in a tirade from Jim Courtney, who writes for a newspaper but vows he will use powers other than that of words: "I will meet them with the pen. I will meet them with the pistol. . . . Yes, even though there is but one hundred and thirty-five pounds of me, I will meet them with my fists!"[24] Gentler voices prevail over Courtney. Their tepid manifesto approves white legislation, but another dissenter says of the manifesto, "There are some of us who do not believe that this expresses the feelings of our race, and to us who believe this, Mr. Courtney has given the use of his press in New York, and we shall print our resolution and scatter it broadcast as the minority report of this convention, but the majority report of the race."[25]

These majority reports and minority reports readily show parallels with Dunbar's own situation. A majority report flattering whites at the heads of publishing establishments represents blacks as laughing minstrels and attracts the caricatures of artists like Kemble. A minority report reaches a narrower audience, results in the author being blacklisted, and shows contempt for the graphic artist. Kemble's picture of the bishop, who blandly figures in a majority report, and Kemble's omission of Kirkman and Courtney, who show the more politicized nature of a minority report, are cases in point. Even the reviews of *The Strength of Gideon* noticed and praised its "realistic" African American images, from the lassitude of plantation "darkies" to the unceasing loyalty of good-natured minstrels. Accounting for these reviews, Gene Jarrett and Thomas Morgan note that "the interspersion throughout the book of E. W. Kemble's caricatures of African Americans featured in the stories certainly contributed to such impressions" of supposed realism: "Most of these reviews miss crucial indications of Dunbar's resistance to pastoral and minstrel imagery."[26] Indeed, at least six reviews make positive references to Kemble's "original," "apt and amusing," "capital illustrations"; none of these reviews observes that Kemble slighted Dunbar's more strident tales.[27] Fictions that whites approved of (conciliatory majority reports) would have received Dodd, Mead's imprimatur and Kemble's embellishments. Fictions that voiced dissent (truer minority reports) would have gone unillustrated, if indeed a publisher like Dodd, Mead had published them at all.

Notice finally, however, that Dunbar has Courtney, the most vocal dissenter in "Council of State," declare in defiance of white politicians that all "one hundred and thirty-five pounds of me ... will meet them with my fists."[28] Since the writer could have assigned his character any words or any bulk he wished, it cannot be accidental that Dunbar and Courtney share the same body weight.[29] Dunbar supplies benign material for majority reports, seems complicit in the racist status quo, and invites belittling caricatures from Kemble. But deep in this very involved short fiction, worded too subtly for Kemble to notice, is an indication Dunbar would throw the full weight of his own being—all 135 pounds of it—into a stinging minority report if he could.

Appearing at first to be a gentler majority report, 1904's *The Heart of Happy Hollow* combines Dunbar's and Kemble's art for what would be Dunbar's last short-fiction collection. Dodd, Mead intersperse Kemble's imagery at regular intervals, thereby eliminating the hundred-page gaps between illustrations that occurred in *The Strength of Gideon*. But, in effect, this also meant placing the images dozens of pages away from the sentences they attempted to illustrate. Since readers were unlikely to hunt for the sentence corresponding to each of Kemble's images, this arrangement discourages those readers from integrating Kemble's visual art with Dunbar's written tales. The images, for their part, highlight sentimental plantation tableaux, while failing to depict any of the stories' signs of racial injustice. A former slave who serves as a witness in a trial finds herself answering questions from a lawyer she knew on the plantation; she cannot accept that "Miss Lou's little Bobby" is now an attorney and cannot defer to his authority in court.[30] A father offers a folk rendition of a biblical proverb wherein he likens his son, who has sold the Democratic Party his vote, to figures who "sol' dere birthrights fu' a pot o' cabbage."[31]

If authority, community, and literacy have changed radically for these characters in the years since slavery, Kemble's illustrations do not reflect the changes. "One Christmas at Shiloh," for instance, revolves around Martha Maria Mixon, for whom "the lessons of slavery had not been idle ones" but taught her to be "industrious, careful, and hardworking."[32] Her husband, Madison, surprises her by abandoning his shiftless youth and becoming a lively, enthusiastic preacher. Instead of depicting this, Kemble chooses to illustrate a scene involving two minor characters, in which Sister Dicey says to Brother Williams, "I don' see yo' back bowed so much by de yoke."[33] Brother Williams, as Kemble depicts him, has an exaggerated waistline, which belies the story's theme of scrupulous industry. Kemble makes Williams a bloated, slack-jawed figure and shows inattention to the tale, which never refers directly to Williams's weight and certainly never assigns him this considerable girth (figure 9.8). Dunbar writes a seemingly less strident collection, and Kemble supplies conventional imagery: he predictably caricatures blacks' bodies and personalities without highlighting their halting but evident social advances.

Two stories indicate that Dunbar altered his approach to rendering fictional folks, even if Kemble never altered his visual treatment of those folks. In "Schwalliger's Philanthropy," the main character is a race-horse tout who is "so short in stature he got the name 'tadpole.'" He has a lisp so prominent that he is left saying "No, thuh, you can't keep a good man down. 'Tain't no use a-talkin', you jeth can't."[34] He seems designed to invite cruel caricatures from Kemble, but the minstrel lisp actually helps hide Schwalliger's shrewd, subtle personality. He listens to a naive black woman fresh from a plantation tell him about two men who tricked her out of her money. He affects a disguise as a country bumpkin, pretends to fall for the same swindlers' schemes, and regains some of the woman's funds. Once Schwalliger assumed the disguise, Dunbar writes, he wore "a very inane smile. He looked the very image of simplicity and ignorance, like a man who is anxious and ready to be duped."[35] Schwalliger acts as a minstrel, and the swindler takes the bait.

In writing the story, Dunbar has him act as a minstrel, and Kemble does *not* take the bait. The artist does not follow suit and does not exaggerate Schwalliger's appearance in the pose of a gullible bumpkin. Instead he shows the tout knowingly eyeing someone outside the picture frame, with his cigar poised in a conspiratorial gesture (figure 9.9). Perhaps Kemble does not sense Schwalliger's comic possibilities. Or perhaps he wishes to be the artist who imposes and manipulates the minstrel mask, not the one who follows another artist's

"'I don' see yo' back bowed so much by de yoke.'"

Figure 9.8: Image from "One Christmas at Shiloh."

lead in fictionally rendering a minstrel show. Dunbar's character knowingly dons the mask, consciously enacts a minstrel routine, and takes advantage of whites in the exchange. Dunbar alters his approach to minstrelsy in his short fiction, and Kemble, if he gets the joke, does not play along.

"The Lynching of Jube Benson" employs the minstrel mask in more tragic circumstances. The story's white narrator, Dr. Melville, describes a lynching he once participated in, but he seems unaware that one of his two white listeners is recording his story for a tabloid newspaper. Melville's tale introduces a gentle slave named Jube who once served Melville and his daughter Alice with a selflessness that recalls Gideon's level of loyalty. But when Alice, mysteriously beaten and bruised, is asked on her deathbed who attacked her, all she has to do is whisper: "That black—" for everyone in the town to accuse Jube of her murder.[36] The formerly rational Melville joins a lynch mob, which Dunbar twice likens to a gathering of beasts. When the men in the mob find Jube, Melville believes the worst about him and prepares to take part when the mob lynches him. "Why did I do it?" Melville rhetorically asks his listeners. "I don't know. A false education, I reckon, one false from the beginning," which leads him to say of Jube, "I saw his black face glooming there in the half light,

Figure 9.9: Image from "Schwalliger's Philanthropy."

and I could only think of him as a monster."[37] Melville offers a psychological understanding of black faces as embodying dangerous, beastly evils, as white observers project their anxieties onto blacks' physiognomies.

This motif continues when the mob of citizens, their faces fully exposed, go to hang Jube. "No one was masked," Melville explains. "We knew each other. Not even the culprit's face was covered, and the last I remember of him as he went into the air was a look of sad reproach that will remain with me until I meet him face to face again."[38] As that haunting look lingers, Jube's brother appears. He arrives too late to save Jube but sheds light on the true identity of the murderer: "We saw in the full light the scratched face of Tom Skinner," whom Melville calls "the worst white ruffian in town—but the face that we saw was not as we were accustomed to see it, merely smeared with dirt. It was blackened to imitate a Negro's."[39] A tale that considers the interpretation of faces concludes with a white murderer's face painted black. Melville finds traces of a white man's skin underneath the murder victim's broken fingernails; he deduces that Tom Skinner, not Jube Benson, committed the crime; and he swears he will never take part in a lynching again. In one story, then, Dunbar dons Dr. Melville's "whiteface" mask, has white listeners face the blanching Dr. Melville as he tells his tale, and places a white murderer in blackface at the center of the tale's melodrama. Having worked with and against minstrel traditions for much of his career, Dunbar now depicts a blackface character who does not laugh in droll comedy or exhibit vaudeville buffoonery but carries out a murder calculated to play upon a white mob's most irrational fears, and to displace guilt upon black men. Importantly, Dunbar offers as evidence of the murderer's guilt traces of white skin beneath the victim's fingernails; guilt is not written on faces—which, as the tale demonstrates, are open to others' psychological projections, and concealed behind masks others can manipulate.[40]

Dunbar symbolically seizes control of the story's many means of racial representation. He has not been sold out or sold his literary interests "down the river," as it were, but has invited clichéd caricatures from Kemble, produced minority reports that elude the cartoonist's pen, and finally manipulated the minstrel mask in words more adeptly than the crude caricaturist could handle that mask in images. Speaking of the poem "We Wear the Mask," Houston A. Baker Jr. has written, "It is as though Dunbar's speaker plays the masking game without an awareness of its status as a game. It seems that he does not adopt masking as self-conscious gamesmanship in opposition to the game white America has run on him."[41] This may be true of Dunbar's persona in this poem, but the short-fiction personae of Schwalliger and Dr. Melville suggest that he eventually "plays the masking game" more slyly and subtly, with fuller awareness and opposition, than his leading readers give him credit for. Dunbar struggles against the theatrical backdrops that Kemble's art imposes until sly minority reports and reinterpreted minstrel masks upstage Kemble's white stereotypes. What appears to be stereotyped minstrel imagery in Dunbar's folks testifies to his efforts to counter Kemble's figures and steal the show.

In *The Voice of the Negro* in 1906, a writer defined a cartoon as "a system of pictorial falsehood long used as an artifice in the presentation and promulgation of principles."[42] The writer, John Henry Adams, regularly contributed columns to the *Voice* entitled "Rough Sketches," in which he described prominent figures and then rendered their likenesses graphically. With some personal authority and vested interest, then, he could continue:

> No people have felt the sting of the cartoon more than we. Almost in any direction can be seen great wide mouths, thick lips, flat noses, glaring white eyes, and to wind up the thing, there close beside the caricatured is the familiar chicken-

I know the pangs which thou did'st feel,
When slavery crushed thee with its heel.
—*Dunbar*

Figure 9.10: John Henry Adams's rendering of a matronly figure to adorn Dunbar's verse.

coop and out beyond that is the rind of the "dervastat'd watah million." These cartoons have done no little toward increasing our persecutions and enemies. The time has come when we must have real live cartoonist amongsts [sic] us to make sentiment. We have the material for the making of any kind of man but after the fellow is made where is he to find encouragement and how is he to live[?][43]

"The time has come," Adams writes in the fall of 1906—less than six months after Dunbar's death—for an African American cartoonist to reverse hateful traditions of exaggeration and stereotypes in pictorial representations. If so, Kemble's representations of Dunbar's short fiction would constitute one of the last cases in which an African American writer had to turn to a white artist for graphic illustrations. Soon after Kemble and Dunbar's unequal, uneasy collaboration, Adams suggests, a black visual artist could begin to validate a black writer's artistry and counter the distortions of cartoonists like Kemble. Indeed,

Dunbar's work originates at the pivotal moment Adams indicates: it survives from one of the last intervals in which black writers had to turn to white artists to give their stories visual expression even as it looks forward to a day when black cartoonists could earn their living illustrating black writers' works.

Authorities such as John Wheatley, Lydia Maria Child, and William Lloyd Garrison had long lent their authority to works by African American writers. They penned introductions that prepared readers to receive a black person's words, attested to the writer's reliability, and took responsibility for any extravagance in a former slave's work. Kemble's work similarly assures white readers of the supposed familiarity of Dunbar's settings. It neutralizes any perceived threats from Dunbar. It licenses readers to find the minstrel humor in what would otherwise be sober subjects. If an authenticating document is "a black message in a white envelope,"[44] these short-fiction collections show editors enclosing Dunbar's message in the envelopes that Dodd, Mead's packaging and Kemble's caricatures provided.

The *Voice of the Negro*, the *Colored American*, and other vanguard venues had also begun their own efforts to free messages like Dunbar's from envelopes like Kemble's. The *Voice*'s editorial cartoons visually ridiculed Theodore Roosevelt's maneuvers in foreign policy. Its caricatures decried Mississippi governor James K. Vardaman's advocacy of lynching. Its illustrations reduced Thomas Dixon Jr., author of the racist tract *The Clansman* (1905), to a bestial "snake in the grass." In the same issue in which Adams mused about the truth value of cartoons, the magazine printed three of Adams's images, including a rendering of an African American matron, accompanying a line of Dunbar's verse (figure 9.10). The matron beams with sentient intelligence and eschews conventional signifiers such as corncob pipes, jolly chuckles at "massa's" jokes, and unthinking subservience. She strikingly contrasts with Kemble's somnambulant mammy (figure 9.4). She does not permit whites to impose minstrel masks or passivity on her but demonstrates blacks authorizing written and visual imagery. Adams's image helps initiate a tradition of "counter-caricature," an appropriation of Dunbar's work, not for cartoons of Kemble's ilk, but for a new and proudly black artistic tradition.

"The time ha[d] come" for black art for black literature—six months too late for Dunbar. Dunbar's folk exhibit the marks of his rhetorical ploys to outstrip Kemble's caricatures, in part because too few contemporary African American caricaturists were empowered to leave their own mark on Dunbar's work. On the one hand, his publishers believed that the visual authorization of artists like Kemble was needed to market an African American comic aesthetic successfully. On the other hand, Dunbar, who clearly did not need these caricatures to succeed, began in these stories to prove his illustrator and white publishing establishment wrong. Kemble's images originated in a tradition of white authenticating documents for black literature; they have survived into a time that instead inspires counter-caricature, a visual arts tradition that defies the misrepresentation of Kemble's art. Penned as ploys to wrest control of minstrel masks from artists like Kemble, Dunbar's stories in turn betray the efforts, and portend the successes, of an author who learned to orchestrate a masquerade of his own.

NOTES

I would like to thank Leonard Spacek, Frederick Karem, Adrienne Gosselin, and Jack LaPlante for their suggestions and recommendations.

1. Paul Laurence Dunbar, "A Coquette Conquered," *Century* 52, no. 3 (1896): 479.

2. For critical interpretations of the Hampton Institute Camera Club's photographs as an aspect of Dunbar's books of poetry, see Jean Lee Cole, "Coloring Books: The Forms of Turn-of-the-Century American Literature," *Papers of the Bibliographical Society of America* 97, no. 4 (2003): 461–93; Nancy McGee, "From Poem to Photograph," *International Review of African American Art* 20, no. 1 (2005): 48–57; and Jeannene M. Przyblyski, "American Visions at the Paris Exposition, 1900: Another Look at Francis Benjamin Johnston's Hampton Photographs," *Art Journal* 57, no. 3 (1998): 60–68.

3. Kemble illustrated the following short-story collections by Paul Laurence Dunbar: *Folks from Dixie* (New York: Dodd, Mead, 1898); *The Heart of Happy Hollow* (New York: Dodd, Mead, 1904); and *The Strength of Gideon and Other Stories* (New York: Dodd, Mead, 1900). Another collection, *In Old Plantation Days* (New York: Dodd, Mead, 1903), appeared with reproductions of B. Martin Justice's illustrations, which had originally appeared with these stories in various American newspapers and magazines.

4. According to Virginia Cunningham in *Paul Laurence Dunbar and His Song* (New York: Dodd, Mead, 1947), Richard Underwood Johnson, an editor of the *Century*, once asked Dunbar how the writer felt about the magazine's comic portrayal of African Americans. In reply, Dunbar wrote, "There is a large humorous quality in [an African American's] character just as there is in that of the Irishman, and I cannot see that a laugh, when one laughs with them, hurts either one or the other" (207). Darwin Turner, in "Paul Laurence Dunbar: The Rejected Symbol," *Journal of Negro History* 52, no. 1 (1967), writes that Dunbar owned one of Kemble's original pen-and-ink drawings (12), and Benjamin Brawley, in *Paul Laurence Dunbar: Poet of His People* (Chapel Hill: University of North Carolina Press, 1936), asserts that he decorated his Washington, D.C., home with prints of Kemble's work (87). He seems, then, not only to have accepted Kemble's artistry as an inevitable facet of his publishing experience but actually to have appreciated Kemble's work. I explore the dynamics of their relationship below.

5. For studies of Kemble's illustrations for writers, including Joel Chandler Harris, Mark Twain, and Harriet Beecher Stowe, see Beverly R. David, *Mark Twain and His Illustrators* (Troy, N.Y.: Whitston, 1986); Elvin Holt, "*A Coon Alphabet* and the Comic Mask of Racial Prejudice," *Studies in American Humor* 5, no. 4 (1986–87): 307–18; and Francis Martin Jr., "Edward Windsor Kemble: Master of Pen and Ink," *American Art Review* 3 (1976): 54–67.

6. Earl F. Briden, "Kemble's 'Specialty' and the Pictorial Countertext of *Huckleberry Finn*," in *The Adventures of Huckleberry Finn*, by Mark Twain, ed. Thomas Cooley (New York: Norton, 1999), 311.

7. Ibid., 318.

8. An anecdote that Dunbar told the *Inter-Ocean* of Chicago provides some idea of his relationship with his publishing house: "I have a novel almost completed ... which is to be brought out this fall by Dodd, Mead. The last time I was in Chicago I told a reporter I was writing it. While in Colorado I wrote a story of 30,000 words which I submitted to an Eastern publishing house. They wrote to say they accepted it with the promise that I give them the novel I was reported to be writing. I was obliged to refuse because it was already sold to Dodd, Mead. The manuscript went to three other publishers and I received the same reply. So you see the reporter is to blame for my still having the manuscript on hand." "Negro Poet's Work," *Inter-Ocean,* May 8, 1900, qtd. in Paul Laurence Dunbar, *Paul L. Dunbar Papers,* ed. Sara S. Fuller (Columbus: Ohio Historical Society, 1972), roll 5.

Dunbar returned to Dodd, Mead, then, even when other houses were willing to publish his work. Their stature as major publishers, their promise of wide audiences, and their legal contractual obligations retained Dunbar's business even as alternative opportunities arose.

9. Since publication of Jay Martin and Gossie H. Hudson's *The Paul Laurence Dunbar Reader: A Selection of the Best of Paul Laurence Dunbar's Poetry and Prose, Including Writings Never before Available in Book Form* (New York: Dodd, Mead, 1975), Kemble's images have been omitted from editions of Dunbar's stories. In their introduction to *The Complete Stories of Paul Laurence Dunbar* (Athens: University of Ohio Press, 2005), editors Gene Anthony Jarrett and Thomas Lewis Morgan explain that they chose to exclude them because they "mirrored the racist images circulating in American popular culture at the turn of the century. The illustrations reflect the kind of misreading that Dunbar tried to address and refute during much of his professional career and that subsequent literary scholars have tried to critique and revise" (xlv).

10. Darwin Turner, preface to *The Strength of Gideon and Other Stories,* by Paul Dunbar (New York: Arno Press, 1969), vii.

11. Paul Laurence Dunbar to Alice Ruth Moore, Feb. 15, 1898, in *Dunbar Papers,* roll 4.

12. For a full reading of the personal dynamics of the Dunbar-Moore courtship—including their two-year correspondence before they met in person, Dunbar's alcoholism, his rape of Moore late in 1897, and their clandestine wedding and subsequent secrecy—see Eleanor Alexander, *Lyrics of Sunshine and Shadow: The Courtship and Marriage of Paul Laurence Dunbar and Alice Ruth Moore* (New York: Penguin, 2001), 112–45.

13. Dunbar writes in early 1897 that an illustrator for the *Star* wishes to improve his illustrations and send both the story and the drawing elsewhere, and in early 1898 that a Dr. Stewart of the Philadelphia *Times* is ready to illustrate his work. Paul Laurence Dunbar to Alice Ruth Moore, Jan. 8, 1897, and Jan. 8, 1898, in *Dunbar Papers,* roll 4.

14. Henry B. Wonham, *Playing the Races: Ethnic Caricature and American Literary Realism* (New York: Oxford University Press, 2004), 22.

15. Dunbar, *Folks from Dixie,* 30.

16. Ibid., 194.

17. Jarrett and Morgan, introduction, xxiv.

18. Dunbar, *The Strength of Gideon,* 24.

19. Ibid., 282.

20. Ibid., 227.

21. Alexander, *Lyrics of Sunshine,* 7.

22. Dunbar, *The Strength of Gideon,* 319.

23. Kemble does not acknowledge Miss Kirkman, but, interestingly, at least two newspaper reviewers did. On May 15, 1900, a Waterbury, Connecticut, paper referred to a woman character "with scarce a tinge of negro blood, who uses her slight connection with the black race for her pecuniary advantage," and on June 1, 1990, the New York *Commercial Leader* called Ms. Kirkman

"a capital example of a woman in politics—that sort of woman who is always going somewhere to get someone to vote for something." See *Dunbar Papers*, roll 5. Given Dunbar's politics and Moore's complexion, this story also invites a biographical interpretation.

24. Dunbar, *The Strength of Gideon*, 334.
25. Ibid., 336–37.
26. Jarrett and Morgan, introduction, xvii.
27. The New York *Evening Post* concluded that Kemble's illustrations were "of their usual excellence" (June 23, 1900), and Philadelphia's *Literary Era* claimed that they were "as original and amusing as anything he has done" (June 1900). The *Spy*, a Worcester, Massachusetts, paper, more extravagantly claimed that "Kemble's apt and amusing illustrations add much to the charm of an already attractive volume" (June 3, 1900), and a Toronto *Star* review followed suit in remarking that "a number of capital illustrations" produced by Kemble's "graphic pencil" increased the volume's appeal (Mar 30, 1901). Boston's *Literary World* gave what was possibly a backhanded compliment when it said, "There are a few illustrations by Kemble which are worthy of their place" (Aug 1, 1900). See *Dunbar Papers*, roll 5.
28. Dunbar, *The Strength of Gideon*, 334.
29. Dunbar's weight in 1899 is estimated to have been about 135 pounds. See Felton O'Neal Best, *Crossing the Color Line: A Biography of Paul Laurence Dunbar* (Dubuque, Iowa: Kendall/Hunt, 1996), 93; and Alexander, *Lyrics of Sunshine*, 43.
30. Dunbar, *Happy Hollow*, 172.
31. Ibid., 249.
32. Ibid., 37.
33. Ibid., 42.
34. Ibid., 244, 245.
35. Ibid., 250.
36. Ibid., 232.
37. Ibid., 236.
38. Ibid., 238.
39. Ibid., 238–39.
40. Scholarship on the nineteenth-century cultural construction of whiteness proposes that it functions as the absence of a racial sign, an unwritten or "unraced" state of being, in opposition to markers that designate others as "non-white." But interestingly, the white murderer in Dunbar's tale leaves behind incriminating signs of his whiteness: Melville finds traces of the murderer's skin beneath the victim's fingernails. Dunbar rewrites whiteness, then, as having its own signifiers and providing tangible incriminating evidence, rather than agreeing with Euro-American authors in presenting whiteness as the absence of any such racial signs.
41. Houston A. Baker Jr., *Modernism and the Harlem Renaissance* (Chicago: University of Chicago Press, 1987), 39.
42. John Henry Adams, "McGowans' Cartoons," *Voice of the Negro* 3, no. 9 (1906): 645.
43. Ibid., 646.
44. William L. Andrews, "The Literature of Slavery and Freedom," in *The Norton Anthology of African American Literature*, ed. Henry Louis Gates Jr. and Nelly Y. McKay (New York: Norton, 1997), 133.

10
"We Know de Time Is Ouahs"
The Power of Christmas in the Literature of Paul Laurence Dunbar

AMY CUMMINS

ONE HUNDRED YEARS AFTER THE POET'S DEATH, Paul Laurence Dunbar and his legacy merit continued literary study and public appreciation. His achievements are demonstrated by the literary quality and range of his work, the critical debates about his ideology and goals, and his influence on other writers. This chapter focuses on an area that has not yet been addressed by scholarship: the significance of Christmas in Dunbar's writings. Dunbar utilized the subject and setting of Christmas in "A Christmas Folksong," "Chrismus Is A-Comin'," "A Back-log Song," "Chrismus on the Plantation," "Christmas in the Heart," "Christmas Carol," and "A Little Christmas Basket"; in the one-act musical "Uncle Eph's Christmas"; and in the short stories "One Christmas at Shiloh," "A Defender of the Faith," and "An Old-Time Christmas." The holiday becomes a platform for Dunbar's social criticism. In building on the topos of Christmas, Dunbar aimed to express truths about life under slavery, to document the impact of racism and economic injustice on African Americans, and to urge reconciliation and charitable giving. Depictions of holiday revelry ironically underscore the true unfreedom of slavery—and of the new forms of slavery in the early twentieth century—as Dunbar's satire rewrites stereotypes.

Under the slavery system in the American South, newspaper notices in the month of December announced the upcoming hiring of servants for the following year, because the end of the calendar year was the main season for hiring slaves for work during the following year.[1] A statement received from a slave in 1862 mentions that on New Year's Day, "a general sale of slaves" would take place.[2] Slaves were hired out to perform labor for which the need was temporary or because the hirer could not afford to purchase and own slaves.[3] The period of service for the hired "servants" could extend from the first of January to the day before Christmas.[4] The practice of hiring out slaves to themselves was prohibited legally yet practiced often, disproving the claim that slaves would not work without compulsion.[5]

In *My Southern Home* (1880), William Wells Brown refers to the "long custom" of providing enslaved persons a week of time off for the winter holidays.[6] Many slaves attended religious revivals, while others would "spend their time at the dances, raffles, cock-fights, foot-races, and other amusements."[7] Jacob Stroyer writes in his 1879 narrative of life in slavery that slaves were expected to perform in particular ways for their masters at Christmas, as at all times. Dancing was obligatory at Christmas, even if one did not believe in dancing.[8] Token gifts were presented to the slaves after they displayed themselves by performing amusements.[9] Slaves often had only Christmas morning to themselves and were "required to devote themselves to the pleasure of their masters" by the afternoon.[10] Any holidays allowed by slaveholders were a performance of benevolence within systemic domination. Holiday revelries were part of the system that controlled "black pleasure by allowing it periodic, approved, expression"; slaveholders intended plantation parties "to inspire respect, gratitude, deference, and, most importantly, obedience."[11]

As Dunbar writes in the story "One Christmas at Shiloh" from *The Heart of Happy Hollow* (1904), enslaved persons knew that any pleasures of Christmas week were followed by "separation and sadness. For this was the time when those who were to be hired out, loaned, or given away, were to change their homes. So even while they danced they sighed, and while they shouted they moaned."[12] In this story, Martha Maria Dixon is part of an active southern church community in the urban North that is preparing for a meaningful Christmas celebration, hoping to approach "the rousing times both spiritual and temporal" typical of winter holidays of the plantation past.[13] When the visiting preacher Martha is hosting turns out to be her long-lost husband, the reunion is a fulfillment of the fantasy that families can be brought together rather than torn apart at Christmas.

Frederick Douglass identifies the Christmas holidays as "safety-valves" that were the slaveholders' "most effective means" of "keeping down the spirit of insurrection."[14] Slaveholders aimed "to disgust their slaves with freedom, by plunging them into the lowest depths of dissipation." Describing Christmas day of 1833, when his term of service to Edward Covey ended, Douglass notes that slaves occupied themselves during the interval before New Year's Day in various ways: some would employ themselves in making useful items, while others would go hunting, but the majority of the slaves participated in "such sports and merriments as playing ball, wrestling, running foot-races, fiddling, dancing, and drinking whisky; and this latter mode of spending the time was by far the most agreeable to the feelings of our master." The slaveholder uses contrivances to get slaves excessively drunk, administering "a dose of vicious dissipation, artfully labelled with the name of liberty" of holidays.[15]

Douglass notes in the section about Christmas in the 1892 work *The Life and Times of Frederick Douglass* that the songs sung by slaves could include a subversive element in the form of lyrics critical of conditions under slavery. Douglass writes that sometimes in the "wild frolic, a sharp hit was given to the meanness of slaveholders," as in a song that shows enslaved singers' awareness of their exploitation: "We peel de meat, / Dey gib us de skin; / And dat's de way / Dey take us in."[16] Rather than gratefully accepting the "crusts" and "skin" they receive on a few holidays, they recognize the lack of freedom of their lives yet must, in Dunbar's words, "wear the mask that grins and lies" in order to survive under slavery.

Douglass's observations about the coercive purposes of the holidays are echoed by Frances Fedric in his 1863 narrative about life in slavery. Fedric writes that at Christmas the slaves would be given "four or five days' holiday" and forced to consume more whiskey than they wanted. Then the slave owner would say to the slaves that their "liberty" during holidays had been used poorly and that they needed "a master, to look after you, and make you work, and keep you from such a brutal state, which is a disgrace to you," to which some of the slaves would agree. "Thus, by an artfully-contrived plan, the slaves themselves are made to put the seal upon their own servitude."[17]

Christmas holidays were especially significant due to the holiday's correlation with slave escapes and retaliation against the condition of servitude. It has been estimated that up to one-third of actual and intended slave revolts were planned for the Christmas season.[18] The parties, "sanctioned disorder," and movements of African Americans provided opportunities to run away or join together for subversive purposes.[19] In 1865, rumored conspiracies of massive "Christmas Riots" in former slave states did not prove true.[20] However, the heightening of emotions was predictable, because freed people believed they would be receiving property and economic rights in the form of land at the end of the war, and because Christmas was associated with changes in routine and symbolic challenges of power.[21]

Dunbar used African American dialect in his literature for several purposes: he endeavored to record aspects of the African American experience, to build a wide audience that would enable him to make a living off his writing, and to develop his poetic craft. Not wanting to be limited in what he could publish, the multidialectical Dunbar expected more recognition for his achievement in "literary" English forms than for his dialect work. He capitulated to expectations that he write in black dialect, despite his artistic frustrations at the constraint. Dunbar did not denigrate his own accomplishments with dialect, telling James Weldon Johnson that he knew he could write in dialect as well as or better than anyone else he knew, and that he had recognized early on "that by doing so I should gain a hearing."[22] Critics praised Dunbar's new poetic diction, and other poets imitated him.[23] But Dunbar's dialect work was a disappointment to "some members of the black middle class who wanted nothing to do with its suggestions of ignorance and naïveté."[24] By the end of the nineteenth century, dialect was viewed as connoting inferiority, "the linguistic sign both of human bondage (as origin) and of the continued failure of 'improvability' or 'progress.'"[25] Twentieth-century critics increasingly condemned Dunbar for adhering too comfortably in his style and content to negative stereotypes of the plantation tradition. Because critical assessments of Dunbar's work vary greatly, and they are "sometimes as much a reflection of the values and concerns of reviewers as they are a measure of his own accomplishments,"[26] it is important to focus on the primary texts.

In the dialect poem "A Christmas Folksong," the holiday season occasions mourning and dread. The narrator of the poem remarks on the warm weather that offers no hint of snow; each of the four stanzas includes a variation on the statement that "It's goin' to be a green Christmas, / An' sad de day fu' me."[27] Marveling at the "feasting" and holiday celebrations in the slave quarters and the "big house," the speaker says that "dancin' times an' spahkin' / Are all done pas' fur me."[28] His lamentations are more than a personal reference. As a folk song calling upon shared traditions, the poem may be read as a warning for enslaved persons to stay alert and never to let down their guards in the brief respite of the holidays.

The mournful tone of "A Christmas Folksong" dwells upon the inevitability of the grave and describes the time of slave hiring that followed the Christmas holidays. Five dead and buried individuals are named, with a suggestion that they were family members of the speaker: "Wid only dis one lef'."[29] The speaker's gravity about the future contrasts to the levity of people who can enjoy a Christmas celebration. The "hungry chu'chya'd" seems eager for more inmates, and the poem closes with the ominous warning that "Befo' de summah beckons / Dey's many'll weep wid me."[30] In addition to the poem's evocation of deaths and family separations as basic features of the African American experience, there is a suggestion that the approach of Christmas day is a sad time because it brings closer the separation of families that is a seasonal ritual at year's end. After a "green Christmas" that may offer some minor pleasures, the temperate weather will bring out more slaveholders to exchange the services of their slaves, and observers to watch the transactions. The speaker of the poem cannot be jovial in the face of such harsh, inescapable realities.

While the popular poem "Chrismus Is A-Comin'" emphasizes positive aspects of the seasonal holidays, it also demonstrates the injustice of slavery. In this text, Christmas, and the week of holidays accompanying it, is eagerly anticipated by the speaker: the first stanza closes with the lines "Chrismus is a-comin' / An' all de week is ouahs," and the last stanza ends with a variation on the same idea.[31] Nevertheless, the claim that the slaves can possess their own week is undercut by the second stanza. The narrator of the poem notes that when the master's son asks about Santa Claus, the question "Meks it kin o' taxin' / Not to break de laws."[32] Because the master's son is so "tryin'" and "pryin'" to the speaker, who is legal property of the slave-owning family and cannot speak harshly to the boy, he is inclined to "tell 'em true," violating prohibitions against honest dialogue between slaves and whites.[33] The speaker could be thinking that all people are equal in God's sight and that slavery is un-Christian. In the next stanza, rather than rebuking the boy, the speaker and his wife reflect upon their own son, who is sleeping. As the parents perceive that even their masters "Got no chile lak dis is, / D'ain't none anywhaih," they honor themselves even though the law does not legally recognize them as a family.[34]

Thus, while the fourth stanza details the pleasures of music, food, and drink that can be had during the week of holidays, "Chrismus Is A-Comin'" cannot be read as acceptance of or nostalgia for the condition of servitude. It is a reminder that slaves can own neither themselves nor their time, despite the changes in routine during the Christmas week. The "Drams to wet yo' whistles / So's to drive out chills" only dull the senses.[35] The text was popular even before being included in *Lyrics of the Hearthside* and the illustrated volume *Poems of Cabin and Field* (both 1899). Under the title "Christmas Is A-Coming," it was published in four different newspapers, including the *New York Times*, in 1897 and 1898, and it was twice published in 1899 under the title "Chrismus Is A-Coming."[36] Double directed, the poem evokes the positive associations of Christmas while also including the subversive element that criticized slavery and racism.

The poem "A Back-log Song" likewise uses a Christmas setting to raise the question of whether slaves can own their time. The ritual of the backlog, or Yule log, involved cutting down a large tree, soaking the log during the year, then lighting it on the morning of Christmas day; this tradition "allowed slaves to exert at least symbolic control over the length of the holidays."[37] In Dunbar's poem, while the carefully chosen and prepared log burns, the slaves have some choice of activities, "Fu' we know de time is ouahs."[38] The illusion of self-direction for a few hours' time is evoked by this tradition: "An' dey ain't no ovahseer an' no other kind o' powahs / Dat kin stop us while dat log is bu'nin thoo."[39] During this brief interval, the "Mastah," "Mistus," and "young folks" are supposedly trying "fu' to mek us feel hit's Chrismus time fu' sho.'"[40]

However, this moment of revelry in "A Back-log Song" only underscores the true absence of freedom on the plantation. As the speaker describes the frenzies of activity—"evah one be runnin,'"—their haste shows how much they value the precious little time they are given.[41] The length of time it takes for one log to burn is fleeting in comparison with a lifetime of enslavement. Dunbar's poetic references to logs and decorated tree boughs allude to the linkage of Christmas trees with the abolition cause. In 1835, Harriet Martineau wrote about the evergreen tree of fellow abolitionist Charles Follen, and the Christmas tree became an important symbol.[42] The National Anti-slavery Bazaars, held during the Christmas season in northern cities after 1839, raised awareness and funds for the abolition movement.[43] These ten-day fairs featured Christmas trees and products created with free labor, including books and artistic works by African Americans.[44]

Dunbar's "Chrismus on the Plantation" (1898) both uses and undermines the stereotyping of the plantation tradition. The setting is Christmas Eve during Reconstruction, "a mighty gloomy day" on which the workers lament because that morning, the man the speaker still calls "Mastah" announced that he will be selling the homestead, where "he'd been paying us sence freedom, but he couldn't pay no more."[45] While everyone is in tears at having to leave the plantation, Ben says that he will not desert the man, who has "been kind" but now is unable to pay them, because the plantation "did suppo't us, and de place kin do it yit."[46] Their labor has supported them, and they want to stay on the land. Speaking on behalf of the workers, Ben says that they will not leave; they vow to remain on the plantation and not to let it be sold, for "Ouah min's was sot to stay, / An' po' ol' Mastah couldn't plead, ner baig, ner drive us 'way."[47] The poem affirms the loyalty of the workers to their former owner and to their plantation—but also to themselves and the site of their hard labors.

Critical judgments of "Chrismus on the Plantation" vary. Paula Bernat Bennett sees it as offering the "conventional treatment of the faithful slave trope," presenting scenes from the slaveholder's perspective, and catering to white supremacist views.[48] Yet the poem must be read as a criticism of slavery and its legacy. In the text, the slaves' refusal to leave is a declaration that slaves possess rights to the land where they worked the soil. Following the Civil War, freedmen spoke of "a right to the land," and in some cases, former slaves claimed plantations for themselves.[49] While the use of dialect might disarm a reader into thinking the former slaves are still, to use Gates's terminology, "objects" instead of "subjects," their decision to remain on the plantation they still work is a seizing of power and land.[50] Dunbar's "Chrismus on the Plantation" also indicts the lack of vocational opportunity outside the agricultural realm of the place where they had been enslaved.

In an alternative reading of "Chrismus on the Plantation," the critic Darwin Turner suggests that the former slaves may be "nostalgic" and loving of their employer but that Dunbar would not have considered his characterizations a perpetuation of "derogatory images" but rather "evidences of a virtue which should be brought to the attention of white readers in the hope of persuading them to stop abusing a people who had served them faithfully."[51] If Dunbar praises such values as compassion and reconciliation in the poem, he makes a connected move with the short story "Nelse Hatton's Vengeance" in *Folks from Dixie* (1898), in which an impoverished white man from Kentucky appears at the door of a black family in Ohio thirty years after the Civil War. In both texts, the formerly enslaved persons have power.

In "Nelse Hatton's Vengeance," the indigent white man, Tom Hatton, seeks food from a person who was previously enslaved by his family, and whom he personally had whipped and beaten. Despite Nelse's angry resentment at the indignities and wounds he suffered when owned by the Hattons, whose family name he has retained in freedom, Nelse's religious beliefs and "warm sympathies conquered."[52] Nelse sees Tom as "the white Hatton," thus linking them together.[53] After much internal struggle, Nelse gives Tom money and his best suit, and the story ends with emotional affirmation. Like some of Dunbar's poetry, the story may be interpreted as accommodating white supremacy, but it equally encourages values of mutual respect and racial reconciliation. The story's title, "Nelse Hatton's Vengeance," indicates Nelse's moral and economic superiority over his former master. From his position of success, Nelse can be generous to others.

Other poetry approaches Christmas nostalgically. "Christmas Carol" refers to the birth of Jesus and uses Standard English.[54] Social criticism is muted in "Speakin' o' Christmas," and the poem contributes to the mythologizing of the season, albeit with exaggerated diction that calls into question the sentimental images. While "Christmas of the long ago" used to be anticipated "weeks an' weeks before it come," the Christmas of today is characterized by "new-styled ways." When the poem ends with "I'd jest like once more to see / Christmas like it used to be!"[55] the reader wonders exactly when this idealized holiday of "Frozen mill-ponds all ashine" and "Every cottage decked out gay" existed.[56] The fact is that the fantasy never existed.

The recently recovered one-act musical "Uncle Eph's Christmas" satirizes stereotypes of African Americans and of Christmas. The play, which takes place during an unspecified time period but on a set with an "Old fashioned Fireplace" that visually suggests the past, is a light entertainment, and Ephram's holiday an occasion for merriment.[57] Ephram is initially dressed in his wife's shirtwaist when he is awakened from a nap by his children, who crowd around, saying, "Christmas gift," an old expression used before the greeting "Merry Christmas," to which Dunbar also refers nostalgically in the poem "Speakin' o' Christmas."[58] The use of this expression in the play may be a pointed reference to the antebellum game called Christmas Gift, in which slaves directly demanded gifts from their owners. The game's brief "gesture of autonomy" arguably provided "a symbolic moment" for overturning "the racial hierarchy," even if the "gifts" received were basic necessities such as winter clothing or food.[59]

When Ephram dispenses homespun remedies, gets drunk on gin, and enjoys wordplay with multisyllabic fabrications, his word games should be heard as more of a parody than a perpetuation of stereotypes. For instance, stage directions describe him as looking around "slyly" then drawing attention to guest Parthenia Jenkins, who passed for white, attended Vassar College, and graduated at the top of her class.[60] As Ephram chooses to use several different mispronunciations of words such as "education," "graduates," and "Vassar College," and Parthenia sings, "I'm the Colored Girl from Vassar," the point is that a trick has been played successfully upon the white power structure.[61] Would audience members catch such fine points? As in "Chrismus on the Plantation," the satire may get lost in the stereotype despite Dunbar's efforts to play on the stereotype rather than to reinforce it.

In his performances of Dunbar's work, poet and scholar Herbert Woodward Martin addresses the question of Dunbar's use of minstrelsy tropes. According to Ronald Primeau, Martin believes that Dunbar's choice to use "tropes of the minstrel show" in his musicals helped "attract an audience who will see and hear his modification, mockery, and other critiques of that stereotyping."[62] Dunbar's "ironic overtones" were intended satirically, "both as a mock of the stereotypical roles and a probing insight into the behavior and motivation of white folks."[63] In the musical, the character of Darky Dan sings a song titled "Czar of Dixie Land," which opens with the claim that white people will not elect black people to office and that white people want "to keep black folks in dey station."[64]

By the time the musical culminates in a cakewalk and a song titled "Possum Is de Best Meat after All," the audience may have lost sight of the fact that Christmas is being honored with a communal gathering of family and friends in an environment of cheerfulness and ample refreshments. When Ephram goes to get more provisions, he returns quite inebriated, with an opossum he says he has captured.[65] The improbably caught opossum parodies a stereotype, although the insistence on the greatness of the opossum, a wild game meat often associated with poverty, may also represent a preference for a familiar food or a reference to an African American tradition. In Dunbar's story "Mt. Pisgah's Christmas Possum," the rural church members plan a communal Christmas feast with four opossums but are foiled by a greedy person who steals three of the opossums to eat by himself.[66] The poem "Christmas" also describes the Christmas tradition of feasting on opossum.[67] Yet the opossum is also a negative symbol of the limited economic opportunities and stereotypes of the rural South.

For instance, a photograph in a December 1901 issue of *Leslie's Weekly* depicts a black man climbing a spindly tree to catch the opossum at the top, presumably for a Christmas dinner; racist imagery associates African Americans with the distant "defeated South" rather than showing them as neighbors.[68] The idea of a black Christmas was perpetuated in periodical illustrations for a northern white audience through racist images showing poor rural African Americans as "exotic natives."[69] That early twentieth-century readers continued to look nostalgically at antebellum white supremacy is evident in the reprinting in 1907 of an engraving from 1857 titled "Winter Holidays in the Southern States," in which the master and mistress watch their slaves dancing. In this picture and many other images, caricatures exaggerate the black people's facial expressions and make body movements appear uncontrolled, in contrast to the "bland and classical" visages and "restrained gestures" of white onlookers.[70] The stereotypes of black Christmas become part of Dunbar's satire in "Uncle Eph's Christmas."

Dunbar's song "Possum Is de Best Meat after All" does not represent benign acceptance of the inferior "meat" of opportunity available to African Americans. The song states that a black man "kin go into de senate, he kin gain a high degree, / But he allus shous 'de possum is de only meat fu me.'"[71] Parodying ideas of what African Americans crave, drawing attention to the fact that a black man cannot so easily get in the Senate—as Darky Dan's song stated earlier—and reminding the audience of Booker T. Washington's acceptance of social segregation, the song points to the effects of enduring prejudices upon African American ambition and achievement. But such subtleties may get buried in the musical's overall tone of jollity. Furthermore, staging these scenes in a musical creates white spectatorship that may seem reminiscent of the way that, according to Stephanie Camp, slaveholders "oversaw" and contained holiday pleasures by "attending and surveilling" the parties of their slaves.[72]

The poem "Christmas in the Heart" establishes the importance of a charitable spirit at Christmastime, coinciding with Dunbar's urging of philanthropy as expressed in "A Little Christmas Basket" and several short stories. "Christmas in the Heart" vividly describes winter weather and floral Christmas decorations then analyzes "a grasping miser" in order to conclude with the point that a person must hold "Christmas in his heart."[73] The importance of brightening other people's lives through well-timed charity is shown in stanza 2, as Dunbar writes, "Even the pauper of the earth / Some kindly gift has cheered to mirth!"[74] The miserly man should be ashamed of himself and fulfill his duty to help others, "For 'Christmas Day' is no mere name."[75]

The emphasis on direct charity to the less fortunate became a major element of the holiday season, benefiting the giver as well as the recipient. The connection between benevolent actions and the Christmas season was established through popular nineteenth-century literature such as Sarah Orne Jewett's holiday stories in magazines of the 1880s and 1890s; Louisa May Alcott's *Little Women* (1868–69); and, most important, the Christmas stories of Charles Dickens, such as *A Christmas Carol* (1843).[76] Ebenezer Scrooge is the predecessor of the miserly man in Dunbar's "Christmas in the Heart." Personal contributions to the less fortunate were known as "old charity," different from modern charity, which involved the disbursement of funds through organizations and social workers.[77] Effective gift-giving builds a fellow feeling between the giver and the recipient, and it should be done through a genuine spirit of personal caring, not from meddlesome aims.[78]

"A Little Christmas Basket" highlights the practical impact of charitable donations. The abstract idealization of Christmas in "Speakin' o' Christmas" is nowhere in evidence in this pragmatic poem. Financial needs are emphasized because bills for food, shelter, and fuel define reality. The speaker shows that words are not enough: "So we want ouah Chrismus sermon, but we'd lak it ef you could / Leave a little Chrismus basket at de do.'"[79] The speaker needs to indicate specific financial needs without alienating the donor. To Dunbar, a true Christian will help those who are less fortunate, not just offer tracts or platitudes. Reassurances that God will provide are inadequate, for "What's de use o' preachin' 'ligion to a man dat's sta'ved to def?"[80] To truly touch the hearts of others, "save yo' sermons an' yo' bref," and offer instead "a little Chrismus basket" with useful items such as food and fuel.[81]

An archetypal illustration of this message of Christmas charity is the short story "A Defender of the Faith," first published in 1901 then printed in

The Heart of Happy Hollow (1904), Dunbar's collection of stories principally set in the contemporary urban North. The message is that people should act in a role of Santa Claus for others and, by doing so, improve the nation for future generations. One Christmas Eve, looking for a story to write about in the newspaper, perhaps to satisfy an audience wanting a stereotypical image of Black Christmas, reporter Arabella Coe walks through the streets of "what was put down on the real estate agent's list as a coloured neighbourhood" inhabited by "people so poor that they were constantly staggering on the verge of the abyss."[82] She eavesdrops on a group of children debating the existence of Santa Claus. The children want desperately to believe in him, but he did not visit their house last year. A young girl wonders aloud, "Maybe Thanty's white an' don' go to see col'red people," but her brother Sam insists, "Dem col'red folks dat's got the money, dem's de only ones dat Santy Claus fin'd, you bet."[83] After Arabella hears the children pray to God to send Santa, and the mother telling the children that Santa Claus may not have presents for them, Arabella decides to help the family anonymously.

Just as Arabella reaches "a parting of the ways" in deciding whether to get involved in the poor children's situation, so too must readers consider how they are honoring the Christmas spirit.[84] Sacrificing the purchase of a much-needed pair of boots, Arabella goes to the store to select gifts for the family, feeling that the alternative is that the children, disabused of a belief in Santa Claus, would "lose their faith forever and from this it will go to other things," perhaps crime.[85] She places the gifts with an explanatory note from Santa Claus outside the family's door. "A Defender of the Faith" demonstrates that the rhetoric of a newspaper article by itself would have done no practical good for the family, although Arabella, like Dunbar, still writes and submits a story. The omniscient narrator does not reveal the content of Arabella's story, ending instead with a statement by Sam's brother Tom, "resplendent in a new muffler" as he sells newspapers on a street corner, that he will punch the head of anyone who denies the existence of Santa Claus.[86]

The Christmas experience of another urban newsboy occasions Dunbar's social criticism in the story "An Old-Time Christmas" from *The Strength of Gideon and Other Stories* (1900). The story's exposé of racial tensions and economic injustice is heightened due to the setting of Christmas at the turn of the century. 'Liza Ann Lewis, ten years a resident of New York City, dreams of showing her son, Jimmy, the Christmas celebrations and "merry-making" she enjoyed in the past.[87] The story opens with her remembering the times "at home when, following the precedent of anti-bellum days, Christmas lasted all the week and good cheer held sway."[88] Because 'Liza Ann affectionately recollects the celebrations, and the music, gifts, dancing, and good food, the story might initially appear to reinforce the untruth that African Americans were content when enslaved. But 'Liza Ann's nostalgia for the "feast-days," themselves a re-creation of past traditions, is partly due to the expense of food in the city, and the story quickly shows the irony in her "tears of memory and longing" after she hears through the window a man's voice singing "The Old Folks at Home," with lines such as "Still longing for the old plantation, / An' for the old folks at home."[89] By the time 'Liza Ann hears the voice again singing at the end of the story, she has learned a hard lesson about the forms of unfreedom experienced by African Americans at the turn of the century, a reminder of how much more change was still needed to redress economic and social injustices. On Christmas Eve's day, Jimmy, who sells newspapers on the streets of New York, is arrested by a police officer for penny gambling and jailed.

The new forms of oppression faced by the mother and son are reminiscent of situations faced under slavery. With the unhappy ending, the tale subverts conventions of Christmas stories. Because "Her Christmas treasure[,] added to what Jimmy had, paid his fine," the price to get Jimmy out of jail is reminiscent of costs to liberate the enslaved from their masters a half century prior, as well as the system of peonage, under which African Americans who could not pay fines for crimes for which they were convicted were incarcerated.[90] The true meaning of Christmas is dishonored in such a world. The police sergeant alleges that the newsboys are gambling away the pennies tossed to them in charity, undermining the importance of benevolence.[91] The judge refuses to show any leniency, though he has done so for others recently. Far from bringing justice, the judge gives a "stern lecture upon the evil of child-gambling" when the much larger evil is poverty: the mother and son retreat to a home with no coal, no fire, and almost no food.[92]

The injustice exposed in the story "An Old-Time Christmas" is symptomatic of the "new and more dastardly slavery" that Dunbar identifies in "The Fourth of July and Race Outrages."[93] In this 1903 article in the *New York Times*, Dunbar exposes the evils of lynchings in and beyond the southern states; of disenfranchisement, or the denial of voting rights through such means as poll taxes and literacy tests; and of "industrial prejudice," which narrowed employment and economic opportunities for African Americans.[94] Dunbar writes that "For the sake of reenslaving the Negro, the Constitution has been trampled under feet, the rights of man have been laughed out of court, and the justice of God has been made a jest and we celebrate."[95]

The ironies of Independence Day had been revealed in Frederick Douglass's 1852 lecture "What to the Slave Is the Fourth of July?" National holidays such as the Fourth of July and Christmas draw attention to political inequalities behind celebrations and to the insufficiency of changes since 1865. Between

1889 and 1932, more than 3,745 persons were lynched in the United States; in 1892 alone, 235 people were lynched, 155 of them African American. From 1901 to 1972, there were no African Americans representing the South in the United States Congress.

Dunbar uses the phrase "new slavery" in a poem describing conditions at the turn of the century. Addressing the South and accusing the entire nation of being complicit in the perpetuation of inequalities, Dunbar's long poem "To the South, on Its New Slavery" from *Lyrics of Love and Laughter* (1903) insists that "not for this, a nation's heroes bled."[96] Dunbar castigates the "newer bondage and this deeper shame" of miseries such as the "crime" of a workingman made "almost too brutish to deplore his plight."[97] This degradation, distinct from the absence of freedom under chattel slavery, denies the full humanity of the African American as citizen, worker, and neighbor.

Christmas was an entry point for Dunbar's social criticism. He evokes the historical reality of winter holidays for enslaved persons as a short interval of illusory cheer and liberty, in the light of impending sales and hiring out of slaves on New Year's Day, and he reveals that the true meaning of Christmas is dishonored by slavery and white supremacy. Dunbar's literature exposes the enduring history and repercussions of slavery, such as family separation, overt racism, the failure of Reconstruction, economic injustice, and social segregation, at the beginning of the twentieth century. He depicts African Americans seizing power and influence. In a variety of prose and poetic texts, Dunbar acknowledges the exploitation of the Christmas season while urging compassion, lessons that readers of the twentieth century must heed in order to develop a true "Christmas in the Heart." Through satire, Dunbar worked with the setting and emblems of Christmas to criticize racism in its historical and present manifestations.

Notes

1. Frederic Bancroft, *Slave Trading in the Old South* (New York: Frederick Ungar, 1959), 147–49.

2. "Statement of a Slave," *New York Times*, Jan. 14, 1862, rpt. in *Slave Testimony: Two Centuries of Letters, Speeches, Interviews, and Autobiographies*, ed. John W. Blassingame (Baton Rouge: Louisiana State University Press, 1977), 171–72.

3. Bancroft, *Slave Trading*, 146.

4. Ibid., 149 n. 7.

5. Ibid., 162–63.

6. William Wells Brown, *My Southern Home; or, The South and Its People* (Boston: A. G. Brown, 1880), 95.

7. Ibid., 97.

8. Jacob Stroyer, *Sketches of My Life in the South, Part I* (Salem, Mass.: Salem Press, 1879), 35.

9. Ibid., 34.

10. Ibid., 28.

11. Stephanie Camp, *Closer to Freedom: Enslaved Women and Everyday Resistance in the Plantation South* (Chapel Hill: University of North Carolina Press, 2004), 65.

12. *The Complete Stories of Paul Laurence Dunbar*, ed. Gene Andrew Jarrett and Thomas Lewis Morgan (Athens: Ohio University Press, 2005), 327.

13. Ibid., 326.

14. *Narrative of the Life of Frederick Douglass, an American Slave, Written by Himself*, in *Norton Anthology of African American Literature*, ed. Henry Louis Gates Jr. and Nellie Y. McKay, 2nd ed. (New York: Norton, 2004), 428.

15. Ibid., 428, 429.

16. *The Life and Times of Frederick Douglass* (1892; New York: Collier, 1962), 144.

17. Frances Fedric, *Slave Life in Virginia and Kentucky; or, Fifty Years of Slavery in the Southern States of America* (London: Wertheim, Macintosh, and Hunt, 1863), 28.

18. Dan Carter, "The Anatomy of Fear: The Christmas Day Insurrection Scare of 1865," *Journal of Southern History* 42 (1976): 358.

19. Stephen Nissenbaum, *The Battle for Christmas* (New York: Vintage, 1996), 291.

20. Eric Foner, *Forever Free: The Story of Emancipation and Reconstruction* (New York: Knopf, 2005), 91.

21. Nissenbaum, *The Battle for Christmas*, 296–97.

22. Qtd. in James Weldon Johnson, *Along This Way: The Autobiography of James Weldon Johnson* (New York: Viking Press, 1968), 160.

23. Henry Louis Gates Jr., *The Signifying Monkey: A Theory of African-American Literary Criticism* (New York: Oxford University Press, 1988), 164.

24. Herbert Woodward Martin and Ronald Primeau, introduction to *In His Own Voice: The Dramatic and Other Uncollected Works of Paul Laurence Dunbar* (Athens: Ohio University Press, 2002), xxii.

25. Gates, *The Signifying Monkey*, 176.

26. Martin and Primeau, introduction, xxi.

27. *The Collected Poetry of Paul Laurence Dunbar*, ed. Joanne M. Braxton (Charlottesville: University of Virginia Press, 1993), 236, lines 9–10.

28. Ibid., 236, lines 17, 15–16.

29. Ibid., 237, line 41.

30. Ibid., 237, lines 35, 46–47.

31. Ibid., 153, lines 11–12.

32. Ibid., 153, lines 15–16.

33. Ibid., 153, lines 17, 19, 24.

34. Ibid., 153, lines 31–32.

35. Ibid., 153, lines 41–42.

36. E. W. Metcalf Jr., *Paul Laurence Dunbar: A Bibliography* (Metuchen, N.J.: Scarecrow, 1975), 34–35, 37–38.

37. Nissenbaum, *The Battle for Christmas*, 357 n. 13.

38. *The Complete Poems of Paul Laurence Dunbar* (New York: Dodd, Mead, 1922), 143, line 13.

39. Ibid., 143, lines 14–15.

40. Ibid., 143, lines 10–12.

41. Ibid., 143, line 26.

42. Karal Marling, *Merry Christmas! Celebrating America's Greatest Holiday* (Cambridge, Mass.: Harvard University Press, 2000), 160.

43. Michael Bennett, *Democratic Discourses: The Radical Abolition Movement and Antebellum American Literature* (New Brunswick, N.J.: Rutgers University Press, 2005), 26, 164 n. 7.

44. Ibid., 40.

45. *Collected Poetry*, 137, lines 1, 6.
46. Ibid., 137, lines 21, 26.
47. Ibid., 137, lines 33–34.
48. Paula Bernat Bennett, "Rewriting Dunbar: Realism, Black Women Poets, and the Genteel," in *Post-bellum, Pre-Harlem: African American Literature and Culture, 1877–1919*, ed. Barbara McCaskill and Caroline Gebhard (New York: New York University Press, 2006), 155–56.
49. Foner, *Forever Free*, 91–92.
50. Gates, *The Signifying Monkey*, 176.
51. Darwin T. Turner, "Paul Laurence Dunbar: The Poet and the Myths," in *A Singer in the Dawn: Reinterpretations of Paul Laurence Dunbar*, ed. Jay Martin (New York: Dodd, Mead, 1972), 70.
52. *Complete Stories*, 62.
53. Ibid., 64.
54. *Collected Poetry*, 278
55. Ibid., 78, 79, lines 17, 19, 60
56. Ibid., 79, 78, lines 62–63, 41, 24.
57. *In His Own Voice*, 115.
58. Ibid., 116; Marling, *Merry Christmas*, 256.
59. Nissenbaum, *The Battle for Christmas*, 281, 273.
60. *In His Own Voice*, 120.
61. Ibid., 121.
62. Qtd. in Ronald Primeau, *Herbert Woodward Martin and the African American Tradition in Poetry* (Kent, Ohio: Kent State University Press, 2002), 159.
63. Ibid., 159.
64. *In His Own Voice*, 122.
65. Ibid., 129.
66. *Complete Stories*, 44.
67. *Collected Poetry*, 269, lines 17–20
68. Marling, *Merry Christmas*, 270.
69. Ibid., 273.
70. Ibid., 257.
71. *In His Own Voice*, 132.
72. Camp, *Closer to Freedom*, 65.
73. *Collected Poetry*, 105, lines 18, 32.
74. Ibid., 105, lines 15–16.
75. Ibid., 105, line 26.
76. Monika Elbert, "Women's Charity vs. Scientific Philanthropy in Sarah Orne Jewett," in *Our Sisters' Keepers: Nineteenth-Century Benevolence Literature by American Women*, ed. Jill Bergman and Debra Bernardi (Tuscaloosa: University of Alabama Press, 2005), 176.
77. Marling, *Merry Christmas*, 149.
78. Elbert, "Women's Charity," 181.
79. *Collected Poetry*, 174, lines 7–8.
80. Ibid., 174, line 13.
81. Ibid., 174, lines 15–16.
82. *Complete Stories*, 351.
83. Ibid., 352.
84. Ibid., 353.
85. Ibid.
86. Ibid., 354.
87. Ibid., 160.

88. Ibid.
89. Ibid., 160–61.
90. Ibid., 162.
91. Ibid., 161.
92. Ibid., 162.
93. "The Fourth of July and Race Outrages," *New York Times*, July 10, 1903, rpt. in *Norton Anthology of African American Literature*, ed. Henry Louis Gates and Nellie Y. McKay, 2nd ed. (New York: Norton, 2004), 928.
94. Ibid.
95. Ibid.
96. *Collected Poetry*, 218, line 65.
97. Ibid., 218, lines 64, 62, 47.

11

Creating a Representative Community

Identity in Paul Laurence Dunbar's In Old Plantation Days

WILLIE J. HARRELL JR.

I too believe a story is a story and try to make my characters "real live people." But I believe that characters in fiction should be what men and women are in real life,—the embodiment of a principle or idea.
—PAUL LAURENCE DUNBAR, LETTER TO ALICE RUTH MOORE,
MAY 23, 1895

BETWEEN 1898 AND 1904, Paul Laurence Dunbar published four volumes of short stories (*Folks from Dixie*, 1898; *The Strength of Gideon and Other Stories*, 1900; *In Old Plantation Days*, 1903; and *The Heart of Happy Hollow*, 1904), adding to his already abundant contribution to American literary studies. Since his death in 1906, scholars have investigated Dunbar's contribution to American literary studies through diverse scopes. Jay Martin and Gossie H. Hudson, for example, examined Dunbar's prose through an assortment of perspectives. Martin and Hudson's *The Paul Laurence Dunbar Reader* (1975) offered various interpretations of Dunbar's role as a writer and his relationship to his people. Martin and Hudson argued that Dunbar was the first African American writer to remove himself from "the influence of racial convention" in America and to appreciate his "identity on its own terms."[1] Herbert Woodward Martin and Ronald Primeau's *In His Own Voice: The Dramatic and Other Uncollected Works of Paul Laurence Dunbar* (2002) continued the examination of some of Dunbar's previously uncollected works to conclude that Dunbar protested against the injustice and the "accommodationist acceptance of slavery and its" effects.[2] More recently, Gene Andrew Jarrett and Thomas Lewis Morgan, in *The Complete Stories of Paul Laurence Dunbar* (2005), find in Dunbar's fiction an articulation of "the social and racial limitations that existed for African Americans" during his time.[3]

To position Dunbar's creativity in its rightful place in historical and literary studies, an examination of the ways in which he sought to represent the black community through his contribution to the short-story genre is of utmost importance. Not available in collections of his work until recently, many of Dunbar's short stories began appearing in popular magazines in the 1890s and often represented the voices of African American characters in both the North and the South.[4] The urgent need to give a voice to the black community was a significant theme in the African American literature around Dunbar's time. Not receiving the critical attention it deserves, Dunbar's short fiction has been regarded as "formulaic, conventional, and pedestrian."[5] Martin and Primeau have argued that Dunbar's short fiction demonstrates his command of an array of dialects, his appreciation of short-fiction conventions, and an "ironic commentary on slavery as well as the hypocrisy of much 'charitable' activity in a society where class division remained sharply drawn."[6]

Dunbar scholarship has had and continues to have a significant impact within and beyond the academy, and for this reason there is an extraordinary demand for the distribution, examination, and assessment of this scholarship. By examining his short stories through the context of community, for example, we are forced to struggle with both the disparaging effects of the "happy darky" myth and the positive effects of community cohesiveness. Dunbar believed that there were special temperaments in the black community that needed to be illustrated by one of the race. Therefore, in his short stories, Dunbar offered his reading public perceptive representations of American racial tensions that he could not offer in his longer fiction.[7] Since his novels, with the exception of *The Sport of the Gods,* appeared not to be racially motivated, Dunbar had an altogether different purpose in his short fiction: he sought to fashion black identity to fulfill the need for the creation of a representative black community. Focusing on Dunbar's short stories published in *In Old Plantation Days,* this chapter adds to the ongoing critical analysis of Dunbar's works and argues that Dunbar's development of representation of black life is keenly presented through the context of community building. It seeks to reveal the complex and often conflicting process of dissemination that characterized and still characterizes the perpetual struggle of representing blackness in ways that some may see as disruptive to forms of black Americanisms. This discussion begins where many of the chapters in this volume begin: Dunbar's use of dialect.

Critics have argued that Dunbar's use of dialect inspired a new black identity. His employment of dialect is rooted in the connection between community and identity. "The southern people have eaten me up wonderfully," he wrote to his mother, Matilda Dunbar, on August 25, 1896, during a reading tour.[8] Although he believed that his representation was graciously received in the black community, many believed Dunbar to be reinforcing the already pejorative image of blackness in America. By employing dialect in his efforts to forge a community, does Dunbar intend to educate whites about the minority linguistic form from the perspective of a black man? Is this a form of internal protection from the dominant hegemonic impositions of white America? Or it is a sort of external restraint, inasmuch as it limits the opportunities of the race? Gavin Jones rightfully argues that Dunbar could only gain literary success by "imitating the predominantly white literary imitation of black speech."[9] Dunbar's employment of dialect was more than simply the reiteration of a "minstrel paradigm" of black inferiority; he cleverly redirects the established "literary conventions" and becomes an astute "overturner of racist stereotypes, and a sensitive recorder of the multiple facets of black consciousness at the turn of the century."[10] Inherent, then, in Dunbar's *In Old Plantation Days* is a negation of the racist ideologies of his time that suggested the innate idiocy and brutish character of the black identity, as his command of language—his succinct and resolute style—confronts the characterizations of authors such as Joel Chandler Harris, Thomas Nelson Page, and Ruth McEnery Stuart. However Dunbar's use of dialect may have varied from that of the Harris-Page-Stuart era, the dialect structure in his short fiction has one constant feature: meaning. The accessibility of black dialect is to a large degree a provision for the implementation of one possible identity alternative, that is, to live in a community where one's experience is formed, understood, and judged by its patterns of speech. No doubt, then, Dunbar's use of dialect in *In Old Plantation Days* positions a persuasive tradition of moral elevation of which he himself was very much a part. His use of dialect and the seemingly "happy darky" was neither an expression of conformity to white American standards nor simply a marketing technique used to engage white readership. Nor did Dunbar's genius and imaginative courage totally deny the romantic or sentimental characterizations of his culture's survivalism. Understanding that the caricatures that white America perpetuated would have to be forcefully removed, Dunbar's portrayal of black reality and identity in *In Old Plantation Days* showed the race in a positive way: it did not mimic or degrade blacks but attempted to prevail over the effect of the centuries-old hegemonic structure of racism that was used to disadvantage the race.

As much as Dunbar struggled to be recognized in a range of genres—short stories, novels, plays, musicals, and essays—he saw himself above all as a poet and found himself challenged to develop a positive representation of his people. Of his volumes of short fiction, the most successful in terms of sales was *In Old Plantation Days*. This can mainly be attributed to his reviewers' acknowledgement of the "optimistic theme of potential interracial peace."[11] Published in 1903, *In Old Plantation Days* developed the distinction between the social and the physical implications of a black community in America during slavery. The volume consisted of twenty-five tales that attempted to establish a black community by placing the everyday trials and tribulations that blacks endured into a recognizable experience. Therefore, community building in *In Old Plantation Days* is directed at the enhancement of identity among the slaves on the plantations. Dunbar sought not to transform the existing discourse of white American writers but to influence fundamental values in changing the public view of the "happy darky." As Jarrett and Morgan suggest, Dunbar resisted "pastoral and minstrel imagery" in his short fiction.[12]

Dunbar began publishing his short fiction during an era that saw both the continuation of established trends of racial characterizations in American literature and the incorporation of novel advancements. Local color realism was in literary vogue in the 1880s, and getting published at all was virtually impossible, regardless of the handicap imposed by blackness, if one did not conform to the established set of narratives. However, by the time *In Old Plantation Days* was published, Dunbar was already an established poet and was able to incorporate subtle protests in his works. He believed that African Americans had to begin to think and operate in terms of entirely new and considerably diverse forms of expression that departed significantly from those of white American writers. Because of their representations of black life, Dunbar realized that the initiative for such changes in the mind-set of the reading public had to come from within the black community. Initially, his short stories seem to fit into the plantation tradition of American fiction. This type of writing sought to create an appealing image of the "happy days" of slavery in the "South through its use of dialect, caricatures, and stereotypes of Black life."[13] Dunbar used moral characters and virtues made public by the dominant social class to address the concerns and problems blacks faced. He refracted these concerns through the lens of his characters' plight in *In Old Plantation Days*. Although the old plantation days had since passed, Dunbar felt that he had a stake in asserting control over the flow, direction, and acceptance of the continuing development of the black community he presented in the stories. Therefore, the cornerstone of his efforts in his short fiction was to uplift the race. As many of his short stories show, Dunbar sought to explore the coldhearted realities that in historical verity characterized black life in turn-of-the-century America. In *In Old Plantation Days*, there are tales that highlight the strength of women and introduce gender politics ("Aunt Tempe's Triumph," "Aunt Tempe's Revenge," "The Brief Cure of Aunt Fanny"), the strength of religion as a community-building vehicle ("The Walls of Jericho," "How Brother Parker Fell from Grace," "The Trousers," "The Last Fiddling of Mordaunt's Jim"), the rebellious slave ("Mr. Groby's Slippery Gift"), and the importance of conjuring to the slave community ("The Conjuring Contest," "Dandy Jim's Conjure Scare"), as well as several other notable tales with considerable power.

Dunbar was born when the failure of Reconstruction was creating institutionalized racism. The son of former Kentucky slaves, Dunbar's conscientious effort to represent his race brought him face to face with American mainstream prejudice and discrimination and the demands to meet its numerous burdens. This would require social change in the American mainstream consciousness; therefore, Dunbar's attempts to represent a black identity became a channel to construct an alternate space for theorization of discrimination and prejudice against blacks, one that allowed African Americans to critique the constraints of representational categories currently unavailable to them.[14] Does Dunbar go against the need for positive representations of black identity by creating characters that seemingly fit the "happy darky" trope? Even if Dunbar was not aware of it, many of his short stories served to create a representative community by forging more than an individual self. In these short stories, Dunbar's focus moves beyond the characterization of the "happy darky" or the subservient Negro to larger sociopolitical issues faced by the turn-of-the-century black community. His use of dialect, for example, intends not simply to respond to blacks' historical voicelessness but to reinforce his protest by bringing to light the hardships of their plight. In his quest to create a representative black community, Dunbar constructs a visionary language and liberation philosophy from the drudges of American racism that began to foster a sense of cohesiveness within the black community. The central problem, then, for Dunbar was the construction of an elevated black consciousness of the racial stereotypes that had been formulated by whites.

Dunbar's attempts to create a representative black community were embedded within a cultural matrix, as he certainly understood that he could not represent the black community without participating in the ongoing debate about race that began when the first twenty Africans became indentured servants. Therefore, by the time Dunbar began to publish his short fiction, the agenda to affirm whiteness at the expense of blackness had been ongoing for nearly three centuries, and throughout the years it had taken on numerous manifestations. *In Old Plantation Days* was intended to show that blacks were not struggling with whites for political rights and that social cohesion among the black community was not high on white America's agenda at the time. If the black community was defined in political, social, and economic terms by whites, then what chance would blacks have to create a community of uplift on their own? This was the problem for Dunbar. According to Roland Barthes, "Representation is not directly defined by imitation: even if we were to get rid of the notions of 'reality' and 'verisimilitude' and 'copy,' there would still be 'representation,' so long as a subject (author, reader, spectator, observer) directed his [or her] *gaze* toward a horizon and there projected the base of a triangle of which his [or her] eye (or his [or her] mind) would be apex."[15] In stories such as "A Supper by Proxy" and "Mr. Groby's Slippery Gift" in *In Old Plantation Days,* Dunbar examines the abundant hardships slaves experienced and illustrates that while some slaves sought to reassure their masters of their contentment, most secretly worked against the institution of slavery.[16]

The desire for community building suggests that people of African extraction see themselves with invigorating strength, that they recognize their personal struggles as being part of the greater efforts of the community they are laboring to strengthen. Those who contribute to this goal, however, can differ extensively in how willing they are to aid in strengthening the community. As is evident in many of his short stories, Dunbar realizes that no overarching norms by which communities could be judged existed—or at any rate, no acceptable norms existed for representing the black community and the degradation they suffered. Martin suggests that Dunbar vigorously and insistently sought to present the struggles of his people "even while he suffered personally from the way in which both his literary career and also his defenses of his people brought him into contact with the racism so pronounced in American culture in the 1890s."[17] Others, however, as Laval Todd Duncan notes, have argued that during his lifetime, Dunbar was seen as a "literary Uncle Tom."[18] Some Harlem Renaissance writers, such as William Stanley Braithwaite, believed that Dunbar's postbellum/pre-Renaissance fiction "dealt only successfully with the same world that gave him the inspiration for his dialect poems."[19] True, Dunbar was aware of the black struggle against white hegemony. Perhaps this is why he was able to draw from those toils knowledge and a desire to appeal to the general public about the social wrongs done to them. *In Old Plantation Days,* for example, is used to enlighten the world of African Americans' plight, to foster a sense of community in which the characters have dignity and the mind-set of communal accountability. African Americans around the turn of the century faced an identity crisis partly because Reconstruction, which was supposedly meant to help them survive without the aid of the master-slave system, had failed. Dunbar positions *In Old Plantation Days* as a vehicle to bring to light the appalling social conditions facing the race. He believed that his artistry "express[ed] the inmost thoughts and feelings of the Negro . . . because literature was the only acceptable form of protest for the Negro" during his time.[20]

Scholars have not been able to confidently identify Dunbar's contribution to the short-story genre. Bert Bender notes that Dunbar reached a "full-blown lyricism in his short fiction." Bender writes: "Dunbar published stories which were more directly expressive of the emotional discontent in black America. These stories are informed by a lyric impulse—Dunbar's dream of freedom and equality for his people—and the impulse arises in reaction to various kinds of real oppression."[21] Jarrett and Morgan, however, suggest that Dunbar "articulated the social and racial limitations that existed for African Americans, while developing multidimensional and positive portrayals of African Americans in order to revise the literary norms of racial presentation."[22] Aunt Tempe and Brother Parker are the most important characters among the pious slaves presented in the stories in *In Old Plantation Days* and are the towers of strength in the life of the slave community. The stories in *In Old Plantation Days* read much like vignettes about the lives of the slaves on the plantations. The first half of these stories are centered on the Mordaunt plantation, while the second half are devoted to Curtis's neighborhood and various neighborhoods nearby. In many of the stories, Dunbar shows us the incidents in the characters' lives that help to shape their identities; however, the stories do not appear in chronological order. For example, when we first meet the Reverend Parker, he is an eighty-year-old preacher on Mordaunt's plantation who is struggling not only with trying to keep the slaves on the path to righteousness but also with trying to maintain his own dignity. In a later story, "How Brother Parker Fell from Grace," we are given a glimpse of Parker as a younger man and how he fell from grace. Parker dies in another tale, "The Last Fiddling of Mordaunt's Jim," but resurfaces in "Mr. Groby's Slippery Gift." Read together, these stories help the reader envision the community through frames.

What is missing in Dunbar's *In Old Plantation Days*, though, is the romanticism and sentimentality of slavery that slave narrators painted for readers in their first-person narratives of the late eighteenth and nineteenth centuries. The dark sides of slavery as an institution are not revealed at all in the stories. Much like female slave narrators, however, Dunbar painstakingly demonstrates the gender politics on the plantations. Aunt Tempe, on Mordaunt's plantation, for example, symbolically acts to redefine gender politics in the first two stories of the collection. Her strength, even though we are led to believe that she is manipulative, is an important aspect of community. Like Harriet Jacobs's grandmother in her 1861 *Incidents in the Life of a Slave Girl, Written by Herself,* Aunt Tempe's position on Mordaunt's plantation gives her certain advantages: strength and self-determination. As the Mordaunt family prepares for the marriage of Miss Eliza, Aunt Tempe, "chief authority and owner-in-general" of the festivities,[23] is worried because she wants to be the one to give her "Lammy" away. Aunt Tempe's actions here contradict the institution of marriage because the father of the bride (or another male figure in the family) is the one who is normally responsible for offering his daughter in marriage.

The discussion of Aunt Tempe is important because it shows the discourse of community as an enabling paradigm for other repressed discourses such as feminism. Aunt Tempe's spirit is solid. She is strong; forthright; and determined to have her way, not to be taken advantage of, and to survive. The character of Aunt Tempe deconstructs the myth that black women were merely mammies without a voice. Her battle with Mordaunt—the fight for representation, self-definition, and respect—is no doubt a battle that black women fought, individually and collectively, and constantly. Even Mordaunt acknowledges the power Aunt Tempe wields over his plantation. "The fact is," he tells her, "half the time I don't know who's running this plantation, you or I. You boss the whole household round, and 'the quarters' mind you better than they do the preacher. Plague take my buttons if I don't think they're afraid you'll conjure them!"[24] Defiant to the very end, Aunt Tempe does not give up. Just before Mordaunt is about to give his daughter away, she interferes. Her acts reflect not so much her devotion and her determination to fulfill the role of the black mammy as her desire to control the lives of both the slaves and the whites on the plantation. Aunt Tempe's strength and self-reliance surface in several of the tales in this volume in the form of other marginalized female characters: Martha in "The Memory of Martha," Aunt Fanny in "The Brief Cure of Aunt Fanny," Anna Maria in "The Way of a Woman," and Maria Ann Gibbs and Lucindy Woodyard in "The Defection of Maria Ann Gibbs." All these women seek to achieve one of two goals: either they seek to acquire some kind of power or they seek to preserve and legitimize what power they have been able to acquire.

Focusing on the problems within the black community caused by the brutal limitations of evangelical religion, several stories in *In Old Plantation Days* highlight the significance of religion in community and social cohesion. Dunbar's own religious idiom helps to shape his artistic expression in these tales as his writing becomes an outlet for religious expression. One of Dunbar's boldest representations of black religious strength is the devout vicar Brother Parker. Parker, raised to be a fighter, was strong in his religious exhortations to the slaves on Mordaunt's plantation. In the stories that center on the life of Parker, religion becomes a positive form of community. In "The Walls of Jericho," for example, the efforts of social cohesion are introduced through the elitist notions held by Parker, who exhibits a profound interest in understanding black life on the plantation. Readers are told that Parker has always been "faithful to his flock, constant in attendance and careful of their welfare."[25]

"The Walls of Jericho," unique because of its allusions to the biblical account of the destruction of the ancient city of Jericho, is perhaps the most illuminating and significant tale of community and social cohesion in the collection. Dunbar's views on black religiosity shine through his use of biblical imagery in the tale. In the biblical story, the walls of Jericho were breached because of the deeds of Joshua, Moses's successor. Joshua told the Israelites to march around the fortified city seven times until the walls tumbled down. After the Israelites laid siege to the walls of Jericho, Joshua cursed the city. "And Joshua charged the people with an oath at that time, saying: 'Cursed be the man before the Lord that riseth up and buildeth this city, even Jericho; with the loss of his first-born shall he lay the foundation thereof, and with the loss of his youngest son shall he set up the gates of it.'"[26] In Dunbar's story, the young Johnson, a free Negro and a "mighty preacher,"[27] obtains permission to hold religious meetings in the woods neighboring Mordaunt's plantation. Because of Johnson's theatrics, Parker's flock deserts him and finds consolation in the young preacher's voice and influence. Johnson asks the worshipers to bring baskets to the nightly services so that they may "serve the body while they saved the soul." The story, then, is centered on the struggle between the old and accepted religious fervor and the new preaching offered by Johnson. "The Walls of Jericho" is impressive in its dramatization of the fervor of the meetings. Every night at the pinnacle of his theatrics, Johnson commands that the baskets be opened, and "following the example of the children of Israel," he asks the parishioners to perform the traditional "march, munching their food, round and round the inclosure, as their Biblical archetypes had marched around the walls of Jericho."[28] Parker, however, is discerning and wise enough to know that the participants are entirely ignorant of the spiritual implications of the performance. "Oh, brothahs, an' sistahs, let us a-ma'ch erroun' de walls o' Jericho to-night seven times, and' a-eatin' o' de food dat the Lawd has pervided us wid," Johnson exhorts. The walls of Johnson's Jericho represent sin, although readers are not told what kind of sin. "Rise up, fu' de Jericho walls o' sin is a-stan'in.'"[29] The story, then, represents a conflict between religious fervor and natural physical desire.

Parker believes the march, which is presented as a religious obligation rather than a traditional practice, to be a farce, a mockery of God. "Dem folks don't know what dey're doin'," he proclaims.[30] Representing the spiritual interests of the plantation, Parker feels that attending Johnson's meetings debases him. However, Parker, Dunbar writes, is "a diplomat" and bears his loss well.[31] In Parker we see a strong claim that the special arrangements made by Johnson to accommodate the religious beliefs of the slaves are demanded by virtue. Tricked into attending one of the meetings by Tom Mordaunt and one of his friends, Master Ralph, Parker attends one of Johnson's meetings only to find that—in a twist of fate—he is the one who seems to be converted by the young preacher's spiritualism. "He found himself joyous," Dunbar writes, "and when Johnson arose on the wings of his eloquence it was Parker's loud 'Amen' which set fire to all the throng."[32] As they begin to march around the "walls of Jericho," something strange happens. Unbeknownst to Parker, Ralph and Tom had previously cut the trees surrounding the figurative forest of Jericho. When the participants are given the order to march, Ralph and Tom blow a loud horn and send the falling trees crashing down, frightening all, even the Reverend Johnson. Parker, however, exhorts his congregation to "Stan' still, stan' still, I say, an' see de salvation."[33] It is Parker's strength, wisdom, and guidance that show Johnson to be a coward, and Parker's meeting house again fills, and the community he worked so hard to construct is reestablished. Parker's conception of recognition is at the root of the Hegelian concept of lordship and bondage in *The Phenomenology of Spirit*. For example, Parker believes that his identity as *the* plantation preacher is established in part by his congregation's acknowledgment of his status as a white man's preacher. Parker cannot be lord of his flock and think of himself in such a manner unless his flock—along with his white master—treats him as such.

The next story in the volume, "How Brother Parker Fell from Grace," also intertwines biblical text and black religious traditions. Jarrett and Morgan's argument that religion in the "slave quarters tends to exhibit the kind of problems found in any society, including envy and sin"[34] can be aptly applied to "How Brother Parker Fell from Grace." In this tale, we are introduced to the younger Parker, who is so "earnest for the spiritual welfare of his fellow-servants that his watchful ministrations bec[ome] a nuisance and a bore" but eventually falls from grace. After his sermon one Sunday morning, Parker seeks out those who went "erway on some dev'ment."[35] Although Dunbar portrays Parker as an extremely gifted preacher, he is not beyond human guile: his negligence and pride cause him to play cards on the Sabbath when challenged by others who Parker feels have also "fallen from grace." The biblical allusion here is to Galatians 5:4, when Paul says: "You have been severed from Christ, you who are seeking to be justified by law; you have fallen from grace." The question to be raised here is, does a true child of Christ ever fall from his grace? For centuries, African Americans were taught that they must live up to an accepted form of behavior in order to preserve their place in the family of God. Likewise, they were taught that one could fall from grace and be forever lost. What Dunbar suggests in this story is that falling from grace does not mean that one's righteousness before God is lost as well. The sinners on the plantation trick Parker into playing cards: "I play you thee games fu' de Gospel's sake." It seems to be his desire to sin, but in actuality he longs to teach the sinners a lesson and bring them back into the good grace of his flock. When Mordaunt is summoned to witness Parker's sin, he is angered "at the hypocrisy of a trusted servant." Dunbar, then, explores the question, what does it mean to fall from grace? The answer is not readily found in the story. What Parker comes to terms with, however, is that the answer lies neither in religion nor in tradition, but in his own spirituality. Mordaunt reminds him of this: "There are times when we've got to meet the devil on his own ground and fight him with his own weapons. . . . But it isn't safe to go into the devil's camp too often."[36] Religion is thus politicized and becomes a matter of prime concern for Mordaunt and his slaves. What is evident in the story is Dunbar's message of reconciliation. If the grace of God is an undeserved favor, then how can one lose it? Parker comes to realize that one cannot.

The most deeply moving, literary, and metaphorical story in the collection is "The Last Fiddling of Mordaunt's Jim." In this tale, Parker becomes ill and Jim, who is the "prime mover in every bit of deviltry" on the plantation, believes that his fiddling and the merriment it creates in the slave quarters are the cause of Parker's sickness. Jim decides, then, to stop playing his fiddle; however, when Parker recovers, Jim begins "o' celebratin'" Parker's "gittin' well." Still bedridden, Parker sends for Jim and apologizes for chastising him earlier for his fiddling. Jim, the "contrite sinner," undergoes a conversion of a mystical sort. Later in the night, Parker's health worsens, and Mandy, Jim's wife, attempts to nurse him. After locking himself in his quarters, Jim "sat there, it seemed, a long while, when suddenly out of the stillness of the night a faint sound struck on his ears. It was as if someone far away were fiddling, fiddling a wild, weird tune. Jim sat bold upright, and the sweat broke out upon his face in great cold drops. He waited. The fiddler came nearer."[37] Terrified and frightened for his life, Jim smashes his fiddle against a chair and cries: "Lawd, Lawd, spaih me, an' I'll nevah fiddle ergin!" The music slowly fades into silence. Later, Jim receives word that Parker has died, and Jim becomes convinced that the devil "tried to fiddle [his] soul erway to hell" and that he would have succeeded had not Jim wrestled in prayer. "From that moment on," Dunbar reveals, "Jim was a pious man."[38] To describe Jim as a "contrite sinner" is ideologically correct insofar as it refers to African American beliefs concerning the Sabbath. "The Last Fiddling of Mordaunt's Jim" ends, however, with a confluence of allegory. Readers find out that Parker's death achieves what he in life could not: conversion of the most "contrite sinner" to the path of righteousness.

Gideon Stone, the same Gideon who appeared in *The Strength of Gideon* (1900), surfaces in *In Old Plantation Days*. Gideon arrives in Washington, D.C., and quickly realizes that racism has become institutionalized in the town. In "The Finding of Martha," Gideon travels to Washington with an understanding that his duty "toward his fellows," much like that of Dunbar himself, "was plain." But he also has another motive: to find his wife, Martha, who left five years earlier seeking freedom among the Union soldiers. Gideon, who we discover in "The Strength of Gideon" carries the name of one of the most prominent heroes in the Bible, is described as an advocate for his people: "Their griefs were mirrored in his own sorrow, and every wail of theirs was but the echo of his own heart cry. He drew people to him by the force of his sympathetic understanding of their woes, and even those who came for his help and counsel went away asking how so young a man could feel and know so much."[39] After finding a congregation in a city troubled by racial tensions, some of the older women in the community seek to find Gideon a wife. They recognize something abnormal, something perplexing and strange, about Gideon's celibacy. It is their understanding that a young devoted preacher like Gideon is "mos'ly the marryinest kin." When they approach Gideon with their concerns about finding him a wife, however, he simply responds: "There's time enough; oh, there's time enough."[40] Although Gideon does not believe in his heart that it will happen, he and Martha do eventually reunite and remarry. Unquestionably, then, the recurrent biblical allusions in *In Old Plantation Days* show that the Bible and its interpretation functioned as an essential model of discourse in the lives of southern slaves.

Although only two tales in *In Old Plantation Days* concern conjuring, the mystical performance of feats requiring the assistance of supernatural powers or forces, there are elements that suggest Dunbar uses the subject of conjuring to serve as a means of fostering community. Dunbar participates in the public portrayal of conjuring, which was a pervasive part of nineteenth-century black life and the focus of writers such as Charles W. Chesnutt. In his *The Conjure Woman* (1899), Chesnutt invents a form for black authority—the refusal to romanticize slave life or the Old South—that allows him to avoid confronting the already established white theories concerning the power of literary traditions (since literary traditions emerge from an oral rather than written tradition). This literary tradition allows him to portray the black plantation community effectively.[41] In the African American community, conjuring requires the possession of "supernatural power by gifted professionals" and is "the means by which persons could tap that power to make it 'work' for them."[42] The idea of conjuring, then, is explicitly linked to the institution of slavery.

Dunbar's "Dandy Jim's Conjure Scare" offers an ideal example of the way in which slaves used conjuring not only as an escape from reality but also for the betterment of the black community. The story is about a slave named Dandy Jim who believes that he has been "conjured" because he is interested in another slave's girlfriend. Jim, a "dark-skinned valet," takes pride in his personal appearance and is "little less elegant than the white man himself." Jim is always well dressed and swift and responsive on his feet. One morning, however, Jim's master notices a change and is surprised to see his slave looking unkempt and dejected. "Why, you look like you'd been getting religion," says Master Henry. Jim feels, however, that his soul has somehow been affected by conjuring. Therefore, he asks his master for a silver dime. Placed in his shoe, the dime will tell him whether or not he has been cursed. However, before Jim can test the silver dime, he is confronted by Sam, who whips Jim.[43] Jim rejoices in the beating he receives from Sam, as he believes that it means Sam did not place a curse on him. As we have seen with Tom Mordaunt and Parker, white acceptance is a significant factor in the creation of a black community. Jim's tale becomes a form of conjure of its own, as he attempts to convince his master that he has been "conjured."

In "The Conjuring Contest," Mam' Henry, "the plantation oracle," provides a connection between black women, conjuring, and literary authority. Dunbar offers readers a tale of conjuring women who serve as a source of power. For the slaves who believe in conjuring, there is a sort of consolation in it, for when all else fails, conjuring is the one thing that can be relied upon to solve the problems facing them. Her authority as a conjurer allows Mam' Henry to exert great influence over the rest of the slaves on the plantation. When Bob, Maria's son, unexpectedly gives up his courtship of Viney to date another woman, Cassie, Mam' Henry intervenes. Thinking that conjuring is the only thing that would cause Bob to date Cassie, Mam' Henry offers her services to counteract the spell. Mam' Henry sees Bob's decision as the act of an untrustworthy individual and believes that he shames Maria's name. She tells Maria to put a piece of silver in Bob's shoe; if the silver turns black, she warns, Bob is "cotched bad." The silver turns as "dark as copper," and Mam' Henry advises Maria to visit Doctor Bass, "de conju' doctah."[44] Soon the spell on Bob is removed, and he and Viney resume their courtship. In Mam' Henry's capacity as advisor and conjurer, she manages to preserve a feminist strategy that validates black female authority. Dunbar's employment of conjuring in these two tales in *In Old Plantation Days* places the suffering of the enslaved Africans in a cultural diasporic gamut.

Other notable themes in the volume include injustice and the psychological consequences of masters and slaves ("A Supper by Proxy," "Mr. Groby's Slippery Gift") and rejection of one's own blackness as opposed to faith that better days lie ahead for blacks ("A Blessed Deceit," "Who Stands for the Gods"). By far, *In Old Plantation Days* is Dunbar's best volume of short stories, yet it is evident from the few scholarly inquiries that have been made into it that very few academics have found it to be a notable addition to his oeuvre. *In Old Plantation Days*, which appeared eleven years after Dunbar's first volume of poetry and three years after his first novel, marked the height of his creativity as a writer of short fiction and signifies his accountability as a representative of his race. However, Dunbar understood that if one is to represent the black community, one must not regard it as backward in its speech, ignorant, and barbaric. In *In Old Plantation Days*, Dunbar demonstrated that the black community has an independent voice, that its voice is expressed in its culture, and that only when that voice is heard will blacks be respected and understood as a cultural group. Dunbar also realized that, partly because of white authors' characterizations of the black voice, the black community had not garnered any appreciation or respect. *In Old Plantation Days* highlights the black community's ability to survive and to develop and maintain its heritage and traditions in spite of the oppression of slavery and discrimination in America. If we study it through this lens, we will be begin to see that *In Old Plantation Days* celebrates the quintessence of the black community's vibrant, compassionate, and religious spirit in Dunbar's illustration of its resilience, its pride, its courage, and indeed its strength.

Notes

1. *The Paul Laurence Dunbar Reader: A Selection of the Best of Paul Laurence Dunbar's Poetry and Prose, Including Writings Never Before Available in Book Form*, ed. Jay Martin and Gossie H. Hudson (New York: Dodd, Mead, 1975), 22.
2. Herbert Woodward Martin and Ronald Primeau, introduction to *In His Own Voice: The Dramatic and Other Uncollected Works of Paul Laurence Dunbar* (Athens: Ohio University Press, 2002), xix.
3. Gene Andrew Jarrett and Thomas Lewis Morgan, introduction to *The Complete Stories of Paul Laurence Dunbar* (Athens: Ohio University Press, 2005), xxxix.
4. Many of these did not appear in collections of Dunbar's work until the publication of Martin and Hudson's *The Paul Laurence Dunbar Reader*, Martin and Primeau's *In His Own Voice*, and Jarrett and Morgan's *The Complete Stories of Paul Laurence Dunbar*.
5. Yolanda Pierce, "That Old Time Religion: Christian Faith in Dunbar's 'The Strength of Gideon,'" *African American Review* 41 (2007): 313.
6. *In His Own Voice*, 215–16.
7. Jarrett and Morgan, introduction, xviii.
8. *Dunbar Reader*, 436.
9. Gavin Jones, *Strange Talk: The Politics of Dialect Literature in Gilded Age America* (Berkeley: University of California Press, 1999), 183.
10. Ibid., 184.
11. Jarrett and Morgan, introduction, xxx.
12. Ibid., xxxix.
13. Pierce, "That Old Time Religion," 313.
14. Thomas L. Morgan, "The City as Refuge: Constructing Urban Blackness in Paul Laurence Dunbar's *The Sport of the Gods* and James Weldon Johnson's *The Autobiography of an Ex-Colored Man*," *African American Review* 38, no. 2 (2004): 214.
15. Roland Barthes, "Diderot, Brecht, Eisenstein," in *The Responsibility of Forms: Critical Essays on Music, Art, and Representation*, trans. Richard Howard (New York: Hill and Wang, 1985), 89–90.
16. Felton O. Best, *Crossing the Color Line: A Biography of Paul Laurence Dunbar, 1872–1906* (Dubuque, Iowa: Kendall/Hunt, 1996), 118.
17. Jay Martin, "Paul Laurence Dunbar: Biography through Letters," foreword to *A Singer in the Dawn: Reinterpretations of Paul Laurence Dunbar* (New York: Dodd, Mead, 1975), 14.
18. Laval Todd Duncan, "White Audience, Black Artist: Paul Laurence Dunbar and the Context of Entrapment" (PhD diss., Harvard University, 1973), ii.
19. William Stanley Braithwaite, "The Negro in American Literature," in *Double-Take: A Revisionist Harlem Renaissance Anthology*, ed. Venetria K. Patton and Maureen Honey (New Brunswick, N.J.: Rutgers University Press, 2001), 15.
20. *Dunbar Reader*, 429
21. Bert Bender, "The Lyrical Short Fiction of Dunbar and Chesnutt," in *A Singer in the Dawn*, 217, 212.
22. Jarrett and Morgan, introduction, xxxix.
23. *Complete Stories*, 202.
24. Ibid., 202–3.
25. Ibid., 211.
26. Josh. 6:26.
27. *Complete Stories*, 212.
28. Ibid., 213.

29. Ibid., 213.
30. Ibid., 214.
31. Ibid., 213.
32. Ibid., 215.
33. Ibid., 215.
34. Jarrett and Morgan, introduction, xxix
35. *Complete Stories*, 216, 217.
36. Ibid., 218, 219, 220.
37. Ibid., 224.
38. Ibid., 226, 227.
39. Ibid., 289.
40. Ibid., 290, 291.
41. Majorie Pryse, "Introduction: Zora Neale Hurston, Alice Walker, and the 'Ancient Power' of Black Women," in *Conjuring: Black Women, Fiction and Literary Tradition*, ed. Majorie Pryse and Hortense J. Spillers (Bloomington: Indiana University Press, 1985), 10.
42. Yvonne P. Chireau, *Black Magic: Religion and the African American Conjuring Tradition* (Berkeley: University of California Press, 2003), 35.
43. *Complete Stories*, 254, 257.
44. Ibid., 250, 251.

PART III

Novels, Identity, and Representation

12
Memory and Repression in Paul Laurence Dunbar's The Sport of the Gods

Jeannine King

Modern life begins with slavery.... These things had to be addressed by black people a long time ago. Certain kinds of dissolution, the loss of and the need to reconstruct certain kinds of stability. Certain kinds of madness, deliberately going mad, ... "in order not to lose your mind." These strategies for survival made the truly modern person. They're a response to predatory western phenomena. You can call it an ideology and an economy, what it is is a pathology.
—Toni Morrison,
 "Living Memory: A Meeting with Toni Morrison"

Paul Laurence Dunbar's *The Sport of the Gods* depicts postbellum declension as Dunbar, beneath the cloak of the plantation novel, tells a tale of national tragedy: the crime of slavery, the false justice of emancipation, and the impossibility of freedom. It is not a novel of resistance. Nor is it a complete submission to Thomas Nelson Page's construct of the plantation narrative and the attendant notions of black subordination and white paternalism. It is a novel of psychological repression and eruption, of subverted violence and memory, and of the inner conflict of the newly emancipated African American. Using the framework of African American migration, Dunbar explores the topography of memory and forgetting in the interstitial spaces of the "new" South and the "corrupt" North. These spaces bleed into the other, creating strange couplings of gambling halls and deserted plantations, urban theaters and southern penitentiaries. In *The Sport of the Gods,* haunted by the unexamined past, the Hamiltons begin to see their social positions with a darker consciousness. The upheaval of the southern order has an apocalyptic tenor as "a good Negro family" moves from exile to revelation.

The phenomenon of trauma has been mapped in a variety of discourses, including psychology, politics, sociology, and history. The work of scholars such as Cathy Caruth, Dominick LaCapra, Shoshana Felman, Dori Laub, and Ron Eyerman attests to the breadth of this field of inquiry. In this chapter, I focus on the trauma of slavery. Ron Eyerman underscores the lasting damage of slavery. He writes, "Slavery was traumatic in retrospect, and formed a 'primal scene' which could, potentially, unite all 'African Americans' in the United States, whether or not they had themselves been slaves or had any knowledge of or feeling for Africa."[1]

One aspect of slave trauma is psychological repression. In *A Dictionary of Psychology*, psychological repression is defined as a "*defence mechanism* whereby unacceptable thoughts, feelings, or wishes are banished from *consciousness*. . . . According to Sigmund Freud, the essence of repression lies simply in turning something away, and keeping it at a distance, from the conscious."[2] This turning away has specific implications within the context of African American history. Through dehumanization, slavery sought to repress the instinct to question, to resist, to love. While this endeavor failed in many respects, it did create a slave pathology, one that Toni Morrison attributes to "predatory Western phenomena."[3] An example of these pathology-creating phenomena is the cultural narrative of tradition that works as a repressive structure on the psyches of African Americans, limiting their ability to speak their own truth. This master narrative becomes one of the most insidious agents of domination. The narrative of legal, historical, and psychological "truth," it attempts to make the victim complicit in this exercise of power. The plantation narrative, in portraying slavery as a benevolent institution, parallels this cultural narrative.

In depicting the psychological impact of domination, Dunbar's writing invokes and upsets the model of the plantation narrative. Furthermore, it presages the work of Richard Wright and other writers of African American realism. Almost half a century later in *Native Son*, Wright would describe the "white force" as a power so pervasive that it becomes a part of the environment. This presence undoes Bigger, the embattled protagonist. "'Well, they own everything. They choke you off the face of the earth. They like God.' . . . To Bigger and his kind white people were not really people; they were a sort of great natural force, like a stormy sky looming overhead, or like a deep swirling river stretching suddenly at one's feet in the dark. As long as he and his black folks did not go beyond certain limits, there was no need to fear that white force."[4] In Dunbar's work, the white force is also powerful. Whites are the arbiters of fate, and the souls of black folks merely sport.

The physical methods of slavery can be clearly delineated. Slave masters held African Americans captive and attempted to control and exploit their bodies. More ambiguous is the psychological damage of slavery: the submission and repression of desire, belief, memory, and subjectivity. In repressing these natural expressions of self, slavery created psychic disorder. One facet of this disorder is repressed memory. Often portrayed as forgetting, this repressed memory was still at work after emancipation. The tension between remembering and forgetting was so strong in the 1880s that African American leaders Frederick Douglass and Alexander Crummell addressed it publicly. According to David Blight, "Douglass and Crummell shared a sense of the dangers and limitations of social memory, especially for a group that had experienced centuries of slavery. A healthy level of forgetting, said Douglass, was 'nature's plan of relief.' But in season and out, Douglass insisted that whatever the psychological need for avoiding the woeful legacy of slavery, it would resist all human efforts to suppress it."[5] While at the end of the nineteenth century Douglass and Crummell delineated both the rationale for forgetting and the inevitability of memory, Richard Wright in the mid-twentieth century described the repercussions of ignoring the past. In "Phychiatry [sic] Comes to Harlem," Wright illustrates the eruptive effect of the repressive memory of slavery: "the repressed need goes underground, gropes for an unguarded outlet in the dark and, once finding it, sneaks out, experimentally tasting the new freedom, then at last gushing forth in a wild torrent, frantic lest a new taboo deprive it of the right to exist."[6]

Using Wright's definition of repressed need and the Freudian concept of the "return of the repressed," I define eruption as *involuntary* acts of subversion. Unlike the more conscious and systematic resistance that occurred during Reconstruction, including political involvement, artistic expression, and even organized violence, eruptive acts are unplanned. Michael Billig describes the response to repression as an "inevitable eruption of an inner instinctive force."[7] In his analysis, the instincts of memory and violence ultimately return, whether called forth or not. The return of the repressed is also described as "the process whereby repressed elements, preserved in the unconscious, tend to reappear, in consciousness or in behavior, in the shape of secondary and more or less unrecognizable 'derivatives of the unconscious.' Parapraxes, bungled or symptomatic actions, are examples of such derivatives."[8] In a cultural context, Eric Berlatsky connects this return of the repressed with collective trauma: "It may be useful to understand the psychoanalytic 'return of the repressed' as itself a cultural narrative that makes sense of trauma."[9] After emancipation, for some southern African Americans, eruption was expressed in ways that recall the return of the repressed. Jane Dailey details random acts of dangerous, unsanctioned behavior by African Americans during and after slavery. Dailey describes "the jostling of whites, profanities and depredations in urban public spaces of the antebellum South, [which] later became acts of an enfranchised and empowered people, during the transition between slavery and the Jim Crow era."[10] These small acts speak to the larger pathology of slavery still extant in the African American community during the postbellum period.

In *The Sport of the Gods*, Dunbar depicts the conflict between slave pathology and the goals of emancipated African Americans, specifically in terms of progress and freedom. The Hamilton family—Berry the butler, Fannie the housemaid, Joe the barber, and Kit the mother's helper—represent the burgeoning black bourgeoisie. They model themselves on the whites they serve. The confident son, Joe, the day after observing a party attended by the town's white elite, "contented himself with devouring the good things and aping the manners of the young men who he knew had been among last night's guests."[11] The Hamiltons separate themselves from the other African Americans in their community. Wearing finery, saving money, and believing themselves to be models of progress, they are actually victims of stasis. As they remain in the space of slavery and under the symbolic "mastery" of their employer, Maurice Oakley, their stasis is a symptom of repression. When Francis, the younger brother of Maurice Oakley, accuses Berry of theft to cover up his own gambling, Oakley ejects the family from the plantation. Their exile engenders a series of eruptions. As a break with the slave system, migration threatened the order and tradition of the South. The end of the war and the official Emancipation Proclamation were seen as the beginning of a transformation. As the "most psychologically dramatic of all manifestations of freedom," migration opened up psychic space for new consciousness.[12] The redemption of the migrating Hamilton family depends on their ability to develop a new consciousness, leave behind the mind-set of the "old-time darky," and surrender illusion.

Paul Laurence Dunbar was caught between subjugation and subversion, the "Old Negro" and the "New Negro." His nickname, the "elevator boy poet," is revealing of the two worlds he inhabited. My work situates Dunbar between these two worlds, finding him in a conflicted space of repression, self-deprecation, and desire. This conflict led Dunbar to question the meaningfulness of his work. In a letter to an active supporter, Dr. James Newton Matthews, Dunbar writes, "With it all . . . I cannot help being overwhelmed by self-doubts. I hope there is something worthy in my writings and not merely the novelty of a black face associated with the power to rhyme that has attracted attention."[13] This insecurity, along with his marital troubles, alcoholism, illnesses, and nervous breakdown, reflects inner turmoil.

By his own admission, Dunbar did not meet his standards of black progressiveness. Modeling the plantation tradition, much of his work romanticized slavery and the South in the vein of Thomas Nelson Page in *In Ole Virginia*, a collection of dialect stories narrated by a faithful ex-slave who reminisces nostalgically about "dem good ole times." Writers in this tradition often presented a willful forgetting of slavery's brutal violence and of slave resistance. The conflict between Dunbar's writing and his inner life plagued him. In the poem "Frederick Douglass," written for the occasion of Douglass's funeral, Dunbar admires the qualities that he believes he himself lacks.

> And he was no soft-tongued apologist;
> He spoke straightforward, and fearlessly uncowed;
> The sunlight of his truth dispelled the mist,
> And set in bold relief each dark hued cloud.[14]

Dunbar's desire to "get a hearing" unquestionably led to writing that was not his "truth." As he told James Weldon Johnson the year he died, "I have kept on doing the same things, and doing them no better. I have never gotten to the things I really wanted to do."[15] From his perspective, he stagnates, caught by the critical success that brought fame and economic, if not psychological, freedom. This stagnation is a facet of Dunbar's own repressed desire to create neither a master narrative nor a slave narrative but to speak his own truth.

In *The Sport of the Gods*, the narrative shifts dramatically between two genres: plantation literature and naturalism, a contrast that parallels the conflict between the repressed, masked self and the erupted inner life.

> First appearing to offer his readers a plantation story at its most conventional, . . . "undercuts the southern code of chivalry and the legendary paternalism of master to servant," so that his characters must go north, a strategy that has personal as well as literary consequences for Dunbar. Having cleared a geographic space, he sends them to a setting that is relatively free of white racial stereotyping and is instead informed by urban naturalism.[16]

In the plantation sections of the novel, stasis defines Dunbar's South. As in his other stories in which southern tradition and honor are upheld despite horrific consequences, whites in *The Sport of the Gods* practice a violent form of conservatism that reflects a desire for stability after the upheaval of emancipation.

One form of this stasis is tradition embedded with violence. In "The Lynching of Jube Benson," Dunbar offers his definition of this tradition through the voice of a white man who knowingly participates in the lynching of a wrongfully accused, devoted servant. "I saw his black face glooming there in the half light, and I could only think of him as a monster. It's tradition."[17]

Dunbar's depiction of the plantation illustrates this tradition, as even after emancipation it is marked only by small changes that provide a cursory nod to social change. Dunbar describes the Hamilton home as "somewhat in the manner of the old cabin in the quarters, with which usage as well as tradition had made both master and servant familiar. But, unlike the cabin of the elder day, it was a neatly furnished, modern house, the home of a typical, good-living Negro."[18] Maurice is one of the most conservative of the old guard of this community, one who has managed to avoid being affected by the outcome of the Civil War. "Maurice Oakley was not a man of sudden or violent enthusiasms. Conservatism was the quality that had been the foundation of his fortunes at a time when the disruption of the country had involved most of the men of his region in ruin."[19] Maurice Oakley demands Berry's conviction and, even when later apprised of Berry's innocence and his brother's lies, invokes the southern tradition of honor trumping justice. He asks, "What is that nigger to my brother? What are his sufferings to the honour of my family and name?"[20]

Tradition controls all the denizens of Dunbar's South, the Hamiltons and Oakleys, the black community and the white. "In the black people of the town the strong influence of slavery was still operative, and with one accord they turned away from one of their own kind upon whom had been set the bane of the white people's displeasure. . . . They have brought down as a heritage from the days of their bondage both fear and disloyalty."[21] The southern blacks unwittingly collude with the white gentry, who wager on the lure of tradition to African Americans. "Why, gentlemen, I foresee the day when these people themselves shall come to us southerners of their own accord and ask to be re-enslaved until such time as they shall be fit for freedom."[22] Dunbar creates, in the Hamiltons, a family that does "ask" for re-enslavement by failing to examine its past and by remaining on the plantation both physically and psychologically. Dunbar shows how their decision to stay leads to destruction and their exile to enlightenment.

Berry, the head of the Hamilton family, leads the family in their loyalty to the South and its promises. "He was one of the many slaves who upon their accession to freedom had not left the South, but had wandered from place to place in their own beloved section, waiting, working and struggling to rise with its rehabilitated fortunes."[23] Untouched by the rupture of emancipation and surrounding migration, Berry and his family are happily complacent, viewing their lives on the plantation with fondness. It is the place where "they had toddled as babies and played as children and been happy and care-free."[24] Despite their ostensible contentment and the idyllic description of their cottage, there are moments of doubt and questioning. This introspection, though quickly suppressed, is the first step to a new consciousness. "There had been times when they had complained and wanted a home off by themselves, like others whom they knew. They had not failed, either, to draw unpleasant comparisons between their mode of life and the old plantation quarters system."[25] But the details of this unpleasantness are ambiguous. Adding to this ambiguity is the conspicuous absence of lynching. As Florette Henri writes, "no picture of the environment in which black people lived in the South of 1900 can be complete without the shadow of the lyncher lurking behind the door."[26] Instead, the Hamiltons find their place almost Arcadian, "a pastoral Eden indistinguishable from the settings detailed by Page and dozens of other plantation writers."[27] The Hamiltons are uprooted only when circumstances beyond their control threaten their place on the plantation and in their beloved home.

Berry's transformation becomes evident even before he leaves the plantation. We first know him as the plantation tradition's cheerful "darky." The "pink" of servants, he is a shining example of the benevolent relationship between white paternalism and black dependence. But the master narrative of the loyal servant cannot be maintained. Before Maurice becomes disillusioned with Berry, he describes the social transformation of African Americans to his brother: "We must remember that we are not in the old days now. The Negroes are becoming less faithful and less contented, and more's the pity, and a deal more ambitious, although I have never had any unfaithfulness on the part of Hamilton to complain of before."[28] This mourning of the Old Negro parallels the historical context in which southern whites decried the upset of social order. Henri writes:

> Young blacks, born a whole generation after Emancipation, were scorned as a worthless lot compared to the old-time darky, who was diligent, faithful, and "orderly"—he knew his place and kept it. "That the 'old-time Negro' is passing away is one of the common sayings all over the South," gently lamented Thomas Nelson Page in the very early years of the century; their former masters, he said, reminiscing about these wonderful old servants and associates "turn away to wipe their eyes."[29]

This narrative of tradition also represses introspection. In prison, when Berry changes to a brooding, contemplative Negro, he signifies a threat to the romance of the South, one in which "'Sambo' must forever replace 'Nat'" Turner.[30] Berry's transformation undermines the postbellum perpetuation of the slave-master construct. "Anxiety was produced by a seeming contradiction within the cherished myth—a contradiction embodied in the disgruntled slave, an image that would have to be confronted daily in one form or another."[31] Like the disgruntled slave, Berry's violence remains beneath the surface.

At first, Oakley's accusation leaves him incredulous.

> Berry turned to his employer. "You b'lieve dat I stole f'om dis house aftah all de yeahs I've been in it, aftah de caih I took of yo' money and yo' valybles, aftah de way I've put you to bed f'om many a dinnah, an' you woke up to fin' all yo' money safe? Now, can you b'lieve dis?"
>
> His voice broke, and he ended with a cry.[32]

The final description of their exchange shifts dramatically as Berry transforms before Oakley's eyes.

> Berry's eyes were bloodshot as he replied, "Den, damn you! damn you! Ef dat's all dese yeahs counted fu', I wish I had a-stoled it."
>
> Oakley made a step forward, and his man did likewise, but the officer stepped between them.
>
> "Take that damned hound away, or, by God! I'll do him violence!"
>
> The two men stood fiercely facing each other, then the handcuffs were snapped on the servant's wrist.[33]

Without physical constraint and the intervention of the law, the confrontation could end with violence. Unlike other renditions of the slave betrayed by a formerly benevolent white "friend," Berry's relationship ends with equalizing anger. While in "The Lynching of Jube Benson," the soon-to-be-lynched servant cries, "W'y, doctah," in the "saddest voice" the doctor had ever heard, Berry takes a dangerously aggressive stance, matching the angry Oakley's "step forward" with his own.[34] Furthermore, Berry asserts an equal right to threaten violence when he "fiercely" faces Oakley and mirrors his actions.

Berry's imprisonment forces him to reenvision his enslavement and emancipation. The disillusionment sloughs away his former self. "As for the prisoner himself, after the first day when he had pleaded 'not guilty' and been bound over to the Grand Jury, he had fallen into a sort of dazed calm that was like the stupor produced by a drug."[35] Berry's stupefaction combines with fainting spells to evoke fear and emasculation. Most important, Berry's loss of consciousness signifies a break with the former self. "Berry was convicted. He was given ten years at hard labour. He hardly looked as if he could live out one as he heard his sentence. But Nature was kind and relieved him of the strain. With a cry as if his heart were bursting, he started up and fell forward on his face unconscious. Some one, a bit more brutal than the rest, said, 'It's five dollars' fine every time a nigger faints.' But no one laughed. There was something too portentous, too tragic in the degradation of this man."[36] Berry's fainting, like his trancelike state, prepares the way for the metamorphosis of a "good-living Negro."[37] When Berry is first imprisoned, his own illusion will not even allow him to believe that he could be convicted. His inability to absorb this information is described psychologically in the language of repression. "Beyond this, apparently, his mind could not go. That his detention was anything more than temporary never seemed to enter his mind. That he would be convicted and sentenced was as far from possibility as the skies from the earth. If he saw visions of a long sojourn in prison, it was only as a nightmare half consciously experienced and which with the struggle must give way before the waking."[38] Like his incredulity when he is first accused, Berry's shock is symptomatic of repression. He behaves as though injustice is a new and remarkable experience, despite a life of enslavement. Repression, in the form of illusion, keeps Berry enslaved years after emancipation.

Migration, in *The Sport of the Gods*, sets off eruptions of involuntary memory. In its chaos, migration—the venture into the unknown (parallel to Berry's periods of unconsciousness)—prohibits stasis. Because of the psychological nature of the Hamiltons' stagnation and commitment to plantation life, Fannie experiences leaving as rupture. After being ejected from her home, she is thrown into tumult. "Her desperation . . . would not let her give way to fear, so she set forth to look for another house. Joe and Kit saw her go as if she were starting on an expedition into a strange country. In all their lives they had known no home save the little cottage in Oakley's yard."[39] After being ostracized by the town, Joe claims that he "always wanted to go north" and encourages his sister and mother to go to New York, a place that carries mythical significance for the family: "They had heard of New York as a place vague and far away, a city that, like Heaven, to them had existed by faith alone. All the days of their lives they had heard of it, and it seemed to them the center of all the glory, all the wealth, and all the freedom of the world. New York. It had an alluring sound. Who would know them there? Who would look down upon them?"[40] The invocation of "all the freedom" that New York promised exposes a lifelong desire that belies their professed contentment on the plantation. The shame of their failure to confront the damages of the slave past is displaced by the shame of their father's incarceration. While Berry undergoes a transformation in the southern prison, Kit, Joe, and Fannie also go through a process of transformation in the form of amnesia. Up North, both children abandon the possibility of ever returning to the Oakley plantation, leaving them free to re-create themselves. However, for Kit and Joe, the first generation born after slavery, the inability to confront the past and surrender their illusions leads to self-destruction. Joe and Kit unconsciously seek to reconstruct the structures of the plantation in the urban bar and the theater, respectively. William Boelhower discusses the city's impact on memory: "The city is an atropic space. The very notion of home is foreign to it. Nor can the urban dweller find philosophical repose in it, since it never sleeps. Above all, the city's dazzling functionalism cancels the mechanisms of memory that once constituted the very raison d'etre of the traditional city. All this produces a loss, a sense of amnesia, a tension in abstentia."[41] In the new urban spaces, Kit and Joe, the hope of a new generation, submit to the city's amnesiac lure.

The urban theater in *The Sport of the Gods* speaks to both repression and the distortion of black expression. Harry Elam Jr. describes the black theater as a dialectic, a site of tension between opposing forces. "Definitions of race, like the processes of theater, fundamentally depend on the relationship between the seen and unseen, between the visibly marked and unmarked, between the 'real' and the illusionary."[42] The tension between the real and the illusionary is particularly relevant. Kit's involvement in the theater allows her to maintain the illusion of the new while she re-creates a distorted version of her southern life in a distorted form. Her observation of something "weird in the alternate spaces of light and shade" reveals the relationship between the oppositions of memory and forgetting, as well as a shift in consciousness.[43] This shift in consciousness is further illustrated in Kit's new name, Kitty, given to her by her mentor, Hattie. As she views the theater's stage, Kit's perception alters. "Without any feeling of its ugliness, she looked at the curtain as at a door that should presently open between her and a house of wonders. She looked at it with the fascination that one always experiences for what either brings near or withholds the unknown."[44] Kit anticipates the house of wonders, the new and the unknown, in ways that defy her former adherence to tradition and morph her character: "At first the girl grew wistful and then impatient and rebellious.

The quick poison of the unreal life about her had already begun to affect her character. She had grown secretive and sly. The innocent longing which in a burst of enthusiasm she had expressed that first night at the theatre was growing into a real ambition with her, and she dropped the simple old songs she knew to practise the detestable coon ditties which the stage demanded."[45] Encouraged by her admirer, Thomas, to sing "some o' the new songs," she surrenders to the new music. The newness of Kit's songs, however, proves illusory. In fact, the "coon ditties" are the urban version of the old songs. Instead of developing a new consciousness or a truly "new song," Kit carries the southern psychologies of repression to the North. Her coon songs render her complicit in the propagation of the southern tradition. They allow her to avoid confrontation of the slave past, a potential source of psychological freedom.

Kit progressively sheds her reserved southern ways along with the memory of her father, whom she does not mention until she encourages her mother to also forget him. Her transformation follows the arc of her growing involvement with the theater, first as spectator and ultimately as performer. Joining a theater company allows Kit to maintain her illusions, still searching for the Promised Land in the "house of wonders." Though gilded and obfuscated by darkness, it recalls the southern "cottage," in which reality is repressed and averted.

Whereas Berry's site of new consciousness is the prison, a place both of and outside southern tradition, Kit's becomes the stage, a place of illusion, anonymity, and amnesia. She is soon hardened to the point where even Thomas, their Hadean guide to the dark spaces of the city, marvels, describing her change as an acquisition of knowledge. "Well, if they don't want to find out things, what do they come to N' Yawk for?"[46] Her disillusionment, however, ends in disassociation rather than new consciousness and knowledge. When her brother is imprisoned, she abandons him, arguing that "She was afraid it might make her nervous while she was in the city. . . . She went on the road with her company before he was taken away."[47] Kit forgets Joe in the same way she represses the memory of her father, maintaining the psychological structure of slavery.

In the North, Joe adopts the bar, the Banner, as his new home. He befriends fellow former southerners who use alcohol to attempt to "wash the memory" from their consciousness.[48] In this space he begins to rationalize his break with the past and establish a pattern of forgetting and false transformation: "Was it not better, after all, that circumstances had forced them thither? Had it not been so, they might all have stayed home and stagnated. Well, thought he, it's an ill wind that blows nobody good, and somehow, with a guilty under-thought, he forgot to feel the natural pity for his father, toiling guiltless in the prison of his native State."[49] At the Banner, memories from the past intrude, but not the memories of "dem good ole times." Instead, an unwilled, disruptive memory illuminates the damages of the slave past: repression, violence, and psychological conflict. Darkened like Kit's theater, the bar facilitates the process of forgetting, aided by alcohol and the company of other migrants. The displaced southerners band together to forget a painful communal past, one symbolized by Sadness, a regular figure at the bar. "'Better known as Sadness,' he said, with an expression of deep gloom. 'A distant relative of mine once had a great grief. I have never recovered from it.'"[50] Sadness's demeanor haunts each of the patrons and represents the inescapable memory of slavery as well as the possibility of redemption.

As the only one who speaks explicitly of the threat of lynching, Sadness embodies the shared history of violence, loss, and mourning. He enlightens Joe: "Now, Mr. Hamilton, let me tell you, and you will pardon me for it, that you are a fool. Your case isn't half as bad as that of nine-tenths of the fellows that hang around here. Now, for instance, my father was hung. . . . A half-dozen fellows whom you meet here every night have killed their man."[51] Sadness even attempts to disabuse Joe of a vestigial commitment to the southern romance by urging him to confront the pain of the past and begin the mourning that comes with consciousness. He warns, "A man must be very high or very low to take the sensible view of life that keeps him from being sad."[52] Despite Sadness's implorations, Joe, in an act of repression, dismisses him and garners only a "false bravery" from his revelations.[53] Instead, Joe adopts self-destructive habits. Following urban customs in the way he used to mimic the white gentry, Joe gambles, drinks, and disconnects from his family and his own consciousness. Fannie becomes disgusted and disowns him: "Oh, go on, . . . go on. It's been a long time sence you been my son. You on yo' way to hell, an' you is been fu' lo dese many days."[54] Sadness is equally disgusted with Joe's dissipation, saying that he was "fool enough to try" to help him.[55]

Made dizzy by his struggle to forget, Joe's quest is temporarily impeded by Minty, a young woman from their town who knows the family history and becomes a physical reminder of the past. Unlike Sadness, who represents the pain of the past, Minty symbolizes its shame. While Sadness offers the possibility of a new consciousness, Minty brings only stagnation and tradition. In this way, her presence jeopardizes even the hope of a new way of thinking: "Somehow old teachings and old traditions have an annoying way of coming back upon us in the critical moments of life, although one has long ago recognized how much truer and better some newer ways of thinking are. But Joe would not allow Minty to shatter his dreams by bringing up these old notions. She must be instructed."[56] With the help of Sadness, Hattie, and the others, Joe subdues Minty. It is only with the confidence and city wisdom of his fellow bar patrons that Joe renders Minty's knowledge obsolete. "She rose hastily and, getting her skirts together, fled from the room."[57] Though the community act shows power, it also underscores Joe's ineffectuality and impotence.

Joe's illusions of equality and bourgeois values also challenge his ability to face his own subjugation. These illusions are introduced when the blacks in his southern community confront him about his sense of superiority. "W'y I hyeah you say dat you couldn't git a paih of sheahs thoo a niggah's naps. You ain't been practisin' lately, has you?"[58] We discover traces of these same illusions when Mr. Skaggs, a white newspaper reporter, visits the bar. Burning with the desire to call him Skaggsy as the others do, Joe is easily enthralled by his claims. "I like coloured people, anyway. It's natural. You see, my father had a big plantation and owned lots of slaves,—no offence, of course, but it was the custom of that time,—and I've played with little darkies ever since I could remember."[59] Joe, who answers in the affirmative when Skaggs asks him if he believes that "there ain't an ounce of prejudice in [his] body," is "unable to understand the amused expression on Thomas' face."[60] Unlike Joe, Thomas and the other city dwellers recognize the falseness of this claim, calling him the "biggest liar in N' Yawk."[61] "Shocked" and unhappy when Thomas reveals this truth, Joe does "not thank him for destroying his romance."[62]

For Joe, repressed memory and avoidance return as displaced violence. "When [Joe] saw his mother's tears and his sister's shame" after his father was imprisoned, "something rose within him that had it been given play might have made a man of him, but, being crushed, died and rotted, and in the compost it made all the evil of his nature flourish."[63] Joe's heroism is thwarted by the unspoken reality of the threat of death. As Thomas L. Morgan writes, "To act on such a dream would lead to Joe's death at the hands of Southern lynch law."[64] While in the South, Joe misdirects this anger toward the blacks who reject him, foreshadowing the irrational murder of his northern girlfriend, Hattie. "'I'd like to cut the heart out of a few of 'em,'" said Joe in his throat."[65] Instead, Joe migrates and takes up the communal process of "wash[ing] away memory."[66] He becomes increasingly morose and, when rejected by his girlfriend, murders her. A literary precedent to Bigger's murder of his girlfriend, Bessie, in *Native Son*, Joe's repressed violence, born of slavery, erupts. The murder and Joe's imprisonment mark the depth of his declension.

Ultimately, even Fannie, the moral barometer of the family, submits to the temptations of New York. In her own way, she also forgets her husband when she decides to marry a physically abusive gambler. Kit encourages her mother to remarry:

"I don't reckon we'll ever see pa again an' you got to do something. You got to live for yourself now."

Her mother dropped her head in her hands. "All right, she said, I'll do it; I'll ma'y him. I might as well go de way both my chillen's gone. Po' Be'y, po Be'y."[67]

Though Fannie's break is more delayed, it is just as complete, so that "in the weeks and months that followed she drifted farther away from her children and husband and all the traditions of her life."[68] Fannie's abandonment of Berry marks an important moment in the Hamiltons' decline and signals his return to the narrative.

After Joe drunkenly discusses his father's imprisonment at the bar, Skaggs's investigative work exposes the Oakleys' deception, leading to Berry's release from prison. His "freedom" is dramatically described: "He had long ago lost hope that justice would ever be done to him. Five years of prison life had made a different man of him. He no longer looked to receive kindness from his fellows, and he blinked at it as he blinked at the unwonted brightness of the sun. The lines about his mouth where the smiles used to gather had changed and grown stern with the hopelessness of the years."[69] Immediately, Berry goes to New York and finds that his wife is remarried. He also learns from Fannie the fate of his children.

"My wife gone, Kit a nobody, an' Joe, little Joe, a murderer, an' then I—I—ust to pray to Gawd an' call him 'Ouah Fathah.'" He laughed hoarsely. It sounded like nothing Fannie had ever heard before.

Berry speaks a new language, one that acknowledges the depths of their darkness and calls into question one of the fundamental tenets of the Old South—religion. When Fannie's new husband dies before Berry can kill him, Fannie and Berry "simply [go] back to each other."[70]

Broken by the dissolution of their family, Berry and Fannie turn to the past together: they return to the plantation and engage in an unexpected play on justice. "New York held nothing for them now but sad memories. Kit was on the road, and the father could not bear to see his son; so they turned their faces Southward, back to the only place they could call home."[71] Though called home, the cottage is transformed by disillusionment and the shift in power caused by Oakley's mental degeneration. That Oakley, the most conservative of the old guard, is driven mad by his own "sport" signals the destruction of the old order. The Hamiltons wait, watch, and listen to his ranting from their cottage. In this way, they finally savor a form of justice, a reckoning.

The ending of the novel has been interpreted as submissive. Rodgers, for example, sees Berry and Fannie's clasped hands as symbolizing loyalty to the past. He states: "In a parodically grotesque imitation of their former existence, Berry and Fannie and [Maurice Oakley's wife] pass their nights sitting together, hands clasped in a pitifully inadequate gesture of loyalty to the system that has failed them. The punishment for their allegiance is to be continually reminded through the shrieking voice of Maurice Oakley echoing across the yard that the price of holding on to that loyalty at all costs is ultimately madness—even more so for the white population than the black."[72] While certainly the Hamiltons' physical presence on the plantation recalls the past, little else remains the same. Instead of a return to the past and to the tradition of loyalty, the conclusion signals the possibility of a subverted social order. Oakley's degeneration is one of the signs of subversion: "It would have been hard to recognise in the Oakley of the present the man of a few years before. The strong frame had gone away to bone, and nothing of his old power sat on either brow or chin. He was a man who trembled on the brink of insanity."[73] While Oakley loses his ability to control his future and is consumed by a corrupt past, Berry and Fannie return to the site of buried memory with new consciousness and a straight aim. Their return mirrors the awakening associated with the return of the repressed. Dina Georgis uses the trauma theory of Cathy Caruth to frame her discussion of repression and eruption: "To return to the site of repressed memory is like waking up from a long sleep. For Caruth, the effect of trauma is sleeping, and a return to the scene of trauma signals freedom because it is followed by a departure from the scene or waking up from a bad dream. In the moment of awakening, death is allowed in and is then left behind so that living can go on."[74]

David Blight discusses Frederick Douglass's belief in confrontation with the past. Douglass's use of violent metaphor, of "blood" and the "crowd," calls to mind a crime scene: "Frederick Douglass wrote that the history of African Americans can 'be traced like that of a wounded man through a crowd by the blood.' Better to confront such a history, he believed, than to wait for its resurgence."[75] In the conclusion of *The Sport of the Gods*, Berry and Fannie Hamilton confront this history at the scene of the crime. In this return, Maurice Oakley, the southern gentleman, is exposed as a madman. The clasped hands, which might have previously signified allegiance, now symbolize a shared recognition of truth and disillusionment. Moreover, Fannie and Berry no longer sublimate their sense of vengeance. Instead they think "of what [Oakley] had brought to them and to himself."[76] Though Berry and Fannie return to the space of slavery, they see it for the first time. In this way, their plantation home does become a "new" South, one constructed by exile, psychological eruption, and revelation.

NOTES

1. Ron Eyerman, *Cultural Trauma: Slavery and the Formation of African American Identity* (New York: Cambridge University Press, 2001), 1.

2. Ray Corsini, *A Dictionary of Psychology* (New York: Brunner/Routledge, 2002), 777.

3. Qtd. in Paul Gilroy, *The Black Atlantic: Modernity and Double Consciousness* (Cambridge, Mass.: Harvard University Press, 1993), 178.

4. Richard Wright, *Native Son* (New York: Harper and Brothers, 1940), 97.

5. David Blight, "'What Will Peace among the Whites Bring?' Reunion and Race in the Struggle over the Memory of the Civil War on American Culture," *Massachusetts Review* 34, no. 3 (1993): 398.

6. Richard Wright, "Phychiatry [sic] Comes to Harlem," *Freeworld*, Sept. 1946, 49.

7. Michael Billig, *Freudian Repression: Conversation Creating the Unconscious* (Cambridge: Cambridge University Press, 1999), 135.

8. Jean-François Rabain, "Return of the Repressed," in *International Dictionary of Psychoanalysis*, ed. Alain de Mijolla (Detroit: Macmillan Reference USA, 2005), 3:1491–92.

9. Eric Berlatsky, "Memory as Forgetting: The Problem of the Postmodern in Kundera's *The Book of Laughter and Forgetting* and Spiegelman's *Maus*," *Cultural Critique* 55 (2003): 143.

10. Jane Dailey, "Deference and Violence in the Postbellum Urban South: Manners and Massacres in Danville, Virginia," *Journal of Southern History* 63, no. 3 (1997): 552.

11. Paul Laurence Dunbar, *The Sport of the Gods* (New York: Dodd, Mead, 1902), 35.

12. James R. Grossman, *Land of Hope: Chicago, Black Southerners, and the Great Migration* (Chicago: University of Chicago Press, 1989), 19.

13. Qtd. in "Paul Laurence Dunbar," in *African American Writers*, ed. Valerie Smith (New York: Charles Scribner's Sons, 1991), 87.

14. Paul Laurence Dunbar, *Lyrics of Lowly Life* (New York: Dodd, Mead, 1896), 9, lines 19–22.

15. Qtd. in James Weldon Johnson, *Along This Way: The Autobiography of James Weldon Johnson* (New York: Viking Press, 1965), 161.

16. Lawrence R. Rodgers, "Paul Laurence Dunbar's *The Sport of the Gods*: The Doubly Conscious World of Plantation Fiction, Migration and Ascent," *American Literary Realism* 24, no. 3 (1992): 47.

17. *The Complete Stories of Paul Laurence Dunbar*, ed. Gene Andrew Jarrett and Thomas Lewis Morgan (Athens: Ohio University Press, 2005), 379.

18. Dunbar, *Sport*, 2.

19. Ibid., 8.

20. Ibid., 196.

21. Ibid., 49.

22. Ibid., 56.

23. Ibid., 72.

24. Ibid., 65.

25. Ibid., 66.

26. Florette Henri, *Black Migration: Movement North, 1900–1920* (Garden City, N.Y.: Anchor Press/Doubleday, 1975), 43.
27. Rodgers, "Dunbar's *The Sport of the Gods*," 48.
28. Dunbar, *Sport*, 25.
29. Henri, *Black Migration*, 74.
30. William Tynes Cowan, *The Slave in the Swamp: Disrupting the Plantation Narrative* (New York: Routledge, 2005), 3.
31. Ibid., 90.
32. Dunbar, *Sport*, 44.
33. Ibid., 47.
34. *Complete Stories*, 378.
35. Dunbar, *Sport*, 57.
36. Ibid., 62.
37. Ibid., 2.
38. Ibid., 59.
39. Ibid., 65.
40. Ibid., 67.
41. William Boelhower, "Ethnographic Politics: The Uses of Memory in Ethnic Fiction," in *Memory and Cultural Politics: New Approaches to American Ethnic Literatures*, ed. Amrijit Singh, Joseph T. Skerrett Jr., and Robert E. Hogan (Boston: Northeastern University Press, 1996), 25.
42. Harry J. Elam Jr., "The Device of Race: An Introduction," in *African American Performance and Theater History: A Critical Reader*, ed. Harry J. Elam Jr. and David Krasner (Oxford: Oxford University Press, 2001), 4.
43. Dunbar, *Sport*, 99.
44. Ibid., 98.
45. Ibid., 130.
46. Ibid., 177.
47. Ibid., 216.
48. Ibid., 212.
49. Ibid., 88.
50. Ibid., 113.
51. Ibid., 146.
52. Ibid., 148.
53. Ibid., 149.
54. Ibid., 140.
55. Ibid., 149.
56. Ibid., 152.
57. Ibid., 158.
58. Ibid., 67.
59. Ibid., 121.
60. Ibid., 122.
61. Ibid., 123.
62. Ibid., 60.
63. Ibid., 57.
64. Thomas L. Morgan, "The City as Refuge: Constructing Urban Blackness in Paul Laurence Dunbar's *The Sport of the Gods* and James Weldon Johnson's *The Autobiography of an Ex-Coloured Man*," *African American Review* 38, no. 2 (2004): 221.
65. Dunbar, *Sport*, 75.

66. Ibid., 221.
67. Ibid., 169.
68. Ibid., 130.
69. Ibid., 242.
70. Ibid., 254.
71. Ibid.
72. Ibid.
73. Ibid., 230.
74. Dina Georgis, "Falling for Jazz: Desire, Dissonance, and Racial Collaboration," *Canadian Review of American Studies* 35 (2005): 226.
75. Blight, "Peace among the Whites," 398.
76. Dunbar, *Sport*, 255.

13
A Little Something More Than Something Else
Dunbar's Colorist Ambivalence in The Sport of the Gods

DOLORES V. SISCO

ALTHOUGH PAUL LAURENCE DUNBAR'S first three novels center on white characters, the fourth novel, *The Sport of the Gods* (1902), focuses on the rise and fall of the southern black Hamilton family as they leave their rural home and encounter the urban perils of northern migration. Dunbar's short novel is now recognized as the first depiction of the shift of black populations from the rural South to the urban North, and the short novel gives an almost documentary depiction of the rise of black urban culture. Although one can find fault with the novel's structure (and the attempt at the type of literary naturalism achieved by his white contemporaries), sustained critical assessments of the poet, author, and essayist's works have been terribly few and far between. The lack of concerted critical attention, unhappily, is a condition that belies Dunbar's stature in African American writing. "His reputation," Darwin T. Turner writes perceptively, "has suffered from those who have been blinded by a single work or who have failed to discern his attempts at ironic protest."[1] *The Sport of the Gods* was believed to be lacking in true black political protest by later critics of African American literature who argued that black artistic endeavors should follow a black aesthetic of political protest against the lived conditions of blacks in America. Although the critical consensus has been that the novel should be hailed as the first depiction of the black migration, this chapter argues that the novel offers a more intriguing reading that directly challenges the construction of traditional American masculinity, especially the unique challenges of late nineteenth-century black masculinity.

The problem of an objective critical analysis of *Sport*, of course, has to do with the writer's ambivalence over race at a time when the subject of race was at the forefront of American political and cultural life. Although critics like Addison Gayle Jr. accused Dunbar of selling out the race by pandering to the prevalent plantation fantasies and derogatory myths about blacks, the author was also trapped between competing (and fluid) contemporary models of a black masculinity that sought parity with whites. Equally troubling was the fact that Dunbar, who Turner rightly argues is "far more bitter and scathing... than his reputation suggests,"[2] hints at a darker side not revealed in his sunny odes to black plantation life. Although Turner's assertion is made in the context of a different aspect of the novel, I find the assessment useful as an antidote to the racially offensive traditional plantation genre. Furthermore, Dunbar also manages to question the imitative values of the new southern mercantile class as they rewrote a fantasy world of masculine southern gentility. Although later critics of African American literature have routinely dismissed Dunbar as a black writer who pandered to the racist notions of his white readership, overlooked in his last novel is a perceptive criticism directed at a black societal structure that devalued those black men who did not come close to the prevailing standards that characterized the New Negro.

My reading of *The Sport of the Gods* aims to uncover Dunbar's implicit construction of a model of masculinity based on white male supremacy and phenotypical affinities with whites by explicitly attacking its adoption by the black community. One problem—as I read Dunbar—is that the model of white male aristocracy is at its core one of degeneration and debasement, which belies the plantation fantasies of courtliness and genteel prewar manners. However, this is not to say that the masculine ideals of protecting the weak or, for that matter, of standing up to political oppression are the wrong models to emulate. For the descendants of former slaves who were stripped of their rights of manhood—especially their right to protect black women—submitting to the backward turn of racial subordination was clearly not an admirable option. But as a member of the black community, Dunbar's quarrel was with the terms of exclusion of the models of black manhood, the boundaries of which were circumscribed by color and class. I argue that *Sport* is a novel of vindication, not only for the exclusion of black men from the standards of traditional American masculinity, but also a personal vindication for an author personally conflicted over the stigma of race. Thus, Dunbar's project with his last novel was a difficult one at a difficult time as southern white males reimagined their own masculinity in the aftermath of the Lost Cause.

"Negro domination," explains Eric J. Sundquist, "did, in fact, threaten the manliness of the white southerner, though not in the way it was often represented."[3] At a time when race relations were at their worst, the thought of peacefully sharing political rights with black men was seen as a renewed attack on white manhood, and the vengeance of a war-defeated white southern manhood was quick and brutal. Disfranchisement was the order of the day after the South's defeat in 1865, and by 1877, American white men were able to resolve their sectional differences on the bloody backs of African Americans. The burning cross and the lynch rope (among other punitive devices) were thought necessary to stifle or derail any attempts by black men to hold the Constitution to its promises, even as the federal government turned a blind eye to the more sadistic and egregious southern outrages that continued throughout the post-Reconstruction era. The protection of white southern womanhood was the excuse used by white men eagerly anxious to assert a beleaguered manhood that they believed would prevent rampant "Negro outrages"[4] to occur after losing a war fought in order to maintain black submission. As Sundquist suggests, "Rape was the mask behind which disfranchisement was hidden, but it was part of the larger charade of plantation mythology that set out to restore southern pride and revive a paradigm of white manliness that the legacy of the war and the economic and political rise of blacks during Reconstruction had called seriously into question."[5] Although the acts of violence and illegal subterfuges by southern white males made southern black life no better than it had been under slavery at times, blacks also had to contend with the vicious "academic" sociological studies that determined them unfit and undeserving of American political and social rights. This was especially true in the case of the recognition by whites of a politically and socially potent manifestation of black masculinity as the old canards of the ungovernable sexual depravity of blacks reached a point of national white hysteria. The majority of the books and pamphlets that purported to offer scientific evidence of the true nature of black men were given long and impressive titles that bespoke the authors' erudition; however, many were straightforward and to the point, like Charles Carroll's *The Negro a Beast*, published in the same year as *The Sport of the Gods*.

With the exception of the racial histrionic imaginings of Thomas Dixon Jr., creative literature was (by comparison) "kinder" to black males as a new genre fed a white reading public primed to forgive the South for its crimes against black humanity. The ideology of the happy plantation with benevolent and courtly masters and docile, happy slaves was a profitable reiteration for dozens of hack scribblers in hundreds of novels and short stories that were calculated, points out Sundquist, not so much to entertain but to assure northern whites that "blacks were under control."[6] The plantation tale thus restored the natural order, where the prerogatives of white masculinity could be refashioned (with a great deal of white-washing) for a new white male agenda. But there was a darker aspect to these tales of dialect-speaking, shuffling "old darkies," an aspect that I suspect may have contributed to the animosity directed toward the most famous black writer in the plantation genre by later critics of African American literature: the unmistakable fact that the "model" black characters in these tales were effectively "neutered" black men. White fears of rampant (young) black men bent on racial revenge did not appear in the tales of kindly whites and trustworthy and dependent old black men who longed for the days of "slave irresponsibility," when they did not have to trouble themselves with the complications of voting or demanding their rights. Although Jim Crow never made an ugly appearance in these tales, the plantation mythology—together with the scientific racist screeds—merely made their white readers aware of its necessity as another tool in the arsenal for racial social regulation.

At the very least, Dunbar should be recognized for his attempt at changing the image of black men in many of his short stories that deal with both rural and urban black life, but with *Sport*, the author makes an explicit break from the traditional in order to reveal a text of misdirection. "Fiction has said so much in regret of the old days when there were plantations and overseers and masters and slaves," writes Dunbar at the start of the novel. The plantation trope, declares Dunbar, is "tiresome iteration," a warning that can be assumed to be the author's attempt to break with the very genre that made him a celebrated author.[7] Instead of dismissing the novel, as Gayle suggests, as blanket acquiescence in white evaluations of blacks in general, we can see in *The Sport of the Gods* a more bitter hand at work.[8] "Careful examination," points out Turner, "reveals Dunbar to be far more bitter and scathing, much more a part of the protest tradition than his reputation suggests." Turner continues: "Even if Dunbar had been completely free to write scathing protest about the South, he could not have written it, or would have written it ineptly. His experiences and those of his family had not compelled him to hate white people as a group or the South as a region."[9] But Turner obviously misjudges Dunbar's purpose in deconstructing the southern mythology of cavaliers and gracious ladies: "Fiction has said so much in regret of the old days when there were plantations and overseers and masters and slaves," begins *The Sport of the Gods*,[10] and fiction has had so much to say about the postbellum honor code of the planter class.

"The ... notion of honor," explains Bertram Wyatt-Brown, "became the more familiar one, associated with the upper ranks of Southern society from the eighteenth century through the Civil War."[11] The legendary code of the old southern aristocracy was readily adapted by the new mercantile class, who both despised and envied the class they blamed for the South's degradation under Reconstruction. However, in practice, the code, as noted by many historians of the period, was breached more often than not, as many utilized the southern code to paper over their own class insecurities and their lack of ancient ancestral pedigrees. The elements of "(1) honor as immortalizing valor, particularly in the character of revenge against familial and community enemies; (2) opinion of others as an indispensable part of personal identity and gauge of self-worth; (3) physical appearance and ferocity of will as signs of inner merit; and (4) defense of male integrity and mingled fear and love of woman" were crucial in regulating a code of conduct that easily accommodated the new mythology of plantation tales that former slaves were now valued employees and family dependants, points out Wyatt-Brown.[12] "And of all these fictions," argues W. J. Cash in his *The Mind of the South* (1941), "the most inevitable and obviously indicated was just that one which we know today as the legend of the Old South—the legend of which the backbone is, of course, precisely the assumption that every planter was in the most rigid sense of the word a gentleman."[13] Cash's descriptions are apt when we consider the contours of behavior that shaped the usual plantation fantasy. Although the code of conduct for southern male behavior can readily be seen as the basis for the racial excuses that justified white male violence against perceived enemies (African American men) of white racial wholeness, it is just this code that Dunbar condemns in the novel's white male characters, and one that proves detrimental in its misapplication for white and black men alike.

While participating in the existing market for dialect poetry, Dunbar was often ambivalent about his fame as a "Negro" poet. His very existence as a poet, and more especially as a representative of black manhood, could not escape the ongoing contemporary debates about the nature of black men. As much as he might have wished to be regarded as just an American poet, Dunbar could not erase the dark color of his skin in a race- (and color-) conscious world, nor could he fail to recognize the racial ideology accepted by the majority of whites. When he entered the burgeoning market for plantation tales, Dunbar's distinctive African features were the selling point of critic William Dean Howells's critical evaluation of the young writer's work. At a time when the *only* interest in African American lives came primarily from white fabulists and racist propagandists, Howells declared Dunbar the "real thing" by emphasizing his racial characteristics, gathered from a photograph of the poet. "The face which confronted me when I opened the volume was the face of a young negro, with the race traits strangely accented: the black skin, the woolly hair, the thick out-rolling lips, and the mild, soft eyes of the pure African type. One cannot be very sure of the age of these people, but I should have thought that the poet was about twenty years old; and would have been worth, apart from his literary gift, twelve or fifteen hundred dollars under the hammer."[14] Howells's acclaim for Dunbar's work is, of course, muted by the decidedly racist description he uses to "market" the poet's racial status by explicitly pointing to his worth as chattel in familiar language his white readers would readily grasp. For Dunbar, the accentuation of race, the reminder of slavery, and (in his case especially) the darkness of his skin only contributed to a racial self-consciousness that permeated his social relationships and no doubt contributed to an uneasy accommodation with his growing fame. From a reading tour in London, Dunbar wrote his mother of the respect and civility with which he was received by Europeans, who accepted him on the same grounds accorded to any white man of genteel breeding. Dunbar assiduously followed the prescriptives for the public face of black masculinity dictated by a color- and class-conscious black middle class, but the standards were, nevertheless, bound by the dictates of race that American racial ideology declared off limits to black males. Thus, for Dunbar, Howells's praise was decidedly a mixed blessing. On the one hand, the poet gained a wider audience, but on the other, he felt that the critic "has done me irrevocable harm in the dictum he laid down regarding my dialect verse."[15]

In *The Color Complex: The Politics of Skin Color among African Americans*, Kathy Russell, Midge Wilson, and Ronald Hall cite a study done in the 1940s on color stereotyping among black teenagers. The teens were found to utilize 145 different terms to distinguish a wide variety of skin shades within the African American population. What the study indicated was that "in general, light to medium skin tones were linked to intelligence and refinement, while dark skin tones suggested toughness, meanness, and physical strength."[16] Although the study was done in the 1940s, these sentiments are not dissimilar to those held by blacks at the dawn of the twentieth century. Early twentieth-century guides on black middle-class behavior stressed the importance of genteel behavior in order to counteract the myth of black masculine disorder. Eleanor Alexander points to one 1902 guide as an example of black middle-class dictates: "Women were to accept nothing less than the 'Christian Gentleman.' Such men were not only religious, they were industrious, highly respectable, brilliantly educated, well trained, and extremely polished. These men were so polished, wrote the author, that they were 'as smooth as a mirror, and you can see your face in that mirror as well as the best looking glass.'"[17] Although he was accomplished by any measure, Dunbar would never see a white face in the mirror, even in the best of looking glasses.

After centuries of a deeply entrenched racial hegemony that placed a premium on European features, blacks themselves often believed what experience with racist values painfully taught them—and Dunbar was no exception to a well-learned lesson. "People of color," writes Alexander, "were taught that they had been enslaved because God had cursed them. Dark skin was a sign of the curse, and it made them inferior to whites."[18] What novelist Alice Walker termed "colorism" remains one of the most troubling aspects of "double-consciousness" in black America: that of "seeing oneself through the eyes of another" when the "other" is also African American.[19] The very fact of intraracial colorism underscores the psychic damage of a racial hegemony that devalues the African racial phenotype. Deeply conflicted by his own skin color, Dunbar—because of his new celebrity—was adopted as an "ornament" by an elite class of African Americans who embraced their "white" heritage while holding those with distinctive African features (like Dunbar's) as reasons for self-separation or—too often—derision. As self-proclaimed black elites who professed themselves to be the equals of whites in culture and taste, many were proud of the young poet's accomplishments, but as the son of two racially unmixed ex-slaves, Dunbar must have felt uneasy in their presence, no doubt aware of their pointed and often vocal hypocrisy regarding color and class. "A self-ordained group," continues Alexander, "these men and women engaged in uplifting the usually darker-skinned, less fortunate African Americans, even though many also distanced themselves from this group. The reason for this attitude . . . was that the two groups had little or nothing in common."[20]

That the dark-complexioned Dunbar internalized the racist dogma concerning black skin should not be surprising to many African Americans. "Few issues were more emotion-laden in the black community," writes Willard B. Gatewood, "than those relating to the color prejudices and preferences of blacks themselves."[21] Dunbar took no position in the debate across the color line about whether or not fair-skinned blacks were naturally superior because of their "white-blood." As Howells pointed out the poet's unmistakable "authenticity," the staunch detractors of color elitism thanked God that Dunbar was racially unmixed. "Among the dark-skinned Negroes regularly cited as proof that the 'full-blooded Negro' was the intellectual equal of either whites or mulattoes [was] . . . the poet Paul Laurence Dunbar."[22]

But Dunbar was torn about his position as a racial representative. Although there have been exceptions, black leaders during Dunbar's time were invariably much lighter skinned than the masses they presumably led. Moreover, as Dunbar knew too well, successful African American men whose outward appearance did not fit the profile for success were often given a pass as long as they understood and practiced the rules of masculine conduct. The well-known phenomenon of a class of blacks who were accorded "privileges" by the dominant white culture, point out the authors of *The Color Complex*, resulted in "a leadership pool of light-skinned Blacks with both money and education. Within that pool, it was often those Blacks light enough to pass who became the Black community's most vocal and active leaders."[23] Furthermore, these light-skinned males became the models for an idealized black masculinity as they met intransigent white racism on its own ground of national political rights.

In her account of the troubled marriage of Paul Laurence Dunbar and Alice Ruth Moore, Eleanor Alexander points to the poet's reference to himself in correspondence with his mother as "your ugly black boy" as a manifestation of his fixation on the ugly stigmas attached to the "pure" African type. Alexander surmises that Dunbar "was uncomfortable with the racialized self and had an intense inferiority complex."[24] Using the pre-marriage correspondence between Dunbar and his color-conscious wife, Alice Ruth Moore, Alexander paints the image of an unsteady beginning of a marriage doomed to fail because of the racial ambivalence of both parties. Although Dunbar fell in love with a picture of the fair-skinned Alice, he tellingly omitted to send her a picture of himself, most likely in the hope that his words and budding celebrity might ease the shock of his darkness and clearly defined African features. As Alexander notes, Dunbar's ambivalence about skin color no doubt contributed to the quick demise of the marriage; the "white" skin of his wife and her antipathy to black skin no doubt instigated bouts of physical abuse, actions clearly indicative of Dunbar's simultaneous attraction to and resentment of intraracial color hierarchies.

In his own assessment of *The Sport of the Gods*, Myles Hurd takes issue with critics like Addison Gayle Jr. who blame the ultimate fall of the Hamilton family on the negative aspects of the city. Such a reading, Hurd concludes, leads to "confusion over the extent to which the Hamiltons themselves are held responsible for what happens to them after their migration." Hurd continues: "Because Joe and Kit display the same negative traits in New York that were apparent to their fellow black townspeople in the rural South, we have grounds for arguing that the Northern city does not actually shape their lives as much as the narrator suggests."[25] Just what does Hurd believe to be the ultimate cause of the family's misfortune? Hurd argues that Dunbar points to the family's "excessive pride," which accounts for the "unwillingness of the other blacks in the Southern town to befriend them." As Hurd argues, Dunbar's depiction of the reaction of the Hamiltons' fellow blacks to Berry's arrest and imprisonment suggests that the arrest "can almost be regarded as a punishment he deserves because of his family's excessive pride."[26] However, I would suggest that the source of the Hamiltons' pride—the source of their "good fortune" in employment and their social status in their small black community—is undoubtedly the result of their light skin coloring and their mistaken belief in their "pride of place" in a color and class hierarchy.

Dunbar was neither the first African American nor the last to critique the long-held secret about skin color and the resulting class divisions among blacks in print. Although the criticisms of "blue vein society" exclusivity often took the form of oral protests among those on the receiving end of intraracial animus, many black newspapers railed against the practice at a time when the need for a public face of black political unity was most urgent. As the historian Gatewood points out, the more vocal black critics of a light-skinned supremacy often chose to believe the worst about so-called black aristocrats. Gatewood argues, "They might vehemently deny that mulattoes were intellectually superior to blacks, but they accepted and embellished upon other aspects of white notions about 'mixed-bloods.'" As one editor opined, "there was no use talking about the color prejudice of white folks because it could not equal the color prejudice among colored folks, for no one would call a dark-skinned man a 'nigger' so quickly as a light-colored dude."[27] The black journalist John E. Bruce took on the existence of "white fever" by ridiculing the so-called black elite's racial pretensions and their "narrow escape from being born white." According to Gatewood, "He ridiculed the pride they manifested in their blue veins, small hands, finely chiselled features, 'good' hair, and 'aristocratic insteps.' . . . He thought it absurd that those who were actually 'the illegitimate progeny of the vicious white men of the South' should attempt to pose as 'representatives of the better class of Negroes.'"[28] Dunbar, as a reporter for several black society pages, had a firsthand view of the color and class bias among the black elites. I would suggest that the racially ambivalent writer, who was so painfully self-conscious of his own African phenotype among the color-conscious black aristocracy, expressed his bitterest feelings in the one novel that contained black characters as he tapped into intraracial animosities that escaped the notice of whites.

Although Dunbar does not explicitly accuse the Hamilton family, as a whole, of colorism, the reaction of Berry's fellow blacks does support the author's protest against colorist ideals. Berry Hamilton's black community is a case in point. Falsely accused of stealing a large sum of money from his "indulgent" white employer, Berry—"an honest, sensible negro, and the pink of good servants"—is arrested, quickly found guilty of the theft, and sentenced to the penitentiary. With Berry still protesting his innocence, the remaining Hamiltons are forced from their comfortable home on the Oakley plantation. Significantly, Berry Hamilton is stripped of his minor leadership role and social standing in the black community. The black community refuses to believe in Berry's innocence and fails to rally around Fannie Hamilton and the children, Kit and Joe. As the treasurer of his lodge, Berry's fiduciary responsibilities are checked with suspicion by his lodge brothers "when they should have been visiting him with comfort, and they seemed personally grieved when his books were found to be straight."[29] Even the black church, the bedrock of the black community, turns its back on the unfortunate family. "The A.M.E. church, of which he had been an honest and active member, hastened to disavow sympathy with him, and to purge itself of contamination by turning him out. His friends were afraid to visit him and were silent when his enemies gloated. On every side one might have asked, Where is charity? And gone away empty."[30] Although Dunbar plausibly explains the lack of sympathy for the unfortunate Hamiltons as an incidence of either rank "jealousy" or, worse, the "strong influence of slavery," where "If they had sympathy, they dared not show it," such a contention hardly justifies the level of animosity directed at the family. Although the matter of skin color is not *explicitly* stated in the black community's lack of charity for the Hamilton family, the matter of intragroup class position suggests the long legacy of color privilege.

To Berry Hamilton's peers, he is "Mistah Rich Niggah," and the family many believed held itself above the rest now experiences the common lot of the majority of southern blacks. Not unlike the "mulatto aristocracy," the Hamilton's fatal flaw appears to be their mimicking and adoption of white attitudes and values as the path to American inclusion, which is based on their distancing from the darker-skinned masses. The fortunate senior Hamiltons inculcate the same (white) class values in their children—albeit, as we see later, with drastic results. Young Joe, especially, is affected by the values he learns "from scraping the chins of aristocrats, and rather too early in life bid fair to be a dandy." Young Kit is also placed above her peers with "the prettiest clothes of any of her race in the town." Thus Berry's fall is greeted not by the sympathy of a community used to the ways of white folks, but by community derision for a family that has set itself apart by "gittin' so high dat dey own folks ain' good enough fu' 'em."[31] But it is on the shoulders of young Joe Hamilton that Dunbar places the most rancor toward the colorist ideals of a community that judges black masculinity on its close imitation of whites in a bid to overturn racial animosity.

After his father's downfall, young Joe is "crushed" by the ignominy of the elder Hamilton's fate, and as Dunbar foreshadows what is to come, adversity does not make Joe a better man: "Dandy as he was, he was loyal, and when he saw his mother's tears and his sister's shame, something rose within him that had it been given play might have made a man of him, but, being crushed, died and rotted, and in the compost it made all the evil of his nature flourish."[32] The "quality mannahs" that Berry felt were "de p'opah" thing for his son to acquire are, significantly, the manners Joe has learned from young, dissolute white dandies like Francis Oakley, who, instead of following the southern code of honor by confessing to his older brother that he has wasted his allowance, lets Berry take the blame for stealing his money. "He was a handsome man, tall, slender, and graceful. He had the face and brow of a poet, a pallid face framed in a mass of dark hair. There was a touch of weakness in his mouth, but this was shaded and half hidden by a full mustache that made much forgivable to beauty-loving eyes."[33] The physical description of Francis can also be applied to the black elite as Dunbar has experienced and perceptively observed them. Moreover, by detailing the moral weakness of Francis Oakley, Dunbar is in a position to argue the inherent degradation of the former "planter class" (as I detail below), a class whose tissue-thin values of gentility were often adopted as models for a new post-Reconstruction black masculinity, a model that Joe has been encouraged to emulate.

Although the novel is not explicit in detailing the colorism of the Hamiltons, the accusation, I would argue, is reserved for the character of young Joe as Dunbar demonstrates the resentment of darker-skinned blacks toward the supposed supremacy of light-skinned males. Joe is unaware of the depth of black hostility that greets him as he looks for work to support the family in the forced absence of Berry. Trained as a barber, and forced to quit his job because of the shame of Berry's incarceration, Joe turns to the black community for work—"because all the white folks are down on us"—a condescension for Berry Hamilton's son. "He had never shaved a black chin or put shears to what he termed 'naps,' and he was proud of it. He thought, though, that after the training he had received from the superior 'Tonsorial Parlours' where he had been employed, he had but to ask for a place and he would be gladly accepted."[34] But the black community has not forgotten the intraracial color and class lines the Hamiltons, especially Joe, have practiced, and he ("a white man's bahbah") is derided for his anti-black attitudes. "W'y, I heah you say dat you couldn't git a paih of sheahs thoo a niggah's naps. You ain't been practisin' lately, has you? Oh, yes, you're done with burr-heads, are you? But burr-heads are good enough fu' you now."[35] Bereft of a community and under suspicion by formerly "friendly" whites, the family moves to New York in order to better its fortunes but is destroyed by the moral corruption of urban life.

Later critics found *The Sport of the Gods* "anti-urban." Critic Addison Gayle Jr. explicitly argues in *The Way of the New World: The Black Novel in America* that the novel reflects Dunbar's feeling that city corruption was more debilitating to the political future of blacks than the bigotry and violence of the South.[36] In his biography of the poet and novelist, Gayle writes: "In no other novel does the city come under as fierce an attack from Dunbar's pen.... The city is portrayed as the center of evil, vice, sin, and corruption. Into this hellhole falls the family of Berry Hamilton, a victim of the southern plantation system, whose daughter and son are ruined by this hostile environment."[37] Thomas L. Morgan, however, takes a more complex view of Dunbar's characterization of the city; unlike Gayle, who sees the city as the only space available for black freedom, Morgan understands Dunbar's urban space as one of possibilities that are "just as unavailable as" those offered by "the space of the pastoral South."[38] Dunbar reveals: "They had heard of New York as a place vague and far away, a city that, like Heaven, to them had existed by faith alone. All the days of their lives they had heard of it, and it seemed to them the center of all the glory, all the wealth, and all the freedom of the world. New York. It had an alluring sound."[39] And the novel does depict not a rise in the fortunes of the Hamilton family but a more devastating reversal in moral fortune as the city beats them back to the rural South. Thus, Kit and Joe (as read by Gayle) are "ruined" not so much "by this hostile environment" as by what they bring to this environment. Depicting the uncertainties of city freedom allows Dunbar to expose not only the Hamiltons' inherent moral weakness and lack of black community feeling but also the internal tensions that, publicly, many African Americans wished to believe had been long eradicated.

The Hamiltons are soon swept up in the excitement of New York black urbanity as they seek an alternative to the closed-mindedness of their rural black community. "To the provincial coming to New York for the first time," warns the author, "ignorant and unknown, the city presents a notable mingling of the qualities of cheeriness and gloom."[40] Although Fanny and Kit are at first wary of their new black community, Joe quickly succumbs to what he sees as a new model of swaggering black masculinity, but it is a masculine model already rooted in him by the standards of black masculinity from home. "Why should those fellows be different from him? Why should they walk the streets so knowingly, so independently, when he knew not whither to turn his steps? Well, he was in New York, and now he would learn."[41] But soon Joe makes himself believe that he has an advantage over these urban black males similar to his "advantages" over the southern blacks back home: his light color and close associations with whites. "One might find it in him to feel sorry for this small-souled, warped being," Dunbar explains, "if it were not that he was so blissfully, so conceitedly, unconscious of his own nastiness. Down home he had shaved the wild young bucks of the town, and while doing it drunk in eagerly their unguarded narrations of their gay exploits. So he had started out with false ideals as to what was fine and manly. He was afflicted by a sort of moral and mental astigmatism that made him see everything wrong.... He gave to all he saw a wrong value and upon it based his ignorant desires."[42] Joe soon becomes an habitué of a Bowery dive frequented by "sporting" men and women and white thrill-seekers who consider the Banner Club a bastion of black cultural authenticity. "Here the rounders congregated, or came and spent the hours until it was time to go forth to bout or assignation.... Among these, white visitors were not infrequent,—those who were young enough to be fascinated by the bizarre, and those who were old enough to know that it was all in the game."[43] The naive Joe, flush with his new feeling of urban "manhood," is greeted by a new black community of grifters and con men who pay his pretensions of color and class no mind: "They were polite. They treated him with a pale, dignified, high-minded respect that menaced his pocket-book and possessions."[44] For the denizens of the Banner Club, the southern code of masculine honor is something adhered to by rubes and "old-time darkies," and urban manhood is fashioned from a different perspective designed for survival. It is at the Banner Club—"an institution for the lower education of negro youth"[45]—where Joe's weak ideals lead him to further disaster.

Joe's infatuation with the easy-going Hattie Sterling leads to a large part of his education under the rough-and-tumble auspices of the Banner Club, and against the half-earnest warnings of the barkeep, Sadness. "It was very plain to him now that to want a good reputation was the sign of unpardonable immaturity, and that dishonor was the only real thing worthwhile. It made him feel better."[46] Thus Joe comes to recognize the code of honor for what it really is, but he has already made the choice of applying it to his own life, like so many of his white southern counterparts. Hattie, older and wiser than Joe, makes a huge impression on a youth eager to demonstrate his manhood with a new breed of woman: "She was a good-looking young woman and daintily made, though her face was no longer youthful, and one might have wished that with her complexion she had not run to silk waists in magenta.... Nothing could keep her from being glorious in his eyes,—not even the grease-paint which adhered in unneat patches to her face, nor her taste for whiskey in its unreformed state."[47] The affair proceeds quickly as Joe spends his hard-earned money on good times with Hattie and forgets his duties to the Hamilton household as male protector. Puffed up with masculine self-importance, Joe considers Hattie's choice in male companionship a good one. "She had taught him much, because it was to her advantage to do so. His greenness had dropped from him like a garment, but no amount of sophistication could make him deem the woman less perfect. He knew that she was much older than he, but he only took this fact as an additional sign of his prowess in having won her."[48] The implication here is that because of his "good looks" (i.e., European features), Joe is a fine catch for a woman "much older than he," although because of his further degradation, the gender expectations are brutally reversed as Joe is forced to trade his looks for financial support from Hattie and his sister, Kit.

Hattie's opinion of Joe reflects the attitude of the Banner Club: "She liked him in a half-contemptuous, half-amused way. He was a good-looking boy and made money enough, as she expressed it, to show her a good time, so she was willing to overlook his weakness and his callow vanity."[49] But as Joe's inner weakness overtakes him, Hattie is no longer amused by the former "good-looking boy." "No one had ever looked at you," she angrily tells a drunken Joe, "until I picked you up and you've been strutting around ever since, showing off because I was kind to you, and now this is the way you pay me back. Drunk half the time and half drunk the rest."[50] In just five years Joe has hit rock bottom and, after moving in with Hattie, becomes a drunken wreck who cadges drinks from the customers of the Banner Club. "He was so ready to go down that it needed but a gentle push to start him, and once started, there was nothing within him to hold him back from the depths. For his will was as flabby as his conscience, and his pride, which stands to some men for conscience, had no definite aim or direction. . . . He did not work, and yet he lived and ate and was proud of his degradation."[51] After Hattie throws him out, Joe returns to the only place where he knows he will be treated like a man and finally gets up the courage to prove his manhood by returning to her flat. "The realisation of what he was, of his foulness and degradation, seemed just to have come to him fully,"[52] and in his frustrated rage he murders the woman who has discarded his manhood.

I began this essay by arguing for an alternative reading of *The Sport of the Gods* as Dunbar's explicit criticism of the terms that shaped a new model of a black masculinity for the twentieth century. The point of the argument is that Dunbar was forced to redirect his criticism of plantation mythology by directly challenging the colorist ideas of the upper stratum of black America. Impelled by the belief that imitative modes of behavior would eventually lead to the path of full civil rights, many black elites sought to regulate and possibly erase the so-called bad behavior of their darker fellow African Americans. In an age of virulent racist propaganda, it was felt that regulation of black behavior (or, as one elite termed it, "niggerisms") should be avoided at all costs. Furthermore, we must contend with the resentment of darker-skinned blacks who accepted some of the worst myths about mixed-race individuals, who, in turn, were as racist as the whites they chose to emulate as they sought to sever their ties to the darker masses. But while many European values were worthwhile on paper, in reality too many were only figments of a white imagination. This is the milieu of which Dunbar was a part, and his last novel carefully notes the connection between a skewed set of values and the reality of those values as shared by both whites and blacks in the twin images of Joe Hamilton and Francis Oakley.

Albeit on a higher level than Joe, Francis Oakley—the typical southern gentleman of southern legend—goes against the code of honor by "allowing" the hapless Berry to take the blame for stealing his missing money. When Berry falls under suspicion, Francis half-heartedly defends him: "I would trust Hamilton anywhere . . . and with anything."[53] However, his brother, firmly believing in the old southern code of manly honor, and thinking his brother, in defending Berry, exhibits the best of southern chivalry toward the downtrodden, quickly reveals the lie at the heart of goodwill between white masters and their dutiful black servants:

> That's noble of you, Frank, and I would have done the same, but we must remember that we are not in the old days now. The negroes are becoming less faithful and less contented, and more's the pity, and a deal more ambitious, although I have never had any unfaithfulness on the part of Hamilton to complain of before.
> . . . The old negro knew nothing of the value of money. When he stole, he stole hams and bacon and chickens. These were his immediate necessities and the things he valued.[54]

A year after Berry is incarcerated, Maurice Oakley receives a letter from Francis, who supposedly is away in Paris, studying art. "First, now, it might be a notice that Frank had received the badge of the Legion of Honor,"[55] but the fateful letter does not involve "honor."

The expected code of southern honor, argues W. J. Cash, "is a fundamentally narrow and incomplete one. . . . These ideas, representing the highest product of aristocracy, and constituting perhaps its only real justification in the modern world, are only imperfectly adumbrated or are missing altogether."[56] The idea of "*noblesse oblige* and chivalry"[57] professed in legend and in the countless fantasies of idealized southern men is a myth stripped of its validity by Dunbar as a stricken Oakley finally reads his brother's confession: "You will remember that I begged you to be easy on your servant. You thought it was only my kindness of heart. It was not; I had a deeper reason. I knew where the money had gone and dared not tell." Francis's "deeper reason," like the predicament Joe Hamilton finds himself in with Hattie, is that he has been spending his money on a woman he cannot honorably marry: "Perhaps I would have been successful had I not met her, perhaps not."[58] It is implied that this woman whom Francis cannot give up is most likely a prostitute:

> When a man does not marry a woman, he must keep her better than he would a wife. It costs. All that you gave me went to make her happy.
> ... I would have asked you for more, and you would have given it; but that strange, ridiculous something which we misname Southern honor, that honor which strains at a gnat and swallows a camel, withheld me, and I preferred to do worse. So I lied to you.[59]

Finally, Francis vows that he will be no more: "Do not plead with me, do not forgive me, do not seek to find me, for from this time I shall be as one who has perished from the earth; I shall be no more."[60] The confession triggers a stroke as Maurice Oakley realizes the blow to the code of southern manhood, but as his wife asks, "What of Berry?" the elder Oakley succinctly demonstrates one of the realities of the code as it is practiced: the defense of family must come first. "What of Berry? ... What is Berry to Frank? What is that nigger to my brother? What are his sufferings to the honor of my family and name?"[61]

Maurice Oakley ends his life as a gibbering madman as his feverish brain tries to keep the secret of the family's lost honor, a tale (oddly enough) reported by the white New York newspaper reporter looking for a "sob story," who coaxes the whole tale out of a drunken Joe at the Banner Club. But in his demented ravings, the truth of the secret is confirmed, and even as Oakley in his madness continues to hide the letter on his person, neighboring whites rally to support the tattered shreds of Oakley's honor: "Even then they would have smothered it in silence, for the honor of one of their best families; but too many ears had heard."[62] And too many eyes have failed to read Paul Laurence Dunbar's indictment of the demoralizing effects of imitating values that are best left to the pages of fiction.

Close friend and fellow poet James Weldon Johnson cautioned his fellow black artists about airing black dirty laundry in public at a time when he felt art should exhibit the New Negro in the best light. Along with W. E. B. Du Bois and Alain Locke, Johnson fervently believed that African American cultural expressions would undoubtedly lead the way to full American acceptance—but only if blacks themselves refused to publicize internal faults or cater to the white marketplace for demeaning black caricatures. "They feel that other groups may afford to do otherwise," he warns, "but, as yet, the Negro cannot. This is not to say that they refuse to listen to criticism of themselves, for they often listen to Negro speakers excoriating the race for its faults and foibles and vices. *But these criticisms are not for the printed page. They are not for the ears and eyes of white America.*"[63] Johnson's advice, fortunately, was not taken by Dunbar. The significance of *Sport* is that it *does* explicitly critique Black "faults and foibles and vices" through its awareness of a doubled audience—that is, white readers read the surface-level meaning of the text, but for many black readers, Dunbar's text reads as a subtle criticism of masculine ideals of color and class—but provides a subtext readily accessible to perceptive black readers. Although such a specialized reading for multiple audiences may fall prey to the charge of black "insiderism," I would counter this charge with a reminder of the legacy of internal black criticism that continues to this day. The literary importance of *Sport* is that it is a precursor to Wallace Thurman's *The Blacker the Berry* and the late twentieth-century works of Alice Walker and Toni Morrison, which all deal with the issues of intraracial color and class consciousness, regardless of the presence of the ears and eyes of white America. The novel signals the beginning of a necessary and significant attempt to eradicate one of the most demoralizing and debilitating effects of white racism: intraracial color and class bias and its confluence with a black code of masculinity for a new age.

Notes

1. Darwin T. Turner, "Paul Laurence Dunbar: The Rejected Symbol," in *The Black Novelist*, ed. Robert Hemenway (Columbus, Ohio: Charles E. Merrill, 1970), 35.
2. Ibid.
3. Eric J. Sundquist, *To Wake the Nations: Race in the Making of American Literature* (Cambridge, Mass.: Harvard University Press, 1993), 425.
4. Ibid., 416.
5. Ibid., 416–17.
6. Ibid.
7. Paul Laurence Dunbar, *The Sport of the Gods* (New York: Penguin, 1999), 1.
8. See *Oak and Ivy: A Biography of Paul Laurence Dunbar* (Garden City: Doubleday, 1971) for Gayle's discussion of *The Sport of the Gods*.
9. Turner, "The Rejected Symbol," 35, 36.
10. Dunbar, *Sport*, 1.
11. Bertram Wyatt-Brown, *Honor and Violence in the Old South* (New York: Oxford University Press, 1986), 27.
12. Ibid.
13. W. J. Cash, *The Mind of the South* (New York: Knopf, 1941), 63.
14. Qtd. in James B. Stronks, "Paul Laurence Dunbar and William Dean Howells," *Ohio Historical Quarterly* 67, no. 2 (1982): 97.
15. Ibid.
16. Kathy Russell, Midge Wilson, and Ronald E. Hall, *The Color Complex: The Politics of Skin Color among African Americans* (New York: Anchor Books, 1992), 66.

17. Eleanor Alexander, *Lyrics of Sunshine and Shadow: The Tragic Courtship and Marriage of Paul Laurence Dunbar and Alice Ruth Moore* (New York: New York University Press, 2001), 82.
18. Ibid., 41.
19. Alice Walker, "If the Present Looks Like the Past, What does the Future Look Like?" in *In Search of Our Mothers' Gardens: Womanist Prose* (San Diego, Calif.: Harcourt Brace, 1983).
20. Alexander, *Lyrics of Sunshine and Shadow*, 46.
21. Willard B. Gatewood, *Aristocrats of Color: The Black Elite, 1880–1920* (Fayetteville: University of Arkansas Press, 2000), 155.
22. Ibid., 159.
23. Russell, Wilson, and Hall, *The Color Complex*, 34–35.
24. Alexander, *Lyrics of Sunshine and Shadow*, 40.
25. Myles Hurd, "Blackness and Borrowed Obscurity: Another Look at Dunbar's *The Sport of the Gods*," *Callaloo* 4, no. 1–3 (1981): 91.
26. Ibid., 93.
27. Gatewood, *Aristocrats of Color*, 158.
28. Ibid., 165.
29. Dunbar, *Sport*, 27.
30. Ibid., 28.
31. Ibid., 3, 29.
32. Ibid., 34.
33. Ibid., 7.
34. Ibid., 37.
35. Ibid., 38.
36. Addison Gayle Jr., *The Way of the New World: The Black Novel in America* (Garden City, N.Y.: Anchor Press, 1976), 56.
37. Ibid., 151.
38. Thomas L. Morgan, "The City as Refuge: Constructing Urban Blackness in Paul Laurence Dunbar's *The Sport of the Gods* and James Weldon Johnson's *The Autobiography of an Ex-Colored Man*," *African American Review* 38 (2004): 220.
39. Dunbar, *Sport*, 43–44.
40. Ibid., 46.
41. Ibid., 49.
42. Ibid., 57.
43. Ibid., 67.
44. Ibid., 64.
45. Ibid., 66.
46. Ibid., 86.
47. Ibid., 71.
48. Ibid., 75.
49. Ibid.
50. Ibid., 115.
51. Ibid., 113–14.
52. Ibid., 119.
53. Ibid., 14.
54. Ibid., 14–15.
55. Ibid., 104.
56. Cash, *The Mind of the South*, 76–77.
57. Wyatt-Brown, *Honor and Violence*, 38.

58. Dunbar, *Sport*, 180.
59. Ibid., 109.
60. Ibid., 110.
61. Ibid., 111–12.
62. Ibid., 138.
63. James Weldon Johnson, "The Dilemma of the Negro Author," in *The New Negro: Readings on Race, Representation, and African American Culture, 1892–1938*, ed. Henry Louis Gates Jr. and Gene Andrew Jarrett (Princeton, N.J.: Princeton University Press, 2007), 381 (emphasis added).

14
Mobile Blacks and Ubiquitous Blues

Urbanizing the African American Discourses in Paul Laurence Dunbar's The Sport of the Gods

MICHAEL P. MORENO

AT THE DAWN OF THE TWENTIETH CENTURY, African Americans—well over two million, according to Houston A. Baker Jr.[1]—were migrating from the American South in record numbers to new locations throughout the North, the Midwest, and the western states. Lured by the promise of true emancipation and social justice, many families traversed difficult and unaccommodating terrains into industrialized urban spaces in the hope of securing new opportunities for themselves and for subsequent generations. Accordingly, this diasporic movement, at once external and internal, signaled a new era in the cultural production of black American consciousness through the articulation of the migration narrative, an artistic genre that transformed African American literature and set it on a course for wider recognition. As one of the first of these narratives to remold and resituate a mobile black community for the new century, Paul Laurence Dunbar's *The Sport of the Gods* (1902) designs a landscape of social justice that redefines and reinterprets the role of agency and subjectivity among urban and rural blacks and between blacks and whites. His novel recasts the African American archetype in literature and underscores how new forms of black consciousness and conditions engendered innovative constructs of the African American narrative. On the surface, the novel highlights the story of an African American family moving from bad to worse. However, viewed through the lens of postbellum dichotomies—North and South, black and white, industrial urbanism and agrarianism, spirituality and the blues—Dunbar's characters migrate back and forth along these narrative axes as they search for concrete identities in the wake of early American modernism. The novel is one of the first narratives to articulate the modernist black urban identity and its postbellum origins.

Part of what constructs black identity in the migration narrative can be comprehended by way of an examination of the disparate spaces generated by these postbellum dichotomies. Two antipodal locations in *The Sport of the Gods* that assist in defining the political, racial, and classificatory climate of the black community in the early twentieth century are the leisure bars that frame the discursive communities for southern whites and northern blacks. The first of these antithetical spaces is the Continental Hotel, located in the rural South and patronized by the "old regime"[2] of white plantation owners; the second is the urban Banner Club frequented by the African American professionals, artisans, gamblers, and stage performers of New York City. As black bodies moved from southern white spaces, they carried with them a legacy of disenfranchisement and dispossession. In the novel, this legacy produces an active "blues" vocabulary that renders the Continental Hotel and the Banner Club not so much societal contrasts as a discursive nexus of race, geography, spirituality, and ideology through which new languages for articulating psychological lynching and industrial alienation are forged. Despite new horizons of liberty for blacks after emancipation and laws relating to segregation, cultural and juridical practices on the part of the hegemonic apparatus of the Reconstructionist South created for blacks "the awesome burden of being 'free' in a racist society when one is black," according to James H. Cone.[3] As such, the vocabulary of the blues serves as "secular spirituals," Cone contends, for those emigrating from the new chains of disenfranchisement and searching for a new connection to the self and to the diasporic African American community at large.

The opening chapters of Dunbar's *The Sport of the Gods* commence with the indictment of Berry Hamilton, the longtime black servant of the white southern Oakley family. After an unfair investigation into the matter of in-house theft, Maurice Oakley, an industrious plantation owner whose savvy business practices have ensured his family's continued postbellum fortune, is convinced that his loyal butler is responsible for stealing money from the bedroom bureau of his younger half-brother, Frank. Despite Hamilton's innocence, the white judge and grand jury find Hamilton guilty and sentence him to ten years of hard labor. The shame and injustice scar the rest of the Hamilton family, which is comprised of Fannie, Berry's wife; Joe, the eldest son; and Kitty, the younger daughter. After Hamilton's sentencing, they are asked to vacate the small cottage on the Oakleys' property. Evicted from their home and spurned by the black community, the three make their way up to New York like fugitives on the run from southern social injustice. In New York, news of the patriarch's incarceration soon reaches the social and labor circles of the Hamiltons' northern home. This causes the Hamilton family to disintegrate slowly. Although Berry is finally released by the novel's end, his family has broken apart: Fannie marries an abusive man, Joe is arrested for murder, and Kitty runs off with a chorus line. With no other place to go, Berry and Fannie, whose second husband dies abruptly, return to their southern cottage and to the daily haunts of Maurice Oakley's insane wails of shame, a shame generated by Frank, who, it is revealed, gambled the money away in an attempt to pay his debts.

At the heart of this misery and seemingly anti-urban narrative is the ubiquitous blues. Misunderstood, unsung, and forgotten by these characters, the lyrical blues not only "encompasses the psychological state of someone who is exploited, abused, dominated, and dispossessed" but as a force is collected and composed by artists who draw from the narrative well of African American exploitation, abuse, domination, and dispossession. When an artist sings the blues, a metanarrative is generated that speaks of community and commonality, for "the blues in not a passive migrant";[4] rather, the genre is an active agent responsible for acclimating the migrant and redefining his or her new urban identity.

From the novel's inception, this blues metanarrative is challenged by the patriarchal hegemony of white male aristocrats, men who construct themselves as "sovereign subject[s]" in the postbellum South and who maintain that "the African American is . . . a mere object, as a body, a commodity, or chattel."[5] This patriarchal discourse is confirmed in the social exchange that transpires at the Continental Hotel shortly before Berry Hamilton's trial. In this leisure space, members of the old regime of southern gentlemen reinforce each other's convictions of the intellectual and physiological inferiority of African Americans. Sipping their drinks, the gentlemen assert the racist discourse that trickles down to the white mobs and fuels their appetite for lynchings, acts of disenfranchisement of the southern black community, and operations of social injustice. For the patrons of the Continental Hotel—an ironic title for men who reveal their intellectual provinciality regarding the governance of the postbellum South—crafting a rhetoric that would sustain firm control over African Americans by rendering them sociopolitical orphans in need of patriarchal counsel and ideological discipline would ensure the patrimony's continued role as purveyor of the larger southern symbolic "family." According to Casey Inge, the "disciplinary patronage" represented by the Continental Hotel gentlemen in Dunbar's novel "is naturalized by retrogressionist rhetoric, which imagined African Americans as degenerating into a state of savagery without the firm guidance of the white hand, and by eugenic or naturalist accounts, which viewed the sympathetic bond between black and white as the only hope for moral salvation."[6] As such, the southern patriarchs maintain that their position of power and privilege is a natural feature of governance, thus solidifying their dominance in the social and economic constellation of the American South.

This hope for order and civility is expressed by Horace Talbot, one of the Continental Hotel's loyal patrons and "a man who was noted for his kindliness towards people of colour."[7] Talbot's speech to his peers echoes the racist rhetoric of intellectual superiority and exposes the mistaken belief fed by this rhetoric in African Americans' inability to comprehend the meaning and application of freedoms theoretically granted to them by the Fourteenth Amendment. Talbot believes that the North erred in the aftermath of the Civil War by "turning these people loose upon the country . . . without the knowledge of what the first principle of liberty was. The natural result is that these people are irresponsible. They are unacquainted with the ways of our higher civilisation, and it'll take them a long time to learn."[8] (Likewise, Talbot envisions the return of sojourning blacks to the white fold of the pre–Civil War southern political family as a prodigal son's return to his father's benevolent protection: "I foresee the day when these people themselves shall come to us Southerners of their own accord and ask to be re-enslaved until such time as they shall be fit for freedom.")[9] This patriarchal egalitarianism mixed with an ironic sense of social justice comforted the purveyors of the southern aristocracy while it blinded them to the humanity and agency of African Americans. Indeed, men like the patrons of the Continental Hotel facilitate the creation of trauma that eventually produces the blues narratives that circulate throughout the diasporic African American community.

Although Berry Hamilton's alleged crime initiates the dialogue in the Continental Hotel, Hamilton's circumstances are symbolic of the indictment of the entire black community, for "All niggers are alike," asserts Beachfield Davis, another member of the old regime participating in the gentlemen's conversation, "and there's no use trying to do anything with them."[10] The utter "depravity" and "irresponsibility"[11] of Hamilton's actions are emblematic of all African Americans' incapability of ascertaining right from wrong, according to this retrogressionist rhetoric. As such, the Continental Hotel functions as a socio-spatial engine for the manufacturing of a paternalistic and racist discourse in the late nineteenth-century white South, a discourse that (re)criminalizes all African Americans and robs them of their liberties and their agency and denies them justice while ensuring a perpetual social lynching that scars black bodies with a sense of inferiority and alienation.

Abandoned by the black community and dispossessed by the whites, the remaining Hamiltons are forced to leave the sedate confines of the Oakley plantation to search for work and a new life. For the banished Hamiltons, New York City represents a Promised Land that would salve the wounds of abuse and criminalization and redirect their lives through an enterprise of opportunity and equality. "They had heard of New York as a place vague and far away, a city that, like Heaven, to them had existed by faith alone. All the days of their lives they had heard of it, and it seemed to them the center of all the glory, all the wealth, and all the freedom of the world. New York. It had an alluring sound. Who would know them there? Who would look down upon them?"[12] Despite the economic pulls of opportunity and unjust pushes from discrimination that brought thousands of African Americans from the South to the northern and western states at the end of the nineteenth century, "many of the social evils"—and financial evils—"which oppressed blacks in the rural areas and small towns of the South were not automatically removed simply by moving to a different city, state, or region."[13] Indeed, the Hamilton family soon comes to discover this during their tenure in New York City.

While the American city slowly entered a boom in material wealth at the turn of the twentieth century, it achieved a modernist aesthetic that manifested itself in the mass production of industrial and domestic goods. Thus, the philosophy of production gave birth to the various machines that accelerated life and manufactured the illusion that the common citizen could participate in this new America. Underscoring this theme of mechanization, the Hamilton family takes the train out of the South and into the North. A paradigm of masculine American power and virility, the locomotive serves to thrust these migrants into the enclosure of the urban whirlpool of New York.

Engaged in this shared power of mobility, African American men and women migrants experienced the train through different lenses of interpretation and artistic expression. According to Hazel V. Carby, "the train, which had symbolized freedom and mobility for men in male blues songs, became a contested symbol. The sound of the train whistle, a mournful signal of imminent desertion and future loneliness, was reclaimed as a sign of women too were on the move."[14] This disjunctive climate of masculine opportunism in the North and feminine dispossession of the South is marked by Fannie, Kitty, and Joe's silent responses to riding the train northward: "As the train drew out of the station, [Joe] did not look back upon the place which he hated, but Fannie and her daughter let their eyes linger upon it until the last house, the last chimney, and the last spire faded from their sight, and their tears fell and mingled as they were whirled away toward the unknown."[15] The fact that these experiences are now becoming internalized for the Hamiltons is significant in that not only the body but equally the psyche of the migrant is reorganized by the socio-technological changes in time and space within the realm of northern urban culture.[16]

For the Hamiltons, their initial impressions of the urban sensations of New York create "a notable mingling of the qualities of cheeriness and gloom"[17] that signify the paradoxical landscape such a space generates. Unlike the wide-open parcels of the rural South, the urban North dramatically contains and restrains its dwellers while offering them a voyeur's visual feast of "the bustling mob"[18] gliding down streets, alleyways, and sidewalks, as if vessels effortlessly charting their way through an urban delta. Concerned for her family's moral and psychological welfare, Fannie maintains that "the very bigness of [New York] frightened her and made her feel alone"; [19] however, "Joe and Kitty were more concerned with what they saw about them than with what their future would hold."[20] Indeed, the city is in constant flux between varying experiential degrees of perspective and interpretation. The city stimulated an immediate connection to events swirling about the observer and invited his or her participation. Past and future were irrelevant in the modernist city, for new beginnings promised great things to come but firmly rooted the urban dweller in the present. As such, Dunbar's novel pays great heed to how the psychological apparatus of the neophyte migrant would find negotiating the urban terrain both challenging and intriguing.

In an effort to understand how the discursive architecture of the migrant narrative constitutes a site of mobility, it is important to survey the paradigms of the ancestor and stranger figures in *The Sport of the Gods*. In her seminal work, *"Who Set You Flowin'?" The African-American Migration Narrative,* scholar Farah Jasmine Griffin posits that ancestors and strangers play an integral role in articulating the cultural, gendered, and spatial relations constructed and deconstructed by the migrant narratives themselves. Whereas the ancestor figure has the ability to provide "the new migrant a cushion with which to soften the impact of urbanization,"[21] the stranger "possesses no connections to the community,"[22] for he or she is a product of the northern urban culture and inhabits a site of "critical consciousness" as a "cosmopolite."[23] Both the ancestor and the stranger are complex components in the literary web of the migration narrative, since both may conversely be engineered through the form of individuals, songs, memories, or geographical spaces. Often, however, these configurations cross over and "exist in the same figure" despite being "polar opposites."[24] The ancestor and stranger, as such, provide the migration narrative with a dialectical frame that locates and situates the migrating characters within overlapping sites of power and incarceration.

In Dunbar's *The Sport of the Gods,* the debonair William Thomas, a train porter who welcomes the Hamiltons to New York City and recommends appropriate lodging, serves as the stranger in contrast to Fannie Hamilton's role as the ancestral southern paragon of morality and familial community to her unacclimated children. It is Thomas, "a loquacious little man with a confident air born of intense admiration of himself,"[25] who first introduces the Hamilton family to the African American theater, and then young Joe Hamilton to the Banner Club. Believing that he "had suddenly stepped into the place of the man of the family,"[26] Joe views his introduction to the urban life as an opportunity to mold himself into a cosmopolite rather than as a means to protect his family, as his father might have done during a geographical relocation from the country to the city. True to his task as the novel's stranger figure, Thomas facilitates the emergence of Joe's urban identity with the veiled intention of making overtures to Joe's attractive sister, Kitty. This in turn renders Thomas's character suspect, for he operates not on the premise of strengthening the newly arrived family, nor with the intention of animating the growing black community in Harlem. Rather, Thomas's role as stranger in the narrative demonstrates an opportunistic consciousness in urban culture, one antithetical to community building.

Although Thomas hosts the Hamiltons on urban outings, his offerings "of (mis)guidance, advice, and a new worldview"[27] entice Joe into the rhythmic undertones of urban pleasures and decadence that fuel Joe's desire to mimic "the swaggering, sporty young negroes"[28] he has been observing along the street corners and row-house stoops. Consequently, Joe's "induction" into the Banner Club affords him the chance to abandon the rural tenets of southern virtues in favor of the more intoxicating acceleration of urban vices.

A New York pool hall and nightclub, the Banner Club functions as the geocultural antithesis to the posh southern Continental Hotel, for the Banner Club is "a social cesspool, generating a poisonous miasma and reeking with the stench of decayed and rotten moralities. There is no defense to be made for it. But what do you expect when false idealism and fevered ambition come face to face with catering cupidity?"[29] As a discursive nexus for rural naïveté and urban adroitness, the Banner Club operates in the social production of communal suspension, in which the club's patrons are exposed to negotiating strategies that may ensure their survival in the urban terrain of the North. Houston A. Baker Jr. calls this nexus a "matrix" and maintains that such a location "is a point of ceaseless input and output, a web of intersecting, crisscrossing impulses always in productive transit. Afro-American blues constitute such a vibrant network" and function as "the multiplex, enabling *script* in which Afro-American cultural discourse is inscribed."[30] The Banner Club, then, architecturally frames the black urban community by producing variable gravitational pushes and pulls among its patrons, discursive exchanges that can provide an urban milieu with a blues language for articulating the psychological lynching of alienation and political disavowal of black confinement within the city limits of New York. Indeed, part of the education of the migrant involves learning this new urban language, a blues discourse, and this is something Joe does not seem to comprehend fully in *The Sport of the Gods*.

Bringing Joe to the Banner Club serves a double purpose for Thomas. On the one hand, there is a gaming atmosphere among the club's patrons in which duping and deceiving naive outsiders serves as sport, for cleverness and mental dexterity always win the approval of the patrons. On the other hand, the "parasites [who] came there to find victims, politicians for votes, reporters for news, and artists of all kinds for colour and inspiration"[31] formed an assemblage of abraded human interaction where the blues was literally and figuratively performed as a means of negotiating this Janus-faced terrain. These performances—whether they were on stage behind a tinkling instrument, crooned through a microphone, or transpiring at a dark corner table behind a whiskey glass—created a public space for both newly arrived and longtime African American urban dwellers to mesh with the sounds, rhythms, and beats of the mechanized city. Moreover, "the performance of the blues often offered a type of safe space in the North which allowed for community and regrouping as well as providing a transitional space where migrants could make the transition from Southern migrant to urban dweller."[32] This sense of crossing over—and crisscrossing mobility—characterizes the language and actions of those who initially welcome Joe Hamilton into the unfurling folds of the Banner Club.

Phrases and actions possess a double meaning, and salutations take on deeper political and cultural resonances—all blues narrative devices that are completely lost on Joe. As Thomas introduces Joe to the various patrons of the club, each is able to cadge free drinks from the gullible young southerner, for "a smart man don't need to show nothin'. All he's got to do is to act."[33] The figure who buttresses the social architecture of the Banner Club is a young man by the name of Sadness. He is the last to meet Joe and the first to make a memorably odd impression on the newcomer. Regarding Joe with a paradoxical countenance of "innocent gloom," Sadness reveals that "a distant relative of mine once had a great grief. I have never recovered from it."[34] Perplexed by this awkward exchange, Joe quickly dismisses the revelation under the sardonic cloak of the others' laughter. As Sadness's character develops through *The Sport of the Gods*, readers learn that he is burdened by the sorrow of his father's lynching in Texas. Sadness becomes the quintessential bluesman in the novel and performs as a musical "barometer of the experiences of black people in the United States."[35] Nevertheless, Joe's greatest obstacle is his inability to be reached by these blues lyrics—renderings that come subtly from those around him.

In many respects, the Banner Club offers the New York dwellers a site of interaction and discourse, for it is above all a location that provides many with a "home life which is so lacking among certain classes in New York."[36] Soon after this "shearing [of] another lamb"[37] in the discursive slaughterhouse of the Banner Club, Thomas leads Joe, who is by now a little poorer and a little drunker but none the wiser, to the nucleus of this social terrain. In the upstairs space of the club, "the lower education of [this] negro youth"[38] continues among the small tables and churning live music. This is where the blues becomes animated not only in songs sung by the evening's various performers, but also by the swaying, drinking, and laughing bodies who "can experience the new urban rhythm of life as one of the communitas, in a kind of modern urban 'tribal ritual' . . . in which the worries of everyday life are suspended."[39] As such, Joe is politely ushered by the club's proprietor to a table where he "can see everybody that comes in"[40] and be in a position that might allow him to begin to absorb the urban performances and vocabularies of this suspended public milieu. Indeed, *The Sport of the Gods* makes the case that it is imperative for "the black population to formulate its own values and rely, regardless of white perceptions, on its own distinct voice."[41] The many bodies who inhabit the Banner Club night after night are manipulated "by a pragmatic city expressed in popular forms [and] consumed as information and entertainment" by the popular media venues.[42] Accordingly, this distinct voice, an urban blues voice, defines the narrative of the northern city through the lens of the quotidian black experience. Both the Banner Club and the Continental Hotel, then, can be defined as geopolitical nexuses of power and survival. Whereas the social space of the hotel employs static performances—the same men gathering for the same drinks to discuss the same issues over and over again—to ensure a consistent public display of consensus, the club relies on its capacity to reinvent positions of power among its variable patrons, thus underscoring its ability to churn and move like the blues.

While Dunbar weaves the blues fabric of the Banner Club as "a mediational site where familiar antinomies are resolved (or dissolved) in the office of adequate cultural understanding,"[43] he also demonstrates how the crisscrossing of racial relations further complicates the politics of exchange in the black archipelago of New York. The only identified white male patron of the club is Skaggs, a guileful yellow journalist for the New York *Universe,* which is a Hearst-esque newspaper bent on circulating stories for mass consumption regardless of their reliability or credibility. In the novel, Skaggs's presence in the club signifies the ubiquity of white penetration into black culture regardless of geography. As in the South, there was a racial double standard for mobility in the northern cities. Whereas blacks were relegated to confining pockets within the urban landscape, whites enjoyed the privilege of crossing the color barriers and patronizing various establishments regardless of the dominant racial composition of such spaces. Later on in the early twentieth century, whites would control many of the popular Harlem nightclubs and black tenements, often charging exorbitant rents. According to Claude McKay's important work on the history of the growing black community in New York City entitled *Harlem: Negro Metropolis,* "Blacks willingly paid from a hundred to two hundred per cent more than did the whites [in rent]. And they paid promptly in those days. They were eager to prove that they were good tenants, worthy of living in a better residential district. Penned in the gangster-ruled blocks of lower Manhattan, they were bound to expand or explode."[44] The racial imbalance in urban ownership, patronization, and mobility suggests that African Americans had to design alternative social and spatial orders to combat segregation and produce new forms of agency within the growing community.

Part of the hegemonic privilege of whites allowed for white mobility in both black and white spaces. However, that white presence could never fully be trusted or accepted in the black community. Despite the fact that Skaggs has "been invited to join some of the swell [i.e., white] clubs" in New York, he'd "rather come down here and fellowship right in with" the club regulars, the reporter tells Joe upon meeting him. After inventing a story about being raised on a slaveholding plantation, he states that he's "played with darkies ever since [he] could remember." Skaggs appropriates a racially egalitarian guise when he comes to the Banner Club in an effort to blend in with the African Americans. However, "it was the same old story that the white who associates with negroes from volition usually tells,"[45] according to the narrator, to explain his presence in the bar, where he would look for an exotic story to spill across the pages of his newspaper. Nevertheless, Joe is completely taken with a white man who seems so cordial to a black man and appears to be so honest and forthcoming, something unique from his experiences of southern white men. Thomas insists that Joe, who has been duped by the reporter's lie, not take what Skaggs says seriously. However, Joe, unable once more to untangle the language of deceit, maintains that "Thomas was jealous of the attention the white man had shown him and wished to belittle it."[46] In taking this position, of course, Joe plays directly into the hands of white hegemony: a black man's desire for power is mistakenly predicated on attention or acceptance from the white community. Joe's need to participate in the illusory topography of a racially equal and empowering northern world is so strong that he is willing to barter his integrity along with his common sense for a taste of this paradisiacal dream he's harbored since arriving in New York. For Joe Hamilton, the northern city cannot bear any resemblance to the rural South, lest he discover that black liberty is a social and political facade.

The evening culminates when Joe is introduced to Hattie Sterling, who is "altogether lovely to him, and his delight was the more poignant as he recognized in her one of the girls he had seen on the stage a couple of weeks ago."[47] At this juncture, Thomas relegates the responsibility of the stranger-guide to Hattie, who, in her role as singer/lover, draws Joe farther away from his mother and sister and pulls him closer to the culture of the Banner Club. However, this bliss is short lived. Although "Joe is thrilled with his new set of friends and falls in love with the illusion of his popularity,"[48] a former resident of the Hamiltons' southern community by the name of Minty Brown makes her way into their social circles and threatens to reveal the secret that the Hamilton patriarch has been incarcerated for stealing. Here the South clashes with the North in the migrants' world and compromises the new identities being cultivated in the urban environment. This was integral to the black migrant's experience. "Black migration toward the end of the [twentieth] century clearly revealed . . . that improving one's economic position was easier than escaping social injuries. The curses of second-class citizenship were to follow blacks regardless of their choice of destination."[49] As such, Minty Brown's presence is double edged, for it is a reminder that the Hamiltons are linked to criminal behavior in the white world and that they have been expelled by the southern black community.

In Joe's broken world, where the nightmares of the South now collide with the dreams of the North, the blues haunt the soul. James H. Cone suggests that "the personification of the blues feeling and experience is most revealing: to black folk he is no shadow, but a person whose presence is inescapable."[50] The arrival of Minty Brown and Joe's confession to Sadness are the genesis of Joe's own attempt at articulating a blues discourse within the narrative. Dejected and blaming his mother for her inhospitable reception of Minty Brown, Joe returns to the Banner Club to soak his miseries in alcohol and lament the fact that his mother's arrogance and disavowal of Minty will cause the young woman to reveal his father's crime, thus destroying the reputation he has carefully been sculpting for nearly a year. Indeed, Joe "had no doubt but that the malice of Minty Brown would prompt her to seek out all of his friends and make the story known."[51] The fragile identity he thought he had forged at the Banner Club would suddenly mean nothing. Where then would he turn if his surrogate family abandoned him? As though on cue, the "sadly gay" Sadness enters and sits down beside Joe, ordering himself a drink on "Mr. Hamilton's" tab. Desperately in need of redemption, Joe reveals his troubles, which are the source of his own sadness. Dunbar's eleventh chapter, in which the conversation between Joe and Sadness transpires, is appropriately titled "Broken Hopes," for it reads like a blues song and underscores Joe's "desire . . . to tell this man the whole truth"[52] about his current misfortunes and troubled past.

To return to Farah Jasmine Griffin's construction of the ancestor-stranger dichotomy in the migration narrative, it is the character of Sadness who simultaneously embodies both of these figures in *The Sport of the Gods* and offers a metaphorical link between the northern and southern experiences. Since Joe has completely divorced himself from the ancestral space—through his rejection of both his geographical southern home/identity and his disassociation from his mother, he requires a balance that will return his psyche to a platitude of symmetry. Sadness, as a paragon for blues itself, attempts to reinterpret the Banner Club as a "safe space" for Joe through the blues revelation he utters; Joe's mental incarceration and alienation have relegated him outside the parameters of African American communalism. Whereas locations such as the Banner Club serve as "spaces of retreat [from], healing [of], and resistance" to the historical, physical, and psychological trauma experienced by the greater black community, Joe has transformed the club into a "provincial" space that does "not encourage resistance but instead" helps him become a "complacent [subject] whose only aim is to exist within the confines of power that oppress" him.[53] Because of Joe's individual quest to become something on his own, he now finds himself alone and suffering with no manner through which to articulate this emotion or express it constructively. Blues, then, can become both the ancestor, who recalls the idyllic southern home of memory, and the stranger, whose sounds produce the syncopated rhythms of the lonesome city. However, Joe is too far removed to hear the blues in his own words and therefore remains alienated from himself and the black community.

Despite his educational year in "the New York nightclubs," Joe has learned absolutely nothing about being a black urban dweller, much to Sadness's disappointment. Observing "his companion through a wreath of smoke,"[54] Sadness demonstrates an urban version of what W. E. B. Du Bois has called a "double consciousness" in the African American. According to Dickson D. Bruce's critical essay on Du Bois's philosophical construction of black consciousness, such a state involves the experience of

> A "two-ness" of being "an American, a Negro; two warring ideals in one dark body, whose dogged strength alone keeps it from being torn asunder."
> ... Du Bois referred most importantly to an internal conflict in the African American individual between what was "African" and what was "American."
> ... For Du Bois the essence of a distinctive African consciousness was its spirituality, a spirituality based in Africa but revealed among African Americans in their folklore, their history of patient suffering, and their faith.[55]

Here, double consciousness, like the dual role of the ancestor/stranger, serves as an appropriate metaphor for the post-emancipation condition of the African American. Du Bois suggests that blacks are not truly liberated despite the language of the law; rather, they are statically incarcerated in a new slavery experience. The great irony is that one is free when one is no longer a slave, and yet the African American is still unable to fully enjoy the promises of the Fourteenth Amendment despite his or her constitutional liberty.

Sadness's *urban* double consciousness, one that moves from a spiritual base in the South to a blues system in the North, stems from his paradoxical ancestor-stranger role in Dunbar's *The Sport of the Gods*. As the embodiment of the blues, Sadness is afforded a level of enlightenment since he is able to articulate/sing of the pain endured by the rural and urban black communities, for his own father was lynched in Texas, which suggests that he suffers from the psychological lynching this entails. "I am ungratefully sad," he relates to Joe. "A man must be very high or very low to take the sensible view of life that keeps him from being sad. I must confess that I have aspired to the depths without ever being fully able to reach them."[56] Unable to heal this misery and trauma, African Americans sought comfort in the blues in both performing and participating in its artistic deliverance. Indeed, blues performativity "acted as a means of conveying community, of invoking common experiences and values,"[57] and Sadness underscores this artistry by personifying what the blues is: mobility, healing, and collectivity. His urban double consciousness allows him to view not only Joe's circumstances, but the narratives of all disenfranchised blacks he encounters, through a lens that magnifies the collective experience in the individual, the macrocosm in the microcosm.

Using random patrons of the Banner Club to illustrate his final lesson to Joe, Sadness recites the tragic stories of individuals who have committed major and petty crimes and continue to inhabit the safe space of the bar. Like quintessential blues songs, the narratives confirm how the black body suffers by invoking the memory of their crimes: Viola, who "two years ago wrenched up an iron stool from the floor of a lunch-room, and killed another woman"; Barney, who "has been indicted twice for pocket-picking"; and Wallace, who "know[s] already how to live on others as they have lived on him." These individuals are not meant to serve as models of morality. Rather, Sadness's lesson is inverted much like the "lessons" of a blues song, for the narratives he shares with Joe demonstrate the vulnerability of human beings—particularly black urban dwellers, who experience a psychological lynching from the dispossessing policies of civic containment and alienation in New York. Thus, Sadness explains, "in this life we are all suffering from fever, and no one edges away from the other because he finds him a little warm. It's dangerous when you're not used to it; but once you go through the parching process, you become inoculated against further contagion."[58] This revelation serves only to create a fissure in the larger sphere of African American experience and knowledge.

Sadness's lesson for Joe, then, is not that he should measure or argue for or against the discursive features of virtues or vices or relegate experiences to individual case scenarios; rather, the task is to permit the discursive features of the blues narrative to build upon each other in order to generate a more fluid and informed discourse through which to examine the psychological lynchings all black bodies encounter. The same argument can be posited for the blues experience. "No black person can escape the blues, because the blues are an inherent part of black existence in America. To be black is to be blue."[59] Likewise, the lynching of one is the lynching of all. Joe, however, fails to align his burden with those of others or to recognize that there is a community inhabiting safe spaces such as the Banner Club that shares in this suffering. Concerning this tragic failure on Joe's part, Susan Bausch argues the following: "The problem with the Banner Club is not the company Joe keeps, as much as what he chooses to glean from their counsel. Joe does not take away the strength to withstand their common oppression but rather their tacit permission to accept his own degradation. The devastating result of this lesson is that Joe abandons his self-respect and cultivates his rage at the unjust system that imprisoned his father and limits his own opportunities."[60] As such, his rage, shame, and disavowal of his family and history alienate Joe from his community and set him on a path toward imminent social death. Regardless of Joe's incomprehension of Sadness's blues metanarrative, Sadness himself sustains the encapsulation of the traumatic collective burden that has metaphorically migrated through the blues tradition from the South to the North. Thus, it is essential to bring together the ideological South and the North in order to articulate the blues and allow it to flourish.

The blues voice is integral in constructing a safe space in the city "where migrants are healed, informed, ministered, and entertained."[61] However, just as this voice can be inverted and ambiguous at times, the voice of the city itself can underscore the oscillation between truth and fiction, reality and fantasy. Here the yellow newspaper, with its half-truths, uses a mass-produced voice to inform larger social spheres of exchange while manufacturing a particular public discourse for these spheres. In Dunbar's *The Sport of the Gods*, Skaggs, the reporter from the *Universe*, is one of the makers of a mass-produced narrative at the turn of the twentieth century. He reencounters Joe Hamilton a few years later at the Banner Club. Dejected, drunk, and still dismayed by his own misery and naïveté, Joe reveals to the coaxing reporter the story of the southern injustice perpetrated against his father. Having struggled "for years to get a big sensation for [his] paper" and secure his position as "a made man,"[62] Skaggs views this as an opportunity to engage in some real investigating and hone his talent as an investigator by creating enticing images of injustice for mass consumption. More important, exposing truth in the Hamilton case would enable the ambitious reporter to rise in the printed world and serve as a laudable herald for the narrative voice of the New York *Universe* as well as the city's white social "universe."

The black community drew strength from the blues and used it as an instrument for crafting an identity with agency and power. Moreover, the blues produces a narrative of resilience and relevance for African Americans that "affirm[s] their existence and refuse[s] to be destroyed by the oppressive environment" and demonstrates that, "despite white definitions to the contrary," whether in the form of juridical malady, as in the Berry Hamilton case, or the commodification of this same event, as represented by Skaggs's yellow narrative in the *Universe,* blacks "defined their own somebodiness and realized that America was not their true home."[63]

Rather than participate in the larger power of the blues, Joe is determined to eradicate it from his world. Driven by his own madness and self-loathing, Joe confronts Hattie after sharing his father's story with the newspaper and blames her for turning him into a creature of "foulness and degradation."[64] As the urban stranger, whose role is to guide and beguile the migrant, Hattie tries to "educate" Joe throughout the novel by exposing him to the urban psychological realities of suffering, loving, losing, and desiring that transpire between men and women—elements that position her as a blues character not only in her profession but in her lifestyle. "The blues woman," according to Hazel Carby, "brought to the black, urban, working class an awareness of its social existence and acted creatively to vocalize the contradictions and tensions of the terrain of sexual politics in the relation of black working-class culture to the culture of the emergent black middle class."[65] Here Hattie's urban character provides a direct contrast and likely alternative to the female ancestor role that Joe's mother originally played.

Despite Hattie's role as the linchpin bringing together these gendered and classificatory identities, she does not reach Joe and fails to acclimate him to the ambiguous vocabulary of the larger city apparatus. Moreover, beyond Joe's simple boyish desire for Hattie, he does not recognize the blues persona that empowers her and makes her a paragon of traumatic expression. Blaming her for his metaphorical deafness and muteness, Joe kills the blues by strangling Hattie, allowing his strumming fingers to give her "the caress of death."[66] In this final musical score of paradoxical desire and disgust, Joe silences the blues at its origin (Hattie's throat) and from his ears forever. Here the cycle of destruction is repeated, for "violence is directed at the victims of racism rather than its perpetrators."[67] As a result, the hegemonic powers that be, that is, the urban northern whites (and southern whites by historical and psychological extension), are able to maintain their positions of power and control over the black archipelago of tenements and taverns in Dunbar's New York City as long as African Americans continue to misdirect their anger and protestations toward members of their own community.

Although the white political and social enclaves appear impenetrable, they are breached and compromised by other white bodies who seek to buttress their own positions within the discourse of hegemonic privilege and power throughout the United States. Skaggs, the reporter in the novel, is an adept instrument in this self-serving exercise. With Joe now incarcerated for the murder of Hattie Sterling, Skaggs decides to pursue the Hamilton case and journeys down South to expose the injustice, thereby ensuring for himself an elevated role in the mass production and consumption of the *Universe's* own narrative of intrigue. Whereas the Banner Club engineers a domain in which the "social structure of everyday life is suspended" and blues, dance, and discourse intermingle in a "community ritual,"[68] the Continental Hotel is equally suspended in a rhetoric of self-preservation and empowerment. However, it is locked within an historical capsule and lacks the dynamism of its northern counterpart, for Dunbar's narrator informs his readers that "five years had not changed the Continental frequenters much."[69] When the old regime welcomes Skaggs, thus "plac[ing] him on terms of equality with many of his kind,"[70] the slick reporter assumes a genteel disposition in order to ascertain the truth in the old Hamilton case from the forthright Colonel Saunders, the only member of the old regime who believes in Hamilton's innocence. Yet Saunders has resigned himself to silence all these years for the sake of the white southern aristocracy's honor, though he secretly revels in his personal theories of law and his "analytical mind," as Skaggs calls it with underlining sarcasm.[71] The vulnerability of the Continental Hotel suggests that hegemonic anatomy is easily permeable, for Skaggs's drive to become a "made man" in the sphere of journalism allows him to employ his racial privilege and "his fine disregard of [southern] ways and means"[72] to unveil the secret of Maurice Oakley's own crime of silence.

Oakley, who has withdrawn from his former social circles, unwillingly relinquishes his secret to Skaggs, who quickly circulates the story throughout the North and the South. Skaggs's exposé leads to Hamilton's release and to the widespread lauding of the *Universe*. Despite this surface act of egalitarianism and justice for the African American community, the *Universe*, like its corporate paramour, Skaggs, sees only the benefit in its assumption of the role as a champion for the oppressed—as long as the oppressed continue to consume the *Universe's* yellow journalism. "The *Universe*," Dunbar's narrator suggests, "had always claimed to be the friend of all poor and oppressed humanity, and every once in a while it did something to substantiate its claim, whereupon it stood off and said to the public, 'Look you what we have done, and behold how great we are, the friend of the people!'"[73] Skaggs, as the novel's white "urban trickster," is just as much an instrument of the city as he is of the newspaper. The city, with its ambiguous boundaries between virtue and vice, incessantly generates a narrative that is simultaneously "sordid and noble,"[74] for justice is ensured at the price of objectification and mob consumption. Indeed, Berry Hamilton is released from prison and "pardoned" for the crime, but he is not deemed innocent, nor is his dignity restored.

As such, the members of the Hamilton family are made into a spectacle for public scrutiny and pity, and their story is syndicated to multiple social spheres and openly dissected on a metaphorical operating table. As such, their lives, their very bodies, have been rendered commodities available for mass consumption by the hand of northern industry. This public spectacle, in many ways, reveals a pop-cultural lynching of a black family more than it illustrates that crime does not pay. Dissatisfied with his abilities and talents as an honest purveyor of knowledge or truth, "Skaggs needs the spectacle of a black family in order to divert attention away from his failings. Just as Mr. Oakley implicates Berry in a scandal in order to cover up his brother's possible 'deviancy,' Skaggs relies on the Hamiltons' exposé to placate his boss's concerns about his own ability as a reporter."[75] The commercialization of knowledge manifests itself in the form of the Hamiltons' various migrations, transgressions, and incarcerations. In so doing, *The Sport of the Gods* provides a modernist frame for the migrant narrative, for Dunbar illustrates how industrialization and commercialization in the northern cities transform not only the behavior and psychology of its urban inhabitants, but also the archaic patriarchal anatomy of the postbellum South.

Woven into the literary and lyrical fabric of *The Sport of the Gods* is the blues, which provides African American characters a language with which to describe the institutional racism that continues today to plague this community in both the South and the North. Although the title of Dunbar's migration narrative may suggest that the novel's victims are "powerless against some Will infinitely stronger than their own," it must be made clear that the actions of some ulterior force, in actuality, stem from "the historical legacy of slavery and the virtual perpetuation of its conditions."[76] Therefore, the continual performance of the blues—and its ubiquity throughout black safe spaces—allows for a spatial and psychological mobility and sustenance within the debilitating sectors of the industrialized city, for not only does the blues mirror and parody the sensations of urban streets and structures; it also reanimates the alienated body and offers a site for collective comfort. More important, it provides the black community with an identity neither compromised by white hegemony nor implicated as a substitute for authentic agency. LeRoi Jones succinctly underscores this point in *Blues People*: "The Negro could not ever become white and that was his strength; at some point, always, he could not participate in the dominant tenor of the white man's culture. It was at this juncture that he had to make use of other resources, whether African, sub-cultural, or hermetic. And it was this boundary, this no man's land, that provided the logic and beauty of this music."[77]

Such musical language as generated by geo-social matrixes like the Banner Club presents the listener and the performer with "instrumental rhythms [that] suggest change, movement, action, continuance, unlimited and unending possibility." As such, this metaphorical marriage between blues artists and audience occurs when the metaphorically lynched body hears and sings the blues, for the harsh urban system offers an unrepentant education, yet not everyone can sing the blues. "Only a *trained* voice can sing the blues."[78] Performing the ubiquitous and ever-mobile blues acclimates the migrant—or blues traveler—to the contradictory layers of the modernist American city and the layers of the North and the South: the stranger and ancestor, the urban dweller and the migrant, the silence and the blues. Thus, *The Sport of the Gods* forges the literary tropes employed later by blues-styled writers such as Langston Hughes, Ralph Ellison, Jack Kerouac, and Toni Morrison. An early blues narrative such as Dunbar's ensures that this traveler is alive and with agency while incarcerated behind the veils of white supremacy and segregation, for these are the gods who sport with the black mortals.

Notes

1. Houston A. Baker Jr., *Blues, Ideology, and Afro-American Literature: A Vernacular Theory* (Chicago: University of Chicago Press, 1984), 119.

2. Paul Laurence Dunbar, *The Sport of the Gods* (New York: Signet Classic, 1999), 127.

3. James H. Cone, *The Spirituals and the Blues: An Interpretation* (Maryknoll, N.Y.: Orbis Books, 1972), 102.

4. Farah Jasmine Griffin, *"Who Set You Flowin'?" The African-American Migration Narrative* (New York: Oxford University Press, 1995), 19, 56.

5. Casey Inge, "Family Functions: Disciplinary Discourses and (De)constructions of the 'Family' in *The Sport of the Gods*," *Callaloo* 20, no. 1 (1997): 238.

6. Ibid., 232.

7. Dunbar, *Sport*, 29.

8. Ibid., 30.

9. Ibid., 31.

10. Ibid., 30.

11. Ibid., 31.

12. Ibid., 43–44.
13. Daniel M. Johnson and Rex R. Campbell, *Black Migration in America: A Social Demographic History* (Durham, N.C.: Duke University Press, 1981), 68.
14. Hazel V. Carby, "'It Jus Be's Dat Way Sometime': The Sexual Politics of Women's Blues," in *Unequal Sisters: A Multicultural Reader in U.S. Women's History*, ed. Vicki L. Ruiz and Ellen Carol DuBois, 2nd ed. (New York: Routledge, 1994), 335.
15. Dunbar, *Sport*, 45.
16. Griffin, *"Who Set You Flowin'?"* 52.
17. Dunbar, *Sport*, 46.
18. Ibid.
19. Ibid., 49.
20. Ibid., 47.
21. Griffin, *"Who Set You Flowin'?"* 5.
22. Ibid., 7.
23. Ibid., 8.
24. Ibid.
25. Dunbar, *Sport*, 51.
26. Ibid., 45.
27. Griffin, *"Who Set You Flowin'?"* 6.
28. Dunbar, *Sport*, 57.
29. Ibid., 67.
30. Baker, *Blues, Ideology*, 3–4.
31. Dunbar, *Sport*, 66.
32. Griffin, *"Who Set You Flowin'?"* 60–61.
33. Dunbar, *Sport*, 63.
34. Ibid., 64.
35. Griffin, *"Who Set You Flowin'?"* 53.
36. Dunbar, *Sport*, 67.
37. Ibid., 65.
38. Ibid., 66.
39. Günter H. Lenz, "Symbolic Space, Communal Rituals, and the Surreality of the Urban Ghetto: Harlem in Black Literature from the 1920s to the 1960s," *Callaloo* 11, no. 2 (1988): 323.
40. Dunbar, *Sport*, 66.
41. Lawrence R. Rodgers, "Paul Laurence Dunbar's *The Sport of the Gods*: The Doubly Conscious World of Plantation Fiction, Migration, and Ascent," *American Literary Realism, 1870–1910* 24, no. 3 (1992): 54.
42. Charles Scruggs, *Sweet Home: Invisible Cities in the Afro-American Novel* (Baltimore: Johns Hopkins University Press, 1993), 39.
43. Baker, *Blues, Ideology*, 6.
44. Claude McKay, *Harlem: Negro Metropolis* (New York: E. P. Dutton, 1940), 18.
45. Dunbar, *Sport*, 68–69.
46. Ibid., 70.
47. Ibid., 71.
48. Susan Bausch, "Inevitable or Remediable? The Historical Connection between Slavery, Racism, and Urban Degradation in Paul Laurence Dunbar's *The Sport of the Gods*," *CLA Journal* 45, no. 4 (2002): 515.
49. Johnson and Campbell, *Black Migration in America*, 63.
50. Cone, *The Spirituals and the Blues*, 109.
51. Dunbar, *Sport*, 82.

52. Ibid., 83.
53. Griffin, *"Who Set You Flowin'?"* 60, 9.
54. Dunbar, *Sport*, 83.
55. Dickson D. Bruce Jr., "W. E. B. Du Bois and the Idea of Double Consciousness," in *The Souls of Black Folk*, by W. E. B. Du Bois, ed. Henry Louis Gates Jr. and Terri Hume Oliver (New York: Norton, 1999), 236, 238.
56. Dubnar, *Sport*, 83–84.
57. Griffin, *"Who Set You Flowin'?"* 55.
58. Dunbar, *Sport*, 84.
59. Cone, *The Spirituals and the Blues*, 103.
60. Bausch, "Inevitable or Remediable?" 511.
61. Griffin, *"Who Set You Flowin'?"* 55.
62. Dunbar, *Sport*, 117.
63. Cone, *The Spirituals and the Blues*, 105.
64. Dunbar, *Sport*, 119.
65. Hazel V. Carby, "Policing the Black Woman's Body in an Urban Context," *Critical Inquiry* 18, no. 4 (1992): 755.
66. Dunbar, *Sport*, 119.
67. Bausch, "Inevitable or Remediable?" 517.
68. Lenz, "Symbolic Space," 322.
69. Dunbar, *Sport*, 127.
70. Ibid., 131.
71. Ibid., 117.
72. Ibid., 131.
73. Ibid., 137.
74. Bausch, "Inevitable or Remediable?" 515.
75. Dunbar, *Sport*, 148.
76. Bausch, "Inevitable or Remediable?" 522.
77. LeRoi Jones, *Blues People* (New York: William Morrow, 1963), 80.
78. Baker, *Blues, Ideology*, 8.

15
"With Myriad Subtleties"
Paul Laurence Dunbar's Constructions of Social Identity in The Sport of the Gods

JAYNE E. WATERMAN

IN PAUL LAURENCE DUNBAR'S FINAL NOVEL, *The Sport of the Gods* (1902), Skaggs, a reporter from the "yellow" New York *Universe* who is searching for a topic for an exposé about "a poor and innocent negro," notes that he "often find[s] the smallest and most insignificant-appearing details pregnant with suggestion."[1] Although the motives for his journalistic investigations are far from altruistic, Skaggs provides critics with a useful proposal: deep and revealing understandings can be gleaned from the seemingly small and insignificant details of Dunbar's writing. In other words, to appropriate a phrase from one of Dunbar's most famous poems, "We Wear the Mask," it is in the "myriad subtleties"[2] of his texts that Dunbar's voices can be heard and his identification as a black author of late nineteenth- and early twentieth-century America can be found.

Beginning this chapter with the less-than-philanthropic intentions of a rather insidious white character in *The Sport of the Gods* is somewhat unsettling, but in the pages that follow, I will posit that all the characters portrayed by Dunbar reveal and comment on the contemporary and critical interpretations of a popular African American author writing for both white and black audiences. Moreover, in the social framework of the novel, a self-actualization is represented in a fluid, protean form: "an entire metamorphosis," as the narrator notes in the "Frankenstein" chapter.[3] Artifice and actuality, emancipation and oppression, and inclusion and exclusion are used to articulate the formation and deformation of self in the society of *The Sport of the Gods*.

Dunbar's prose explores the trope of the mask, be it that of monster or man, and for the Hamiltons, the Oakleys, and their dialectic discourse with the rural South and the urban North, the mask (in all its multiplicity) idealizes, exaggerates, and destabilizes the performative social complexities of blackness and whiteness. Dunbar's fiction, through satirized stereotypes, explores and implodes the conventions and expectations of racial identity. Essentially, in its paradoxes and ambiguities, everyone wears the mask. In this light, the asides of Dunbar's questionable journalist character provoke a necessary critical disturbance by providing the tools for understanding the complex constructions of social identity for the characters of *The Sport of the Gods,* and for their author.

Before we begin to explore the role of these contrasts and the function of the performative mask in the formation of social identity, it is first necessary to discuss the critical climate that informs such an approach. In general, Dunbar's work has been overlooked and misread by critics unable, or unwilling, to read around and below the surface of his texts. In 1973, writing about the themes of his popular poetry, Jean Wagner displays his frustration and notes critical necessities for a closer reading, claiming that if certain aspects "were to be overlooked, one would risk losing at the same time all that lies behind the specific worth . . . of Dunbar's popular poetry."[4] Almost thirty years later, Susan Bausch, addressing Dunbar's prose, particularly *The Sport of the Gods,* highlights a similar critical oversight: "Unfortunately, Dunbar's use of irony has been largely overlooked," later adding that "the text" of *The Sport of the Gods* "requires a closer reading."[5] Part of the reason for these missed critical opportunities is the subtlety of Dunbar's work. Robert Bone viewed this quality not as a quiet triumph of Dunbar's writing, as in, for example, the racial protest of Dunbar's *The Fanatics* (1901), but simply as an attempt at textual protest that is so hidden and "so carefully veiled that only the subtlest of readers will grasp the point."[6] But this is a necessary veiling, and such a seeming shortcoming should not always be viewed as such. Instead, Dunbar's literary technique is an abstruse subtlety that demonstrates the dexterous skill of the writer and illustrates his ingenuity in circumventing dictated convention.

In Nancy Von Rosk's terms, Dunbar's position as a writer has been "precarious and difficult,"[7] as Bone's commentary attests. Wagner also captures these troublesome qualities, noting that Dunbar's work is "difficult to evaluate fairly. . . . One has a strange but inevitable feeling of embarrassment in turning to him. . . . His contradictions and his complexity have yet to lose their disconcerting quality." As he considers the problem of Dunbar's ambiguities, however, he quickly reasons, "But to be born black, and a poet, in the United States in 1872—was that not ambiguous at the outset?"[8] Ralph Ellison captured the essence of this dilemma and the habits it engendered: "I found the greatest difficulty for a Negro writer was the problem of revealing what he truly felt, rather than serving up what Negroes were supposed to feel, and were encouraged to feel. And linked to this was the difficulty, based upon our long habit of deception and evasion, of depicting what really happened within our areas of American life."[9] As alluded to at the beginning of this chapter, it is crucial to recognize the limitations imposed on and surrounding African American writers in the late nineteenth and early twentieth centuries as well as to acknowledge the quiet circumventions and transgressions that were made within those boundaries.

Clearly, critical readings need to appreciate Dunbar's work in its historical context and as an illustration of literary resourcefulness. Herbert Woodward Martin and Ronald Primeau's recent work *In His Own Voice* (2002) begins to identify this need, noting that many of the long-standing critical debates about Dunbar "are sometimes as much a reflection of the values and concerns of reviewers as they are a measure of his own accomplishments." Furthermore, their introduction offers the astute observation that what commentators find in Dunbar's work "often depends on the ability of an age to understand the constraints imposed as well as the opportunities afforded."[10] Rather than reading Dunbar's texts as problematic contradictions, the "scholarly reflex" as Gene Jarrett describes it, scholars need to open up to readings that allow them to develop a capacity for complexity and multiplicity.[11] Many recent scholars have begun to do just that, working against the ambivalence of Dunbar's literary legacy and exploring the power of his textual ambiguities. The emphasis is on viewing the various messages embedded in his work and regarding so-called textual problems as subtle manipulations that, in the search for a whole sense of black identity, are simultaneously disabling and enabling.

There is more to Dunbar's work than has been discovered: his work does not avoid textual ambiguities but tackles the awkwardness head-on with pluralistic projections of literary selves that both enforce and subvert black identity. His work also shows a keen awareness of the potential found in such equivocations. Throughout poems such as "Comparison," "Differences," "The Paradox," and "The Poet"—who from "A jingle in a broken tongue" "sang of life, serenely sweet, / With, now and then, a deeper note. / From some high peak, nigh yet remote, / He voiced the world's absorbing beat"[12]—Dunbar revisits the ambivalences and complexities of his multifaceted voice, a voice that continues to be heard in his prose. As Shelley Fisher Fishkin argues, "it is a mistake to try and pin a reductive label on Dunbar. His work is more complex than that—and more interesting." She later argues, "We can view Dunbar reductively ... only if we ignore alternative models."[13] Fishkin also works to push Dunbar analysis beyond "silent assertions," to hear his "cultural conversations" and to witness the "additional significance" of his texts.[14] A focus on the construction of social identity in *The Sport of the Gods* builds on this work to illustrate the far-reaching implications of black identity in what has been called Dunbar's most socially conscious novel.

In an interview documented in *Shadow and Act,* Ralph Ellison foregrounds the significance of these connected notions of identity and society to an African American writer. When asked if the search for identity has been an American theme, Ellison answers: "It is *the* American theme." He goes on to note that "The nature of our society is such that we are prevented from knowing who [African American writers] are. It is still a young society, and this is an integral part of its development."[15] The following decade, in *The Negro in American Fiction,* Sterling Brown continued the exploration of these interdependent notions of identity and sociological conditions: "We shall see . . . how stereotypes—that the Negro is *all* this, that, or the other—have evolved at the dictates of social policy."[16]

At the turn of the century, Dunbar centered his work, particularly *The Sport of the Gods,* on this question of racial identity and the dictates of society in a disturbing postbellum and pre–Harlem Renaissance story of deception, distrust, and disintegration. Told through a naturalistic and fatalistic lens, this story is set against the backdrop of the ever-growing prominence of the theories and prejudices of social Darwinism. In 1881, William Graham Sumner of Yale University had set forth a new "science of society" in his essay "Sociology."[17] Subsequent ideas of racial inferiority were developed from Sumner's popular and numerous lectures and books. Dunbar's *The Sport of the Gods* demonstrated the impact of these endemic racial stereotypes. At the same time, he played with these stereotypes to show their excessive, ridiculous, and tragic consequences. As a novelist and social critic, Dunbar highlighted the societal self in its literary estrangements, alienations, constructions, and identifications.

In the chapter ironically entitled "The Justice of Men," the Hamilton family experiences firsthand the complex social codes that work across, and because of, racial lines. After Berry Hamilton's arrest for allegedly stealing money from Frank Oakley, the brother of Maurice Oakley, Berry's present employer and former master, the AME church is the first to renounce its ties with one of its own, "to disavow sympathy with [Berry], and to purge itself of contamination by turning him out."[18] Significantly, the black religious institution of the postbellum period was codified not by biblical law but by the social "laws" of the still-felt institution of slavery: "In the black people of the town the strong influence of slavery was still operative, and with one accord they turned away from one of their own kind upon whom had been set the ban of the white people's displeasure. . . . They did not dare to do it before the sixties. They do not dare to do it now."[19] At the same time, the reasoning for the congregation's renunciation also alludes to social jealousy and racial betrayal that operate within, and across, racial lines. Berry is characterized and chastised as "Mistah Rich Niggah," who "wanted to dress his wife an' chillen lak white folks."[20] In this cacophony of human motivations and societal pressures, complex formations of socially constructed race lines are drawn.

Like his father, Berry, Joe Hamilton is exposed to the same social codes of racially defined ostracism in "Outcasts," the chapter that follows his father's unjust incarceration. "Outcasts" resonates with the same social realities and implications of social alienation, culminating in the remaining Hamilton family abandoning the South for New York City. Unable to get work in the black barbershops in town, Joe is turned away only "to meet the grinning or contemptuous glances of the bellman."[21] Here, the grinning and the contemptuousness express the same sentiment. As in the varied message of the mask that "grins and lies" in Dunbar's "We Wear the Mask," seeming contradictions exist.[22] And it is this compelling contradiction that Dunbar explores in all its social contexts.

In 1927, Robert E. Park, founder of the Chicago school of sociology, researched the idea of social codes in human nature and collective behavior. Alongside conscious role-playing, Park introduced the notion of pretense or masking, which characterizes everyday human interactions. Erving Goffman developed these theories in his major works, *The Presentation of the Self in Everyday Life* and *Stigma*. Adapting Goffman's theories of social interaction, specifically the identification of self in its dramaturgical stage management and notions of shame, this essay proposes to reread Dunbar's *The Sport of the Gods*. Within a theoretical framework that interrogates key episodes of performance in all its illusionary deception, the textual consequences of wearing the wrong performative mask and the ensuing shame and deformation are also explored.

In Dunbar's array of self-projected personae, layers of self take on changeable and fluid states: identity is never fixed but is, instead, always in an unstable and evolving state. In *The Sport of the Gods*, three strategic episodes of performativity are evident: the performativity of fiction, the dramaturgy of everyday life, and the role of theater. As an author, Dunbar understood the scope of his authorial deceptions, which constituted not only the act of writing fiction but also the act of writing for a largely white audience. This masking of the novelist—playing to the milieu of his audience and the expectations of the plantation tradition—occurs throughout the text from the nostalgically viewed South and the urban plight in New York City to the macabre southern homecoming at the end of the novel.

Authorship represents various constructions, reinventions, and developments (as opposed to the often misconstrued contradictions) that provide an artistic creation of self. However, the writer never truly speaks for himself. Instead, the essence of the author is conveyed through an assumed persona, a mask. Like its author, the story is also masked. In *The Sport of the Gods*, the narrative opens with a distinct indication of this masking process: "Fiction has said so much in regret of the old days when there were plantations and overseers and masters and slaves," the novel begins, "that it was good to come upon a household such as Berry Hamilton's, if for no other reason than that it afforded a relief from the monotony of tiresome iteration."[23] Here, the narrative playfully sets a tone of ironic masking. Skaggs's editor at the *Universe*, following the pitch for the Hamilton miscarriage-of-justice story, also candidly comments on this tension: "Yes, it looks plausible, but so does all fiction."[24]

The Sport of the Gods is encoded with constant allusions to various forms of deception and disguise, from the initial discovery that the money is missing and Frank Oakley's later confession to Maurice Oakley of what actually happened to the "stolen" money to the illusion of the theater for Kitty and the delusions of Banner Club popularity for Joe. Essentially, these private and public, personal and societal, theatrical depictions represent a diversion away from the self. At the same time, each character, in his or her everyday performances, enacts, however illusionary, a form of self-expression. Bausch defines this search for identity and belonging as the "off-stage" and "on-stage" spectacle.[25] In their dramatizations, a social front and the staging of a self are projected. After an intimidating arrival in New York City, for example, Joe, "made a decided advance in knowledge, and he swelled with the consciousness that already he was becoming a new man of the world." This is especially marked in the linguistic projections of Joe and Kitty, who drop their provincial accents for the sounds of, and subsequent identification with, "N' Yawk."[26]

In *The Presentation of the Self in Everyday Life*, Erving Goffman discusses the issues of stagecraft and stage management, which "occur everywhere in social life, providing a clear-cut dimension for formal sociological analysis."[27] This sociological analogy of society and performance seems to describe Dunbar's text, in which, as the Shakespearean chapter heading indicates, "All the World's a Stage."[28] Even the Banner Club—"a social cesspool, generating a poisonous miasma and reeking with the stench of decayed and rotten moralities"—provides a profitable site of performativity: "But what do you expect when false idealism and fevered ambition come face to face with catering cupidity?"[29] In Goffman's terms, the Banner Club allows Joe to "implicitly request his observers to take seriously the impression this is fostered before them."[30] The key, Goffman argues, is not reality but "the individual's own belief in the impression of reality" and the subsequent establishment of a social role. Here, the self is not a unified self; instead there are selves for occasions. Racially, institutionally, culturally, and socially, Joe seeks acceptance and identity, so that, as Goffman states, "when the individual presents himself to others, his performance will tend to incorporate and exemplify the officially accredited values of the society."[31] But in the friendship of Sadness and in the love of Hattie, Joe also finds a fulfillment that goes beyond facade.

Goffman's analysis of the "whole machinery of self-production" (social fronts and routines, collective representations, idealized impression management, and the act of staging) also provides an effective lens through which to examine the onstage identity of Kitty Hamilton. Kitty exemplifies the defining role of theater itself, from her singing for the AME church benefit to her participation in the chorus line of the New York stage. She epitomizes the quest for identity through theatricality. In the delusion and illusion of performance, Kitty loses and then discovers herself: "Kitty was enchanted. The airily dressed women seemed to her like creatures from fairy-land. It is strange how the glare of the footlights succeeds in deceiving so many people who are able to see through other delusions. The cheap dresses on the street had not fooled Kitty for an instant, but take the same cheese-cloth, put a little water starch into it, and put it on the stage, and she could see only chiffon."[32] With almost childlike naïveté, Kitty's impressionable gaze simultaneously perceives and is deceived by the theatrical illusion of lighting and make-believe. Kitty becomes fascinated by and pursues her ambition to work in the theater. With the corrupting guidance of Joe's girlfriend, the vaudeville actress Hattie Sterling, and advice that "nowadays everybody thinks stage people respectable,"[33] Kitty eventually overcomes her humiliating and shameful ordeal with Mr. Martin, the casting director, and joins the chorus.

Even though Kitty's newfound theatrical identity recalls the difficult past of female slaves displayed on the auction block, alongside the racial degradation of coon and minstrel shows, Dunbar's narrative does not offer complete condemnation.[34] Instead, the search for a black female identity is articulated at the end of the novel. Although ultimately controlled by the decisions of her male manager, Kitty relishes her relative independence: "From the first time she went on the stage she had begun to live her own life," albeit a life "in which the chief aim was the possession of good clothes and the ability to attract attention which she had learned to crave."[35]

An integral component of this notion of performance and social identification is the mask. Significantly, Goffman begins his investigation of the everyday role of the self with an epigraph from George Santayana, which announces: "Masks are arrested expressions and admirable echoes of feeling, at once faithful, discreet, and superlative." Goffman explores further the multifaceted nature of the mask as an artifice and a natural expression of "the concept we have formed of ourselves—the role we are striving to live up to—this mask is our truer self, the self we would like to be."[36] In the case of Kitty and Joe, their performative masks attest to their determination, however misguided, to belong and succeed in New York society. In Joe's case, this masking is ultimately challenged as a fraudulent facade with tragic consequences. In *Figures in Black*, Henry Louis Gates Jr. also describes the mask as an "essence of immobility fused with the essence of mobility, fixity with transience, order with chaos, permanence with the transitory, the substantial with the evanescent."[37]

For Dunbar's African American, the mask is a means of security and protection on the one hand; on the other hand, it represents pretense and disguise. Nathan Huggins concludes his brief discussion of Dunbar with the revelation of his frustration with the charade of the mask, asking, "How, and when does one call upon the real self to dispel the make-believe and claim humanity and dignity?"[38] Huggins's dismay draws attention to the mask's reductive stereotyping and concealed representation of falsehood. At the same time, Huggins realizes the potential of the mask as an empowering, subversive, and emancipatory agency: "The persistence of the Negro stereotype has tended to make the Negro the one constant through all change and various guises. It has been a great convenience for those who have wanted to find or lose themselves behind the mask."[39]

Throughout *The Sport of the Gods*, Dunbar employs this masking aesthetic for black and white characters alike. The mask is used in multiple ways, in both a physical and a metaphorical sense, demonstrating flexibility, versatility, and adaptability. Black and white characters attempt to hide their true personalities from themselves and each other. Yet the truth is often revealed in the dropping of the mask and the blush of shame or red anger. At the farewell dinner, for example, Claire Lessing, a marriage prospect for Frank Oakley, suspiciously questions Frank's "tell-tale flush" when a dinner guest hints that he has some "dark-eyed mademoiselle" waiting for him when he gets to Paris.[40] At the same time, Frank is contemplating a very different deception that leads to the false accusation of theft in order to protect his own indiscretions.

Goffman considers these alternative social characteristics in *Stigma*. Those who do not depart from societal expectations are deemed "normal"; those who do are considered "abnormal" or "deviant." As Goffman explains, "A discrepancy may exist between an individual's virtual and actual identity. This discrepancy, when known or apparent, spoils his social identity; it has the effect of cutting him off from society and from himself so that he stands as a discredited person facing an unaccepting world."[41] Furthermore, Goffman argues, this "stigma involves not so much a set of concrete individuals who can be separated into two piles, [but] the stigmatized and the normal, as a pervasive two-role social process in which every individual participates in both roles, at least in some connection, and in some phases of life."[42] For example, Berry goes through the process of normalization and stigmatization only to return to a dissatisfying sense of normality at the end of the novel. Other characters in *The Sport of the Gods* fluctuate between normal and deviant roles. When Berry is freed from jail and returns to his wife, Fannie Hamilton's normal societal role as mother and wife is jeopardized by the revelation of her marriage to Mr. Gibson. Likewise, Minty Brown, an ironic symbol of normality in her hometown in the South, is stigmatized by the Banner Club society, who manage to make "the outsider" "feel distinctly uncomfortable."[43]

Huggins notes another defining characteristic of this stigmatization, however, in relation to the notions of performance and masking: "The Negro was the performer in a strange, almost macabre, act of black collusion in his own emasculation.... The theatrical stage itself, more than any other cultural phenomenon, opens a perspective into the pathology of American race relations."[44] Although Huggins discusses the formation of race relations after Dunbar, the connections he draws between performance, theatricality, and pathology are pertinent to the narrative demises of Joe Hamilton and Maurice Oakley in *The Sport of the Gods*. As dehumanized, disabled, and deteriorated deviants, Joe and Maurice exemplify the monstrous creations of society. Lost masks of social decency mark their black and white descent into degeneracy, as the decline of each character is carefully depicted in juxtaposed chapters to reflect their ultimate crimes of self-delusion. After receiving a confession of guilt in a letter that outlines Frank's hypocrisy and lies surrounding the accusations of Berry, Maurice, instead of making amends, decides to bury the secret of his brother's, and thus his own, transgressions in his heart. The "Frankenstein" chapter, with Joe's inhuman transformation and transgression, immediately follows Maurice's revelation. Just before he murders his girlfriend, Hattie Sterling, Joe is described as a "terrible, terrible man or a monster."[45] And later, while Joe's murderous actions render him "without sense or volition . . . a man over-acting insanity,"[46] Maurice's derangement is described: "From a social, companionable man, he became a recluse, shunning visitors and dreading society."[47]

As grotesque formations of their own social projections, Joe and Maurice share a similar monstrous demise. In some ways, their relationship recalls the earlier crippling bond of a black servant, Henry Johnson, and his white employer, Dr. Prescott, in Stephen Crane's "The Monster" (1898). Shelley Fisher Fishkin notes that Dunbar may well have encountered Crane in England when he was working on this reverse plantation story.[48] Ralph Ellison's comments on the Crane story also secure their conceptual connections: "No other Crane fiction—except, perhaps, 'The Monster'—expresses such a violence of disgust with man and his condition, and one feels behind the non-committal mask of the prose a conviction that man exists in the universe ever at the mercy of a capricious fate, a hostile nature, an indifferent and unjust god—*and* his own misconceptions.... Dr. Prescott's loyalty to his oath as a physician and to the man who has saved his son's life cost him his practice, his friends and ultimately his social identity."[49] In his mental derailment and facial disfigurement after his heroic rescue of Dr. Prescott's son from a fire, Henry Johnson becomes a "monster, a perfect monster,"[50] forced by society to wear a "mask, or some kind of veil."[51] Johnson, who earlier in the story is characterized as displaying "the elasticity of his race,"[52] personifies a literal masking. Like the "torn,"[53] "bleeding,"[54] and "tortured"[55] souls depicted in Dunbar's "We Wear the Mask," the monstrous and mask-wearing characters in Crane's short story and in Dunbar's novel epitomize the social punishment for those who transgress societal codes and expectations.

In terms of undeserved punishment, it is fitting to consider the ending of *The Sport of the Gods*, with its final image of the Hamiltons:

> They sat together with clasped hands listening to the shrieks of the madman across the yard and thinking of what he had brought to them and to himself.
>
> It was not a happy life, but it was all that was left to them, and they took it without complaint, for they knew they were powerless against some Will infinitely stronger than their own.[56]

Critics have decried this final passage as unsatisfying and failing to offer a resolution. Such critical discourse has been self-perpetuating. Regrettably, this sense of dissatisfaction lies not in the tone and the intention of Dunbar's words but in the critical misinterpretations and under-interpretations of the conclusion. This chapter has gone some way to arrest the perpetuation of this misreading and redress the imbalance in critical appreciation of Dunbar's work. The final words in *The Sport of the Gods* are realistic in their equivocations. Berry and Fannie have nowhere else to go; in 1902, the fate of African Americans was equally unknown. Moreover, it is important to note that the portrayal of despair and pessimism was not Dunbar's. Rather, his writing was merely holding up a mirror to his society in the same way that he found it necessary to strip both the rural South and the urban North of all their illusions. Ultimately, perhaps, deceit *was* the truth, just as pessimism *was* optimism.

The ending is unsettling, going against traditional, romantic notions of textual restoration and resolution. This disturbing tone replicates, albeit with greater transparency, the disconcerting quality of the novel's opening pages. With the Hamilton cottage garden's atmosphere of quaint romanticism—"Over the door of the little house a fine Virginia creeper bent and fell in graceful curves, and a cluster of insistent morning-glories clung in summer about its stalwart stock"[57]—the opening is just too nice and too perfect for a definite sense of security and comfort. And like the unsettling topic that began this chapter, Dunbar's beginning and ending create a tension in order to capture the reader's attention. Moreover, the portrayal of irresolution in and of itself speaks volumes of a continuing, rather than completed, search for black social identity. Dunbar's writing is comfortable in these ambiguous spaces. Ironically, the text is at its most articulate when it is inarticulate. The text calls on the reader, and the critic, to understand its textual silences, for in these omissions there is a textual unmasking articulated "with myriad subtleties."

NOTES

1. Paul Laurence Dunbar, *The Sport of the Gods* (New York: Signet, 1999), 127, 128.
2. *The Complete Poems of Paul Laurence Dunbar* (New York: Dodd, Mead, 1962), 12, line 5.
3. Dunbar, *Sport*, 113.
4. Jean Wagner, *Black Poets of the United States: From Paul Laurence Dunbar to Langston Hughes*, trans. Kenneth Douglas (Urbana: University of Illinois Press, 1973), 113.
5. Susan Bausch, "Inevitable or Remediable? The Historical Connection between Slavery, Racism, and Urban Degradation in Paul Laurence Dunbar's *The Sport of the Gods*," *CLA Journal* 45, no. 4 (2002): 507, 501. For an extensive discussion of further critical oversights, particularly in relation to *The Sport of the Gods* as plantation tradition writing, see Nancy Von Rosk's "Coon Shows, Ragtime, and the Blues: Race, Urban Culture, and the Naturalist Vision in Paul Laurence Dunbar's *The Sport of the Gods*," in *Twisted from the Ordinary: Essays on American Literary Naturalism*, ed. Mary E. Papke (Knoxville: University of Tennessee Press, 2003), 145–46. In general, see Shelley Fisher Fishkin, "Race and the Politics of Memory: Mark Twain and Paul Laurence Dunbar," *Journal of American Studies* 40 (2006): 286–87.
6. Robert A. Bone, *The Negro Novel in America* (New Haven, Conn.: Yale University Press, 1965), 41.
7. Von Rosk, "Coon Shows," 147.
8. Wagner, *Black Poets*, 73.
9. Ralph Ellison, *Shadow and Act* (New York: Random House, 1964), xxi.
10. Herbert Woodward Martin and Ronald Primeau, introduction to *In His Own Voice: The Dramatic and Other Uncollected Works of Paul Laurence Dunbar* (Athens: Ohio University Press, 2002), xxi.
11. Gene Jarrett, "'We Must Write Like the White Men': Race, Realism, and Dunbar's Anomalous First Novel," *Novel: A Forum on Fiction* 37 (2004): 305.
12. *Complete Poems*, 309, lines 8, 1–4.
13. Shelley Fisher Fishkin and David Bradley, eds., *The Sport of the Gods and Other Essential Writing*, by Paul Laurence Dunbar (New York: Modern Library, 2005), 101, 102.
14. Fishkin, "Race and the Politics of Memory," 285, 299, 301.
15. Ellison, *Shadow and Act*, 177.
16. Sterling Brown, *The Negro in American Fiction: Negro Poetry and Drama* (New York: Arno Press, 1969), 1–2.
17. "Sociology," in *The American Intellectual Tradition: A Sourcebook*, vol. 2, *1865 to the Present*, ed. David A. Hollinger and Charles Capper (New York: Oxford University Press, 1989), 21.

18. Dunbar, *Sport*, 28.
19. Ibid.
20. Ibid.
21. Ibid., 40.
22. *Complete Poems*, 112, line 1.
23. Ibid., 1.
24. Ibid., 126.
25. Bausch, "Inevitable or Remediable?" 514.
26. Ibid., 507, 501.
27. Erving Goffman, *The Presentation of the Self in Everyday Life* (New York: Doubleday, 1959), 15.
28. Dunbar, *Sport*, 91.
29. Ibid., 67.
30. Goffman, *Presentation of the Self*, 16.
31. Ibid., 45.
32. Dunbar, *Sport*, 58–59.
33. Ibid., 59.
34. See Bausch's "Inevitable or Remedial?" for an extended discussion of black women's bodies at slave auctions, particularly her discussion on page 518.
35. Dunbar, *Sport*, 124.
36. Goffman, *Presentation of the Self*, 19.
37. Henry Louis Gates Jr., *Figures in Black: Words, Signs, and the "Racial" Self* (New York: Oxford University Press, 1987), 169.
38. Nathan Huggins, *Harlem Renaissance* (New York: Oxford University Press, 1971), 262.
39. Ibid., 301.
40. Dunbar, *Sport*, 9.
41. Erving Goffman, *Stigma: Notes on the Management of Spoiled Identity* (New York: Simon & Schuster, 1963), 19.
42. Ibid., 137–38.
43. Dunbar, *Sport*, 89.
44. Huggins, *Harlem Renaissance*, 245.
45. Dunbar, *Sport*, 119, 121, 129.
46. Ibid., 121.
47. Ibid., 129.
48. Fishkin, "Race and the Politics of Memory," 303.
49. Ellison, *Shadow and Act*, 75.
50. Ibid., 31.
51. Ibid., 49.
52. Ibid., 11.
53. *Complete Poems*, 112, line 4.
54. Ibid., 113, line 11.
55. Ibid.
56. Dunbar, *Sport*, 148.
57. Ibid.

16
"Nemmine. You Got to Git Somebody Else to Ring Yo' Ol' Bell Now"

Nigger Ed and the Rhetoric of Local Color Realism and Racial Protest in Dunbar's The Fanatics

WILLIE J. HARRELL JR.

> Has the press begun to say anything about the Fanatics? I am very much afraid for it.
> —PAUL LAURENCE DUNBAR, LETTER TO ALICE RUTH DUNBAR, APRIL 8, 1901

> I am so glad of these reviews of The Fanatics.
> —PAUL LAURENCE DUNBAR, LETTER TO ALICE RUTH DUNBAR, APRIL 11, 1901

THE YEAR 1899 WAS A CRITICAL ONE for Paul Laurence Dunbar. In May, he collapsed on a reading tour in New York, reportedly from pneumonia. Shortly after, doctors detected the actual reason for his illness: the deadly tuberculosis strain had begun its progression. Encouraged by his doctors to travel to Denver, Colorado, Dunbar packed his bags and began, along with his wife, Alice Ruth, and mother, Matilda, two separate yet corresponding journeys: a physical one and a literary one. The physical expedition, of course, took him to Colorado to relieve symptoms of tuberculosis. The crisp, fresh air of the mile-high plateau was often prescribed to sufferers of lung infections and other ailments. During his stay there, Dunbar's literary journey commenced when he accepted a position with the *Denver Post,* for which he wrote on his views concerning black migration to the West instead of the North.[1] At the same time, he began writing one of his most controversial novels, *The Fanatics,* which gave him an opportunity to reveal his racial consciousness.[2] As Addison Gayle Jr. has argued, *The Fanatics* freed Dunbar "to deal with black men in novel form on the same terms that they were dealt with by white writers."[3] However, Dunbar was somewhat concerned about how critics would acknowledge such an undertaking.

For some time Dunbar had been exceedingly optimistic about the publication of his long fiction pieces. In an April 17, 1895, letter to Alice Ruth Moore, Dunbar revealed that he was "hopeful at present both for myself and the future of our race in literature."[4] Less than two months later, in a July 13 letter to Henry A. Tobey, Dunbar revealed that he hoped to be able to interpret his race "through song and story, and to prove to the many that after all we are more human than African."[5] Dunbar's growing apprehension about the possibilities for his novels surfaced again in a letter to his agent in July 1900 concerning the publication of *The Fanatics*. Dunbar wrote, "I would expect from this book at least five hundred dollars, because it strikes me as a more serious work and is decidedly longer than *The Uncalled*."[6] Although he was widely criticized for his characterization of the African American community in *The Fanatics*, Dunbar's emergent desire to represent the black community in his long fiction was illustrated in the novel more vigorously than in his previous two attempts, *The Uncalled* (1899) and *The Love of Landry* (1900). In debates concerning racial protest in *The Fanatics*, however, critics have questioned whether or not Dunbar was adhering to the already established depictions of blacks in American literary studies;[7] this is the driving force for the development of this chapter.

Over the past three decades, critics have failed to appreciate Dunbar's veiled racial protest in *The Fanatics*. Those who have suggested that Dunbar's racial protest was a disappointment seemingly misinterpret the purpose of his achievement. Critics' dissatisfaction with Dunbar's characterization of the African American community, for example, seemed to stem from their interpretation of the single black character of consequence in the novel, "the town crier," Nigger Ed.[8] Indeed, Dunbar's characterization of Ed was—and still is—significant—and deserves a closer examination, not only because of *what* Dunbar constructed but also because of *how* and *why* he did so. Dunbar's characterization of Ed was clearly a calculated one, especially since he envisioned *The Fanatics* as a "more serious work" than his previous novels. Dunbar's racial protest actually surfaced through his characterization of Ed, whom he presented as a productive figure who gains the admiration of the white citizens by the end of the novel. In Dunbar's "first confrontation with a black character in his serious fiction," Ed was the key to Dunbar's solution to the artistic question of racial perspective.[9] As Dunbar pointed out in the novel, many blacks were eager to fight in the Civil War in order to secure their own freedoms. However, they were prohibited from doing so until the first executive order of Abraham Lincoln's Emancipation Proclamation was issued on September 22, 1862.[10] As he set the plot of *The Fanatics* at a time when the nation had reached this transformative moment, Dunbar was uneasy about declaring that attitudes toward blacks were not a straightforward matter of the abolitionist North versus the slave-owning South.[11] When Ed is introduced, readers do not learn of the trials and tribulations suffered by those blacks who were soldiers but are given a behind-the-scenes view of the story not told. Ed represents those blacks who did not fight in the Civil War yet had to fight their own personal battles in the racist societies in which they lived. Thus, fighting a war within a war became the motivation behind the creation of the character of Ed.

The rhetoric of any movement—literary, social, or physical—lies in its authority and agency. The ways in which the architects of a movement form their rhetoric and disseminate it to the public determine the degree to which the movement is accepted. The rhetoric of local color realism employed by African American authors was inevitable from the very start; its message was so blurred that it could easily be interpreted to serve the purpose of racists who continued to argue for the domination, dehumanization, and degradation of the black community. In his use of local color in *The Fanatics,* Dunbar focused on "the *structures* of racism and prejudice, rather than on a particular ideological or political position, achieving a subtlety that has been lost on some readers."[12] What African American authors came to realize was that a racial protest could not continue to advance the race by making use of the same language and methods employed by their white counterparts.[13]

Local color realism in nineteenth-century American fiction, however, included good-humored and sometimes romantic representations of everyday life that delved very little, if at all, beneath the external pretense of behaviors and local habits. The characteristic writer attempted to hold a mirror up to reality, to show the world as it was, and to let readers draw their own inferences from this look at reality and local color. Some critics suggested that local color realism was merely neglecting character analysis of the time.[14] Notable local colorists included Francis Bret Harte, James Whitcomb Riley, George Washington Cable, Irwin Russell, Joel Chandler Harris, Mark Twain, and William Dean Howells, although Howells would become better known as an authoritative literary critic than a creative writer. The nucleus of local color themes was centered on geographical humor, folktales, and ballads in local dialect; idealization of form and country life; and dramatic or picturesque western frontier life.

One cannot discuss local color realism without discussing its pejorative effects. Two manifestations of the post–Civil War environment and the popularity of local color realism were the plantation tradition in American literature and the long-lasting popularity of traveling minstrel shows. Both aided in the consolidation of racist caricatured stereotypes of blacks in the minds of white America's reading and viewing public. By the time Dunbar sought acceptance as a writer, both the plantation tradition and the traveling minstrel show were firmly established in American culture. The minstrel show disparagingly lampooned blacks as ignorant, simple, lazy, buffoonish, superstitious, rustic, joyous, overly emotional and gullible, and musical. Meanwhile, the plantation tradition, a genre of literature that nostalgically looked back to the times before the Civil War, idealized the glory days of the munificent plantation master and his appreciative and dedicated slaves who merrily laughed and sang. Kenneth Warren explained the function of the tradition in *Black and White Strangers*:

> The happy-go-lucky darky images of the antebellum South could be contrasted favorably to the images of impoverished, potentially dangerous blacks of post-Reconstruction. Such contrasts were staples of plantation fiction and minstrelsy, both of which were going strong through the 1890s. The needs fulfilled by these images were not solely racial: "For many white audiences the black African was the creature of a pre-industrial life style with a pre-industrial appetite," allowing whites to indulge their nostalgia for a lifestyle that was no longer available to them as they congregated in urban centers. The promise of black America was an assurance that old ways and old pleasures were recuperable. Of course the old ways were beyond recovery.[15]

In his attempt at a validated racial protest, Dunbar had a great deal to contend with in moving away from the stereotypical images previously employed by white authors. Linda Bearss has argued that realism necessitated that he write about what he already knew.[16] Although the novel deals with the effects of the Civil War upon a northern community, it illustrates Dunbar's awareness of the psychology of the small town and the character of the self-righteous northerner.[17] As Gene Andrew Jarrett has argued, Dunbar examined the world through "racial-uplift ideology."[18] Was it Dunbar's true intention to portray Nigger Ed in a pejorative light? Or, in accordance with the established constructs of local color and realism, was that what Dunbar saw when he held up his imaginative mirror to examine antebellum America? It can be argued that because Ed did not step up to control his destiny, he delimited the space for African Americans not only in the town in which he lived but also on a national level. From what readers see, Ed seemingly confirms the "happy darky" myth that had carved out a niche in American mainstream literature and folklore. However, one contemporary reviewer wrote that Ed was "imbued with sterling qualities."[19] Most of Dunbar's portrayal of Ed takes the form of observations by white characters in the text. This does not, however, fully remove Dunbar from his responsibility to the race. Ed, it should be remembered, represented an important figure in the class struggle, a decisive figure in the novel.

Black identity for Ed, as much as it existed in turn-of-the-century America, was a product of guiding principles and procedures in both the North and South. Dunbar had a rather broad understanding of this authority. As Robert A. Bone wrote fifty years ago, Dunbar believed that both North and South could have resolved their differences, "but both sections [were] united and *fanatical* in their determination to keep the Negro in his place."[20] With this in mind, Dunbar used Ed to establish a dialogue between North and South and investigate the methodical oversight of racial prejudice by white authors. Dunbar noted that all Americans could learn from various perspectives on race and social inequality and all could draw insights from the differences among these perspectives. Readers could then generate their own theories on how racial difference is constructed through literature, how racism divides black and white Americans, and how social inequality shaped race.

From its masked development in the oral tradition to its veiled fashion in the poetry and prose of forerunners Phillis Wheatley and Jupiter Hammon to its rhetorical appeal in abolitionists' propaganda to its maturity in the African American novel, racial protest has been a theme throughout the evolution of African American literature. Most African American authors during Dunbar's time wrote their texts with the goal of making a political impact on the mind-set of their readers. One can hardly ignore the racial and sociopolitical motivations behind novels such as Chesnutt's *The Marrow of Tradition* (1901), Sutton Griggs's *Imperium in Imperio* (1899), and Dunbar's own *The Sport of the Gods* (1902). As Dickson D. Bruce Jr. has argued, *The Fanatics*, Dunbar's third novel, "offered an oblique protest against a culture that made unnatural demands on black Americans."[21] The need for Dunbar's creation of Ed had great urgency and as far as racial protest rhetoric was concerned, the story of *The Fanatics* was constructed on a noteworthy frame: black cultural and social identity. Dunbar did not, like writers since and before him, suddenly become enlightened by his insight into racial protest. His creation of Ed was significant for his growth as a novelist of racial protest because *The Fanatics* allowed him to craft a network of social spaces for dealing with racial issues at the dawning of the Civil War.

Inclusion of racial protest in a novel is clearly an author's conscious choice. However, critics' scrutiny of Dunbar's first two novels seemed to be in response to the poetry that had already positioned him in the realm of American literature. Although favored by both blacks and whites, he was a controversial writer because some felt that in employing his unique dialect style, he did not always seek the best interests of the race. Some of his critics found his portrayal of blacks both powerful and derogatory. Dunbar himself was extremely perceptive of how he was positioned in the discourse of representation and identity. He realized that by creating his seemingly "happy darky" characters, he, as a black male, was participating in a culture-wide project of defining the black community through the lenses of white hegemony. Therefore, what we can see in Dunbar's novels is a gradual progression toward a more radical commentary on the effects of slavery and prejudice on African Americans. His first two novels, *The Uncalled* and *The Love of Landry*, have been called nonracial because the main characters are white. *The Fanatics* and *The Sport of the Gods*, however, have been recognized as a manifestation of his racial consciousness, be it a poor representation or a respectable one. Even African American texts that appear not to be a part of the protest tradition were written in a political context, as was clear from much of the critical commentary on Dunbar's *The Fanatics*. Thus, as Pierre A. Walker has argued, "For a critical style to dismiss the closely related categories of form and of literature is to relegate to obscurity an important tradition of African-American literature and an important political tool of the struggle in the United States of Americans of African descent."[22] Dunbar's black contemporaries hoped that racial protest would spark change. The kind of change that they wished to happen, however, was never really spelled out.[23] The same was true for *The Fanatics*.

Set in Dorbury, a small town in Ohio, during the Civil War, the story focuses on two white families: one northern, the other Copperhead.[24] The plot of the novel is centered around two lovers, Mary Waters, daughter of Bradford Waters, a strong sympathizer of the Union cause, and Bob Van Doren, son of Stephen Van Doren, a strong supporter of the Confederacy. Mary and Bob have been engaged for three months and plan to marry. The hostility between the two families, in a contemporary Shakespearean Romeo and Juliet fashion,[25] makes it impossible for the couple to fulfill their dreams. Bob, more for this father's wishes than his own, joins the Confederate army. As to be expected, Mary's father adamantly beckons her to end her engagement to Bob. However, Mary proclaims that her love for Bob cannot be severed so easily. Separated by the "fanaticism" of their fathers, Mary is forced to find refuge within the Van Doren household. After a series of tragic events—the wounding of Van Doren's son and the death of Waters's son—the two families are united in harmony after the war ends. In a veiled manner, Dunbar constructs rather insightful interpretations of American racial issues. On a first reading, one might believe that the white characters are the most important in the novel. However, as Williams has argued, often what Dunbar does not reveal in the text becomes of utmost concern to the novel's "impassioned plea for great racial tolerance and understanding" through "profound judgments on the American social scene, especially of the North."[26]

During Dunbar's time, racial protests in the free North took the form of narratives that enabled groups of people, loosely or tightly connected, to actively engage in protest against an overarching hegemonic power. Racial protests took many forms, among them organizing, activism, and counterpropaganda. In *The Fanatics*, rhetoric of racial protests existed in two types of fanaticism. The first ("for they were all fanatics")[27] signifies, as Bruce argues, that throughout the novel, Dunbar was actually writing about the hegemonic structures that made Ed buffoonish. Ed thus represents a standard basis of comparison that helped reveal not the character of a buffoonish, clownish African American but rather the "character of American race relations." The other is examined through the character of Raymond Stothard, who forms a mob to drive out the group of black refugees who have come from the war in the South. While Van Doren seeks to help the refugees, Stothard's actions entangle both free and refugee blacks in intense conflict, which results in the banning of blacks from the community.[28]

The progression of such subtle resistance to active protest gives *The Fanatics* a thematic concern that stands in contrast to the otherwise episodic quality of the story's plot. For this purpose, protest refers to a culture's ability to oppose adverse conditions, be they political, religious, social, or economic, and to be able to transition out of that predicament. In *The Fanatics*, however, there existed no wide-ranging established foundation for a protest movement in Dorbury. It is not until chapter 14, "The Contrabands," that Dunbar's racial consciousness and racial antagonism become more visible. In this chapter, Dunbar illustrates his understanding that the spaces blacks occupied in the North were but little better than those they had previously inhabited in the South by actively portraying the attitudes of many northern whites concerning the immigration of free blacks into their towns: "Ohio, placed as she was, just on the border of the slave territory, was getting more than her share of this unwelcome population, and her white citizens soon began to chafe at it. Was their free soil to become the haven for escaped negroes? Was this to be the stopping ground for every runaway black from the South? Would they not become a menace to the public safety? Would they not become a public charge and sorely strain that generosity that was needed to encourage and aid the soldiers in the field?"[29] Northern attitudes toward black immigration are succinctly expressed when Stothard, the town's white drunk, complains that the refugees are taking up spaces that should be occupied by the white man:

All the niggers in the South are crowding in on us, and pretty soon, we won't have a place to lay our heads. They'll undercharge the laborer and drive him out of house and home. They will live on leavings, and the men who are eating white bread and butter will have to get down to the level of the black hounds.

... The whole war is on their account. If it hadn't been for them, we'd have been friends with the South today, but they've estranged us from our brothers, rent the country asunder, and now they're coming up here to crowd us out of our town.[30]

As Williams rightfully argued, the blacks who fill in the spaces in Dorbury are used as rhetorical tools in an "apparent local-color tradition: Nigger Ed, the town crier who goes to war, emerges as a warmly human character although he too might prove to be reprehensible to many readers." The story's plot, then, uncovers northern pretenses and protests the "paradoxical position into which most blacks were forced in Northern spaces."[31]

Dunbar's investigation of race relations through Ed examined whether a change in the sociopolitical structure of the antebellum North affected the prescribed set of networks that prejudiced African Americans. If anything at all, Ed fails to demonstrate that to oppose prejudice and racism, there should be a well-connected network of African Americans that could come together under a common interest, as in Chesnutt's *The Marrow of Tradition*. Dunbar's illustration of racial protest in *The Fanatics* portrays a group that had experienced dehumanization and debasement. Readers find, for example, that Nigger Ed is a complicated character. At first glance, Dunbar's depiction of Ed seems to fall in the tradition of boorish, amusing, cheerful, and—most important—loyal blacks in antebellum America.[32] However, a more multifaceted analytical reading of Ed reveals that he was not intended to appear to readers in this fashion. Dunbar's willingness to stand back and record aspects of African American life as he saw it, and with minimal intervention, allowed him to paint for readers the image of a very straightforward character:

Ed was usually good natured, and met such sallies with a grin, but a new cap and a soldier's belt had had their effect on him, and he marched among his derides, very stern, dignified and erect, as if the arduous duties of the camp were already telling upon him. The only reply he vouchsafed was "nemmine, you people, nemmine. You got to git somebody else to ring yo' ol' bell now." The crowd laughed. There came a time when they wept at [the] thought of that black buffoon; the town nigger, the town drunkard, when in the hospital and by deathbeds his touch was as the touch of a mother; when over the bloodswept field, he bore a woman's dearest and nursed him back to a broken life. But no more of that. The telling of it must be left to a time when he who says aught of a Negro's virtues will not be cried down as an advocate drunk with prejudice.[33]

Thus, as Williams argued, Ed becomes "representative to the fanatics of Dorbury of all that they hate."[34] Dunbar's critics have suggested that the type of social identity and categorization elaborated through the character of Ed (as he was seemingly accepting his role in the community until the point mentioned above) is a mechanism that helps explain the town's negative reaction to him. Dunbar's overarching statement concerning racial relations as depicted by Ed was that when a threat is directed at a social identity that an individual feels incapable of escaping, the individual produces a strong self-categorization as a member of a community of degradation. Without risking harm to his life, though, Ed is able to preserve his human dignity in the face of whites' attempts to belittle him. Through his own agency, he seeks to emancipate himself from old behavioral patterns of antebellum America. His desire to no longer ring the bell isn't much, but given the circumstances, it's all that he can do. Thus readers clearly see a man who is beginning to come into his own by resisting racial oppression. What should be problematic for readers is their own response to Ed's coming of age, not the space that Ed occupies in the community. Thus, Dunbar progressively transforms Ed from helpless and ignorant to an individual who engages in subtle resistance.

The support or criticism that Dunbar himself received after publishing *The Fanatics* is also important to the discussion of racial protest. One critic, for example, wrote that Dunbar's use of realism illustrated "excellent judgment. He tells us how pitiful were the conditions of those colored people who sought their freedom in the Northern states."[35] This promising appraisal, though, was overshadowed by negative views. Some critics regarded the character of Ed as the "biggest failure in the book."[36] It is important to understand Ed's plight in being "representative" of all that Dorbury citizens hate.[37] This understanding was critical for assessing the practicability and sustainability of any form of social or racial protest and resistance. In the case of Dunbar's fictive Dorbury, such an understanding is critical if one wishes to understand how public opinion imposed constraints on white behavior and ultimately determined the chance of success of outright racial protests.

By the novel's end, citizens of Dorbury have altered their opinions of Ed. Ed becomes important to the citizens' survival. Should he choose to accept it, his new role would be that of the griot, a highly esteemed position: "There were men who had seen that black man on the bloody fields, which were thick with the wounded and the dying, and these could not speak of him without tears in their eyes. There were women who begged him to come in and talk to them about their sons who had been left on some Southern field, wives who wanted to hear over again the last words of their loved ones. And so they gave him a place for life and everything he wanted, and from being despised he was much petted and spoiled, for they were all fanatics."[38] Dunbar clearly implies certain actions that need to be further analyzed. Ultimately the danger of racial prejudice did not hinge on white America's attempts to strip minorities of their humanity. The danger would come if white America failed to recognize that humanity of black Americans. Ed's awareness of his previous life in Dorbury concerned a critical reevaluation of his self-image. This illustrated transcendence of the racial stereotypes that previously plagued him. Although Ed wins the citizens' admiration and affection, they are all still fanatics: at this point, their fanaticism merely shifts. No longer fanatics in their political views on war and the position that blacks hold in their community, their fanaticism now manifests itself in their views of Ed, whom they no longer regard in terms of the conventional beliefs of the times, but whom they are able to see more through the progressive principles of humanitarianism as a fellow man.[39]

This chapter focused on Dunbar's voice of protest against traditional depictions of African Americans as buffoonish in the country's literary imagination. That being said, the character of Ed deserves one more look. Perhaps Ed is representative of the voicelessness faced by African Americans who chose not to fight in the Civil War, the thousands of men, women, and children across the South whose names did not appear in any history books and whose stories were lost in the vortex of time. What doors were opened to them? Were they traitors to the cause? How did the white community view them? One thing is for certain: Dunbar's rationale for his depiction of the character of Ed was that this character allowed him to catalog the numerous social and political grievances of the black community in the North. To disregard the various ways Dunbar articulated his ideas concerning identity and race in *The Fanatics* is to ignore the extent to which Dunbar successfully confronted the difficulties of creating a constructive representation of his race, an important aspect of his artistic achievement.

Notes

1. Kenny J. Williams, "The Masking of the Novelist," in *A Singer in the Dawn: Reinterpretations of Paul Laurence Dunbar*, ed. Jay Martin (New York: Dodd, Mead, 1975), 180.
2. Also that year, Dunbar published two volumes of poetry, *Lyrics of the Hearthside* and *Poems of Cabin and Field*, adding to his already sizable body of literature.
3. Addison Gayle Jr., "Literature as Catharsis: The Novels of Paul Laurence Dunbar," in *A Singer in the Dawn*, 149.
4. *The Paul Laurence Dunbar Reader: A Selection of the Best of Paul Laurence Dunbar's Poetry and Prose, Including Writings Never before Available in Book Form*, ed. Jay Martin and Gossie H. Husdon (New York: Dodd, Mead, 1975), 428.
5. Ibid., 431.
6. Qtd. in Peter Revell's *Paul Laurence Dunbar* (Boston: Twayne, 1979), 149.
7. American writers who had already begun to offer minstrel representations of blacks in their works include Ruth McEnery Stuart, Thomas Nelson Page, and Joel Chandler Harris.
8. Paul Laurence Dunbar, *The Fanatics*, ed. Lisa A. Long (Acton, Mass.: Copley, 2001), 36.
9. Gayle, "Literature as Catharsis," 147.
10. The first of Lincoln's executive orders was issued September 22, 1862, and declared the freedom of all slaves in all the Confederate States of America that did not return to Union control by January 1, 1863. The second order, issued January 1, 1863, named the specific states to which the first order applied.
11. Revell, *Paul Laurence Dunbar*, 151.
12. Lisa A. Long, introduction to *The Fanatics*, x.
13. Charles W. Chesnutt, in *The Marrow of Tradition*, had been successful in leading a literary protest movement that offered literary representations of blacks that were vastly different from white authors' portrayals of blacks in literature. The burden of shaping the future of black America in the fictional town of Wellington, North Carolina, rests on the shoulders of William Miller, a light-complexioned African American doctor.
14. Guy E. Smith, *American Literature: A Complete Survey* (Totowa, N.J.: Littlefield, Adams, 1970), 101.
15. Kenneth Warren, *Black and White Strangers: Race and American Literary Realism* (Chicago: University of Chicago Press, 1995), 119.
16. Linda Bearss, "Dunbar's Fiction: Transgressing the Limits of Realism to Breach the Horizon of Modernism," *Midwestern Miscellany* 34 (2006): 70.
17. Williams, "The Masking," 184.
18. Gene Andrew Jarrett, *Deans and Truants: Race and Realism in African American Literature* (Philadelphia: University of Pennsylvania Press, 2007), 55.
19. See "Paul Dunbar's War Romance," *New York Times*, April 6, 1901.
20. Robert A. Bone, *The Negro Novel in America* (New Haven, Conn.: Yale University Press, 1958), 41 (my emphasis).
21. Dickson D. Bruce Jr., *Black American Writing from the Nadir: The Evolution of a Literary Tradition, 1877–1915* (Baton Rouge: Louisiana State University Press, 1989), 93.
22. Pierre A. Walker, "Racial Protest, Identity, Words, and Form in Maya Angelou's *I Know Why the Caged Bird Sings*," *College Literature* 22 (1995): 92.
23. Chesnutt's *Marrow of Tradition*, for example, is also based on an historical event (a race riot in the fictional town of Wellington, North Carolina). At the end of the text, readers are left wondering if William Miller, the light-complexioned African American doctor, will take the humane road and save Dodie, Major Carteret's newborn son, even though in the wake of the riot, Miller loses his own child. Reformation is of major concern in the novel. Readers are left to consider whether or not Miller continues to subscribe to his reformist ideas.

24. The separation of the Democratic Party by 1860 did not silence those who were staunch Democrats. Actually, during the secession crisis, northern Democrats were generally more conciliatory toward the South than were Republicans. They called themselves Peace Democrats; their rivals, however, called them Copperheads because some wore copper pennies as identifying badges. The Copperheads were a vocal group in the North who opposed the American Civil War, wanting an immediate peace settlement with the Confederates. For extensive discussions of the Copperheads, see Robert H. Jones, *Civil War Iowa and the Copperhead Movement* (Ames: Iowa State University Press, 1980), and Chuck Leddy's *Copperheads: The Rise and Fall of Lincoln's Opponents in the North* (Oxford: Oxford University Press, 2006). According to Lisa A. Long, the original title of *The Fanatics* was "Copperheads" (8n). Dunbar's papers, Long writes, contain a typewritten manuscript of the novel in progress (*The Fanatics*, xi). See Long's introduction to *The Fanatics* for her discussion of the development of the novel (vii–xxxix).

25. Revell, *Paul Laurence Dunbar*, 151
26. Williams, "The Masking," 183.
27. Bruce, *Black American Writing*, 196.
28. Ibid., 90, 91.
29. Dunbar, *The Fanatics*, 100–101.
30. Ibid., 105.
31. Williams, "The Masking," 185.
32. Jennifer Hughes, "The Politics of Incongruity in Paul Laurence Dunbar's *The Fanatics*," *African American Review* 41 (2007): 299.
33. Dunbar, *The Fanatics*, 34.
34. Williams, "The Masking," 187.
35. Qtd. in Long, introduction, viii.
36. Ibid., ix.
37. Williams, "The Masking," 187.
38. Dunbar, *The Fanatics*, 196.
39. Williams, "The Masking," 187.

Contributors

LENA AMPADU is assistant chair of and professor in the Department of English, Towson University, Maryland, where she teaches composition, Survey of African American Literature, Major Writers of African American Literature, and courses on black women writers. Ampadu also serves as director of the African and African American Studies Program. She received her PhD from the University of Maryland, College Park; her MA from American University; and her BA from Howard University. She has published a number of essays on composition and rhetoric, as well as African American literature. Her specialty is oral traditions in African and African American women's novels.

NASSIM W. BALESTRINI studied American and Russian literatures and cultures in Germany and in the United States. She has taught at the universities of Mainz and Paderborn in Germany, and at the University of California, Davis. She currently teaches in the Department of English and American Studies at Regensburg University. She has published on nineteenth- and twentieth-century American literature, on Vladimir Nabokov's Russian and English works, on teaching American poetry and drama, and on literature and the other arts. Her latest book is titled *From Fiction to Libretto: Irving, Hawthorne, and James as Opera* (2005). A monograph on Nabokov's fiction is forthcoming. Among her current projects are an essay collection on teaching adaptations and a study of poet laureates in North America.

ELSTON L. CARR JR. was born in Dangriga Town, Belize. He grew up in Los Angeles and attended Wesleyan University, where he majored in English. At Wesleyan, he began working as a journalist for the *Middletown Press* and the *Hartford Courant*. Carr has also published his work in the *Los Angeles Times*, the *Los Angeles Times Magazine*, the *Los Angeles Times Sunday Book Review*, and *LA Weekly*. Carr earned an MA in African American studies from the University of California, Los

Angeles. As a PhD candidate at the University of California, Riverside, he focuses on postcolonial literature and theory, American literature, prison literature, and African American and Caribbean literature.

AMY CUMMINS is an assistant professor of English at Fort Hays State University in Hays, Kansas. She holds a BA from the University of North Carolina–Chapel Hill, an MA from North Carolina State University, and a PhD from the University of Kansas. Her scholarly interests include nineteenth-century U.S. literature, education history, and the recovery of neglected authors. Cummins has published work in periodicals such as the *Journal of the Midwest Modern Language Association*, *Eureka Studies in Teaching Short Fiction*, and *Southern Studies*.

WILLIE J. HARRELL JR. is an associate professor of English at Kent State University, where he teaches undergraduate and graduate courses on African American literature and cultural studies. He has published in the *Journal of Canadian Studies*, *Ethnicity and Race in a Changing World: A Review Journal*, the *Canadian Review of American Studies*, *CLA Journal*, the *Journal of International Women's Studies*, and the *Journal of Black Studies*. He received his BS in mass communications from Jackson State University, Mississippi, and both his MA and PhD in English from Wayne State University in Detroit.

JEANNINE KING is an associate professor of English at Saint Mary's College of California, where she specializes in African American literature. She graduated from the University of California, Santa Cruz, with a BA in American studies and earned a PhD in ethnic studies from the University of California, Berkeley.

MICHAEL P. MORENO is a doctoral candidate completing his dissertation on suburban literature at the University of California, Riverside. His areas of interest include spatial theory, twentieth-century American literature, and Latino literature. He has published articles in each of these areas.

MARK NOONAN edits the *Columbia Journal of American Studies* and teaches English and American studies at New York City College of Technology and Queens College. He is the author of *The Place Where We Dwell: Reading and Writing about New York City* and *Reading "The Century Illustrated Monthly Magazine": American Literature and Culture, 1870–1893* (Kent State University Press, 2010).

CORETTA M. PITTMAN is an associate professor of English in rhetoric and composition at Baylor University. Her research focuses on the theoretical and cultural intersections of rhetoric, race, class, and gender. She has published articles on classical rhetoric and race, outsider rhetoric and race, and working-class rhetoric and music. Pittman's articles have appeared in the *Rhetoric Society Quarterly, Agency in the Margins: Stories of Outsider Rhetoric,* and *Phoebe: Journal of Gender and Cultural Critiques.* She also writes about the politics of writing.

MEGAN M. PEABODY is a doctoral student in English at the University of Nebraska–Lincoln. She studies late nineteenth- and early twentieth-century American literature and is interested in investigating systems of subjectivity, especially in literature written by or about marginalized groups like women, African Americans, and immigrant populations.

SHARON D. RAYNOR is currently department chair and an assistant professor in the Department of English and Foreign Languages at Johnson C. Smith University in Charlotte, North Carolina. She completed her doctorate in literature and criticism at Indiana University of Pennsylvania and received both her BA in English and her MA in multicultural literature from East Carolina University. Raynor has written and directed two oral history projects sponsored by the North Carolina Humanities Council entitled "Breaking the Silence: The Unspoken Brotherhood of Vietnam Veterans" and "Soldier-to-Soldier: Men and Women Share Their Legacy of War." She is also a Road Scholar and a presenter for the "Let's Talk About It" book discussion program, both sponsored by the North Carolina Humanities Council. She teaches classes and publishes in the areas of Vietnam War studies, multicultural and contemporary literature, women's studies, and African American studies.

MATT SANDLER is completing a PhD in English and comparative literature at Columbia University. He is currently a visiting fellow at the Program in Louisiana and Caribbean Studies at Louisiana State University.

DOLORES V. SISCO is an assistant professor of English at Youngtown State University, where she currently teaches undergraduate and graduate courses in twentieth-century American studies, women's studies, world literature, and African American studies. Sisco received her BA from the University of Baltimore, her MA from Central Michigan University, and her PhD from Michigan State University. Sisco's research interests include African American literature and popular culture, West African/black British literature, Caribbean literature and theory, and critical race and postcolonial theory. She has most recently published in *Black Women in America* (2005).

ADAM SONSTEGARD is an assistant professor of English at Cleveland State University, where he researches American literary art's mediation of (and mediation by) visual art work. A graduate of Washington University in St. Louis and a former lecturer in the writing program at the University of California, Davis, he has published articles in *Texas Studies in Language and Literature*, *Arizona Quarterly*, and *Studies in American Fiction*.

JAYNE E. WATERMAN is an assistant professor of English at Ashland University in northern Ohio. She specializes in nineteenth- and twentieth-century American literature and culture, and her current research is concerned with regional literature, particularly the literature of the Midwest. She is working on an interdisciplinary monograph that considers the literary career of the overlooked Ohio author Louis Bromfield and has written introductions to two of his most recently reissued novels—*The Strange Case of Miss Annie Spragg* (1928) and *The Rains Came* (1937).

Index

Adams, John Henry, 132–34
Adventures of Huckleberry Finn, The (Twain), 117–18
Alcott, Louisa May, 147
Alexander, Eleanor, xviin1, xviiin7, 125, 196–97, 198
Alger, Horatio, 100
"All Coons Look Alike to Me" (Cook and Dunbar), 56
Allen, James Lane, 83, 95, 92
"America the Beautiful" (Bates and Ward), 8
Ampadu, Lena, xiii, 3–16
Anderson, Benedict, 51, 58n14
Anderson, Sherwood, 106
Andrews, William L., 114n17, 114n34, 137n44
Angelou, Maya, 13, 16n49
Appiah, Kwame Anthony, xii, xviiin5
Arac, Johnathan, 113n8
A Singer in the Dawn: Reinterpretations of Paul Laurence Dunbar (Martin), x
Atlantic Monthly, 42, 51

Baker, Houston A., Jr., xiv, 50, 51, 115n40, 132, 137n41, 210, 216, 228n43, 229n78
Balestrini, Nassim W., xiv, 17–31
Bancroft, Frederic, 150n1, 150n3
Baraka, Amiri, 118. *See also* Jones, LeRoi
Barthes, Roland, 159
Battle at Fort Pillow (American Civil War), 33, 37, 44
Battle at Fort Wagner (American Civil War), 33, 37, 44, 45
Battle at Olustee (American Civil War), 33, 37, 44

Battle of Antietam Creek (American Civil War), 45
Battle of Brandywine (American Civil War), 18, 41, 42
Bausch, Susan, 223, 228n48, 229n67, 229n74, 229n76, 231, 235, 240n5, 241n34
Bender, Bert, 160
Bennett, Michael, 151n43
Bennett, Paula Bernat, 143, 151n48
Berlatsky, Eric, 175
Berman, Marshall, 112n3
Berry, Torriano S., 46n1, 47n56
Berry, Venise T., 46n1, 47n56
Best, Felton O'Neal, 15n1, 15n8, 15n15, 137n29
Bethune-Cookman College (Daytona Beach, FL), 13
Bethune-Cookman University (Daytona Beach, FL), 14
Billig, Michael, 175
Black and White Strangers (Warren), 245
Black, Daniel P., xviiin4
Blacker the Berry, The (Thurman), 207
Black Samson (Battle of Brandywine, DE), 18–19, 33, 41–43
Blassingame, John W., 55
Blight, David, 187
Bloods, the, 34
Blount, Marcellus, 115n50
Blues People (Jones), 227
Blundell, Mary, 46n9
Boelhower, William, 182
Bone, Robert, 231, 246
Book of American Negro Poetry, The (Johnson), 3, 49–50, 57n1

259

Borders, Florence, 11, 13, 14
Boyesen, Hjalmar Hjorth, 85
Brain, Robert, 16n48
Braithwaite, William Stanley, 159
Brawley, Benjamin, 100, 135n4
Braxton, Joanne M., 50, 57, 57n5, 58n36, 109
Briden, Earl F., 117–18, 135n6
Brooks, Gwendolyn, 14
Brooks, Sara, 13, 16n50
Brown, Sterling, 5, 50, 60, 100, 113nn14–15, 114n34, 115n35, 139, 233; *Southern Road*, 50
Brown, William Wells, 139; *My Southern Home; or, The South and Its People*, 150n6
Bruce, Dickson D., Jr., xviiin2, 52, 58n15, 65, 66, 70n17, 70n20, 105, 221, 246, 247, 253n28
Bruce, John E., 199
Burke, Kenneth, 98, 112n3
Burns, Robert, 111

Cable, George Washington, 85, 244
"Caesar Rowan" (English), 91
Calinescu, Matei, 112n3
Campbell, Rex R., 228n13, 228n49
Camp, Stephanie, 151n11, 152n72
Carby, Hazel V., 214, 224, 228n14, 229n65
Carr, Elston L., Jr., xiv, 49–58
Carroll, Charles, 193
Carter, Dan, 151n18
Caruth, Cathy, 174, 187
Cash, W. J., 195, 205
Cather, Willa, 106
Central High School (Dayton, OH), 84
Century Illustrated Monthly Magazine, 51, 53, 82–97, 116, 117, 135n4
Charles, Ray, 8–9
Chesnutt, Charles W., 6, 73, 98, 113n15, 114n34, 166, 246, 249, 252n13
Chesterfield, Lord (Philip Dormer Stanhope), 102
Chicago Inter-Ocean, 136n8
Chicago Record, 28
Child, Lydia Maria, 134
Chireau, Yvonne P., 169n42
Christmas Carol, A (Dickens), 147
Cities of the Dead: Circum-Atlantic Performance (Roach), 51, 57n13
Civil War, American (1861–65), 17, 19, 21–27, 32–45, 51, 55, 75–76, 77, 85, 144, 213, 243–44, 245, 246, 250, 253n24; battle at Fort Pillow, 33, 37, 44; battle at Fort Wagner, 33, 37, 44, 45; battle at Olustee, 33, 37, 44; battle of Antietam Creek, 45; battle of Brandywine, 18, 41, 42; Fort Sumter, 35
Clansman, The (Dixon Jr.), 134
Clinton, Bill, 13
Clorindy (Cook and Dunbar), 56
Cohen, Octavus Roy, 104
Cole, Jean Lee, 135n2
Color Complex: The Politics of Skin Color among African Americans (Russell et al.), 196, 197
Colored American, 134
Cone, James H., 211, 220, 229n59, 229n63
Confiscation Act (1862), 35
Conjure Woman, The (Chesnutt), 166
Connolly, Joy, 46n3, 46n5, 47n54, 48n76
Cook, William Marion, 56, 107
Cook, William W., 15n4
Cooper, Anna Julia, 113n15
Copperheads, 247, 252n24
Covey, Edward, 139
Cowan, William Tynes, 189nn30–31
Crane, Elaine, 46n6, 46n14
Crane, Stephen, 238
Crow, Jim, 23, 176, 194
Crummell, Alexander, 6, 7, 113n12, 175
Cummins, Amy, xv, 138–53
Cunningham, Virginia, 135n4
Curtis, Cyrus, 101

Dailey, Jane, 176
David, Beverly R., 135n5
David, Jay, 46n6, 46n14
Dayton Tattler, 84
Denver Post, 242
Derrida, Jacques, 50
Dickens, Charles, 147
Dixon, Thomas, 118
Dixon, Thomas, Jr., 134, 193
Dodd, Mead and Company, 117–19, 128, 136n8
Douglas, Ann, 52, 58n17
Douglass, Frederick, 6, 30n12, 45, 90, 99, 139–40, 149, 187
Douglass, Helen, 90, 112
Du Bois, W. E. B., xi, xii, 6, 39, 73, 77–79, 81n12, 98, 100, 104, 114n19, 114n27, 115n40, 206, 221; double consciousness, xi,

188n16, 221; *Souls of Black Folk, The,* xv, 47n37, 75, 78, 81n10, 120

Dunbar, Alice Ruth, 242. *See also* Dunbar-Nelson, Alice; Moore, Alice Ruth

Dunbar, Joshua (father of PLD), 33, 34, 35, 84,

Dunbar, Matilda (mother of PLD), 156

Dunbar-Nelson, Alice (wife of PLD), 110

Dunbar, Paul Laurence (PLD), "Accountability," 53, 55–56; "After the Struggle," 31n42; "Alexander Crummell Dead," 7; "Antebellum Sermon, An," 9, 10, 55, 60, 61, 65–69; "At Candle-Lightin' Time," 89, 93, 109; "At Shaft 11," 120; "Aunt Tempe's Revenge," 157; "Aunt Tempe's Triumph," 157; "Backlog Song, A," 138, 142, 143; "Black Samson of Brandywine," 5, 18, 31n55, 33, 41–43; "Blessed Deceit, A," 167; "Booker T.," 5; "Brief Cure of Aunt Fanny, The," 157–58, 161; "Buggah Man, The," 109; "Chrismus Is A-Comin'," 138, 142; "Chrismus on the Plantation," 138, 143–44, 145; "Christmas Carol," 138, 144; "Christmas Folksong, A," 138, 141; "Christmas in the Heart," 138, 147, 150; *Clorindy,* 56; "Colored Band, The," 9; "Colored Soldiers, The," 5, 21, 32, 33, 36–39, 44; "Comparison," 232; "Conjuring Contest, The," 158, 166; "Conquerors: The Black Troops in Cuba," 27, 28, 31n55; "Coquette Conquered, A," 60, 93, 116; "Cornelius Johnson, Office Seeker," 123–24; "Council of State," 126, 127, 128; "Dandy Jim's Conjure Scare," 158, 166; "Defection of Maria Ann Gibbs, The," 161; "Defender of the Faith, A," 138, 147, 148; "Delinquent, The," 60; "Deserted Plantation, The," 53, 56; "Differences," 232; "Dinah Kneading Dough," 30n33; "Dirge for a Soldier," 23, 24; "Discovered," 60; "Douglass," 5; "Family Feud, A," 120; *Fanatics, The,* xvii, 231, 242–53, 253n24; "Finding of Martha, The," 165; *Folks from Dixie,* x, 119, 121, 144, 154; "Foolin' Wif de Seasons," 89, 92; "Fourth of July and Race Outrages, The," 149; "Frederick Douglass," 6, 177; "Frolic, A," 94; "Fruitful Sleeping of Rev. Elisha Edwards, The," 9, 16n34; "Harriet Beecher Stowe," 95; "Haunted Oak, The," 95; *Heart of Happy Hollow, The,* 128, 139, 147, 154; "How Brother Parker Fell from Grace," 158, 160, 163; *In Old Plantation Days,* xv, 101, 154–69; "Intervention of Peter, The," 120; "In the Morning," 11, 13; "Jim's Probation," 124; *Joggin' Erlong,* ix; "Last Fiddling of Mordaunt's Jim, The," 160, 164; "Lincoln," 25, 26, 27, 31n49; "Little Brown Baby," 11, 12, 109, 111; "Little Brown Baby with Sparkling Eyes," 110; "Little Christmas Basket, A," 138, 147; *Love of Landry, The,* 243, 247; "Lover's Lane," 89; "Lynching of Jube Benson, The," 130, 178, 180; *Lyrics of Love and Laughter,* 27, 150; *Lyrics of Lowly Life,* ix, xiv, 59, 60, 82, 83, 99; *Lyrics of the Hearthside,* 27, 142, 252n2; "Memorial Day," 23, 24; "Memory of Martha, The," 161; "Mr. Groby's Slippery Gift," 158, 159, 160, 167; "Mt. Pisgah's Christmas Possum," 146; "Negro Love Song," 12, 94; "Negro Society in Washington," 104, 113n8; "Nelse Hatton's Vengeance," 120, 121, 144; "Noddin' by the Fire," 93; *Oak and Ivy,* ix; "Ode for Memorial Day," 24, 25, 30n42, 33, 40; "Ode to Ethiopia," 28, 31n55, 115n35; "Of Negro Journals," 113n13; "Old-Time Christmas, An," 138, 148, 149; "Old Warrior," 6; "One Christmas at Shiloh," 129, 138, 139; "On Emancipation Day," 19; "One Man's Fortunes," 101, 123; "On the Road," 93; "Ordeal at Mount Hope, The," 120; "Our Martyred Soldiers," 23, 24; "Paradox, The," 112, 232; "Parted," 89; "Party, The," 11, 60–65; *Poems of Cabin and Field,* 109, 142, 252n2; "Poet and His Song, The," 106; "Poet, The," 49, 89–90, 232; "Possum," 93; "Recession Never," 28; "Remembered," 23; "Representative American Negroes," 73–81, 98, 102–3; "Resignation," 105; "Robert Gould Shaw," 26, 27, 28, 33, 42; "Schwalliger's Philanthropy," 129; "Speakin' at de Cou'thouse," 25, 26; "Speakin' o' Christmas," 144, 145; "Spiritual, A," 25; *Sport of the Gods, The,* x, xvi, xvii, 95–96, 106, 107, 111, 114n34, 155, 173–90, 191–209, 210–29, 230–41, 246, 247; *Strength of Gideon and Other Stories, The,* 122, 124, 125, 128, 148, 154, 155; "Strength of Gideon, The," 165; "Supper by Proxy, A," 159, 167; "To the

Dunbar, Paul Laurence (cont.)
    South, on Its New Slavery," 150; "Tragedy at Three-Forks, The," 123; "Trousers, The," 158; *Uncalled, The*, x, 106, 108, 243, 247; "Uncle Eph's Christmas," 138, 145–46; "Unsung Heroes, The," 21; "Veteran, The," 23, 24, 33, 39–41; "Virginia Reel, A," 53–55, 56; *Voice of the Negro, The*, 132, 134; "Walls of Jericho, The," 158, 161; "Warrior's Prayer, The," 33, 44; "Way of a Woman, The," 161; "We Wear the Mask," xi, 4, 57, 116, 132, 230, 234, 239; "When Dey 'Listed Colored Soldiers," 22, 23, 24, 33, 36; "When Malindy Sings," 5, 7, 8–9, 11, 12; "Whistling Sam," 22, 23; "Who Dat Say Chicken in Dis Crowd?" 56; "Who Stands for the Gods," 167
Duncan, Laval Todd, 159

Eggleston, Edward, 85
Elam, Harry, Jr., 182
Elbert, Monika, 152n76, 152n78
Ellison, Ralph, 98, 227, 231, 233, 238
Emanuel, James A., 20, 25, 29n1, 30n13, 30n17, 30n24, 31n44, 31n45
Emerson, Ralph Waldo, 87
English, Thomas Dunn, 91
Epstein, Dena, 16n32
Equiano, Olaudah, 7, 15n23
Eyerman, Ron, 174

Fedric, Frances, 140
Felman, Shoshana, 174
55th Massachusetts Infantry (American Civil War), 35
54th Massachusetts Infantry (American Civil War), 34
54th Massachusetts Regiment (American Civil War), 27, 32, 35, 43–45
Figures in Black (Gates), 237
Fine Clothes to the Jew (Hughes), 112n5
Fishkin, Shelley Fisher, 232, 238, 240n5
Flint, Allen, 42, 43, 47n57
Follen, Charles, 143
Foner, Eric, 151n20, 152n49
Foote, Mary Halleck, 85
Fort Sumter, 35
Fortune, T. Thomas, 73, 98
Franklin, Aretha, 8

Franklin, Benjamin, 101, 102, 104
Frazier, E. Franklin, 113n8
Frederickson, George, 113n6
Freud, Sigmund, 53, 58n9, 174

Gaines, Kevin, 113n12, 114n17
Garland, Hamlin, 85
Garland, Judy, 8–9
Garrison, William Lloyd, 134
Gates, Henry Louis, Jr., xiv, 12, 13, 16n47, 16n51, 50, 51, 57n7, 82, 96n2, 143, 237; *Signifying Monkey: A Theory of African-American Literary Criticism, The*, 50, 57n7, 82, 96n2, 151n23, 151n25, 152n50
Gatewood, Willard B., 113n8, 197, 199
Gayle, Addison, xviii1, 191, 194, 198, 202, 207n8, 242
Genette, Gérard, xiv, 61
Georgis, Dina, 187
Gibbs, Mifflin Wistar, 79
Gilder, Richard Watson, 85
Giovanni, Nikki, 14
Gissendanner, John, 11
Glory (film, 1989), 32
Goffman, Erving, xvi, 234, 235, 236, 237
Gone with the Wind (Mitchell), 91
Good Housekeeping, 51
Gooding, James Henry, 35
Greener, Richard Theodore, 79
Griffin, Farah Jasmine, 215, 220, 227n4, 228n16, 228n27, 228n32, 228n35, 229n53, 229n57, 229n61
Griggs, Sutton, 246
Grimké, Sarah, 22
Grimké Weld, Angelina, 22
Grossman, James R., 188n12

Hall, Donald, 34, 46n8
Hall, Ronald, 196
Halttunen, Karen, 114n25
Ham (son of Noah), 20, 33, 38
Hammon, Jupiter, 246
Hampton Institute Camera Club, 117, 135n2
Harlem: Negro Metropolis (McKay), 219
Harlem Renaissance, xvii, 3, 14, 49, 159, 233
Harper, Frances, 57, 114n34
Harper, Michael, 14
Harper's Monthly, 83, 87, 116
Harper's Weekly, 51

Harrell, Willie J., Jr., 154–69, 242–53
Harris, Joel Chandler, ix, 59, 83, 85, 92, 94, 118, 135n5, 156, 244, 252n7; "Free Joe and the Rest of the World," 92; "Night with Uncle Remus," 94; "Rainy Day with Uncle Remus, A," 92
Harris, Johnnie Mae, 11
Harte, Bret, 85, 244
Hartman, Saidiya, 114n17
Harvard University, 43, 102
Hawthorne, Nathaniel, 113n10
Hegel, Friedrich, 163
Henri, Florette, 179, 189n29
High School Times (Central High School, Dayton), 84
Hoberman, John, 45, 47n51, 48n75
Hofstader, Richard, 103, 114n22
Holiday, Billie, 8
Holland, Josiah G., 85, 87
Holmes, Oliver Wendell, 87
Holt, Elvin, 135n5
Howells, William Dean, ix, 59, 82, 83, 84, 87, 89, 90, 95, 99, 105, 113n15, 116, 195–96, 197, 244
Hudson, Gossie Harold, xviin1, xviiin9, 29n1, 57n6, 136n9, 154
Huggins, Nathan, 237, 238
Hughes, Jennifer, 253n32
Hughes, Langston, 6, 14, 15n12, 99, 112n5, 227
Hurd, Myles, 198
Hutchinson, George, 97n35

Ikonné, Chidi, 113n15
Imperium in Imperio (Griggs), 246
Incidents in the Life of a Slave Girl, Written by Herself (Jacobs), 161
Indianapolis Journal, 84
Inge, Casey, 212, 227nn5–6
In His Own Voice (Martin and Primeau), 232

Jackson, Mahalia, 8
Jacobs, Harriet, 161
James, Henry, 113n15
Jarrett, Gene Andrew, 128, 136n9, 154, 157, 232, 245
Jennie Dean Elementary and High School (Manassas, VA), 13
Jewett, Sarah Orne, 147
Jim Crow, 23, 176, 194
Johnson, Daniel M., 228n13, 228n49

Johnson, James Weldon, 3, 6, 14, 49–50, 53, 60, 105, 107, 114n32, 141, 177, 206–7
Johnson, Richard Underwood, 135n4
Johnston, Francis Benjamin, 135n2
Johnston, Mary, 92
Johnston, Richard, 92
John Wesley Hoffman Junior High School (New Orleans), 13
Jones, Gavin, 95, 156
Jones, LeRoi, 227. *See also* Baraka, Amiri
Jones, Robert H., 253n24
Jordan, Vernon, Jr., 13

Kealing, H. T., 73
Keats, John, 113n8
Keeling, John, 22, 30n29, 50, 53, 63, 69n12, 69n15, 70n23
Kemble, Edward Windsor, xv, 93, 116–37
Kerouac, Jack, 227
Kersten, Holger, 59, 63, 69n3, 70n16
Kilgore, Willie Mae, 13
King, Grace, 83, 92
King, Jeannine, xvi, 173–90
Kipling, Rudyard, 13

LaCapra, Dominick, 174
Ladies' Home Journal, 101
Laub, Dori, 174
Lawson, Victor, 113n9
Lears, T. J. Jackson, 85, 96n6
"Le Cimetiére marin" (Valéry), 111
Leddy, Chuck, 252n24
Lembcke, Jerry, 33, 46n4, 47n55, 48n77
Lenz, Günter H., 228n39, 229n68
Leslie's Weekly, 146
Lewis, David Levering, 105, 114n31
Lewis, Sinclair, 106
Lincoln, Abraham, 35, 45, 243, 252n10
Lippincott's, 102
Little Women (Alcott), 147
Locke, Alain, 206
Logan, Rayford, 112n2
Logan, Shirley Wilson, 81n14
Longfellow, Henry Wadsworth, 87
Long, Lisa A., 252n12, 253n24
Loomis, Charles Battell, 96n18
Lorde, Audrey, 57, 118
Lorimer, George Horace, xv, 101, 102, 103, 104, 114nn18–20, 114n23, 114nn26–27

Lott, Eric, 53, 54–55, 58n12, 58n25, 58n35
Love and Theft: Blackface Minstrelsy and the American Working Class (Lott), 53, 58n12, 58n25, 58n35
Lowell, James Russell, 87
Luker, Ralph, 114n17

Macon, J. A., 92
Mapanje, Jack, 15n7
Marling, Karal, 151n42, 152n58, 152n77
Marrow of Tradition, The (Chesnutt), 246, 249, 252n13, 252n13, 252n23
Martineau, Harriet, 143
Martin, Herbert Woodward, xviii n1, 30n10, 145, 154, 232
Martin, Jay, x, xvii n1, xviii n8, xviii n9, 28, 29n1, 30n12, 31n56, 50, 57, 57n6, 80n2, 136n9
Maryland, Isaac, 41
Matthews, James Newton, xvii, 82, 84, 88, 176
Maultsby, Portia, 15n29
Maxwell, William J., 115n40
McGann, Jerome, 113n8
McKay, Claude, 219
McGee, Nancy B., 22, 30n26, 135n2
Meier, August, 100, 101, 113n11, 114n17
Militia Act of 1862, 35
Militia Act of 1792, 35
Miller, Monica, 115n40
Mitchell, Margaret, 91
"Monster, The" (Crane), 238
Montford Point Marines, 34
Moore, Alice Ruth, ix, xviii n1, 110, 119, 125, 136nn11–12, 198, 243. *See also* Dunbar-Nelson, Alice; Dunbar, Alice Ruth
Moore, Jacqueline, 114n17
Moore, Josie Nell, 11
Moreno, Michael P., xvi, 210–29
Morgan, Thomas, 128, 136n9, 154, 189n64, 202
Morris, Harrison S., 102
Morrison, Toni, 173, 174, 207, 227
Moses, 10, 66–68
Moses, Wilson J., 115n35
Muir, John, 85
Murray, Albert, 98

Nalty, Bernard, 43, 46n10, 48n65, 48n67
National Anti-slavery Bazaars, 143
National Association of Colored Women, 79
Native Son (Wright), 174, 185

Nature and Elements of Poetry, The (Stedman), 87
"Negro Artist and the Racial Mountain, The" (Hughes), 99, 112n5
Negro, New, 3, 115n40, 176, 179, 192, 206
Negro, Old, 176, 179
Negro Problem, The (Washington et al.), 73, 98
Negro Thought in America, 1885–1915 (Meier), 100
Nelson, Cary, 112n3
Newell, Peter, 116
New York Commercial Leader, 136–37n23
New York Evening Post, 137n27
New York Times, 30n12, 51, 149, 150n2, 153n93, 252n19
Nissenbaum, Stephen, 151n19, 151n21, 151n37, 152n59
Noonan, Mark, xv, 82–97
Norris, Frank, 101
Nunley, Vorris L., 16n35

Octopus, The, (Norris), 101
Ole Virginia (Page), 177
Opportunity, 100
Ormand, Kirk, 46n9
Outlook, 51

Page, Thomas Nelson, ix, 59, 83, 85, 90, 96n18, 118, 156, 173, 177, 179, 252n7; "Marse Chan: A Story of Ole Virginia," 92; "Meh Lady," 92
Park, Robert E., 234
Peabody, Megan M., xiv, 59–70
Peterson, Carla, 114n17
Pharaoh (and Moses), 66–67
Phenomenology of Spirit, The (Hegel), 163
Philadelphia Literary Era, 137n27
Philadelphia Times, 136n13
Philips, John Edward, 16n32
Philomathean Society, 84
Philosophy of Literary Form, The, (Burke), 98
"Phychiatry [sic] Comes to Harlem" (Wright), 175
Pickering, Julia, 92
Pittman, Coretta M., xiv, 73–81
Poe, Edgar Allan, 13, 87, 99, 113n10
Poems Here at Home (Riley), 85
Poets of America (Stedman), 87
Presentation of the Self in Everyday Life, The (Goffman), 234

Primeau, Ronald, xviiin1, xviiin7, 30n10, 145, 154, 155,232
Prince Hall African Masonic Lodge, 36
Pryse, Marjorie, 169n41
Przyblyski, Jeannene M., 135n2

Rabain, Jean-Francois, 188n8
Rachel (Grimké Weld), 22
Rampersad, Arnold, 112n5
Ramsey, William M., 20, 25, 30n14, 30n20, 60, 69n4
Raynor, Sharon D., xiv, 32–48
Reagon, Bernice Johnson, 15n26
Reef, Catherine, xviiin1
Revell, Peter, xviiin1, 114n19, 252n11, 253n25
Revolutionary War, American (1775–83), 17, 18, 19, 44
Reynolds, Paul, 102, 114n19
Riley, James Whitcomb, xv, 82, 83, 84, 85–90, 93, 244; "All-Kind Mother, The," 86; "Back From Town," 86; "Boy's Mother, A," 86; "Home Again," 89; "Home Ag'in," 86; "In Swimming-Time," 86; "Our Hired Girl," 86; "Poet of the Future, The," 86–87; "Raggedy Man, The," 86; "Some Poems by Boys," 86; "When She Comes Home," 86
Riordan, Bill, 101
Roach, Joseph, 51, 58n13
Robinson, Smokey, 4
Rockwell, Norman, 101
Rodgers, Lawrence R., 188n16, 189n27, 228n41
Roosevelt, Theodore, 101, 134
Russell, Irwin, 59, 83, 92, 244
Russell, Kathy, 196

Saint-Gaudens, Augustus, 44
Sanchez, Sonia, 14
Sandler, Matt, xv, 98–115
Santayana, George, 236
Saturday Evening Post, xv, 51, 101, 103, 104, 113n8, 122
Saunders Redding, J., 31n55
Scholnick, Robert J., 96n12
Schultz, Pearle Hendrikson, xviiin1
Scott, Gloria, 12
Scott, Walter, 111
Scribner's Monthly, 83, 85, 90–91
Scruggs, Charles, 228n42, 229n73
761st Tank Battalion, 34

7th Regiment, 43
Shadow and Act, 233
Shakespeare, William, 12, 98, 247
Shaw, Robert Gould, 25, 27, 32, 33, 42–43
Sherman, Joan R., 113n15
Signifying Monkey: A Theory of African-American Literary Criticism, The (Gates), 50, 57n7, 82, 96n2, 151n23, 151n25, 152n50
Simon, Myron, 59, 69n2
Sisco, Dolores V., xvi, 191–209
Skinner, C. M., 18
Slave Community: Plantation Life in the Antebellum South, The (Blassingame), 55
Smalls, Robert, 76–78
Smitherman, Geneva, 16n43
Smith, F. Hopkinson, 83; *Colonel Carter of Cartersville*, 92
Smith, Guy, 252n14
Smith, Wilford H., 73
Smoked Yankees, 34
Sonstegard, Adam, xv, 116–37
Souls of Black Folk, The (Du Bois), xv, 47n37, 75, 78, 81n10
Spanish-American War (1898), 17, 27–29
Stanhope, Philip Dormer (Lord Chesterfield), 102
Stedman, Clarence Edmund, xv, 83, 84, 87, 89; "Beauty," 88; "Creation and Self-Expression," 87; "Faculty Divine," 87; "Imagination," 87; "Melancholia," 87; "Oracles Old and New," 87; "Truth," 88; "What Is Poetry?" 87
Stewart, Maria, 6, 15n14
Stigma (Goffman), 234
Stowe, Harriet Beecher, 22, 56, 135n5
Stroyer, Jacob, 139, 150n8
Stuart, Ruth McEnery, ix, 83, 92, 156, 252n7
Sumner, William Graham, 233
Sunday, Billy, 101
Sunday Journal, 119
Sundquist, Eric, 50, 56, 57n4, 58n32, 192, 193

"Talented Tenth, The" (Du Bois), 78–79
Taylor, Bernard, 75
Taylor, Lois, 11
Terrell, Mary Church, 6, 79
Thornton, Ruth, 13
369th Infantry (Harlem), 34
Thurman, Wallace, 207

Ticknor, William D., 113n10
Tobey, Henry A., 243
To Wake the Nations: Race in the Making of American Literature (Sundquist), 50, 57n4
Triple Nickels, the, 34
Trudeau, Noah, 35, 43, 44, 46n11, 48n64
Tuan, Yi-Fu, 52–3, 58n19
Turner, Darwin T., 61, 69n6, 99, 113n8, 135n4, 136n10, 144, 191–92, 194
Turner, Nat, 180
Turner, Victor, 52, 58n18, 58n34
Tuskegee Airmen, 34
Tuskegee Institute, 7
Twain, Mark (Samuel Clemens), 104, 107, 108, 117, 135n6, 244
Twelfth Night (Shakespeare), 98

Uncle Tom's Cabin (Stowe), 56, 119
"Unconscious, The" (Freud), 53
Underground Railroad, 35

Valéry, Paul, 111
Von Rosk, Nancy, 231, 240n5

Wagner, Jean, 18, 20, 22, 31n55, 85, 231; *Black Poets of the United States: From Paul Laurence Dunbar to Langston Hughes*, 29n2, 30n15, 30n27, 31n55, 96n5, 113n15
Walker, Alice, 197, 207
Walker, Margaret, 12
Walker, Pierre A., 247
Warren, Kenneth, 113n15, 245
Washington, Booker T., xv, 6, 7, 15n22, 73, 77, 78, 81n7, 98, 99, 100, 146
Waterman, Jayne E., xvi, 230–41
Way of the New World: The Black Novel in America (Gayle), 202

Western Association of Writers, 84
We Wear the Mask: Paul Laurence Dunbar and the Politics of Representative Reality (Harrell), ix, x, xi, xiii, xvii
Wheatley, John, 134
Wheatley, Phillis, 6, 15n13, 29n3, 246
Wheat, Valerie J., 60, 69n5
White, George H., 79
White, Landeg, 15n7
Whitman, Albery Allson, 112n5
Whitman, Walt, 87
Whittier, John Greenleaf, 82, 87
"Who Dat Say Chicken in Dis Crowd?" (Cook and Dunbar), 56
"Who Set You Flowin'?" The African-American Migration Narrative (Griffin), 215
Wiggins, Lida Keck, 80n3
Wilde, Oscar, 107
Williams, Daniel H., 79
Williams, Kenny J., 249, 250, 252n1, 252n17, 253n37, 253n39
Wilson, Midge, 196
Wonham, Henry B., 120, 136n14
Woods, Granville T., 79
Worcester Spy, 137n27
Wright, Kai, 36, 41, 46n13, 46n16, 47n52, 48n69
Wright, Richard, 174
WWI (1914–18), 45
WWII (1939–45), 45
Wyatt-Brown, Bertram, 194–95

Zafar, Rafia, xviiin3
Zumthor, Paul, 15n6

www.ingramcontent.com/pod-product-compliance
Lightning Source LLC
Chambersburg PA
CBHW021821300426
44114CB00009BA/270